Ye shall be as gods

Ye shall be as gods

Humanism and Christianity
~~~
The Battle for Supremacy in the American Cultural Vision

Larry G. Johnson

Copyright © 2011 by Larry G. Johnson.
All rights reserved.

Published by Anvil House Publishers, LLC
Owasso, Oklahoma
www.anvilhousebooks.com

Printed in the United States of America.
Cover: Whitley Graphics
Cover Photo: iStockphoto.com

The stories in this book are based on facts resulting from extensive research and from the author's personal experiences.

ISBN: 978-0-9839716-0-3

Library of Congress Control Number: 2011916969

To my sons, Philip and Curtis,
fellow contrarians.

Contents

Preface	ix
Acknowledgements	xi
I – THE BOOMERS	**1**
Introduction – One Boomer's Journey	3
1 The Baby Boomers – Growing Up	9
2 Boomers – The Fifties	27
3 Boomers – The Sixties – Ye shall not surely die	43
II – WORLDVIEW	**67**
4 Worldview: Christianity vs. Humanism	69
5 The Fingerprints of God	77
6 The Judeo-Christian Tradition and the Rise of Western Civilization	87
7 The Renaissance and Enlightenment: Progress and Perfection – Science and Reason	95
8 Colonial American Heritage	115
9 The American Founders and Their Beliefs	129
10 The Roots and Rise of Modern Humanism	139
11 The "Why" – Worldviews of Humanism and Christianity	157

III – HUMANISM IN AMERICAN INSTITUTIONS — 169

12 Religion – The Power of Religion in American History — 171

13 Religion in the Public Arena – Mention Jesus Christ and "…all hell breaks loose" — 181

14 Government – "…America is not a Christian nation" — 199

15 Government – Liberalism and Progressivism in America — 213

16 Government – Humanism and the Rise of Socialism — 237

17 Science – Naturalistic Evolution — 259

18 Human Sciences and the Secularization of America — 277

19 American Education — 289

20 American Family – Marriage and Family — 305

21 American Family – Feminism and the Roles of Men and Women — 323

22 American Family – Abortion — 341

23 American Family – Homosexuality — 353

24 Popular Culture — 367

IV – YE SHALL BE AS GODS – SUMMARY, STATUS, AND DIRECTION — 383

25 Differences between Christian and Humanist Worldviews – A Summary — 385

26 Christianity and Humanism – Endgame in America — 401

Notes		417
Bibliography		449
Index		467

Tables

Table 1	United States – Live Births, Birth Rates, and Fertility Rates – 1930-2000	31
Table 2	America's Vietnam Chronology – April 30, 1945 – April 30, 1975	60-61
Table 3	Women with Children under Age 18 – Presence or Absence of Spouse	318
Table 4	No Spouse Present – Reasons for Absence	318

Preface

> And the serpent said unto the woman, Ye shall not surely die: For God doth know that in the day ye eat thereof, then your eyes shall be opened, and *ye shall be as gods*, knowing good and evil. Genesis 3:4-5 KJV. (emphasis added)

This temptation became the first dark cloud on the horizon of man's idyllic existence in the unfolding drama that ended with his fall and separation from his maker. The serpent's whispered words were the seeds of humanism planted in the fertile field of man's free will. Sensual man was the victor that day for the fruit of humanism was pleasant to the eye and good to eat. The serpent sealed the deal with an offer of wisdom to tempt the root of pride within man. Sweet revenge the serpent chuckled. The pride that cost him his place in the heavens would now rob God of his precious creation. The serpent had rebelled against God and was cast down. Now man had rebelled and was cast out and separated from God for whom he had been created. Henceforth in sorrow and by the sweat of his brow, man must wrest from the cursed ground the herb of the field amidst thorns and thistles. At the end of his days he discovered another of the serpent's lies that had been mixed with truth—he would surely die.

This book is the story of two worldviews—humanism and Christianity—that are contending for supremacy in America's central cultural vision. An understanding of this conflict is central to understanding who we were, from whence we came, who we are now, and understanding the swift transformation occurring within America's central cultural vision. To a significant degree this conflict impacts daily the life of every American, and many of them are not conscious of the tactical and strategic maneuvers of the combatants in the swirl of life around them.

In Part I we look at the events and circumstances that created the Boomer generation of whom many became the finest flower of the humanist philosophy during the last half of the twentieth century. In Part II an examination is made of the predominant Judeo-Christian worldview and the sources and development of the worldviews of colonial Americans and the American Founders. Part II ends with a look at the roots and ascendency of modern humanism. In Part III the impact of humanism on American institutions—religion, government and politics, family, academia, economics, art, culture, and society in general—are described and examined. Part IV begins with a summarization of the differences between humanism and Christianity and some of the key concepts as redefined by humanists. The present-day status of the Christianity in America and America's central cultural vision will be explored. Finally, the cultural choices that lay before America will be examined along with the means by which the over-arching Judeo-Christian banner may be restored above the central cultural vision of America.

Acknowledgements

This book is a product of many influences—a lifetime of family, friends, acquaintances, experiences, observations, reading, study, and thought. Amongst all of these, none have been more important than my immediate family—my wife Sherryl and sons Philip and Curtis. They have been my anchors and encouragers. But in living my life and the day-to-day writing of this book, there has been an even greater constant and indispensable anchor responsible for anything good and true in this book. John Leax also knew of Him and described His influence best.

> Since Christians, artists as well as evangelists, have within them the power of the Holy Spirit, it is only logical to conclude that artists who bring everything into captivity for Christ write--just as they live--under the direction of the Holy Spirit...Their poems are not private; they are images incarnated for themselves and for the community in which they live.[1]

---

[1] John Leax, "Becoming a New Creation," *Grace is Where I Live: The Landscape of Faith & Writing*, (La Porte, IN: WordFarm, 2004).

Part I – The Boomers

We start with the ending. Part I is a description of the Baby Boom generation and what that generation has meant to America in the context of the on-going conflict of worldviews. To write of one's own generation is difficult. I am a Baby Boomer and writing in this section primarily about my generation and its impact on America. To look at ourselves and see from whence we came and why we have become who we are as a people and nation is difficult in the sense that we can be overly influenced by our upbringing, friends, acquaintances, faith or lack thereof, personal experiences, education, and many other things. In other words, we may stand too close to the canvas we attempt to paint. However, there is a counter-balance in that we are eye-witnesses to that of which we speak, and those same influences and experiences, if we are careful and thoughtful, can add clarity with which one looks at our history and give assurance that one is speaking the truth. To judge the impact of the those influences and experiences on the contents of this book, the reader should know the author's worldview and how it was formed, and to that end the setting and events of the author's formative years are discussed in the Introduction.

Introduction – One Boomer's Journey

My father's family was considered poor even by the standards of the Great Depression. During that time, my father's mother, my grandmother, cared for a sick husband and five children, cleaned people's houses, and did laundry and sewing for others. When she was in her eighties, she told me of an incident that she experienced during the Depression. There was no food to feed her family. So she went to the back door of a little restaurant at closing time in the small rural town of Collinsville, Oklahoma, where they lived. She asked for any leftover soup. It was some fifty years later, but she still called it the worst day of her life. Her attitude may seem strange to a twenty-first century citizen with a typical entitlement mentality prevalent in United States today, but such were the people of the Greatest Generation and their ancestors.

By ninth grade in 1937, my father had to quit high school and work on a dairy along with his brother to help support his father, mother, and sisters. He was always sensitive about his lack of a formal education. His father died of tuberculosis in 1944 after being sickly and not able to do much work for a number of years. My father was not in the military during World War II. He worked on a dairy, an occupation that was considered critical to the war effort. His older brother was in the Army and fought in New Guinea. I sensed that my father regretted he was not able to do so. Resentment is perhaps a better word to describe his feelings, but my father never voiced his resentment except once through an offhand remark.

My mother and father were married on Christmas Eve 1944 at my mother's parents' dairy farm. They started a small dairy near her parents' farm between Owasso and Collinsville in early 1945. My father's brother returned from the war in late 1945, married, and began working on a job. My father's mother believed that since he didn't go to war, my father owed half of his dairy to his brother. I am not sure of my father's feelings about this for he never spoke of it, but he sold his dairy cattle and farm equipment and gave half of the proceeds to his brother in the late 1940s. He then started over.

I was born in October of 1945, at the leading edge of the Boomer generation. I grew up in awe and respect for what my parents' generation had survived and accomplished. While growing up on a dairy farm, I attended the small rural Owasso school. There I learned much about the sacrifice of the World War II generation and prior generations of Americans as I read books and was taught honor, duty, patriotism, and love of country during those formative years. I was overwhelmed by the magnitude of the sacrifice while watching early black and white television accounts of the war such as *Victory at Sea*. For me and those in my small world, patriotism and love of country were as natural as breathing.

I graduated from Owasso High School in 1963 along with thirty-eight of my classmates and became the first of my family to attend college when I enrolled that fall at the University of Tulsa. It was during that first semester while playing soccer in a physical education class that I heard of the assassination of President Kennedy. Before I graduated in June of 1967, the world I knew growing up was changing dramatically. In my junior year during the spring of 1966 I had gone to the Dallas Naval Air Station for two days of physical examinations and tests with hopes of entering Navy pilot training upon graduation the following spring. That never materialized, and upon graduation in May 1967, I enlisted in the Army and was soon bound for armor officer's candidate school (OCS). During the middle of August I traveled by bus for most of twenty-four hours to Fort Knox, Kentucky, for basic and advanced training. Upon arrival, I was told that the armor school was full and that I could transfer to another OCS program at another base or just stay in as an enlisted man. I chose the latter, and two days shy of five months later I stepped off of a plane at Tan Son Nhut Air Base in South Vietnam. My military occupation specialty (MOS) was 11E20 or mechanized infantryman.

For some inexplicable reason, I recall that my first glimpse of Vietnam was on a television news cast in 1960. Eisenhower was still president, and the newscast showed about 200 American soldiers who were acting as advisors to the struggling South Vietnamese Army. The soldiers were living in little two-man pup tents and wore fatigues not designed for jungle warfare. President Kennedy escalated the number of soldiers in Vietnam to more than 15,000 troops prior to his

Ye shall be as gods

assassination. Two of my high school classmates died in Vietnam in the early stages of the buildup that began in 1965. I arrived in Vietnam on January 13, 1968, two weeks before what proved to be the pivotal event of the war—the Tet Offensive. I was assigned to one of the combat units in the First Infantry Division. While processing in at Di An, a couple of soldiers came to find some out-processing members of the unit I was to join. They wanted them to identify the bodies of two soldiers killed while members of that unit. For some reason, perhaps known only to God, I was reassigned to Headquarters Company. The company was located in Lai Khe, a rubber plantation and small village about thirty miles north of Saigon and near one of the points of the infamous Iron Triangle. The Iron Triangle was sixty square miles of enemy stronghold laced with an estimated 150 miles of tunnels, many built decades earlier. Such was the periodic but regular barrage of rockets and mortars that Lai Khe became known among the troops as Rocket City. If possible, field troops tended to avoid coming to the base camp during the first half of 1968. I recall that during one week twenty-five soldiers within the camp were killed by rockets and mortars. Whether this occurred during the mini-Tet beginning May 5th or at some other time, I do not remember. My first night in Lai Khe was spent sleeping on a concrete pad awaiting the erection of a tent. I slept through the first few rounds of a mortar attack before I realized what was happening. For the newcomer, it was easy to confuse the in-coming mortar explosions with out-going artillery rounds.

Lai Khe was at the edge of an area about twenty-miles in diameter where approximately one-half of all defoliants such as Agent Orange were sprayed during the war. The peak years for defoliant use were from 1967 through 1969. I spent many nights on perimeter guard duty looking across at a tree line 100 yards away. The expanse of jungle between the perimeter and tree line was completely devoid of vegetation, and giant Rhone plows had leveled any trees and brush to give a clear field of vision and line of fire.

Keith Ware was a major general and commanding general of the First Infantry Division. A World War II Metal of Honor winner, it was said that he didn't need to go to Vietnam to get his four stars. The Army has a history of placing generals who are destined to be its top leaders in command of the First Infantry Division at some point in their careers. In civilian clothes, the spectacled general could have easily passed for a mild-mannered college professor. On September 13th, General Ware was heading north by helicopter from Lai Khe toward Quan Loi and on to Loc Ninh where he had been directing a fierce battle against the North Vietnamese Army. For two days the general had repeatedly directed his helicopter to fly over the battle zone at minimum altitude to effectively direct the battle. Five minutes out from Lai Khe, his helicopter was hit by anti-aircraft fire and crashed. All were killed including the Division Sergeant Major, Division G-3, both pilots, and other enlisted soldiers. The co-pilot was Chief Warrant Officer William Manzanares, and he was scheduled to complete his year in country and rotate back to the States in a couple of days.[1] Some of the officers had 'liberated' some steaks from Army supplies meant for the higher ups in Saigon, and we grilled them as a going away party a night or two prior to his death. Little did we suspect his home going would be in a body bag.

Death came easily, often, and in all sorts of ways in 1968 Vietnam. A fellow member of our company was having words with a soldier who had just returned from the field and was preparing to rotate back to the U.S. The Headquarters Company soldier let his M-16 barrel drop across some sandbags as it pointed at the other soldier. The rifle accidentally discharged, killing the soldier. The Headquarters Company soldier was court-marshaled and spent six months in the Army's Long Binh Jail (called LBJ) near Saigon. During that time, the military prisoners rioted and took control of the interior of the prison for a number of days. Many were killed in what was predominantly a race war between blacks and whites. Racial tensions continued to grow in Vietnam along with incidents of "fragging" (rolling a live grenade under the bunk of a disliked officer or non-commissioned officer).

Another incident occurred on the perimeter post I regularly guarded at night. It happened on a night I was off duty. The soldier guarding that section encountered a Viet Cong infiltrator leaving the base camp. The infiltrator was attempting to duck walk through the coils of razor wire when he was spotted. The soldier's M-16 rifle jammed, and the VC shot him with a pistol. Although wounded, the soldier wrestled with the VC and finally strangled him but only after he bit a chunk out of the VC's head as though it were an apple.

The South Vietnamese were a remarkable people. They had been at war for a more than a quarter of a century. In spite of corrupt regimes and past failures, I generally found many of them to be sincere and dedicated to defending their land against the North Vietnamese. Many South Vietnamese soldiers fought courageously and with distinction.

A year is a long time in a combat zone, and for some, it was a lifetime cut short. Some short-timers, those nearing the end of their year in-country, became excessively nervous or superstitious. But for most, that day would come when they would head back to the "world." Most troops were transported on chartered civilian aircraft staffed by civilian airline personnel. Stewardesses who tended civilians one day may be aboard a jet filled with 200 to 250 soldiers the next day, many of whom were just hours off the battlefield. Such was that day in January 1969 when the plane carrying me and over 200 other survivors lifted off the tarmac at Tan Son Nhut. The long awaited hour that was dreamed of for 365 days had arrived. Yet, it still seemed a dream for not one word could be heard anywhere on the aircraft as the plane climbed over the South China Sea. The eerie silence persisted for several minutes as though to speak would awaken us from our dream. Finally, one of the stewardesses came on the intercom and said, "Well, how about it guys?" The response was instantaneous and could only be described as pandemonium. The shouts, screams, and laughter lasted for several minutes. We were going home!

A little over four months later I was in graduate school. In many ways life seemed unchanged from my undergraduate college days. There were many of the same TV programs I watched while in college. The space program continued, and Neil Armstrong would leave his footprints on the moon as we watched the live news coverage on a summer afternoon in July 1969. Less than a month later the nation moved from fascination with the heavens above to the mud wallow below known as Woodstock and its haze of drugs, open and unbridled sex, and rock and roll. Although the routine of life seemingly had changed little, there was a growing sense within that something was amiss. As a graduate teaching assistant, the young faces that stared back at me looked very much the same as others with whom I had gone to school. I realized my feelings of disquiet were not caused by the individual students for they were younger and personally unknown to me. It was the face of the generation of which I was a part that had changed in the two tumultuous years I had been away. Although a year in a combat zone can change a person, the things I knew and believed in had not changed. The unidentified stirrings within me that something was amiss became the subject of this book over four decades later.

Chapter 1

The Baby Boomers – Growing Up

In 1936, President Franklin Roosevelt wrote, "There is a mysterious cycle in human events. To some generations much is given. Of other generations much is expected. This generation has a rendezvous with destiny."[2] Sixty-two years later that generation was labeled as the greatest.

Much has been written and said about the Greatest Generation, a term that has gained almost universal acceptance following Tom Brokaw's book, *The Greatest Generation*. For it was this generation that grew up during the depravations of the Great Depression, fought a world war, persisted in blocking Soviet threats and aggression in a prostrate post-war world, and built the world's greatest peacetime economy. Following the Allied victory in 1945, the United States stood at the pinnacle of world power. But unlike any other time in history, that generation acted not as victors but as a good and honorable people who poured their resources and energies into helping devastated nations and their starving peoples around the world. And, they didn't retreat in the face of new dictators and despots as they fought the hot war in Korea and the cold war in other parts of the world, primarily against the USSR and its satellites. Following World War II, they married; went to schools, colleges, and universities in record numbers; and birthed approximately eighty million children who became known as the Baby Boomers. And through all of this, "They stayed true to their values of personal responsibility, duty, honor, and faith."[3]

The Greatest Generation produced seven American Presidents with an age span from the youngest to oldest of only 16 years, and these men collectively inhabited the Oval Office for thirty-two years. The generation's heroes included Charles Lindbergh, John Kennedy, and Ronald Reagan, the soldiers of World War II and Korea. But in the minds of some of their children, the Greatest

Generation became the much maligned Fifties generation described as bigoted, materialistic, intolerant conformists.

William Strauss and Neil Moore published *Generation – The History of America's Future* in 1991. The authors attempted to anticipate the future by looking to the past. They identified what they believe are eighteen American generations spread over four hundred years of American history, from the Puritans forward to the publication of their book. The authors have also identified four generational peer personality types that they believe recur and follow each other in a fixed order or generational cycle.[4]

The G.I. generation, now called the Greatest Generation, was born from 1901 through 1924 (24 years and 63 million members). They are called the "civic" types and described as believers in public harmony, cooperative social discipline, friendly, optimistic, and having community spirit.[5]

The Silent generation was born from 1925 through 1942 and is characterized as other-directed and adaptive. They have been described as being fair, open-minded, and non-judgmental. The Silents were a small generation in both numbers and years (eighteen years and 49 million members). They were profoundly impacted by the Great Depression and perhaps felt squeezed as the middle child between the G.I.s and the mammoth Boomer generation. The Silents generally led a deprived childhood during the Great Depression and were too young to greatly impact the events of World War II. The Silents would always reside in the shadow of the G.I.s and pampered Boomers.[6] Their generation would not produce any man to inhabit the Oval Office of the Presidency.

Strauss and Moore placed the beginning of the Boomer generation in 1943 and ending at the close of 1960. Although only nineteen years in length, the Boomers burst on the scene in record numbers (79 million members). Boomers knew they were different from their older G. I. and Silent parents and older brothers and sisters. They are idealists with unyielding opinions about all issues and are exceptionally judgmental.[7] Other beginnings of the Boomer generation have ranged from as early as the Japanese attack on Pearl Harbor on December 7, 1941, to January 1, 1946. Although Strauss and Moore point to December 31, 1960 as the end of the generation, others have variously designated the end of the generation as occurring at the end of 1962, the assassination of John Kennedy in

November 1963, or as late as the end of 1964. For purposes of this book, we shall generally consider the Boomers to be those born between the end of 1945 and the end of 1964. The Boomers have produced three presidents.

Karl Mannheim was a 1930s social scientist that believed "...that decisive events in their early years could shape the consciousness of an entire generation...Early impressions tend to coalesce into a natural view of the world."[8] Others would restate Manheim's "decisive events and impressions" by referring to a generational cohort who grew up and came of age together and "...shared experiences during formative years that have a common and lasting effect on values and lifestyle decisions of a group of people."[9] We shall compromise and call those things that give a face to a generation as *significant shared events and formative experiences*.

The Boomer view of the world would be like no other. As a group, it would be both applauded and castigated. Yet, the Boomers cannot be totally blamed nor credited, depending on one's point of view, for the changes wrought to American society beginning in the 1960s. In reality, the Boomers are the product of philosophies and concepts that had been struggling for ascendancy before the Europeans came to the North American continent. What made the Boomers different was the occurrence of a series of significant shared events and formative experiences that came together in a unique time and place—the perfect storm as it might be called. This series of significant shared events and formative experiences would ultimately result in dramatic changes in family life and child rearing, education, culture, religion, politics, and government. The significant shared events and formative experiences all occurred in time of unprecedented prosperity. For good or ill, out of this swirling cauldron of change came the Boomers.

We begin with two significant shared events and formative experiences of the Boomers that resulted from the direct influence of two men—Benjamin Spock and John Dewey. Spock would profoundly influence the home and Dewey would dramatically change education, and their influences among others would contribute to major cultural shifts in America.

Within the first year Boomers began appearing, Spock published his *Common Sense Book of Baby and Child Care*. Released in the spring of 1946, three quarters of a million copies sold by year's end. His influence on child rearing in America and around the world cannot be overestimated. Quoting one of his biographers:

> In terms of sheer influence, what president, general, or tycoon could claim to have affected the fundamental way we bring up our children and carry on our species? In historical volumes found in every library, Dr. Spock's name is in the list of those who have changed our world.[10]

Ben Spock was born in a three-story house in New Haven, Connecticut, on May 2, 1903. His father was a prosperous lawyer and soon became a member of the legal department of J. P. Morgan's New York and New Haven Railroad. As his father progressed up the corporate ladder, Ben's mother dominated the Spock household and its operations as the family grew to six children—Ben the oldest, four sisters, and one brother who was next to the youngest. To the daughters, Ben's father was affectionate and discipline was tender. To the boys, their father was distant and reserve with no hugs, kisses, or displays of other affection. Ben's mother had descended from a family with a long line of prominent Yankee lawyers, bankers, and well-to-do businessmen. Unfortunately, Ben's grandfather on his mother's side was a philandering alcoholic that abandoned his wife and six children for long stretches of time. One of his mother's sisters had a child out of wedlock. Harboring anger and bitterness at the abandonment by her husband, Ben's grandmother would often beat his mother and her siblings and lock them in closets for the least infraction. In later years Ben's grandmother withdrew substantially from the lives of her children.[11]

Ben's mother was a good but domineering mother and a firm disciplinarian. She was strong-willed and determined that her life would be different than that of her mother's life. There were always maids to assist with managing the large household, but Ben's mother felt her role was to raise her children. She was a stern, but loving taskmaster. She loved Ben the most, and her love and discipline were especially focused on him. Though occasionally complaining to his brother and sisters of their mother's strict nature and demands, Ben was aware of his mother's special love and concern for him. He knew he was a mother's boy.[12]

Summers were spent on the coast of Maine. Back in New Haven, the children attended a series of private schools. The family moved to a majestic home in the finest section of New Haven, and Ben attended Phillips Academy in Andover, Massachusetts, whose ancient roster included names such as Quincy and Lowell of Massachusetts and Washington and Lee from Virginia. John Hancock had signed the school's incorporation papers. Following two years at Andover, Ben entered Yale in the in the fall of 1921. Ben's father was now the General Counsel of the New York, New Haven, and Hartford Railroad, a pillar of New Haven, and he had been a Yale man. Ben wanted to surpass his father's accomplishments.[13]

Ben worked as a counselor at a home for crippled children in Newington, Connecticut, during the four summers while attending Yale as an undergraduate. During the summer following his freshman year, his life and the lives of millions would change as a result of a chance encounter in an upstairs bedroom of the old converted house occupied by the children's home. As Ben watched a simple operation on a 10 year-old polio victim's leg, he was greatly impressed with the orthopedic surgeon's skill and the sense of good that was derived from helping the child. Dropping thoughts of becoming an English professor or an architect, Ben decided he would become a doctor. "I decided at that moment it would be a good career. I didn't know the difference between pediatrics and orthopedics. But after my first undergraduate summer, I decided to be a children's doctor."[14] While at Yale, Ben became a member of the elite secret society Scroll and Key, a member of the Yale Rowing Crew that won the Gold Medal at the 1924 Paris Olympics, and met his future wife Jane Cheney.[15]

Benjamin Spock graduated from Yale in 1925 and entered Yale Medical School. After completing his second year, Ben and Jane married in June 1927. In the fall, the newlyweds moved to an apartment in the Greenwich Village neighborhood of New York City as Ben had transferred to Columbia Medical School.[16] Jane Cheney's great grandfather was Horace Bushnell, a graduate of Yale and brilliant Congregationalist minister. Favoring a more humanistic approach to God, his writings greatly influenced Ralph Waldo Emerson and many of his contemporaries. Jane's mother married Bushnell's grandson John Cheney of the wealthy silk manufacturing family. When Jane was only a young girl, her father would contract syphilis and die at age forty-nine following a long period of decline including partial paralysis, mental deterioration, and psychotic behavior. Jane and her younger sister often suffered physical and verbal abuse from their father during this time.[17]

Religion did not play much of a role in the Spock's family life. Ben and his siblings attended Sunday school with other neighborhood children as a matter of routine, but their parents did not belong to a church nor attend regularly.[18] Ben had briefly thought of joining the clergy and said to Jane that, "I must make you a speech sometime Jane to show you what a good minister I'd make." On another occasion Ben's views on Christianity were revealed as he, his best friend Geo Dyer, and Harry Bingham, another pal, were having a heated discussion in Ben's dorm room one night. Dyer, an avowed agnostic, was attacking Harry Bingham, the most conservative of the trio. Ben and Harry accused Dyer of being the best Christian they knew, a charge Dyer heatedly denied. For the next three hours the men discussed the sorry state of Christianity and religion in general.[19]

Politically, Ben and Jane's conservative roots were abandoned in the late 1920s. While at Bryn Mawr, Jane was an admirer of socialist Norman Thomas. She joined the American Labor Party and hosted several organizational meetings in New York. Ben and Jane, like so many of the intellectuals of the era when Stalin's abuses were hidden, became enamored with Marxism in the 1930s. Ben's two sisters were convinced that Ben and Jane had joined the Communist Party. One sister claimed she actually saw his membership card, and the other recalled "cell" meetings being held at their apartment. Ben supposedly quit the party when ordered to stop associating with his affluent classmates on Wall Street. Decades later, while admitting to joining the American Labor Party, Ben denied the accusations that he was a member of the Communist Party.[20]

Spock graduated from Columbia Medical School in 1929 at the top of his class. He entered an internship at Presbyterian Hospital that was associated with Columbia. The Spocks continued to receive financial support from Ben's parents after Ben's graduation. Jane supplemented their finances by getting a job as a research assistant to Dr. George Draper, a friend of Ben. Through psychoanalysis Draper attempted to determine the connection between a patient's susceptibility to physical ailments and psychology. Jane interviewed patients and delved into their personal lives, and at the suggestion of Draper, she agreed to undergo psychoanalysis to become a more perceptive interviewer. For several months she was very absorbed and happy about her new understanding of human behavior. However, her moods began to change, and she became increasingly distraught and experienced bouts of crying. Draper felt she had become too emotionally involved in her patient's histories, and she left the job. However, her weekly psychoanalysis sessions would last for years. Even though Jane's experience was painful, Spock became fascinated by Freud's theories on emotional development.[21]

The various methods of raising a child in America had swung like a pendulum during the centuries since the European arrival on the continent. Following the strict model imposed by the Puritans and Calvinists in which the evil nature of the child must be stamped out, John Locke wrote a book on child-rearing that stressed a more moderate approach and viewed the child as a blank slate awaiting the effects of good parenting. This movement continued into the 1800s when reform-minded ministers pushed for a more nurturing environment. The progressives spawned by this movement moved beyond child-rearing to social causes to rescue the young through various reforms in areas such as child labor, nutrition, and housing and the creation of organizations such as the Children's Aid Society and the Boy Scouts. Ironically, it was Horace Bushnell, Jane's great grandfather, who wrote *Christian Nurture* and greatly influenced the humanistic move toward moderation. However, by the 1920s the psychologists had taken center stage as the experts on child-rearing. G. Stanley Hall and Dr. Holt would preach that a "...child's fate was as much determined by heredity and evolution as any formula offered by religion or reformists." Their prescriptions reflecting the influences of Darwin and Pasteur involved no kissing, playing, and rocking for toddlers. In his 1928 book, John B. Watson would treat the child as malleable, that each child's behavior could be controlled through conditioning in the same manner as Pavlov's dog. Watson promoted scheduling, little emotional attachment, gentle rapping of the hand to correct inappropriate behavior but not as a punishment.[22]

Such was the world of behavioral psychology in which Spock found himself. Given the difficulties in starting a practice in 1932 during the midst of the Great Depression, Spock decided to get additional psychological training in pediatrics. He took a one-year psychiatric residency in a New York City hospital. Spock was psychoanalyzed by Bertram Lewin, a member of the New York Psychoanalytic Group, but unlike Jane, he found it more of an intellectual rather than an emotional experience. His doubts about psychoanalysis were dispelled, and he fully embraced Sigmund Freud's theories in his work as a pediatrician. Caroline Zachry, a New York Psychoanalytic Institute member and educator/psychologist at Columbia, would encourage Spock in developing his child-rearing methods. Zachry embraced Freud's theories and the views of Columbia's John Dewey on childhood development. These views were anti-traditionalist and challenged memorization and rigid discipline in school. Rather, the individual child should determine the curriculum as opposed to an administrator. The primary purpose of school was to teach children how to cooperate and get along and in the world.[23] Thomas Maier, a Spock biographer, wrote:

> Pragmatic believers like Zachry and Spock preferred more liberal adaptations of Freud, sprinkled with Dewey's brand of progressive education. As historian Nathan G. Hale Jr. later commented, these idealistic Americans inspired by Freud "insisted there were no bad children, only children who had been mishandled by misguided parents." This melding of Freud and Dewey, another historian noted, showed how the "traditional American hospitality to messianic ideas corresponded with the optimistic mood of Progressivism."[24]

The stage was set for Spock to write *The Common Sense Book of Baby and Child Care*. In late 1941, Spock began writing his book that would at its completion include 507 sections and become a reference manual of virtually everything known about parenthood and pediatrics. Contrary to Calvinists and behaviorists, Spock's book offered a progressive philosophical view of children as essentially good at heart, not little villains or formless lumps of clay waiting for impressions. Spock applied the principles found in psychoanalysis throughout his book, and of all the experts relied upon, Freud would exert the largest influence. Conservative teachers, while unsure of Freud and his psychoanalytic concepts, would quickly adopt Freud's theories if put in plain English.[25] To this end, Freud's name was deliberately omitted. As Maier wrote, "Masking Freudian theory in friendly phrases and American Colloquialisms proved to be one of the most masterful aspects of Spock's book."[26]

During the unrest of the 1960s two decades after the book's first publication, the section on a child's discipline and punishment became the most controversial. Freud's psychoanalytic view of individual conscience called the superego was very much in evidence in the book. Spock and his book would be one of the major targets of the backlash against the massive revolt and civil disobedience by many students occurring on college campuses and elsewhere in America. Americans perceived that the Boomer generation had been raised in an aura of permissiveness generated by the advice given in the *Common Sense Book of Baby and Child Care*, a charge Spock would always deny.[27]

With regard to discipline, the psychoanalytic view of the individual conscience was reflected in Spock's book. Freud's belief that mankind's brutish instincts were kept in check because people desired to be loved and get along in society.[28] Likewise, Spock contended that, "The thing that keeps us from doing 'bad' things to each other is the feelings we have of liking people and wanting them to like us. In other words, if a child is handled in a friendly way, he wants to do the right thing, the grown-up thing, most of the time."[29] Spock's emphasis is on discipline based on a child's desire to be good and get along in society, and he is very light on punishment. These principles are readily apparent from several excerpts from his 1945-1946 edition:

> A 2-year-old baby shouldn't be worrying about the consequences of his actions. This is the period when he is meant to learn by doing and having things happen. I'm not advising that you never warn your child in words, but only that you shouldn't be leading him out beyond his depth with ideas.
>
> Frequent tantrums are more often due to the fact that the mother hasn't learned the knack of handling the child tactfully.
>
> Then where does punishment fit in? People who have specialized in child care feel that it is seldom required.

But even if we admit that we don't always do a good job of leading our children, and that we turn to punishment instead, that doesn't mean that punishment can be highly recommended.

However, I'd go light on the legalistic, "take-the-consequences" kind of punishment before 6, and I wouldn't try to use it at all before the age of 3. You don't want a small child to develop a heavy sense of guilt. The job of a parent is to keep him from getting into trouble, rather than act as a severe judge after it's happened.

In the olden days children were spanked plenty, and nobody thought much about it. Then a reaction set in, and parents were taught that it was shameful. But that didn't settle everything. If an angry parent keeps himself from spanking, he may show his irritation in other ways, for instance, by nagging the child for half the day, or trying to make him feel deeply guilty. I'm not advocating spanking, but I think it is less poisonous than lengthy disapproval, because it clears the air, for parent and child.

I wouldn't advise putting a child in his room for punishment—that makes it seem like a prison.

If you seem to be needing to punish your child frequently, something is definitely wrong in his life or you are using the wrong methods. You need a wise outsider to help you—a children's psychiatrist.

In general, remember that what makes your child behave well is not threats or punishment but loving you for your agreeableness and respecting you for knowing your rights and his. Stay in control as a friendly leader rather than battle with him at his level.[30]

The Freudian concepts permeate the book and would quietly indoctrinate a generation. Maier wrote:

Spock's liberating message was that they could be any type of parent they wanted to—the ultimate choice being left to them, rather than medical experts, religious leaders, or their own families. Parenthood, as he presented it, was a solemn moral obligation that also could be fun and carried on with a cheerful confidence. As Spock's book seemed to suggest, what red-blooded American didn't want a better life, a better world, for their children?[31]

But those red-blooded Americans read more into Spock's advice than was intended. In 1957, Spock revised the book under the title *Baby and Child Care*. The two greatest changes concerned child discipline and the advice on "self-demand" feeding in which doctors recommended that parents only feed the baby when he was hungry. Although mentioned in his first book, Spock's reservations grew over time.

> Parents in throwing off the old ways, seemed to plunge headlong toward the opposite end of the child-rearing spectrum. Instead of autocratic rigidity, parents were now letting the baby rule the roost, all in the name of enlightenment. The idea of self-demand spread like a virus infecting parental judgment in other areas. Some parents applied this self-demand approach to sleeping schedules, usually with disastrous results. Spock heard many horror stories of little tykes allowed to stay up all night, far beyond a reasonable bedtime, until they collapsed with fatigue…In this new extreme, kids were kings, and mother and father merely did their bidding…When he inquired with parents, they told him, "But I thought we were meant to do what the baby wanted."[32]

The revised edition's section on discipline was expanded and contained clarifications, additions, and deletions. Several sections tempered and clarified statements made in the first edition. It was necessary to add a section entitled "Some common misunderstandings about discipline. Spock wrote:

> The parents who have had more trouble with the new ideas are usually those who haven't been too happy about their own upbringing…They haven't wanted their own children to feel that way about them. So they have welcomed new theories. They often read meanings into them that went beyond what the scientists intended—for instance, that all that children need is love; that they shouldn't be made to conform; that they should be allowed to carry out their aggressive feelings against parents and others; that whenever anything goes wrong it's the parents' fault; that when children misbehave the parents shouldn't become angry or punish them but should try to show more love.[33]

But with regard to punishment, in spite of his protestations, Spock was unyielding:

> The American tradition of spanking may be one cause of the fact that there is *much* more violence in our country than in any other comparable nation—murder, armed robbery, wife abuse, child abuse…In the olden days, most children were spanked, on the assumption that this was necessary to make them behave. (emphasis added) In the twentieth century, as parents and professionals have studied children here and in other countries, they have come to realize that children can be well-behaved, cooperative, and polite without ever having been punished physically—or in other ways.[34]

Spock's book contains much valuable and practical information for young parents, and millions of young American families would embrace Spock's prescriptions following World War II. To some extent, his preachments, even in the areas of discipline and punishment, have merit in the encouragement of loving ways of rearing children.

In spite of the book's merits, Freud's ideas and philosophy would permeate *The Common Sense Book of Baby and Child Care*. That Spock's book would create a seismic shift away from the Judeo-Christian tradition and its doctrine of fallen man cannot be disputed when one considers Freud's worldview. This departure from tradition is evident in Freud's writings:

...let us return once more to the question of religious doctrines. We can now repeat that all of them are illusions and insusceptible of proof. No one can be compelled to think them true, to believe in them. Some of them are so improbable, so incompatible with everything we have laboriously discovered about the reality of the world, that we may compare them—if we pay proper regard to the psychological differences—to delusions.[35]

With Dr. Spock's advice couched in a fatherly, homespun, and seemingly common sense approach, young American parents devoured his book following World War II. It was estimated that one in five American mothers had acquired Dr. Spock's book. Adding those mothers who borrowed the book from a friend or the library, this number approached one in three mothers raising "Spock babies." One poll found that almost two-thirds of new mothers had read *Baby and Child Care*. And by the end of the 1950s, America had also absorbed indirectly many of Freud's theories about human nature. "Newspapers and magazine columns, among them Spock's monthly essays, offered a squeaky-clean version of Freud, what historian Nathan G. Hale Jr. called 'the popularized American Freud', a 'sanitized' Freud who was 'the author of most of the gifts of liberal culture—progressive education, psychiatric social work, permissive child raising, modern psychiatry, and criminology'."[36]

In addition to Freud, John Dewey's ideas on progressive education would strongly influence Spock. One measure of John Dewey's impact on American education can be judged by the level of criticism that was provoked by his teachings. In March, 1959, President Eisenhower wrote, "Educators, parents, and students must be continuously stirred up by the defects in our education system. They must be induced to abandon the educational path that, rather blindly, they have been following as a result of John Dewey's teachings."[37] For an individual deceased for seven years to have his work and philosophy receive the stinging rebuke of a sitting president, that individual's influence on American life must be viewed as substantial. And Eisenhower's feelings regarding Dewey's educational theories were echoed by many prominent Americans. One of the most vocal critics of Dewey's educational theories was Admiral Hyman G. Rickover, the father of the nuclear Navy. Rickover wrote two books on education[38] and testified before Congressional Committees regarding the failure of the American educational system.

John Dewey's admirers called him the greatest American philosopher and the philosopher of American democracy. His views and teachings during his exceptionally long career would influence many facets of American life—art, knowledge, education, morals, politics, science, and religion—and publication of his writings spanned seventy years. The breadth of change during Dewey's lifetime is astounding. Dewey was a grocer's son born in Burlington, Vermont, on October 20, 1859, while James Buchanan was president, a year and a half before Abraham Lincoln's inauguration. With remembrances of the Civil War, he would live to see two world wars and the atomic age by the time of his death in 1952, just five years before Sputnik would herald the beginning of the space age.[39]

Following two years teaching high school in Pennsylvania, Dewey entered graduate work at John Hopkins University in 1882. He received his PhD in 1884 and began teaching courses in ethics, history of philosophy, logic, and psychology at the University of Michigan. With the exception of one year spent at the University of Minnesota, he would stay at Michigan until moving to the University of Chicago in 1893 as the head professor in philosophy. Dewey made his final move in 1905 to the Department of Philosophy and Psychology at Columbia University in New York City from whence he would retire in 1930. During those years he was associated with the University's Teachers' College, and shortly after his arrival at the University he would be "recognized as the leader of the 'progressive movement' in education." Following retirement, he would remain at Columbia as Professor Emeritus in Residence.[40]

He became a social activist during his years at the University of Chicago. His involvement in social causes and organizations included the Jane Addams Hull House social settlement in Chicago, founding of the American Association of University Professors and the National Association for the Advancement of Colored People, organization of the American Civil Liberties Union, and participation in the women's suffrage and anti-war movements. He called for the formation of a third political party during the Great Depression. Dewey was also in demand as a speaker and consultant. He lectured in Japan and China in 1919 and 1920. He was invited by the Turkish government to evaluate their educational system in 1924. The Soviet Union requested the same evaluation in 1928. In 1937, he would chair the hearings conducted by the Commission of Inquiry into the Charges Made against Leon Trotsky and his son in the Moscow Trials. Dewey had little sympathy for Trotsky's ideology, but he felt Trotsky deserved a fair trial. The "Dewey Commission" found Trotsky not guilty of treason and murder although Stalin had tried and convicted the men in absentia during the 1936-1937 political trials.[41]

Dewey's parents were Congregationalists, and his mother was noted for her piety. She often inquired as to her son's and his friend's spiritual health. According to Dewey, her periodic question "Are you right with Jesus?" would cause an "inward laceration of spirit." As a young man Dewey abandoned Christianity, God, and the concept of sin and guilt. The resentment at his mother's inquiry into his childhood faith continued to grow throughout Dewey's life.[42] Following the abandonment of his faith in early adulthood, Dewey searched for a comprehensive philosophical system to replace the dualism of Western philosophy that separated "...mind from body, experience from intuition, fact from value, and reason from science."[43]

Many writers find it difficult to label and explain the philosophy of John Dewey. Most often called pragmatism, the philosophy has been described as one that reflects dissatisfaction with traditional philosophy. Pragmatists believe that philosophy must accomplish something by addressing the problems of the world and therefore emphasizes action. Pragmatists attempt to use the methods of scientific inquiry to evaluate philosophical ideas. Lastly, pragmatists attempt to change traditional concepts of value and science in order to bring reconciliation of the two.[44]

Other names have been ascribed to Dewey's philosophy including instrumentalism, experimentalism, empiricism, naturalism, and functionalism. Robert J. Roth de Dewey's philosophy as one of naturalism in that..."man with his habits, institutions, desires, thoughts, aspirations, ideals, and struggles is within nature, an integral part of it...and insists...on man's continuity with nature and on the fact that man can achieve self-realization only in and through nature." Effectively, Dewey is saying that the human being survives and develops only in and through his material environment.[45] In summarizing Dewey's philosophy, Roth states:

> Nothing can be admitted which transcends the possibilities of concrete, human experience. There is no absolute, no transcendent being, no extra-mundane reality...there is no room for a supernatural religion...and that "supernatural" means that which transcends the possibilities of concrete human experience and involves an absolute being.[46]

Hence, we have the dominant theme of John Dewey's philosophy—human self-realization accomplished through interaction with nature. "In this consists man's happiness which is nothing less than the gradual development of man's capacities as he acts in and through nature."[47]

From this philosophical theme Dewey addressed art, education, morals, politics, science, and religion. As regarding education, Dewey's philosophy would have a profound and lasting impact both in America and internationally. Sidney Hook, one of Dewey's great admirers and defenders, summarized Dewey's educational philosophy. From this philosophical theme Dewey addressed art, education, morals, politics, science, and religion."[48] Quoting Hook:

> It is this theory of experience which underlies Dewey's conception of man as a creature who, although bound by the antecedent conditions of his existence, can within limits redirect and redetermine both the world and himself and become morally responsible for those things which his thought and action can influence.[49]

The second central idea of Dewey's philosophy, according to Hook, is democracy in education, "...an equality of concern for each individual in the community to develop himself as a person." As such, the individual, in harmony with their fellow human beings, would maximize their distinctive growth. To Dewey, this concern for the individual would mean a "moral equality." Under Dewey's educational democracy, such equality would mean that individuals would *not* be held to a common base for comparison in respect to quality. In other words, common and quantitative standards are inapplicable for comparison of student achievements. Additionally, moral equality means "...intrinsic qualities which require unique opportunities and differential manifestation..." Said another way, the essential nature of a thing may be approached in non-traditional ways and interpreted differently, that is, there are no "right" or "wrong" answers.[50]

Dewey's third central idea was that the ways human beings learn can be discovered through scientific psychological study. Critics were skeptical that "psychological and sociological research has established enough 'truths' about the nature of the child and the learning process to provide infallible guides to methods and even content in the education of the very young."[51] In fairness, the arguments of both sides of this issue have some merit. Scientific and sociological research may discover better methods of teaching children. However, knowing the worldview of Dewey and the imposition of that worldview into the educational system, the concerns of Dewey's critics are real.

Psychology, published by Dewey in 1896, was the first American textbook on the "revised" subject of education. It became the most widely read, quoted, and used textbook in American schools of education. Beginning with his twenty-five-year affiliation with Columbia University's Teachers' College, Dewey's "...writings shaped the 20th Century U.S. curriculum..."[52] His ideas on education would extensively permeate American education, and the results are still being felt today.

The impact of Dewey and Spock on the Boomers during their formative years is incalculable. Given their beliefs and worldview, it is undeniable that a major cultural shift of seismic proportions was in the making. But there were other factors that would contribute to this cultural shift.

Chapter 2

Boomers – The Fifties

Born in October 1945, I am at leading edge of the Boomer generation. As previously mentioned, I grew up on my parent's Oklahoma dairy farm about three miles from Owasso, a hamlet of two hundred to three hundred people at that time. Five miles in the other direction was Collinsville, a fairly sizable town of a thousand or two. More importantly, it had many stores and a night-life, at least on Thursdays and Saturdays when families from the many surrounding farms as well as townspeople would gather to do much of their shopping. Stores would stay open late including the movie theatre (which we were not allowed to attend), small restaurants, barber shops, grocery stores, appliance stores, and Henry's Five and Dime where one could spend hours determining how to spend fifty cents on pencils, candy, comic books, and trinkets. We traveled to town on Saturday night in the back of a flatbed truck as we didn't own a car. Parallel parking was allowed in the center of the street as well as diagonal parking down both sides. We watched people as they walked up and down the sidewalks while visiting, shopping, window-gazing, and generally passing the time. If we were lucky, reasonably well behaved, and the budget permitted, we would get an ice cream cone or bottle of pop.

By 1949 we began noticing a group of people who began assembling each week in front of one of the plate glass store windows on Main Street. We had heard about the beast, that mesmerizing cyclops that stared back at the spectators gathered before it. Rather quickly these strange creatures began appearing in homes around the area. By 1951, our family had adopted one, and life would never be the same. With the exception of the movie theatre, Thursday and Saturday evenings saw Main Street windows darkened and the streets substantially deserted, as the stores were no longer open late. Within two years of television's first appearance, the social and shopping patterns of America had completely changed. Television would have an impact on American society far greater than could have been imagined by those walking along a pre-TV Main Street in Collinsville on a Saturday night in 1949. TV ownership would mushroom from one hundred thousand in 1948 to fifty million by 1959.[53]

Our third significant shared event and formative experience in the creation of the Boomers was television. Historian Daniel Boorstin wrote, "Of all the wonders of TV, none was more remarkable than the speed with which it came. Television conquered America in less than a generation..." Gutenberg's printing press would take five hundred years to reach its full impact.[54] Only one household in one hundred had a television in 1948.[55] The percentage of American homes having a television grew to nine percent within two years, sixty-five percent by 1955, and eighty-six percent by 1959.[56] By 1959, a majority of all Boomers had been born, and the oldest Boomer children were in their middle teens. And television was the Boomers' nanny.

From primitive peoples huddled around communal campfires in the millennia of the past to the generations of the early twentieth century, children received most of their values and worldview from their parents, and the local church and community almost universally reflected those same values and worldview. Children in colonial America and the post revolution United States attended local schools whose teachers and textbooks strongly reflected the parents' values. The effects of the progressive school of education were not substantially felt in most parts of the nation before 1940. During the first half of the twentieth century books and newspapers and even radio were still the province of the adult world. Even from the advent of motion pictures in the 1920s through the end of World War II, the movie industry's influence on the molding and shaping of a child's worldview was somewhat limited and generally supportive of the parents' values and worldview. However, with the advent of television, there was a new member of the family seated at the communal campfire. The American child would be exposed to substantial external influences for long periods of time each day. In a series of exceptional essays published in 1981 about television as a social and cultural force, Richard Adler wrote:

> The TV set has become the primary source of news and entertainment for most Americans and a *major force in the acculturation of children*...Television is not simply a medium of transmission, it is an active, pervasive force...a mediator between our individual lives and the larger life of the nation and the world; between fantasy and fact; between old values and new ideas; between our desire to seek escape and our need to confront reality.[57] (emphasis added)

By 1958, the average American watched over five hours of television each day with children watching (becoming acculturated) about the same number of hours as adults although at different times.[58] Michael Novak called television a "...molder of the soul's geography. It builds up incrementally a psychic structure of expectations. It does so in much the same way that school lessons slowly, over the years, tutor the unformed mind and teach it 'how to think'." To Novak, television is a "homogenizing medium" with an ideological tendency that is a "vague and misty liberalism" designed "however gently to undercut traditional institutions and to promote a restless, questioning attitude." Television served its masters, the state and the great corporations, even when exalting "...the individual at the expense of family, neighborhood, religious organizations, and cultural groups...that stand between the isolated individual and the massive institutions."[59] The "restless, questioning attitude" is an excellent description of what the Boomer children of the 1950s would exhibit in the 1960s. Many historians and sociologists believe that the greatest number of significant shared events and formative experiences that defined the Baby Boomers as a distinctive group was provided by television—more than the influence of parents and more than the massive numbers that form the Baby Boomer cohort.[60]

It is interesting that television shows in the 1950s are almost universally maligned as being a vapid depiction of the American family in all of its saccharine sweetness and depiction of life in general in which the good guy always prevails. Yet, tune into any cable system and it is not difficult to find reruns of the programs popular in the 1950s—Father Knows Best, Leave It to Beaver, Adventures of Ozzie and Harriet, Davy Crockett, Roy Rogers, Make Room for Daddy, Perry Mason, and Superman to name a few. Most of these programs are considered "family friendly" and to mild degree grant deference to the values and worldview of the Boomers' parents' generation as the nation drifted toward a mass culture. Television of the 1950s and early 1960s presented life in America the way it should be and, to a lesser extent, the way it was for many—male dominated families, high marriage rates, low divorce rates, and multiple children. Children saw a world in which challenges could be met, problems conquered, and wrongs righted.[61]

When the 1960s arrived, Boomers were told that all was not well with the world, and because all was not well, the Boomers' parents' view of the way things should be was no longer acceptable. Boomers were told that the way to fix the problems, to right the wrongs, was to reject their parents' ways and worldview and plot their own future. And it was television that gave a face to the Boomers' sense of generational identity and separated them from every past generation.[62]

The Boomer generation was the first to have a defined sense of themselves because of its enormous size. According to Steve Gillon the Boomer cohort was "…the single greatest demographic event in American history—more significant, even, than the staggering loss of life during the Civil War."[63] A large part of the generation that came of age in the 1930s postponed marriage and childbearing due to the severe financial difficulties caused by the Great Depression. This group joined the returning soldiers and sailors of World War II in establishing families and bearing children.[64] But only half of the Boomer baby production came from the late-nesting members of the Greatest Generation and early-nesting Silents. The other half resulted from remarkably high levels of fertility.[65] The peak year for Boomer births was 1957 with 4,300,000 live births and a fertility rate of 122.7 births per one thousand *women aged 15-44 years*. Only 1947's birth rate of 26.1 births per one thousand *population* exceeded that of 25.3 births per one thousand for 1954 and 1957.[66] After 1957, most Boomer children were born to large Silent-headed families as opposed to the older Greatest Generation members.[67]

Table 1 reflects the remarkable increase in live births, birth rates, and fertility rates for the Boomer cohort from 1946 through 1964 in comparison to the sixteen-year period prior to the boom and

	Table 1 United States Live Births, Birth Rates, and Fertility Rates 1930-2000		
Years	Average Number of Live Births Per year	Average Birth Rate Per Year (1)	Average Fertility Rate Per Year (2)
1930-1945	2,595,375	19.9	82.6
1946-1964	4,004,229	24.3	113.4
1965-2000	3,686,787	15.8	71.0

Note (1) Birth Rates are live births per 1,000 population.
Note (2) Fertility Rates are live births per 1,000 women aged 15-44 years.

Data derived from source:
US Center for Disease Control: Table 1-1. Live Births, Birth Rates, and Fertility Rates, by Race: United States, 1909-2000
http://www.cdc.gov/nchs/data/statab/t001x01.pdf
Accessed: September 24, 2009

the 36 year period following the boom. It must be remembered that the total numbers of Boomers depends on the starting point and ending point of the Boomer years. However, the number of Boomers born is generally considered to be between seventy-six million and eighty million. As remarkable as the numbers are, the birth rate and fertility rates are just as astounding when compared to the preceding and following periods. Size of the Boomer cohort was, in itself, a significant shared event and formative experience. As one writer stated, "Once you're a market—especially a really big market—you can change history."[68] Business was quick to capitalize on this huge market.

By using television, marketers talked directly to Boomers, bypassing their parents. Boomers also commanded attention in education, too. California built one entire school per week during the 1950s, and 1954 saw construction of 60,000 new classrooms. This bulge would occur again at the college level in the 1960s. This growth was repeated across the United States throughout the 1950s.[69] Boomers became accustomed to being the center of attention and getting what they needed and wanted. And what they wanted was to set the agenda.

Dr. Joshua Zeitz of Cambridge University has identified three causes of the baby boom. Two of the reasons have been discussed. First, the postponement of marriage and childbearing during the Great Depression and World War II that led to a bunching of family formation by this older group immediately after World War II. Second, this bunching occurred at the same time the younger service men and women returning from the war began family formations. Dr. Zeitz's third cause of the baby boom is the phenomenal prosperity experienced by America starting in World War II and continuing through the 1950s.[70] At the end of World War II America found itself at the pinnacle of world power, both militarily and economically. It was the sole nuclear power, and its lands and industry were untouched by the ravages of war. It was a giant nation full of natural resources. James Patterson, Brown University historian, wrote "...economic growth was indeed the most decisive force in the shaping of attitudes and expectations in the postwar era."[71] And to Boomer children prosperity became a significant shared event and formative experience that would profoundly impact their generation, perhaps more so than their parents. J. Walter Smith and Ann Clurman in their book *Generation Ageless* wrote:

> The economy, not protests, is the central dynamic shaping the shared generational character of Baby Boomers. The starting point for Boomers was their shared expectations about the future, rooted in the robust economic growth of their formative years. They took for granted a world of unbridled economic optimism, unprecedented abundance, and wide-ranging prosperity...Boomers grew up with a presumption of economic security, and thus a sense that the future could be taken for granted and would assuredly turn out to be a brighter place than yesterday or today.[72]

The presumption of economic security and the taking for granted of continued economic optimism, abundance, and prosperity that would last forever created a new mindset in America, especially among the Boomers. In 1965, the first year after the Boomer generation officially ended, Charles Reich wrote: "Society today is built around entitlement." In other words, there was a firm popular expectation that some specific or general outcome will occur, whether or not it is formally embodied in law. These expectations include professional licenses, executive contracts, stock options, social security pensions, and education, and most of the more important entitlements flow in some form or fashion from government. But, whether private or from government, "…to the recipients they (entitlements) are essentials, fully deserved, and in no sense a form of charity."[73]

To the growing and prosperous middle class of the 1950s, life was good, and there was no end in sight. Unemployment averaged 4.5% for the entire decade and at its worst during the recession of 1957-1958 inflation rose to only 6.8%.[74] For the first time in their lives, and perhaps their parents' lives, they owned a home of their own with an automobile in the driveway. And not just any old clunker, by the late 1950s it was a shiny new one with lots of chrome and fins. Those cars would soon cruise down the new Interstate Highway System approved by Congress in 1956.

The first homes of the men and women who fought World War II were criticized as little boxes made out of ticky-tacky, looking all the same. Malvina Reynolds wrote "Little Boxes" after she had driven by some of the post-World War II construction of homes around Daly City, California. The song gained renewed popularity in the 1960s as folk singers would ridicule the supposed mindless conformity of American society in the 1950s.[75] Never mind that the severe housing shortage made those little boxes all looking just the same appear as mansions to the young families. Political scientist James Q. Wilson probably expresses the feelings of most of the average Boomer parents about their new post-war homes, ticky-tacky or not. He writes about living in suburban Southern California, not New York City.

> People who live in Southern California are not richer or better educated than those who live in New York; the significant point about them is that they don't live in New York, and don't want to. If they did, they—the average Los Angeleno (my family, for example)—would have lived most of their

lives in a walkup flat in, say, the Yorkville section of Manhattan or not far off Flatbush Avenue in Brooklyn. Given their income in the 1930s, life would have been crowded, noisy, cold, threatening—in short, *urban*. In Long Beach or Inglewood or Huntington Park or Bellflower, by contrast, life was carried on in a detached house with a lawn in front and a car in the garage, part of a quiet neighborhood, with no crime (except kids racing noisy cars), no cold, no smells, no congestion.[76]

Suburbanization would result in one other cultural shift—the decline of the extended family as children living with or near their parents in inner cities began moving to the suburbs. The extended family dissolved into the nuclear family consisting of a mother, father, and children. Instead of three or four generations living in close proximity, only two generations would live in a household, and that arrangement would end as the parents' children went off to college or married and moved away.[77] Critics also point to the suburban exodus that left the cities with fewer middle-class neighborhoods and an increase in poverty, drugs, and crime.[78]

Prosperity had given the Boomer parents a piece of the American dream—a home of their own filled with Boomer kids. And these homes would be in the suburbs, not the crowded city. And the prosperity of the 1940s and 1950s would continue and accelerate into the 1960s.[79]

Closely allied with prosperity was another significant shared event and formative experience of Boomer children—the spectacular technological achievements of the late 1940s and 1950s. World War II sparked the rapid technological advances mostly of military orientation including the atom bomb. The technological advances did not slow following the war but shifted along more consumer-oriented paths. The splitting of the atom for destructive purposes would now be put to peaceful uses. The first transistor was designed and built in December 1947, and further developments would lead to a Nobel Prize for Physics. Swanson's TV Dinners appeared in late 1953 with sales of twenty-five million per year by 1955. The first xerographic method photocopier was introduced in 1958.[80] The medical field received its share of technological miracles as antibiotics helped conquer tuberculosis, diphtheria, whooping cough, and measles. In 1955 Dr. Jonas Salk developed the first vaccine effective against polio that had struck an average of thirty-nine thousand Americans each year. By the end of the decade, polio was virtually eliminated in the United States.[81]

Not all history-altering discoveries in the 1950s were made in the United States. Two Cambridge research scientists announced that "they had discovered the secret of life." In April 1953, James Watson and Francis Crick described the double-helix structure of the DNA molecule in the scientific journal *Nature*.[82]

Jet travel, interstate highways, automatic washers and dryers, and television made their appearances between the end of World War II and the end of the 1950s. Air conditioning was virtually unknown in America before the war except in some major public buildings. Beginning in the post-war period, the installation of air conditioning grew steadily, first in public buildings and then homes. By 1980, three-fourths of the homes in the south and half the homes nationwide would have air conditioning.[83]

Among all of the technological developments of the 1950s, none rank higher in memory of the early Boomers and their parents than the occurrences on the evening of October 4, 1957. It was also on an October night nineteen years earlier that Orson Wells' Mercury Radio Theatre on the Air created a series of simulated news bulletins reporting an invasion by Martians. The adaptation of an episode of H. G. Wells' *The War of the Worlds* was so realistic in describing the terror spread by the invading Martians that thousands panicked. But the NBC radio network announcer of 1957 was not presenting fantasy when he said, "Listen now for the sound that forever separates the old from the new." The "beep-beep" chirping sound that came from outer space was produced by a man-made, man-launched satellite as it circled the earth. Even more unnerving to Americans was that Sputnik I was launched by the Russians. The twenty-three inch diameter, 184-pound silver-colored satellite with four trailing antennae could do nothing more than transmit meaningless signals as it circled the earth in an elliptical orbit every ninety-six minutes. Not only could it be heard, reflections of sunlight from Sputnik I's metallic skin could be seen near the horizon with the naked eye if conditions were right in the early morning or early evening. The atomic age had begun with a tremendous blast in the New Mexican desert in 1945. Twelve years later, the space age would sound its arrival with a simple three-tenths of a second beep. Ironically, the quintessential 1950s television program *Leave It To Beaver* would premier later that same evening. Now, the very safe world of The Beaver would coexist with a very unsettled and nervous world created by Sputnik.[84]

The impact of Sputnik I on America cannot be overestimated; it was monumental and launched the space race. Suddenly, America's supreme confidence in its technological superiority was shaken. Almost immediately, science, technology, and engineering programs were substantially changed and received huge funding increases. The increases in science and engineering led to the development of microelectronics technology eventually paving the way for computers and the Internet. The shift of funding would come at the expense of consumer goods, perhaps fueled by the uneasy feeling of conspicuous consumption that had grown among the Depression-era parents during the prosperous years of the 1950s preceding Sputnik. Sputnik also created the impression that America was weak, complacent, that a "missile gap" existed between America and the Russians, and that the Eisenhower-Nixon administration was responsible. These impressions were erroneous, as they would later be understood in context of the times. However, John Kennedy would capitalize on these misconceptions and narrowly win the presidential election of
1960. In reality, Eisenhower was far more concerned about averting nuclear war, a very real concern during the middle and late 1950s, than beating the Soviets into space. Even so, America was also on the verge of space exploration with its scheduled launch of the Navy's Vanguard satellite in November 1957, but due to rocket problems of weight and design, the launch was delayed until 1958. Forty years after the first Sputnik, NASA chief historian Roger D. Launius wrote that "…the Soviet announcement changed the course of the Cold War…Without Sputnik, it is all but certain that there would have not been a race to the Moon, which became the centerpiece contest of the Cold War."[85]

Writing of America's response to the launching of Sputnik, Simon Ramo, space pioneer and cofounder of the company that became TRW, Inc., stated the event, "…was comparable to the reaction I could remember to Lindbergh's landing in France, the

Japanese bombing of Pearl Harbor, and Franklin D. Roosevelt's death."[86]

In this and the previous chapter, six areas of significant shared events and formative experiences from 1945 to 1960 have been identified that shaped the Boomers of the 1960s and beyond: child rearing techniques influenced by Benjamin Spock that instilled a spirit of permissiveness; a progressive, humanistic educational model based on John Dewey's teachings; the advent of television and its attendant acculturation of children; the exceptionally large and dominating Boomer cohort; unparalleled prosperity; and a burst of technological advances. Each of these influences can be seen in the Boomer personality that emerged by the middle to late 1960s.

It has become the accepted fashion among many Boomers and the institutions they represent to demean the decade of the 1950s and to a lesser extent the late 1940s. Derogatory descriptions abound in their derisive denunciation of the era: conformity, rigidity, hypocrisy, bigotry, repression, prudishness, and materialism to name a few. Before we leave the decade of the 1950s, we should examine these charges.

One of the central charges is that it was a decade of blind conformity and willful authority. Leonard Steinhorn writes in his book *The Greater Generation* of the stereotypical conformist white male of the 1950s. Steinhorn likens those men to that of the William H. Whyte's character in The Organization Man, "...a yes-man...who got ahead, and questioning authority was a fast track to unemployment." In Steinhorn's view, "Men climbing the corporate ladder were expected to act and dress a certain way—the proverbial man in the gray flannel suit—and company culture revolved around slavish obedience to the boss's will." Let's examine Steinhorn's supposed 1950s yes-men in the gray flannel suits. These are the same men and women who were soldiers and sailors that sloughed through four years of combat in World War II. They stood up to the worst the enemy had to offer. They assaulted the beaches at Normandy and destroyed Nazi tyranny in Europe. They fought on the seas and in the jungles of Asia and the islands of the Pacific. Can Mr. Steinhorn really believe these men and women would cower from an overbearing boss for fear of losing a job? As to "slavish obedience", again these men and women were raised in a different era and were taught respect for authority. Second, these men and women were veterans of the military, trained to follow orders. Military training emphasizes that the mission comes first, not the individual. Others stayed on the home front including millions of Rosie the Riveters who worked long hours to assist in accomplishing the country's mission of winning the war. They were fearless, focused on the mission, had a strong work ethic, and a healthy respect for authority. And they carried these qualities into the postwar workplace. It was normal for those men and women to work hard toward the accomplishment of the corporate mission. Thus, the better description of the 1950s American man and woman would be one of respect for authority and a focus on mission, not slavish obedience. One wonders at the outcome of World War II had Mr. Steinhorn's Boomers carried to the battlefields overseas and factories in America their number one attitude of a constant questioning and challenge of authority.[87]

The Greatest Generation and Silent Generation adults of the 1950s have been described as materialistic. Again, we must look at the history of these people. Many were children or young adults during the depravations of the Great Depression. Then along came World War II with millions living a Spartan soldier's life on the battle fronts of the world while those at home coped with shortages and rationing of goods and services. They came out of World War II much older and wiser than most generations beginning family life and working careers. Hard work and prosperity made it possible to own a home of their own, to drive a car of their own, have adequate food for their families, and with a little left over for some of life's simple pleasures. All of this catching up was crammed into a short ten to fifteen years as they approached middle age. Yet, there was a tinge of materialism that began creeping into American life at the close of the 1950s. President Eisenhower recognized this and cautioned America about "worshiping material success", and because of this excessive preoccupation with material success the Commission on National Goals was created. The president's fear was that America could "become emptied of idealism" because of the focus on materialism. To combat national aimlessness, the Commission was charged with restoring a sense of purpose and direction in the country.[88]

But the preoccupation for material success or materialism is not an exclusive obsession of the 1950s generation. The late 1800s, the 1920s, and the Yuppies of the 1980s are all examples of periods of excessive emphasis on materialism. For a true picture of Boomer claims of rampant 1950s materialism as compared to Boomer virtue, we return to Smith and Clurman's *Generation Ageless*.

> The economy, not protests, is the central dynamic shaping the shared generational character of Baby Boomers…Boomers didn't have to aspire to the American Dream; they felt they were born into it…they championed a new notion: that of an unfettered, indulgent, absorbed, celebratory self.[89]

Another charge leveled against the era of the 1950s was rampant bigotry, racism, and repression. Such charges have been made against every generation in America since the Europeans first stepped foot on the continent. There was a measure of racism and repression as had there been in every generation since our founding. America's record has been far from perfect, but with each successive generation there was progress on achieving the nation's ideals regarding racial equality. It will never be achieved in one generation and, given the human condition, it may never be achieved completely. However, there was progress in the 1940s and 1950s in moving toward the American ideals with regard to discrimination and racism. A sampling of the road to equality includes President Truman's July 1948 integration of the armed services and a separate executive order calling for fair employment policies in federal government civil service jobs. The Equal Rights Amendment for Women was adopted by the Senate in January 1950. In June of that same year the Supreme Court ruled against segregation in public universities. To enforce anti-discrimination clauses in federal employment contracts, President Truman established the Committee on Government Contract Compliance in December 1950. In December 1952, the Supreme Court upheld a lower court ruling barring discrimination on interstate railways. The Supreme Court prohibited restaurants from refusing service to black patrons in a June 1953 ruling. The landmark ruling handed down in May 1954 in Brown vs. Board of Education struck down separate-but-equal doctrine that allowed racial segregation in public schools and other facilities. In April 1956, the Supreme Court reversed a lower court ruling on a South Carolina law and thereby forced racial integration on public buses. President Eisenhower sent the 101st Airborne Division to Little Rock, Arkansas's Central High School to protect black students attempting to integrate Little Rock's schools.[90] And the progress made in the 1960s on race and poverty were the products of that 1950s generation that has been so maligned. The oldest Boomers were nineteen at the time of passage of the Civil Rights Act of 1964.

A minimal understanding our nation's history in the twentieth century will reveal Steinhorn's assertions as spurious when he says "...Baby Boomers and Greatest Generation Americans witnessed the same society and its many flaws. One made the choice to accept and defend the status quo. The other made the choice to advance the principles of democracy, equality, and freedom, the founding principles of our country..."[91] Which of the generations truly advanced the principles of democracy, equality, and freedom? Was it the Boomers who occupied a frightened professor's office or college administration building during a sit-in or the generation that survived a depression, fought a world war, rescued a prostrate world following the war, obtained an education that included the wisdom of their patrimony, and reared a family?

The Greatest Generation and Silent Generation who raised their children in the 1950s were no different than those of prior decades. The 1950s fell short of reaching the ideals of the nation. But what generation's reality doesn't fall short of their ideals? Perfection is a goal that will never be achieved. The sin is to not continue the journey and build on the work of those gone before. The sin is to derail the process through impossible demands of instant and total perfection. Because of a significant repudiation of their patrimony, Mr. Steinhorn and his like-minded Boomers separated themselves from all generations of Americans prior to the 1960s. For the Boomers and others critics, the 1950s are an excuse, a bogeyman, to justify the abandonment of their heritage. Steinhorn and his concurring Boomers self-servingly spout platitudinous lip service to high ideas of freedom, equality, and adherence to the ideals of the Founders. Yet, there is a disconnect. The evidence does not support their sentiments, and their arguments fail on one or more levels: ignorance of the history of the nation; early youthful gullibility of Boomers in accepting their like-minded seniors' thoughts, ideas, and concepts; or worse, a knowing and selfish rejection of the ethics and values of their ancestry.

Steinhorn makes an exceptionally revealing statement about the general mindset and attitude of the Boomers—that of entitlement—which had become pervasive by the end of the twentieth century. He writes, "The problem is that the reality of Greatest Generation America fell far short of the ideal—the America that Boomers beheld wasn't even close to the America they were promised."[92] (emphasis added) What generation was ever *promised* anything? Each generation is given the cultural heritage of all that have gone before. Each generation is given the opportunity to do great and good things, and they should do better for they stand on the shoulders of their ancestors. Each generation receives an opportunity, not a promise nor an entitlement.

The 1950s was a very crowded and busy decade and anything but dull. America emerged from World War II at the pinnacle of prosperity and world power, but almost immediately we were pulled into a cold war as the Russians stole America's atomic secrets and raced towards nuclear parity and world domination. The first three years of the decade were consumed by the Korean War along with the internal and external threats of communism. Duck and cover drills along with home fallout shelters stocked with provisions to survive a nuclear winter became common. America took those in stride. After all, we won the war, hadn't we? America could lick anybody. Families with carloads of Boomer kids were driven to elementary schools bulging at the seams. By the end of the decade millions of Americans took to the road and discovered motels and Disneyland. Above all the American can-do attitude reigned supreme. If we had a problem, we could fix it. If we couldn't fix it, we would invent something better. And Americans were good at inventing things. A fresh, new decade was dawning. On the last day of the decade, December 31, 1959, a young senator from Massachusetts prepared to announce his entry into the presidential race to be decided eleven months later.[93]

Chapter 3

Boomers – The Sixties – Ye shall not surely die[94]

John Kennedy was the first of the seven Greatest Generation presidents. From his election in November 1960, Greatest Generation presidents would occupy the White House for the next thirty-two consecutive years. Each of their resumes lists service in the military. Only three of the nine presidents of the twentieth century preceding the Greatest Generation presidents served in the military (Theodore Roosevelt, Harry Truman, and Dwight Eisenhower). World War II was the defining moment of the Greatest Generation and their presidents, and to them "Duty, Honor, Country" was a worldview *not* conceived in the ivory towers of academia, constructed by ideologues bent on building a utopia, or social engineers tweaking the mechanisms of society. The Greatest Generation's worldview was born in the cauldron of economic chaos and threats from maniacal despots attempting to enslave the world, and their worldview rested on their patrimony that was birthed in Western civilization.

John Kennedy defined his generation in his inaugural address when he said the Greatest Generation was a part of, "...a new generation of Americans: born in this century, tempered by war, disciplined by a hard and bitter peace, proud of our ancient heritage and unwilling to witness or permit the slow undoing of those human rights to which this nation has been committed."[95] These words would not have conflicted with the worldviews of his predecessors—Eisenhower and Truman. Yet, the election of Kennedy signaled a new era in America—an expectancy of something new, bright, young, and hopeful. Perhaps as an unconscious omen of the coming youthful mindset, the difference in ages of Eisenhower and Kennedy was almost twenty-seven years, the largest age gap in America's history between an outgoing and an incoming president. Dwight Eisenhower was born in 1890, and John Kennedy was born in 1917. The twenty-seven year span would eclipse by five years the next closest age gap

(George H. W. Bush and Bill Clinton) at twenty-two years. No other age gap between an outgoing and incoming president exceeded twenty years with most being fifteen years or less.

Americans and their Boomer children liked the young Kennedys. There were young children instead of grandchildren in the White House. Via television, Jacqueline Kennedy would give the nation a tour of her renovations of the White House, as might any proud young mother with a new home. It was the 1950s writ new. Dubbed Camelot, it would last less than three years and end with the president's assassination in November 1963. But Camelot was not all that it seemed. Well hidden from the country, serious physical problems and marital infidelity would belie the image of youthful vigor and devoted father and husband as projected by the President. At Kennedy's death, the oldest Boomer was almost eighteen, and the last of the Boomers would be born only thirteen months later.

Boomers did not come in the "one size fits all" variety. The stereotype of the 1960s Boomer was and remains sex, drugs, rock 'n' roll, protest, rebellion, and dropping out. That's the television version that has burned itself into our collective memory banks. But, as Richard Croker wrote in *The Boomer Century,* regarding Woodstock, the giant end-of-decade party at Yasgur's farm, "...as many as 400,000 of us attended, which means, of course, that 77,600,000 of us did not."[96] In reality, most of the Boomer generation did not identify with the Boomers at Woodstock and those attending in spirit if not body.

With regard to the Boomer dichotomy in America, David Gergen has said that the protesters:

> ...did not represent the majority of the people in their generation. So if you actually look at the polls on Vietnam, you'll find that the people who hung in the longest in support of the war, who stayed there the longest with approval ratings, were actually people between eighteen and twenty-four. And the crevices we saw opening up in the sixties and seventies have become canyons today. People are at war with each other for cultural values. And very importantly, the sixties and seventies brought us the Vietnam War, and the Vietnam War put an ax right down the middle of this

generation...because some people went and some people didn't. And the people who went resent those who didn't.[97]

Therefore, the Boomer cohort cannot be treated as an undifferentiated whole. To do so would overlook numerous minority opinions that are just as important even though they may not be shared by all in the cohort.

Yankelovich, Inc. has tracked and surveyed lifestyles and value trends in the consumer marketplace since the early 1960s. Baby Boomers, a term coined by one of the co-founders of the company, have been studied by the firm longer and in more depth than any other research organization. In 2006 Yankelovich conducted an extensive study of the diversity of Boomer hopes, dreams, and aspirations. To accomplish the study Boomers were separated into discrete attitudinal groups, each with a distinctive set of first priorities. The study used 174 items that measured attitudes across an extensive set of values and ambitions broadly defined as spiritual, personal, and societal.[98]

At one end of the Boomer spectrum of attitudes and values were the Straight Arrows, the largest group which comprises about one-third of the all Boomers. Straight Arrows are the most conservative (approximately 69%), hold traditional values, consider religion as important and a source of comfort in life, and have a strong sense of ethical clarity. Straight Arrows have the highest rejection of premarital sex and free-spirited nonconformity. At the other end of Boomer spectrum are those Yankelovich describes as Re-Activists which comprise less than one-sixth of the Boomers. Approximately sixty-five percent of Re-activists have a liberal or radical orientation. Re-activists rank highest in societal priorities and social causes. The other four attitudinal groups comprise the remaining half of the Boomers. Their values and priorities tend to fall between the two ends of the Boomer spectrum of values held by Straight Arrows and Re-Activists.[99]

Straight Arrows would have been more likely than Re-activists to be working or serving in the military during the 1960s. Re-activists have almost fifty percent more of their group who attended college or graduated from college (approximately 60%) as compared to the Straight Arrows (approximately 40%).[100] These findings indicate that Re-activists would have been more likely to have participated in the protest movement as well as remain in college longer to avoid the draft. This view appears to have merit when one considers that much of the protest and rebellion occurred on college campuses during the 1960s. And it is the college educated Re-activists that have had the greatest influence on society and culture through politics, the arts, education, and media since the 1960s.

The study revealed no divergence of attitudes between younger and older Boomers. In other words, younger and older Boomers tend to be found in the same proportions across all attitudinal categories. The study also reflects attitudes and values held at the time of study in 2006.[101] This raises the question with regard to possible changes, if any, of the attitudes and values within a group between the 1960s and the 2006 study. Even if there were some changes of attitudes within a group between the 1960s and 2006, the study gives ample justification for the belief that a large percentage of the 1960s Boomers did not identify with the attitudes and values of the stereotypical 1960s radical.

Robert Bork described that element within the Boomer generation that Smith and Clurman called the Re-activists.

> They didn't go just into the universities. The radicals were not likely to go into business or the conventional practice of the professions. They were part of the chattering class, talkers interested in policy, politics, and culture. They went into politics, print and electronic journalism, church bureaucracies, foundation staffs, Hollywood careers, public interest organizations, anywhere attitudes and opinions could be influenced. And they are exerting influence.[102]

For purposes of this book, Boomers will be considered as those generally reflecting the attitudes and values of the Re-activists. Three reasons support this decision. First, it is the values and attitudes of the Re-activists that appear to have prevailed to a great degree in American society, at least in the short term. Second, most defenders of the Boomer generation (Re-activists) incorrectly assume they represent the values and attitudes of the entire Boomer cohort. Third, the prevailing humanistic Boomer values and attitudes (Re-activists) that strive for ascendancy in American culture are merely the latest skirmishes in a much larger and older war. One of the purposes of the book is to look at that larger war and how those prevailing Boomer values and attitudes relate to that war.

What is the Boomer agenda? Leonard Steinhorn gives as good of a summary as anyone in his book, *The Greater Generation*. He claims, "Boomer culture has embraced diversity, liberated women, demolished discriminatory barriers, democratized institutions, freed up individual expression, fought for a healthier environment, and annulled the shame of being different."[103]

Irrespective of the desirability of the type of changes sought and manner in which they were attempted or achieved, Boomers like to characterize their generation as creating the changes out of whole cloth. Steinhorn essentially confirms this view when he wrote:

> In the 1960s, both Baby Boomers and Greatest Generation Americans witnessed the same society and its many flaws. One made the choice to accept and defend the status quo. The other made the choice to advance the principles of democracy, equality, and freedom, the founding principles of our country—they made the choice to end the hypocrisy of proclaiming but not observing our national ideals, to address the gap between the promise of American life and the reality of that life for so many Americans…Baby Boomers deserve even more credit for enriching democracy and fulfilling its promise when neither war nor catastrophe nor crisis nor necessity compelled them to do it…It was the Baby Boom generation that chose to tackle them, to hold the country to its grand ideals, to agitate for justice when it would have been easier to remain docile and silent, and we are a better nation because of that. It is why this generation's accomplishments eclipse what came before it, and why the Baby Boom must be recognized as *the Greater Generation*.[104] (emphasis added)

In light of Steinhorn's statement, the Apostle Paul's admonition to the church at Corinth appears appropriate. "For who sees anything different in you? What have you that you did not receive? If then you received it, why do you boast as if it were not a gift?"[105] Perhaps reflection on the shortcomings of the Corinthians would be beneficial to all Boomers who tout their generation's superiority. Such claims of superiority are indicative of much of the harsh Boomer criticisms of their parents and the decade of the 1950s.

The Boomer generation's claim to be the ones who were responsible for all of the great social and political revolutions of the 1960s is a myth. Boomers were merely the foot soldiers for change, not the catalysts. For the most part, 1960s Boomers were merely puppets whose strings were pulled by their humanist puppet masters. In essence, "...boomers adopted what others had conceived", and they put their numbers and enthusiasm behind those conceptions and made them important.[106] Boomers had been conditioned and trained by the significant shared events and formative experiences of the late 1940s and the 1950s. As one writer stated, "Probably never before in human history has a society brought together such a large number of potential dissidents...under conditions that so greatly facilitated their mutual influence."[107] But, members of prior generations were the true catalysts for revolution. For good or ill, the generals of the prior generations dictated the marching orders to the impressionable Boomer troops of the 1960s. As Croker wrote, "They (Boomers) just seemed to us to be such powerful agents of change that we can't help but blame them and credit them with things that probably were beyond their control."[108] However, as the Boomers moved into the 1970s and beyond, they began taking the swords from those prior generation revolutionaries to fight the revolution on their own terms. Three broad currents or campaigns would define that war in the 1960s: cultural change, race, and war.

Fred Kaplan's book *1959-The Year Everything Changed* strongly suggests that the seeds of cultural upheaval of the 1960s were planted in the 1950s and in particular 1959. According to Kaplan, "...it was a year when chains of all sorts were broken...in politics, society, culture, science, and sex. 1959 was the year when the shockwaves of the new ripped the seams of daily life...when categories were crossed and taboos were trampled, when everything was changing..."[109]

The sexual revolution would explode in the late 1960s. However, Alan Petigny in his book *The Permissive Society – America 1941-1965* wrote that the sexual revolution really began during World

War II with the great influx of women (four million) into the labor force to fill the vacancies of the twelve million men away at war. The incidence of single motherhood grew forty percent during the first half of the 1940s, from 7.1 to 10.1 babies born per one thousand unmarried women of childbearing age. He also contends that the upswing in pre-marital sex really began in the 1950s as opposed to the 1960s. The misapprehension occurred because the 1950s were a less candid era, and it was during the 1960s that the participants were more open about such activities. There were also indications that sex was becoming a commodity in America during the 1950s. Two high profile examples were the creation of *Playboy* magazine in the early 1950s and the opening of the first Playboy Club in February 1960, both exceptionally successful ventures.[110]

The birth control pill has been called a major factor in promoting the sexual revolution of the 1960s. However, this influence was due to the pill's profound impact on attitudes towards sex and conception and not so much the actual usage of the pill. First marketed in the United States in the summer of 1960 by the pharmaceutical company G. D. Searle, pill usage grew dramatically but diminished in the late 1960s and early 1970s due to its link with serious health problems.[111] The pill as a significant contributor to the sexual revolution is unquestioned. However, given the already growing level of premarital sex, merchandizing of sex, growing focus on sex in the media, more liberal definitions of obscenity in the arts, and the coming of age of the Baby Boomers, the sexual revolution would have occurred with or without the pill.

Just as the pill would contribute to the sexual revolution, so too would the dramatic changes in the arts and media. New offerings in literature, film, books, comedians, and music assaulted the boundaries of traditional morality. In *The End of Obscenity*, Charles Rembar wrote that, "...beginning in 1959, the law within the space of seven years made a profound and radical change" with regard to what is considered obscene. The three Supreme Court cases that challenged and overturned existing obscenity laws were *Lady Chatterley*, *Tropic of Cancer*, and *Fanny Hill*. As a result of these cases, three tests to determine the presence of obscenity would thereafter be applied: was the appeal predominantly prurient, was it patently offensive, and was there an absence of serious social value. Unless a work failed all three tests, the First Amendment would prohibit suppression. With regard to the last of the three cases Rembar wrote, "The 1966 *Fanny Hill* decision produced the cry, pained or joyful, as the case might be, 'The lid is off!'"[112]

There was a strong link between the student conflicts of the 1960s and a "...more liberal and permissive sexuality which cut social taboos to ribbons, and attitudes and behaviour which in general called into question and opposed the established social order."[113] The Free Speech movement was perhaps the closest manifestation of the 1960s rebellion that could be considered Boomer inspired and Boomer led. The Free Speech Movement that began on October 1, 1964 at the University of California's Berkeley campus when Mario Savio rallied his fellow protestors as he stood on top of a police car that had been immobilized by the masses of protesters. The protesters occupied a campus administration building in December and similar protests would spread to other campuses across the country. Initially to protest the arrest of a civil rights activist for defying the University's prohibition against political advocacy, Savio's impassioned speech was a milestone in the early history of the New Left (as opposed to the Old Left groups such as the Communist-led Du Bois Club, the Independent Socialist Club, and the Young People's Socialist League). Although the communist movement benefited from the Free Speech Movement according to FBI director J. Edgar Hoover, there were only a relatively few members who were communists or close to the Communist Party including the upper levels of the FSM involved in the movement.[114] FSM's attack on the University's authority to control the speakers allowed on campus would ultimately result in vast changes to academic government, student rights, and a new definition of the university. The shock waves that spread from the FSM would merge with the civil rights movement and Vietnam anti-war protests and create cauldrons of rebellion on campuses across America in the middle and late 1960s and early 1970s.

Walter was a friend of mine. Walter was black, and he came to Owasso Grade School at the beginning of the fourth or fifth grade following the Supreme Court's ruling on Brown vs. Board of Education that ended the separate but equal doctrine and allowed segregation in public schools. If I remember correctly, no other black children attended Owasso Public Schools at that time. By all standards Walter and his siblings' presence in our school was a non-event. There was only one grade of about thirty kids for each grade level, and Walter was in mine. Walter and I were part of the local Future Farmers of America chapter during the fall of 1959, our freshman year, and I was just turning fourteen. Several of us including Walter exhibited our livestock at the local Tulsa County Fair, Walter with his hog and me with my dairy cow. While at the fair, a half dozen of us rode in a pickup driven by an older boy to go to a local restaurant and get something to eat. That day we drove a half-mile east of the fairgrounds to a small, family operated diner with perhaps a half dozen booths. The six of us crowded into one booth and were busy deciding if we were going to eat anything other than a hamburger, fries, and a bottle of pop, which we never did. The proprietor came over and whispered into Walter's ear as we pored over the menus. Almost without our noticing him, Walter quietly got up and followed the owner through the kitchen door only three paces from our booth and sat inside the open door at a little ledge in plain sight of his friends. It seems the proprietor had said that, "there were some who were not ready for the change." Who "they" were was unclear, as I don't remember more than one other booth being occupied, and I don't recall the owner having talked with them since our arrival. Almost fifty years later I still can feel the initial stupor of incomprehension followed by an extreme feeling of embarrassment for Walter and for us as I realized what had happened. Little if anything was said for the remainder of the meal. We left and said nothing of the incident to Walter or he to us.

Certainly with regard to minorities, all was not well in American society following World War II, but prosperity had prompted a dramatic postwar drop in racial, religious, ethnic, and sexual discrimination. Color lines were broken in major sports in the late 1940s and early 1950s.[115] By all prior standards, racial equality advanced significantly during World War II, the late 1940s, and during the decade of the 1950s. A number of the executive, legislative, and judicial actions, many previously mentioned, were steadily tearing down the barriers to racial equality. Significant milestones included the Supreme Court decision that outlawed school segregation in 1954, the Civil Rights Act of 1964 barred discrimination in public places and employment, and the Voting

Rights Act of 1965 removed obstacles to voting by blacks. The seeds for all of these changes were planted and nourished in the 1940s and 1950s. The attitudes of Americans about race, religion, minorities, ethnic groups, and discrimination in general were changing for the better, and their change of attitudes was followed by action.

By the early 1960s there appeared subtle changes in the fight for equality. Later in the decade the changes would be anything but subtle. With regard to equality, America advanced but at an uncertain, halting, if not fitful pace. Robert Samuelson in his exceptional *The Good Life and Its Discontents* states that this uncertainty resulted from the shifting definition of what equality meant. This uncertainty grew as "...equality of condition and outcome were increasingly seen as essential for equality of opportunity." Samuelson lists three reasons for this new view of equality. The first cause was the civil rights movement of the 1960s. The excessive resistance to equal treatment before the law in the south became a morality tale, good versus evil played out daily on the evening news. Such injustice in the defense of inequality produced a belief that equality could be ended by political and judicial action. Second, there was a growing belief that equality of opportunity required a leveling of social conditions and as a consequence the importance of individual effort was devalued. Third, the changing definition of what constituted equality resulted in courts becoming the arbiters of social policy. In their new role as social engineers, the courts determined that what once were worthy goals became legal rights.[116]

But this new, disquieting definition of equality created another victim. In the march to equality of condition or outcome, the higher goal of racial harmony and brotherhood has been trampled. However, there can be no racial harmony and brotherhood without meaningful progress toward the ideal of racial equality.

The high ideals espoused by Martin Luther King in his eloquent "Letter from the Birmingham Jail" on April 16, 1963, and in his "I Have a Dream" speech four months later in Washington, D.C. drew Americans toward the goal of racial equality, harmony, and brotherhood.[117] However, that progress was severely undermined by events that included the later riots and destruction in dozens of American cities during the 1960s, the rise of the Black Power movement, the race hucksterism of some black and white politicians and civil rights leaders, and the ever growing governmental attempts at leveling society. Such leveling must ultimately lead to socialism with resulting declines in quality of life and standards of living, and loss of trust in government and its institutions. Ultimately, socialism breeds disharmony and erodes the foundations of a civil society that result in loss of freedom.

    A close examination of King's defense of his acts of civil disobedience, written from his jail cell in Birmingham, reveals a clear and unmistakable reliance on the principles of the Declaration of Independence and that those principles apply to all Americans. Equally important, King pointed out the most fundamental basis for our republican form of government was a social contract made under the authority of a higher law, not simply a social contract between the people and those who govern.[118] King called segregation morally wrong and sinful. And it was not the ephemeral amorphous morality of humanists.* King espoused the Biblical moral code that flowed from the Biblical teachings of Jesus Christ, preached by the Apostle Paul, and expounded upon by Saint Augustine and Saint Thomas Aquinas. Certainly King would have rejected Steinhorn's belief that, "...it was never enough to change policies or enact laws. Boomer idealism *demanded* that assumptions, norms, and attitudes change as well..."[119] (emphasis added) King understood that attitudes and assumptions are changed through an acceptance of and adherence to those very norms Steinhorn would change. King's rejection of the imperious imposition of new norms is abundantly evident in his closing paragraph of his Birmingham jail letter to his fellow clergymen.

> I hope this letter finds you strong in the faith. I also hope that circumstances will soon make it possible for me to meet each of you, not as an integrationist or a civil rights leader, but as a fellow clergyman and a Christian brother. Let us all hope that the dark clouds of racial prejudice will soon pass away and

---

* For purposes of this book, the terms "secularist" and "secular humanist" may be used interchangeably with the more general term of "humanist." Likewise, "secularism" and "secular humanism" may be used interchangeably with the more general term of "humanism." Attention to more specific definitions of "humanist" and "humanism" will be given in a later chapter.

the deep fog of misunderstanding will be lifted from our fear-drenched communities and in some not too distant tomorrow the radiant stars of *love and brotherhood* will shine over our great nation with all their scintillating beauty. Yours for the cause of Peace and Brotherhood.[120] (emphasis added)

While striving for equality, Martin Luther King, Jr. recognized the greater goal of racial harmony and brotherhood and that to achieve such harmony required a recognition and observance of those norms that are based on the Judeo-Christian tradition.

King stood against the various black nationalist groups wallowing in despair, bitterness, and hatred and that advocated violence. Fearing a racial nightmare, King believed his non-violent protests stood between the violent black nationalists' ideologies and millions of Negroes.[121] However, many within and without the civil rights movement wanted nothing to do with King's non-violent methods or his reliance on the norms of Judeo-Christian tradition. The four years between 1964 and 1968 were the most intense period of civil unrest since the Civil War. Racial violence flared in North Philadelphia during the summer of 1964 when a confrontation between a black motorist and a policeman resulted in two deaths, widespread looting, and the burning of six hundred mostly Jewish businesses. In August 1965, only five days after the signing of the Voting Rights Act, rioting in the Watts section of Los Angeles left thirty-four dead and forty-five million dollars in property damage. During the summer of 1966 thirty-eight ghetto neighborhoods were destroyed across the nation leaving seven dead, four hundred injured, and five million dollars of property damage. The summer of 1967 proved the most deadly with twenty-five killed and twelve hundred wounded in Newark. In Detroit, riots left forty-three dead while four thousand fires destroyed much of the city. Over sixty percent of the Detroit rioters were between the ages of fifteen and twenty-four.[122]

Whatever King's hopes were for racial harmony and brotherhood died with him when an assassin's bullet cut short his life on April 4, 1968 at the young age of thirty-nine. Rather than an abundant harvest of equality resulting from racial harmony and brotherhood, the nation embarked on a quest for equality through the efforts of thousands of politicians, judges, bureaucrats, and social engineers, each armed with a magnifying glass and carpenter's level.

Such efforts have become endemic in American society and exacerbate the loss of racial harmony and brotherhood. In the quest for greater equality of outcome, Samuelson points to two problems that persist for America at the turn of the millennium. First, government resources are not adequate and never can be. "Government cannot do everything for everybody. People (or institutions) must do some things for themselves." The perceived failure of government leads to less trust in government. Second, Americans generally favor more fairness and equality in national life. But their generosity weakens and shrinks when the government's efforts to help one group impinge on another.[123]

    I lost track of Walter after high school. I was told that he died a number of years ago. It would have been nice to sit with Walter once again in a restaurant over a hamburger, fries, and a pop with Dr. King's radiant stars of love and brotherhood shining upon us.

    Two men sat in a tea shop in a remote dusty village on the southern border of China. The oriental, "...a frail, stooped old man with a wispy beard who wore rice-mat sandals and baggy trousers held up by a string," said to the young American, "Welcome, my good friend." The old man's name was Nguyen That Thanh, but it was not the name he gave the American. The American was Major Archimedes L. A. Patti, and he had been personally sent by General William "Wild Bill" Donovan, the head of the clandestine Office of Strategic Services, to establish an intelligence network in the peninsula of Indo-China in the closing days of World War II. The old man, "the General" as he was known, wanted something, too. He had led a rag-tag band of exiles in a remote part of Asia known as French Indo-China. The exiled group had immediately contacted the new American authority to relay the General's message that he "needed American recognition." The two men talked long into the evening, the old man enjoying the American's cigarettes while discussing practical means of cooperation. The General was determined to drive out the Japanese and the French. Major Patti could only assure the old man that his strict objective was to harass the Japanese. Ho Chi Minh, the alias used by the General, and Major Patti agreed on that common aim. Major Patti was the first American soldier specifically assigned to Vietnam. The General was Ho Chi Minh who eventually became the first president of Vietnam. The men had mutual interests, and Major Patti felt that "much good" would come from the meeting. The date was April 30, 1945. Thus began America's involvement in Vietnam.[124]

Ho Chi Minh had lived in New York City for a brief time and thirty years later encountered the Americans again in Southeast Asia. When arrested by the Nationalist Chinese for being a suspected Communist, U.S. diplomats obtained his release in early 1943. At that time the Americans were secretly working with and aiding both the Chinese Communists and Chinese Nationalists in the fight against the Japanese. Ho Chi Minh, grateful for the American help, provided both intelligence and translation services. Minh had a second occasion to be grateful to the Americans for saving his life. Extremely ill from the effects of malaria in 1945, the OSS provided quinine and sulfa drugs.[125]

The Americans had an extensive file on Ho Chi Minh and knew he was a communist. In his reports to Washington, Patti said that Minh was not a "hardened Communist but foremost a nationalist." Born in 1890, Ho left his native land in 1911 and co-founded the Communist Party of France in 1920. Jean Longuet, the son-in-law of Karl Marx, assisted Minh as he traveled Europe as the Communist Party's expert on colonial issues. He spent two years in Moscow as a delegate to the Communist International where he met Lenin. Leaving Moscow in 1925, the next several years were spent in various communist posts. He was a friend of Communist Chinese leader Mao Zedong. During 1941, Minh and a band of Vietnamese guerrillas led by Vo Nguyen Giap, a history teacher, gathered in the village of Chingsi in southern China to form the League for the Independence of Vietnam that became known as the Viet Minh. He returned to Vietnam in 1945 for the first time since his departure thirty-four years earlier.[126]

American policy envisioned an end to colonialism after World War II. However, the leaders of Allied powers at the conferences at Cairo, Teheran, and Yalta adamantly opposed Roosevelt's interim trusteeship status for former colonies pending independence. Roosevelt, weak and sick, was unable to press America's demands. He died April 12, 1945. Major Patti's instructions on leaving Washington that same month were specific: "…not to assist the French in re-occupying Indo-China in any way whatsoever." But the dropping of atomic bombs on Japan brought a surprisingly quick end to the war on August 10th. Minh arrived in Hanoi on August 26th, a day after he had proclaimed independence for the Democratic Republic of Vietnam in the hills of Tan Trao, while accompanied by the American OSS guerrilla group that had joined with and trained Minh's guerrillas in fighting the Japanese.[127]

Independence Day was set for September 2nd, and Minh urgently sent for Patti to obtain American support. Upon arrival, Minh presented Patti with three sheets of paper. Unable to read them, Minh began to translate. Patti described the scene.

> So I just listened carefully and I was shocked. I was shocked to hear the first few words of our own Declaration of Independence, especially in reference to the Creator. He had the words life and liberty kind of transposed and I worked it out for him a little bit and I said, "I think this is the way it should be."[128]

Pronounced publicly in Hanoi on September 2, 1945, and etched in Bronze in Hanoi's museum of History were these words, "All men are created equal. They are endowed by their creator with certain inalienable rights, among these are Life, Liberty and the pursuit of Happiness." Regarding Minh, Patti would state, "He meant it—definitely. It was also a gesture to the American government. But he meant it. This was exactly what expressed his thoughts, his views. He wanted his people to be happy, he wanted them to be free. He knew they had been in chains for a long, long time."[129]

With two hundred thousand Chinese Nationalists occupying North Vietnam, Minh faced a dilemma. Believing colonialism to be dying and the French weak, Minh compromised by allowing fifteen thousand French soldiers to provide order and replace the two hundred thousand Chinese Nationalist troops. The French-Vietnam agreement was signed on March 6, 1946 only after substantially all of the Chinese had left Vietnam. The agreement provided a definition of independence for Vietnam with the fine print to come later. The French had agreed to withdraw her troops in the north in installments over a five-year period, or by 1952. In exchange, the Viet Minh would end Guerrilla activity in the south. Negotiations were to reconcile the two power bases—Saigon and Hanoi. However, in less than a year Minh was conducting guerrilla warfare, a campaign that would last eight years and involve the Americans who supported the French due to larger geo-political reasons.[130]

The first American presence in Vietnam ended less than a year after it started. The only American present at the signing of the French-Vietnam agreement on March 6th was Major White, the American consul. As the transition between the departing Chinese and the arriving French warships and soldiers was occurring, Major White described Ho Chi Minh.

> At the epicenter of all this sat Ho Chi Minh…his beard was then wispy and his manner curiously detached. The United States, Ho said, was in the best position to aid Vietnam in the postwar years. He dwelled at some length on the disposition of Americans as a people to be sympathetic to self-determination. But he said he felt the US government would find more urgent things to do…that, after all, Vietnam is a small country and far away.[131]

America's march to war in Vietnam was gradual and relatively insignificant until the early 1960s. It began by aid to the pro-French Vietnam funneled through France along with supplying a group of U.S. military advisors in 1950. Military equipment was sent in 1951. In July 1954, Vietnam was divided between North and South Vietnam at the seventeenth parallel. In October, President Eisenhower sent U.S. aid directly to South Vietnam. In February 1955, U.S. advisors begin direct training of the South Vietnamese military. Viet Cong attacks in South Vietnam caused the first U.S. casualties in July 1959.[132] U.S. troops in Vietnam were less than a thousand at the end of 1959 and 1960 but grew to three thousand by the end of President Kennedy's first year in office in 1961. A timeline of events is shown in Table 2. America's involvement in Vietnam was gradual but accelerating. The increasingly rapid growth of advisory personnel and aid of the United States evolved into a full-fledged and direct war against the North Vietnamese Army and Viet Cong insurgents in the south.

The geo-political domino theory was the main justification for concern over the loss of South Vietnam to communist North Vietnam. President Eisenhower first espoused this theory in 1954 in describing the consequences of a loss by the French in its war in Vietnam. It was believed that if Vietnam fell under communist control, other countries in the region (Laos, Cambodia, and Thailand) would fall to communism. This was a continuation of the policy President Truman followed in aiding Greece and Turkey to prevent the spread of communist regimes in eastern Europe. Effectively, the domino theory was a subset of the larger containment policy that had been the basic U.S. strategy since the end of World War II for responding to Soviet military and political power in Europe and other communist-led movements in the world.[133]

The point of no return occurred in March 1965 when President Johnson committed the first combat troops. Between December 1964 and December 1965, troops in Vietnam grew from twenty three thousand to one hundred eighty one thousand. The war peaked in 1968 in numbers of troops, deaths, battles, and by most other statistics by which war is measured.[134]

For America, the events of 1968 would be the most remembered. On both the home front and in Vietnam, it was an unbelievably tumultuous year—peace marches, sit-ins, protests, college campuses in turmoil, assassinations of Martin Luther King and Robert Kennedy, riots at the Chicago Democratic National Convention, capture of an American ship (Pueblo) by North Korea and imprisonment of its crew, decision of Lyndon Johnson to not seek a second term as president, beginning of the Paris peace talks, Tet Offensive, My Lai Massacre, and riots that set aflame a hundred U.S. cities.

The North Vietnamese Tet offensive began on January 31st. It would prove to be a significant military victory for the Americans and South Vietnamese with thirty-seven thousand enemy troops killed. However, the cost to America was two thousand five hundred soldiers killed in action.[135] Americans troops experienced the bloodiest week of the war in February during the Tet Offensive—five hundred forty three were killed in action and two thousand five hundred forty seven were wounded.[136] The Tet Offensive marked the beginning of a critical change of attitude about the war in the minds of many Americans. A Harris poll of Americans in late March revealed that sixty percent viewed the Tet Offensive as a defeat for U.S. objectives in Vietnam.[137]

Table 2
America's Vietnam Chronology

Date	Event
April 30, 1945	Major Archimedes Patti met with Ho Chi Minh, Vietnamese Guerrilla leader and future president of the Democratic Republic of Vietnam.
July 16, 1945	Major Patti and 50-man OSS Guerrilla group parachute into North Vietnam to train and assist Ho Chi Minh in driving out the Japanese.
September 2, 1945	Ho Chi Minh declares Vietnam's independence. However, Ho enters an agreement with the French for Vietnam to be a "free state" within the French union.
February 1950	The United States Recognizes the Vietnams.
March 1950	The U.S. makes the first financial aid, channeled through France, to pro-French Vietnam.
June 1950	First U.S. military advisors sent to Vietnam.
September 1951	U.S. aid to France for Vietnam substantially increased and includes military equipment.
October 1954	President Eisenhower sends aid directly to South Vietnam.
February 1955	U.S. begins direct training of South Vietnam's army. The last French troops leave in April 1956.
July 1959	First U.S. casualties occur from Viet Cong attacks at Bein Hoa.
December 1959	U.S. troop strength in Vietnam less than 800.
November 1960	John Kennedy elected President of the United States.
May 1961	Kennedy announces U.S. troop use in Vietnam under consideration.
December 1961	U.S. troop strength in Vietnam approximately 3,000.
December 1962	U.S. troop strength in Vietnam approximately 11,000.
November 1963	President Kennedy assassinated.
December 1963	U.S. troop strength in Vietnam approximately 15,000.
August 1964	North Vietnamese torpedo boats attack U.S. destroyers in the Gulf of Tonkin. U.S. Congress passes Gulf of Tonkin resolution giving wide military powers to President Johnson.
November 1964	President Johnson re-elected.
December 1964	U.S. troop strength in Vietnam approximately 23,000.
March 1965	First American combat forces arrive at Danang.
March 1965	Sustained bombing of North Vietnamese targets begins.
November 1965	U.S. and North Vietnamese troops engage in battle for first time.
December 1965	U.S. troop strength in Vietnam approximately 181,000.
May 1966	Thousands demonstrate against the war in Washington, D.C.
December 1966	U.S. troop strength in Vietnam approximately 400,000.
December 1967	U.S. troop strength in Vietnam approaches 500,000.
January 1968	USS Pueblo, Navy intelligence gathering vessel, and 83-man crew captured by North Korea.
January 1968	Tet Offensive begins on January 31st.
February 1968	Highest weekly toll of the Vietnam War: 543 Americans killed in action and 2,547 wounded.
March 1968	My Lai massacre of 200 unarmed villages by Lt. William Calley and a platoon of U.S. soldiers
March 1968	President Johnson announces he will not seek re-election.
April 1968	Martin Luther King assassinated on April 4. Riots occur in cities

Table 2
America's Vietnam Chronology

	across the nation in which 46 would die.
April 1968	Tentative peace talk letters exchanged between the U.S. and Hanoi.
June 1968	Robert Kennedy shot on June 5th by a Jordanian, Sirhan Sirhan, due to Kennedy's pro-Israeli speeches. Kennedy dies on June 6th.
August 1968	Chicago Democratic Convention disrupted by heavy anti-war demonstrations that result in riots.
October 1968	President Johnson ends bombing of North Vietnam.
November 1968	Richard Nixon elected as President
December 1968	U.S. troop strength in Vietnam approximately 536,000.
July 1969	President Nixon and Ho Chi Minh exchange secret letters in which agreement to work for peace is reached.
July 1969	Apollo astronauts Neil Armstrong and Buzz Aldrin land on the Moon.
August 1969	400,000+ gather for the Woodstock Music Festival on a 600-acre farm near Bethel, New York.
September 1969	Ho Chi Minh dies.
November 1969	Washington, D.C. anti-war protest attracts 250,000.
December 1969	U.S. troop strength in Vietnam approximately 475,000.
April 1970	50,000 demonstrate in Washington, D. C. to support President Nixon's handling of the war.
May 1970	Amid widespread campus demonstrations in the U.S., four Kent State students killed by National Guardsmen.
December 1970	U.S. Congress repeals Gulf of Tonkin resolution.
December 1970	U.S. troop strength in Vietnam approximately 334,000.
April 1971	500,000 anti-war protesters demonstrate in Washington, D.C.
May 1971	Paris peace talks begin fourth year but still in deadlock.
December 1971	U.S. troop strength in Vietnam approximately 157,000.
June 1972	Five men break-in at the Democratic Party offices at the Watergate Hotel in Washington, D.C. The men are arrested.
August 1972	Last American combat units leave South Vietnam.
November 1972	President Nixon re-elected.
December 1972	Paris peace talks breakdown.
December 1972	U.S. troop strength in Vietnam approximately 24,000.
January 1973	Peace talks resume and an agreement is signed. President Nixon suspends military action against North Vietnam.
February 1973	U.S. military forces leave South Vietnam. Final POWs arrive in Philippines.
August 1974	President Nixon resigns as a result of the Watergate scandal. Gerald Ford becomes the president.
April 1975	Cambodian government surrenders to Communist Khmer Rouge.
April 30, 1975	Saigon falls. South Vietnam's government surrenders.
December 1975	Vientiane, Laos, captured by Pathet Lao resulting in all of Indo-China being under Communist rule with the exception of Thailand.

Source: Some material extracted from: Michael Maclear, *Vietnam* (New York: Tess Press, 2003), pp. xiv-xvi.

By the end of 1968, the number of American troops in Vietnam was five hundred thirty six thousand, just below the peak number of troops in Vietnam during the entire war reached in early 1969. President Nixon was inaugurated in January 1969, and troop strength would be reduced by sixty-one thousand by year's end. Dramatic troop reductions would continue over the next three years: one hundred forty-one thousand in 1970, one hundred fifty-seven thousand in 1971, and one hundred thirty-three thousand in 1972. Only twenty-four thousand troops remained in Vietnam by December 1972. A peace agreement between the United States and North Vietnam was reached in January 1973, and all American military forces left the country in February.[138]

But the war between the two Vietnams would continue for another two years after the Americans left. Saigon fell and the South Vietnamese government surrendered on the same day—April 30, 1975—exactly thirty years to the day after Major Patti and Ho Chi Minh sat drinking tea, smoking cigarettes, and believing "much good" would come from their meeting in the remote little border village in southern China.

The Cambodian government also surrendered to the communist Khmer Rouge in April 1975. By the end of the year, the Laotian government was overrun by the communist Pathet Lao. Much of French Indo-China was now under communist rule. The dominoes had fallen. The suffering and loss of life in the various Indo-China wars would pale in comparison to the victors' killing fields and harsh re-education camps.[139]

In Vietnam, the price of peace was truly high. Approximately one and one-half million Saigon government officials and supporters were forcibly sent to harsh rural development areas resulting in great social upheaval, deprivation, and loss of life. Two hundred thousand senior officials and military officers were sent to prisoner of war camps euphemistically called "re-education camps, in which many would remain for years."[140]

Added to the cost of "peace" was the Cambodian genocide by the communist Khmer Rouge that killed one million seven hundred thousand of their countrymen, about twenty-one percent of the Cambodian population, between 1975 and 1979.[141] War continued in the region when communist Vietnam invaded Cambodia in December 1978 and remained until 1989. In retaliation for Vietnam's invasion of Cambodia, China attacked in February 1979 but withdrew within one month after conducting a scorched earth campaign.[142]

The Laos domino fell in December 1975. Its fall was the result of the Paris cease fire agreement between America and Vietnam and subsequent pressure that the Royal Lao government share power with the communist Lao Patriotic Front. American forces were removed from Laos, but forty thousand North Vietnamese soldiers remained. Under this pro-Vietnamese protective umbrella, the clandestine efforts of the Pathet Lao moved it toward ascendancy.[143]

The Thailand domino wobbled but did not fall. The Communist Party of Thailand attained its greatest membership and support in the early 1970s with over four million followers, approximately ten percent of the population. With up to fourteen thousand armed fighters, the CPT acted as a state within a state. The Chinese gave considerable assistance to the revolutionaries, and in 1965 China's foreign minister stated that Thailand was its next target for revolution. However, China's own Cultural Revolution would divert its attention. China restored diplomatic relations with Thailand, and Mao Zedong assured the Thais that it should not worry about support of the Thai Communist Party by China. Several years later China's new strongman told another Thai premier that, "I am proud to say that the domino theory does not apply to Thailand anymore." The Thai Communist Party dissolved in the 1980s due to the loss of support from China and Vietnam.[144]

The reasons for the Vietnam War and the reaction to that war are still being debated today. Vietnam was the first television war, and the passions, animosities, recriminations, and bitter feelings about the war for many of the supporters and protesters of the era run as strong and deep today as in the 1960s. Many said the war was not winnable while others believe it was definitely winnable. Some called it a civil war; others believed it was communist aggression. Some called the domino theory flawed as it applied to Vietnam in spite of the subsequent spread of communism in Southeast Asia.

A rush to war without adequate deliberation was blamed by many while others would claim America failed to bring the full force of its military might early in the conflict. The Tonkin Gulf resolution and the war's escalation in 1965 would be blamed on White House deceit. Politicians would be denounced for a lack of a will to win.

Some would cite faulty intelligence or lack of reliance on available intelligence. The questions of why we were in Vietnam, how the war was waged, and why South Vietnam fell will never be satisfactorily answered. However, the war produced one undeniable truth that a divided America can never win a war.

The advocates of peace at any price discovered this truth and employed it to great effect in the Vietnam struggle. The Vietnam War was the catalyst that pulled the Boomers into the streets, gave voice to a generation, and divided America. The Boomers became the pawns in the creation of the great division that still afflicts the nation. The Boomers and their puppet masters must carry a significant responsibility for the misery and loss of life in Southeast Asia during the 1960s and 1970s, both during and after the Vietnam War. Whether they accept the responsibility or not, history's verdict is that they gave aid and support to the enemy and divided a nation.

For most people memory tends to fade or become fuzzy over the years. However, certain long-ago incidents stand out in sharp relief as though they happened only yesterday. This vivid recall of long ago events is often the case with regard to life in a combat zone. Not only important or life threatening events, but small things, mostly meaningless, often lodge themselves in one's memory. One such incident occurred as I was processing in at the First Infantry Division administrative headquarters at Di An. Most newly arrived troops were understandably nervous about what lay ahead. The tension was often relieved by horseplay, especially among young men in their late teens or early twenties who would face life and death situations in a matter of days. I recall a jovial, fair-skinned, blond-haired kid from Nebraska. He seemed to be the life of the party as we processed through to our units. One year later to the day as I was processing out at Di An, I saw that young man again. Wary, emotionless eyes stared into space, and the deadpan expression on his face was anything but jovial. Probably still a teenager, he looked to be well into his thirties with bleached-out, whitish hair. War changes people. I'm sure that his quiet, withdrawn demeanor and the dramatic changes in his countenance were only a small hint of the inward trauma that had sucked the joy, hope, and innocence from his young life. Not all death occurs on the battlefield. Some spend the remainder of their lives nursing emotional as well as physical wounds, dying a little each day.

This seemed to be especially the case with the soldier that served in Vietnam.

America was much like the young Nebraska soldier. The decade of the 1960s began with youthful exuberance, a bright and hopeful time. A young president challenged us to "ask not what your country can do for you, ask what you can do for your country." However, when the last troops left Vietnam in February 1973 after a dozen years of war, Americans were a scarred and unsure people. Over fifty-eight thousand American soldiers had given all in death and another three hundred and one thousand were wounded. Allied forces' deaths (South Korean, Australian, New Zealand, and Thailand) added another five thousand two hundred to the body count. These numbers were dwarfed by approximately one and one-half million North and South Vietnamese soldiers and civilians killed during the long conflict.[145] There were other casualties of war. The Canadian government estimated that between thirty and forty thousand young American men of draft age escaped to Canada to avoid the draft.[146] Other sources report much higher estimates. The joy, hope, and innocence of the early 1960s were a distant and haunting memory of what might have been.

The Baby Boom generation became the greatest demographic occurrence in American history because of their large numbers.[147] Consequently, the Baby Boomers have become the largest ripple in the undulating fabric of American's growth as it unrolls into the future. The events and occurrences that profoundly influenced the Boomers and their worldview and that of their parents, the Greatest Generation, have been examined. The consequences of those influences played out in the 1960s in three major arenas: culture, race, and war. The simultaneous unfolding of these conflicts created a perfect storm of turmoil and change in America.

The oldest Boomers experienced their thirtieth birthday at the end of 1975—the age beyond which one is not to be trusted anymore according to one Berkeley protester in 1964.[148] They had succumbed to the ancient lie first whispered in the Garden—Ye shall not surely die. By the mid-1970s, as disquieting thoughts of mortality began troubling the Boomers, they began snipping the strings held by their puppet masters, cutting their hair, shaving their beards, and getting jobs. Like the rebellious prodigal son of the Bible, many Boomers came back to the cultural home of their parents. But many of the unrepentant leaders of the rebellion would assume positions of power and leadership in America and find new ways to challenge their cultural ancestry. Their worldview has changed America, and much of that change is questionable.

The Boomer legacy was summed up by Governor Mitch Daniels of Indiana at his 2009 commencement address to the graduating class at Butler University.

> As a generation, you are off to an excellent start. You have taken the first savvy step on the road to distinction, which is to follow a weak act. I wish I could claim otherwise, but we Baby Boomers are likely to be remembered by history for our numbers, and little else, at least little else that is admirable...Today, if you are thinking about standing on the shoulders of the past generation, I'd say "Please don't"...live for others, not just yourselves. For fulfillment, not just pleasure and material gain. For tomorrow, and the Americans who will reside there, not just for today.[149]

Part II – Worldview

The challenge to the Judeo-Christian worldview by the Boomers is not a new occurrence. For hundreds of years a conflict has existed within Western civilization between those that believe in a transcendent God and those that do not. Part II examines the predominant Judeo-Christian worldview of Western civilization that has reigned through three-quarters of the last two millennia and the challenge for supremacy in the American cultural vision by humanism with the help of its accomplices, the Renaissance and Enlightenment. We shall study the sources and development of the worldviews of colonial Americans and the American Founders. Lastly, we will examine roots and ascendency of modern humanism.

Chapter 4

Worldview: Christianity vs. Humanism

It was not conceivable to my young mind during the 1960s that Americans would ever drift from the principles upon which the nation was founded. I knew there were external threats to America—the Cold War and potential for nuclear annihilation. I also recognized that there were subversive or internal threats. But, the American character that had been shaped by the principles upon which the nation was founded was solid. We would persevere. Hadn't we been birthed by the Greatest Generation? It is now four decades later, and one must wonder if the course of the nation which has drifted from those principles can be corrected.

That is one of the purposes of this book—to examine the competing worldviews and the reasons for the shift in worldview away from that of the Founding Americans. It is not primarily about the Boomers and their story for they are merely the poster children for what's happened to America. More importantly, this book is about why and how the change of worldview occurred and the consequences thereof for America. Therefore, this book is essentially about worldview and more specifically about the change of worldview as it relates to America.

When I looked at those students under my tutelage as a graduate teaching assistant back in 1969 and 1970, I most likely had never heard of the term "worldview." To confirm my suspicion, I looked at my old college dictionary, Webster's Seventh New Collegiate Dictionary, copyright 1963.[150] There was no listing for "worldview", but there was a definition for "weltanschauung." The more modern dictionaries now list "worldview" and give a cross-reference to its German roots. Weltanschauung is the German word for "worldview" and originated in the mid-1800s. It means a conception of the course of events in, and of the purpose of, the world as a whole, forming a philosophical view or apprehension of the universe; the general idea embodied in a cosmology[151] (the universe as an orderly system). "Worldview" has gained currency and is often used in ordinary discourse.

Worldview is "...the comprehensive framework of one's basic *beliefs* about *things*." Things include the world, human life, social morality, education, family, and God. Beliefs are not just innocuous feelings, opinions, or hypotheses. Beliefs are claims to a certain kind of knowledge one is willing to defend, that is, those beliefs to which one is committed. In other words, beliefs have to do with one's convictions. Lastly, worldview deals with *basic* beliefs about things—ultimate questions with which we are confronted, matters of general principle. Terms such as "ideals", "ideology", and "system of values" are too narrow and ineffective in defining worldview as the terms themselves connote certain elements of specific worldviews.[152] Worldview can also be defined as an overall perspective or perception (of reality or truth) from which one sees, understands, and interprets the universe and humanity's relation to it. Simply put, a worldview is a person's beliefs about the world that directs his or her decisions and actions.

Why must we concern ourselves with worldview? The beliefs one holds tend to create a pattern, design, or structure that fit together in a particular way. This structure or order generally has a coherence or consistency; although, inconsistencies may exist within one's worldview. This coherence, consistency, or order within one's worldview gives orientation and direction for living life. If a person's actions and beliefs are not consistent, the conflict must be resolved or over a period of time a person's integrity and mental health will be diminished.[153] Therefore, a person must discover what is true and live a life compatible with that truth.

The average Joe or Jane may dismiss any thoughts or concerns about worldview and believe that it unimportant and/or should be left to the philosophers and politicians. Yet, they complain about assaults on their particular beliefs as the culture wars are fought in the media, in the halls of business and commerce, and in the seats of government. If Joe or Jane were asked what his or her worldview is, the questioner may receive a blank stare. Yet, Joe and Jane do have worldviews even though they may not be able to articulate those views. These views rise to the surface when faced with issues of life that challenge their individual worldview. Conflict, frustration, and disorder in their lives arise because they do not relate some of their actions (e.g., decisions in the voting booth) to outcomes in society with which they may not agree (e.g., pornography, late term abortion, and homosexuality). They may take great exception to society's direction (society's order) in relation to their worldview (how they believe the world is ordered). Yet, through ignorance, laziness, apathy, neglect, or a myriad of other reasons, a society may slide into a predominant worldview in which the prevailing cultural vision does not align with Joe or Jane's worldview or that of a majority of a society's citizens.

As we have stated, the beliefs forming a worldview about life and the universe are held by individuals. The collective worldviews of individuals generally form a society or nation, and one dominant worldview usually will exist and order society accordingly. As other groups with different or competing worldviews enter a society or nation, the resulting tensions and friction between the groups may lead to conflict. Therefore, worldview is exceptionally important. Colliding worldviews have plagued man since his creation. Wars are fought because of conflicting worldviews. Nations rise and fall because of worldviews. Freedoms are won or lost because of worldviews. Worldviews may shift or change from generation to generation, something that will be examined in this book. Such changes may lead to greater order or greater disorder.

Are all worldviews equal in value? Even those that worship at the shrine of diversity, inclusion, and tolerance must answer with a resounding no. Then how do we decide what is the correct or best worldview? The value of a worldview will be determined by whether or not the worldview's answers to life's most important questions are determined to be true. The coffee house philosopher may smugly pose the question, "What is true? What is false?" in an attempt to make such answers appear incomprehensible or irrelevant. However, it is human nature to search for truth, to attempt to know what is real. This is well stated by Albert M. Wolters:

> One of the unique characteristics of human beings is that we cannot do without the kind of orientation and guidance that a worldview gives. We need guidance because we are inescapably creatures with responsibility who by nature are incapable of holding purely arbitrary opinions or making

entirely unprincipled decisions. We need some creed to live by, some map by which to chart our course. The need for a guiding perspective is basic to human life, perhaps more basic than food or sex.[154]

Some worldviews may contain elements of truth but will ultimately fail if enough leaven of false premises is mixed with the true. Also, it must be remembered that many holding false worldviews are not interested in truth. Revelation of truth will not necessarily change their worldview as such a change may endanger their position within the group or society holding that worldview. This seems to be a pervasive affliction of the majority of America's politicians of recent times.

Professor Robert P. George is a Harvard trained lawyer and holds an earned doctorate in legal philosophy from Oxford University. George is the McCormick Professor of Jurisprudence and Director of the James Madison Program in American Ideals and Institutions at Princeton University. With past service as a Judicial Fellow at the Supreme Court of the United States and a past Presidential Appointee to the United States Commission on Civil Rights, Professor George is no lightweight in the arena of ideas. Professor George wrote a penetrating book about the modern clash of worldviews. In his *Clash of Orthodoxies*, George quotes James Kurth who sharply and convincingly presents the battle as not one between the world's major civilizations (the West, the Islamic world, and Confucian East) but a clash within the civilization of the West. This clash is between those holding the Judeo-Christian worldview and those who reject this worldview in favor of a humanist orthodoxy (of which feminism, multiculturalism, lifestyle liberalism, and gay liberationism are examples).[155]

Professor George points out that those holding the secular worldview often depict the battle as being between those persons of "faith" and those of "reason." While upholding the importance of faith, centrality of God's revealed Word in the Bible, and Christian tradition, Professor George challenges the humanists through a philosophical defense of Christian morality and establishes that Christian moral teaching is rationally *superior* to orthodox secular or humanist moral beliefs.[156] Unlike the humanists' worldview, faith and reason are not in conflict within the Judeo-Christian worldview.

The real conflict is between faith allied with reason on the one hand and emotion and imagination on the other.[157] Much of modern America including a large portion of the Christian church attempts to keep one foot in each camp. They follow a dualistic worldview that limits the influence of faith to personal piety, efforts of the clergy, to the future kingdom, or a liberal social gospel. All other realms of human activity are considered humanist or worldly and within the province of reason and outside of religious or sacred influences. Areas excluded from divine influence include the family, politics, business, art, education, journalism, thought, emotion, plants and animals, and inanimate matter.[158] The dualistic view may exist for a while, but as with the disappearance of the Judeo-Christian worldview in much of the northern European continent, there will ultimately be only a single view that substantially excludes Christianity.

A second tactic used by secularists is to present secularism as a "…a 'neutral' doctrine that deserves privileged status as the national public philosophy." In other words, secularism is supposed to be a view independent of tradition and that represents an arena upon which various traditions (Judaism, Christianity, Marxism, etc.) can compete for the allegiance of the people. But, as George points out, secularism is just another player in the battle of worldviews. And, as stated above, the major combatants in the West are the secular humanists and those adhering to the Judeo-Christian worldview.[159]

In the West, secularists' tactics have been extremely successful in the battle between worldviews. With Americans exhibiting a pervasive ignorance of American history and tradition and with an almost universal assault by the government, media, and academia, the Judeo-Christian concepts of government, sexuality, human life, religion, and morality in public life have been battered. Perhaps there is no more stinging indictment of the age than that of Aleksandr Solzhenitsyn: "If I were called upon to identify the principal trait of the entire twentieth century, I would be unable to find anything more precise and pithy than this statement: Men have forgotten God."[160]

Whittaker Chambers wrote one of the great books of the twentieth century. Published in 1953, *Witness* is a brilliant and moving account of Chambers' defection from the Communist Party in the United States in the late 1930s, his coming to the Christian faith, and his testimony against Alger Hiss, a Communist spy who had risen to one of the highest levels of American government. In his book's forward in the form of a letter to his children, Chambers called the Hiss-Chambers case a "...critical conflict of faiths."[161] Speaking of the Communist faith, Chambers said,

> ...it is a simple, rational faith that inspires men to live or die for it.
>
> It is not new. It is, in fact, man's second oldest faith. Its promise was whispered in the first days of the Creation under the Tree of the Knowledge of Good and Evil: "Ye shall be as gods." It is the great alternative faith of mankind. Like all great faiths, its force derives from a simple vision. Other ages have had great visions. They have always been different versions of the same vision: the vision of God and man's relationship to God. The Communist vision is the vision of Man without God.
>
> It is the vision of man's mind displacing God as the creative intelligence of the world. It is the vision of man's liberated mind by the sole force of its rational intelligence, redirecting man's destiny and reorganizing man's life and the world. It is the vision of man once more the central figure of the Creation, not because God made man in his image, but because man's mind makes him the most intelligent of the animals. Copernicus and his successors displaced man as the central fact of the universe by proving that the earth was not the central star of the universe. Communism restores man to his sovereignty by the simple method of denying God.
>
> The vision is a challenge and implies a threat. It challenges man to prove by his acts that he is the masterwork of the Creation—by making thought and act one. It challenges him to prove it by using the force of his rational mind to end the bloody meaninglessness of man's history—by giving it a purpose and a plan. It challenges him to prove it by reducing the meaningless chaos of nature, by imposing on it his rational will to order, abundance, security, peace. It is the

vision of materialism. But it threatens, if man's mind is unequal to the problems of man's progress, that he will sink back into savagery (the A and the H bombs have raised the issue in explosive forms), until nature replaces him with a more intelligent form of life.

It is an intensely practical vision. The tools to turn it into reality are at hand—science and technology, whose traditional method, the rigorous exclusion of all supernatural factors in solving problems, has contributed to the intellectual climate in which the vision flourishes, just as they have contributed to the crisis in which Communism thrives.[162]

Chambers' conflict of faiths continues in the twenty-first century but without Communism's label. Different letters have been substituted for those in front of the *ism*. But whatever the name, it is still the second oldest faith—man without God, and Chambers' diagnosis of mankind's condition is just as relevant today as it was sixty years ago.

Chapter 5

The Fingerprints of God

The Danakil Depression in Ethiopia has been called the hellhole of creation. It is one of the hottest, driest, most isolated and desolate places on the planet. Located within the Great Riff Valley of Africa, the lowlands sink to a depth of 300 to 400 feet below sea level. The region is inhabited by the Danakils, a nomadic people who subsist in this land of volcanoes near the Red Sea and the Horn of Africa. Three expeditions through the region between 1875 and 1884 were wiped out by the fierce Danakils. In 1928, British explorer Lewis M. Nesbitt was the first to lead the most extensive expedition into the 150 by 400-mile Danakil Depression. Three months after Nesbitt, two European associates, and fifteen natives had begun their trek from the northern end of the Depression, the group found themselves in a cave at the base of a ravine to escape the burning sun. Soon the party was surrounded by Danakil tribesmen. Nesbitt and his party escaped annihilation through the efforts of a very old Danakil tribal chief. Suni Maa was described as an ancient, half-alive mummified skeleton wearing only a dirty loin cloth and crude sandals. During three days of talks and negotiations, the old tribal chief explained that strangers coming to their lands are killed because they encroach on their territories. Asked if the Englishman and his party were in danger, Suni Maa replied, "In great danger indeed, especially with the younger men who are avaricious, and whose short life has not yet raised them above the soil to which they cling. They do not know that there are things, not of this world, but mysterious and superior, and worthy of being sought to the exclusion of everything else."[163]

How is it that a primitive, illiterate, and uneducated man as was Suni Maa could have such a profound, insightful perspective on the life and death realities of the world? The ancient Danakil perceived a truth that was beyond the senses and transcends time. Its source is the same God of truth that Moses and the Children of Israel encountered in the Sinai—the God of Judaism and Christianity.[164] The Apostle Paul wrote of this perceived truth.

> For it is not the hearers of the law who are righteous before God, but the doers of the law who will be justified. When Gentiles who have not the law do by nature what the law requires, they are a law to themselves, even though they do not have the law. They show that what the law requires is *written on their hearts*, while their conscience also bears witness and their conflicting thoughts accuse or perhaps excuse them on that day when, according to my gospel, God judges the secrets of men by Christ Jesus. Romans 2:13-16 RSV. (emphasis added)

A worldview must be conditioned by wisdom and common sense and therefore is not a matter of education or intellectual brilliance. A worldview that lacks wisdom and common sense is not workable. A workable worldview is one that is coherent or consistent and gives orientation and direction for living life. Academic disciplines such as theology and philosophy are scientific and theoretical whereas worldview is a matter of the shared daily experiences of mankind. As Albert Wolters wrote, worldview is "...an inescapable component of all human knowing...It belongs to an order of cognition more basic than that of science or theory."[165]

What are those things that Suni Maa thought to be mysterious and superior and worthy of being sought to the exclusion of everything else? We call those things the norms, the permanent things, to which mankind must adhere in order to live. It is a moral order that transcends time. It is not instinct. It is not learned behavior through time although the recognition and practice of those norms are important to keep those norms visible and alive for following generations. Richard Weaver wrote that both modern cultures and primitive have "...powerful feelings of 'oughtness' directed toward the world..." The norms or permanent things are applicable to all of mankind and to all ages. In the revelation of the order of the universe to the Hebrews, it pointed back to the beginning of mankind when all men knew of good and evil.[166] But as time advanced man's understanding of good and evil diminished.[167] The revelation to the

Hebrews and the first century Christians, recorded over a 1,600-year span of time, gave illumination, order, and meaning to those pre-revelation norms or permanent things and which mankind perceived and endeavored to know. Together, the norms or permanent things and the revelation of the order of the universe as created by God form an "…inescapable component of all human knowing."

The Ethiopian tribesman of the twentieth century would have common ground with a brilliant Roman philosopher-statesman of two thousand years ago—the modern day tribesman living as his forebears had thousands of years ago and the philosopher of two millennia ago with an intellect that is counted among the greatest of the ages. Marcus Tullius Cicero (106-43 B. C.), the most famous lawyer of ancient times, was a Roman philosopher and statesman who lived during the century preceding the birth of Christ and concurrent with the collapse of the Roman Republic into a dictatorship. He wrote:

> True law is right reason in agreement with Nature, it is of universal application, unchanging and everlasting; it summons to duty by its commands, and averts from wrong-doing by its prohibitions…We cannot be freed from its obligations by Senate or People, and we need not look outside ourselves for an expounder or interpreter of it. And there will not be different laws at Rome and at Athens, or different laws now and in the future, but one eternal and unchangeable law will be valid for all nations and for all times, and there will be one master and one rule, that is, God, over us all, for He is the author of this law, its promulgator, and its enforcing judge.[168]

A favorite author of the Founders, Cicero was a proponent of Natural Law, the Creator's order of things. The Creator endowed man with a rational or reasoning power that is unique to his species, and this reasoning power allows man to recognize and identify the rules of correct or right conduct that coincide with the Natural Law. Observance of these rules of conduct in the areas of government, justice, and human relations will lead to a stable society.[169]

During the turmoil in America of the late 1960s and early 1970s, Russell Kirk wrote *The Roots of the American Order*, a book of exceptional scope and insight into the origins of America. Summarizing the words of Simone Weil, Kirk states that "…order is the path we follow, or the pattern by which we live with purpose and meaning. Above food and shelter, she continues, we must have order. The human condition is insufferable unless we perceive a harmony, an order in existence." Kirk identified two roots of order: the order of the soul (moral order) and the order of the republic (social order), and they are intricately linked and dependent on each other. Disorder of one leads to disorder of the other.[170]

Who is this God to whom we refer? He is the Supreme Being that created the universe. He existed before the universe and time. In His creation of the universe, a certain order was implemented. The norms are called by other names including universals, permanent things, eternal truths, and first principles. Actions that conflict with this Supreme Being's laws will bring disorder and distress to one's life. Did Suni Mai know the God of Judeo-Christian tradition? No, but he knew there were things worthy of being sought to the exclusion of everything else, things that if ignored or violated would bring disorder and pain. But the Ethiopian tribesman and much of the modern world remain ignorant of or reject the revelation of who God is and His plan for man's redemption from his human condition. Thus, man lives in various states of confusion and disorder as he seeks solace through various false gods and ideologies only to find continued disorder. He recognizes and experiences disorder but has not the will or knowledge to find order.

We get a picture of God by looking at the norms upon which His creation is founded. As C. S. Lewis wrote, His truths are moral laws "...which they (man) did not write, and cannot quite forget even when they try, and which they know they ought to obey." Knowledge of God comes more from an understanding of the moral law than from the universe. Examples of the laws of right conduct include fair play, good faith, honesty, and truthfulness.[171]

As societies organize themselves, the modes of right conduct are eventually codified and became the laws of those societies. These modes of conduct generally revolved around those things recognized as permanent things or the intrinsic order. The Anglo-Saxon influence within the British Isles began around A.D. 450. It was at this point that Anglo-Saxon law began to grow and over time reflect those permanent things leading to intrinsic order.[172] The essence of these laws that grew over the next thirteen hundred years was described by William Blackstone.

Blackstone's *Commentaries on the Laws of England* were derived from his lectures at Oxford University in the 1750s. Blackstone said, "...when the Supreme Being formed the universe and created matter out of nothing, he impressed certain principles upon that matter, from which it can never depart, and without which it would cease to be."[173]   According to Blackstone, these principles dictate rules of action and applies to animate and inanimate objects. These "laws of nature" must invariably be followed by the universe and the created matter therein. Man was the noblest of the creatures and singly endowed with reason and free will. Therefore, the Creator also laid down certain laws of "human nature"; the laws of good and evil to which the Creator and all of his creation conform. Unlike the rest of creation, man through his free will was allowed to constrain his actions, conform to and be in obedience to the Creator's laws of human nature. Man's faculties of reason were to be used to discover those laws as far as necessary for the conduct of man's actions...the living of a life. Blackstone stated that the laws of human nature are so "inseparably interwoven" with the happiness of each individual that man's happiness cannot be obtained without observing and adhering to those laws. But, as Blackstone would say, "our first ancestor" transgressed or failed to conform his actions to those eternal laws of human nature. Therefore, his reason and that of subsequent generations were impaired, flawed, unclear, clouded, or unreliable in finding the laws of human nature from whence one may successfully guide his life.* Subsequently, the Creator allowed man to discover and enforce those laws through the revealed or divine law as found "only in the holy scriptures." Blackstone states that from these twin

---

*The Apostle Paul wrote to the Romans of the deplorable condition of the Gentiles. Paul states that even though the Gentiles did not have the revelation of the Hebrews, they were guilty of violation God's laws evident in eternal power and deity as revealed in nature. "For what can be known about God is plain to them, because God has shown it to them. Ever since the creation of the world his invisible nature, namely, his eternal power and deity, has been clearly perceived in the things that have been made. So they are without excuse; for although they knew God they did not honor him as God or give thanks to him, but they became futile in their thinking and their senseless minds were darkened. Claiming to be wise, they became fools, and exchanged the glory of the immortal God for images resembling mortal man or birds or animals, or reptiles." [Romans 1:19-23 RSV.]

pillars of the law of nature and the law of revelation, all human laws must rest.[174] The essence of Blackstone's treatise is that there are certain truths that are intrinsic and timeless, and those truths are essential elements that provide a coherent and rational way to live in the world.

Only a worldview that aligns with those timeless truths will allow its adherents to live in a harmonious relationship with nature and those around them. As stated, there are two kinds of laws (truths), the laws of nature and norms (laws of human nature).[175] Let's start with the physical realm's laws (natural sciences such as physics, chemistry, and biology) that must be obeyed or those that violate those laws risk undesirable consequences. If my worldview states that I disbelieve in the law of gravity, and I proceed to jump off of a cliff in the Rocky Mountains without the requisite hang-gliding equipment, I will prove the falsity of my worldview and have time to reflect upon the error of my beliefs at the local hospital (or mortuary while others would be doing the contemplating, not I).

Norms flow from God's laws of culture and society and are timeless truths that lay outside the physical realm. Unlike obedience to the laws of nature, man has a choice as to whether to obey or disobey the norms or laws of human nature. But as with the laws of nature, violation of the laws of human nature also has negative consequences. Irrespective of a society's belief or non-belief in a transcendent God, most societies recognize certain norms to be important. Consequently, most societies deem certain actions to be bad (e.g., stealing, murder) and will impose consequences (penalties, imprisonment, or death) on those who violate its collective worldview. Other norms such as the nuclear family, fair play, and honesty are deemed to be good. Almost all societies have a worldview that laws (truths) for nature and humankind have been established by a divine creator. However, the Judeo-Christian tradition is unique in that the God of the Bible is not subject to but created the world order. Secondly, the Judeo-Christian tradition teaches that the laws of nature and norms for mankind are universally valid. Some are general rules or laws such as the Ten Commandments and others are particular to a specific time and place.[176]

Some will argue that a society's worldview should not impact an individual's actions that are private and that do not affect society or other individuals therein. Such assumptions that private actions do not affect a society and its worldview are most often false. As an example, the recreational use of drugs (although a private action) has generally been viewed (worldview) by society as bad, and society has enacted laws to prohibit such use. In other words, the truth is that recreational drug use disrupts the harmony within a society and is injurious to the social well-being of all even though it may be considered a private act. On the other hand, if that society's worldview deems recreational drug use to be acceptable, the validity of the truth will not be changed, and that society will suffer the consequences of such usage because society's worldview is in conflict with the truth (natural law).

Arguing from a Judeo-Christian worldview, Christopher Badeaux's words bring into sharp focus the importance of the search for the correct worldview.

> The Lord made the Universe according to a set of hidden but largely discernable rules, and those rules produce specific, predictable outcomes once the rules and variables are known. Furthermore, all things are made ordered—oriented if you prefer—to not only the Lord, but also to decent and right outcomes…Our consciences and our natural inclinations are manifestations of this intrinsic order; disregarding them gives rise to disorder. Indeed, even doing things that are right and good can be taken to extremes that place one outside of that natural order. When we step outside of that order, as anyone who has lived with someone suffering through, say, anorexia or alcohol addiction can tell you, the disorder radiates outward in a spiderweb-crack pattern of pain.[177]

As a society develops a worldview, it consequentially develops a system of moral codes and laws whereby it enforces what it believes is right and good for society. Once again, it must be remembered that worldview must align with (to use Badeaux's words) those hidden but largely discernable rules that produce specific, predictable outcomes to orient or bring order to a society, that is, to make a civil society civil. When a society ignores or abandons those discernable rules that bring order to a society, one begins to see the tatters as the cohesive fabric of that society begins to unravel and shred.

Every worldview or belief system must answer certain questions: What is the nature and structure of our world and how does it function? Where are we heading? What shall we do (values)? "How should we attain our goals? "What is true and false?[178] Charles Colson and Nancy Pearcey, in their book *HowNow Shall We Live?*, reduces to three questions what any worldview must answer: "Where did we come from, and who are we? What has gone wrong with the world? What can we do to fix it?" Answers to these questions allow one to evaluate any area of life (e.g., family life, politics, science, education, the arts, and popular culture) and how each area aligns with one's worldview.[179]

C. S. Lewis gives an excellent framework for identifying the position of the various players in answering these basic questions that each worldview must answer. The first major division is between those who believe there is no god (the minority) and those that believe there is a god or gods. For those that believe in God there are two additional divisions. The Pantheists believe that God is beyond good and evil; the wiser one becomes the less you want to call anything good or bad. The Pantheists believe that the universe is animated by God and is part of the universe, and without the universe there would be no God. Some religions (Hinduism) and philosophers (Hegel) hold these beliefs. The other view is that God created the universe and is involved with his creation. This view is held by the world's major religions: Jews, Christians, and Mohammedans. Christians believe that God existed prior to the universe that was made by him.[180]

Although Lewis's framework is necessary and helpful, certain terms must be defined to better describe worldview positions and battle lines in the twenty-first century. Theism holds that the universe was created by a transcendent God. Theism's opposite is naturalism (along with its close twin, materialism), which implies that nature is all that exists. Therefore, life arose by chance and evolved into human life. Naturalism is the gospel of the humanists and is the dominant worldview today. Three other terms must be examined: modernism, post-Christian and postmodernism. Modernism dominated American culture for most of the twentieth century. Modernists were little concerned about social issues and ideology and tended to be leaders in business, government, science, and the military. Technology and material success were their most important goals. But as the century progressed, America began sliding into both the post-modern and post-Christian era. By post-Christian is meant that Judeo-Christian truths are no longer the basis of American and other Western cultures as it relates to public philosophy and moral consensus. One step beyond is postmodernism. Postmodernists hold that there are no universal truths and believe all social constructions are shaped by class, gender, and ethnicity in which all viewpoints, lifestyles, and beliefs are equally valid.[181] Theism and naturalism are the labels applied to the combatants, much as Allies and Axis powers identified the combatants in World War II. Modernism, post-Christian, and postmodernism identify the stages through which the war has progressed. Again using the World War II analogy, any observant present-day proponent of the Judeo-Christian truths must believe that their cause is somewhat akin to that of the Allies after Dunkirk or Pearl Harbor at the beginning of America's war with Japan.

    One more comment on terms is needed. The term "Judeo-Christian" has been used extensively to this point. However, the term may be too broad to accurately define the contest between worldviews that is being fought in America, for the battle is really between the Christian worldview and those who hold the humanist worldview. Christianity fully encompasses the Judeo-Christian values, but not all who claim to accept the Judeo-Christian ethic are joined to the battle for various reasons. Some may give lip service to the term for ancestral reasons but give little or no credence to that worldview as reflected by the manner in which they live their lives. Others may give only half-hearted support due to their dualist tendencies thereby allowing it to occupy only a small portion of their worldview. Unfortunately, there are large numbers of people in the Christian community that are not joined in the battle.

    As can be seen from the above discussions, the clash of worldviews in the West is primarily between the humanist view and those holding to the tenets of Christianity. And this battle centers primarily on America as many parts of the West have already surrendered to the humanists. Because the major conflict of worldviews in the West is between the Christian and the humanist worldviews, the differences and conflicts between Christianity and the worldview of other religions will not be examined except on occasions where those religions intersect with the larger conflict.

Therefore, it is beyond the scope of this book to make those examinations of other religions except for the religion of humanism. However, C. S. Lewis cautioned that, "If you are a Christian you do not have to believe that all the other religions are simply *wrong all through*...all religions, even the queerest ones, contain some hint of truth...As in arithmetic—there is only one right answer to a sum, and all other answers are wrong; but some of the wrong answers are much nearer being right than others."[182] (emphasis added) The abundant weight of evidence is more than enough to say that Christianity, in comparison with other religions, has demonstrated its considerable superiority in providing the kind of orientation and guidance that a worldview must give in order to answer all of the basic questions of life.

What is the Christian worldview? God existed before the universe was created, and then God created the universe and all that is within it including the laws that govern that creation. Unlike all of the other elements of his creation, man was created with a free will. This part of the Christian worldview is called Creation. Mankind's free will allowed man to think and act in ways that were contrary to God's plan and will for His creation. When man acted in ways contrary to God's laws (truths), such disobedience to God's laws was called sin, and as a result decay and death entered into God's creation. This is called the Fall, and it affected not only man but all of God's creation. But as God is a loving God, he created a way through His son, Jesus Christ, which allows man to bring order to the chaos he created. This is called the Restoration. There you have the basic elements of the Christian worldview: the Creation, the Fall, and the Restoration. No other worldview recognizes the true nature of the human condition and provides a means whereby man can return to a proper orientation to God's laws and plan. It answers the questions of where we came from and who we are, what went wrong, and how we get out of the chaos and restore order to our souls. The Founders held this worldview and built a nation on the principles that flow from it.

Chapter 6

The Judeo-Christian Tradition and the Rise of Western Civilization

There are those that still look back past the billowing clouds of secularism and humanism that attempt to obstruct the view of their patrimony. Above the din of laughter and derision of modern times, they cock their ear and strive to hear those ancestral voices of truth and certainty sent down to us from former times.

Those ancestral voices of truth and certainty are found in the revelation to the Hebrews and first century Christians. The revelation to the Hebrews and subsequently to the world was recorded over sixteen hundred years. The last books were written in the first century following the death and resurrection of Jesus Christ at the beginning of the Christian diaspora. The Apostle Paul was taken to Rome and martyred. Yet his blood and the blood of Christian martyrs watered the roots of Christendom such that by the beginning of the fifth century half of the Roman Empire professed Christianity. Yet, Roman civilization remained unregenerate and fell, as Augustine said, because of a want of order in the soul.[183]

Christianity survived and the Gentiles received what the Jews rejected. To the twenty-first century citizen of the modern world, this survival appears both a puzzling and remarkable occurrence. "How was it that a religion so exacting, austere, and contemptuous of worldly goods with an emphasis on charity and chastity win the masses of the ancient world" and continue to do so today? Russell Kirk gives three reasons for Christianity's triumph. The first reason was Jesus' concern for the poor—the humble, the meek, the powerless, the oppressed—those who submitted themselves to God's will. Also, Christianity triumphed because of its universal appeal, unconnected with political systems as were the pagans. To the contrary, Christianity acted as a mediator and connection between peoples, states, cultural stages, and centuries. Lastly, Christianity taught people how to find a harmony in their souls during this earthly life coupled with the hope of eternal life thereafter.[184]

With the decline and fall of the western half of the Roman Empire by the end of the fifth century, the material and cultural center of Christianity moved to Constantinople, the heir of Greece and Rome. Yet, a remnant of the Christian heritage of the western portion of the Roman Empire was pushed northward into the sparse and hostile forests of France and western Germany. The inhabitants were Gauls whom the Romans had conquered and brought civilization at the beginning of the Christian era. To this group was added a smaller number of Teutonic invaders that had come from the east and hindered for a time the building of an organized social life and assimilation of the Mediterranean culture. Life was harsh in the pioneer wilds of northern Europe at the beginning of the Middle Ages around A.D. 500. It was also the beginning of what was called the Dark Ages—a time when life was focused on the physical demands of survival and less on those tasks required of a cultivated society. Compared to the remainder of the civilized world, these simple agricultural people of France and Germany would appear backwards if not uncivilized. Yet, out of such stock grew Western civilization, and by Western civilization is meant Christendom.[185]

Because the Western peoples began with so little and struggled under harsh conditions, the Dark Ages would not end until the eleventh century. In that five-hundred-year span of time, there were still only a few million inhabitants in forests of France and hardly a million in the clearings of Britain. However, from about 1100 to 1300, the men of Western Europe built a cohesive and somewhat refined civilization, and the broad and general characteristics of their medieval society remained for centuries. Those characteristics and viewpoint, worldview if you will, became the ideas and ideals that are the foundations of modern Christendom. As towns grew and people had more of both leisure and material possessions, intellectual curiosity grew.[186]

The seeds from whence the early European Renaissance sprang were planted with Europe's first ventures of expansion through the Crusades in the twelfth and thirteenth centuries which brought it into contact with civilizations much more advanced in learning from classical Greece and Rome.[187] When the Renaissance came, the Europeans' earlier experiences had whetted their curiosity. And it was the later Renaissance that continued into the sixteenth century that would challenge man's fundamental way of thinking in the seventeenth and eighteenth centuries.[188]

The Middle Ages that began a thousand years before with the fall of Rome in 476 ended in 1453 when Constantinople fell to the Turks. The Byzantine scholars and nobles fled to Italy and brought a new "humanism" centered on ancient Greek civilization, an essentially pagan view of human nature, concerned with the present as opposed to the focus of the medieval church and institutions on other-worldliness.[189] Some historians have called the contributions of ancient Greek civilization the pre-eminent source of influence in the making of this world..."the seedbed of almost all that played a dynamic part in shaping the world we still inhabit."[190]

The ancient Greeks considered man to be the center of existence. Reason, not emotion, was the true fountain of knowledge, and the emphasis on reason to attain the improvement of humanity is called humanism. From the Europeans' renewed interest in the culture of ancient Greece's classical civilization came the essence of the new humanism—the "dignity of man" or man regenerate, a philosophy that saw man only a little lower than the angels and capable of descending to brutish lower forms of life but with the capability to become godlike. This was the beginning of Christian humanism—not a dethronement of God but the belief that through the moral disciplines of humanistic learning one struggles toward God. But as Kirk wrote, "...the seed of intellectual arrogance, overweening self-confidence, was sown. A time would come when man would take himself for the be-all and end-all." The heresies of the immigrants from the fallen Byzantine Empire accelerated the Renaissance and hastened the end of the Age of Faith.[191]

Western civilization owes a great debt to the monks in the monasteries scattered throughout medieval Europe. For it was they who kept the flame of civilization ablaze during the centuries of the Dark Ages. From these pockets of civilization came the eleventh century monastic schools and cathedral schools, and out of these schools came the first universities in the early thirteenth century. Two of the great thirteen century Christian philosophers charged with the search for universal truths were Albert the Great and his pupil, Thomas Aquinas. They were the first supporters within the Church of the teachings and thought of Aristotle which would profoundly alter the course of the Catholic Church and Christianity.[192] But with the coming of the universities came also the seeds for the destruction of the medieval focus on realism—the existence of universals—by clearing the path for the Renaissance and later the Age of Enlightenment. In fourteenth century England, this undoing was occasioned by William of Ockham and his nominalist doctrine that denied the existence of universals through the separation of philosophy from theology.[193]

The Church was also changing during the twelfth and thirteenth centuries. It moved from a largely local institution under the direction of an abbey here or there to a more centralized system under papal authority.[194] But with centralization came abuses, and these abuses would coincide with the fall of Constantinople to the Turks in 1453 after centuries of classical and Christian civilization. Thus, the stage was set for the seismic changes in the Church. In the midst of the challenges of the Renaissance and the later Enlightenment, the Protestant revolt occurred. The Reformation was not a challenge to the universals but a call to reform within the Church and a return to the fundamental principles of the gospel of Jesus Christ. The troubles within the Church were fortuitous for the ideologies that sought its demise.

Although others had held beliefs and taught Christian doctrine in line with the Reformation prior to the sixteenth century, the Reformation is recognized as beginning in October 1517 when Martin Luther nailed his ninety-five theses to the door of the church in Wittenberg, Germany, six decades after the fall of the eastern half of the Roman Empire. When Luther pounded the nails into the door, little did he know that his actions would ignite a revolution that would change much of the world. His doctrine of the priesthood of all believers would shake the foundations of the Christian church. With an agony of mind, Luther had striven to attain the righteousness as the Apostle Paul had done through endless confessions and ascetic practices. In this desperate spiritual quest he experienced a "conversion" in which he saw the truth of justification by faith only through the grace of God as opposed to works. The Roman church's penitential system had deteriorated to such a point that forgiveness became a matter of gifts of money. His crusade for spiritual liberty would also have the unintended consequence of promoting both political and intellectual liberty as well.[195] However, as we shall see in a later chapter, the seeds of political and intellectual liberty had already been planted by the Church's thirteenth century incorporation of the classical Greek heritage into the Church.[196] This incorporation of the classical Greek heritage marked the beginning of the humanistic Renaissance.

The courts, universities, and even the papacy of the Church had departed from the medieval other-worldliness and philosophies to participate in the things of the world. The popes of the early Renaissance were patrons of the Renaissance arts and culture and participated in the sins of pride and vice. The trappings, traditions, and practices of the Church had worthwhile beginnings in man's desire to please God. Yet, these had become encrusted with man's ideas and wisdom and had over time grown away from the original purposes. The proponents of the Reformation were desirous of a return to the tenets of a medieval world-view and the revelation that culminated with the simple teachings of the Nazarene who was the Messiah. The Reformation was the product of the abhorrence of decadence within the Church and the Church's flirtation with the new doctrines and enticements of the Renaissance. From these twin afflictions arose Luther and ultimately the establishment of Protestantism. Protestant reformers were attempting to revive and reassert the teachings of the early church. So too were the reformers of the Catholic Reformation that followed close on the heels of the Protestant reformers, and both reformations were reactions to the excesses and willful naturalism of the Renaissance. Both reformations were united in their desire to return to the teachings of the early church and a true understanding of the human condition.[197]

Following Luther's priesthood of all believers, the Protestant church emphasized that every man should study the Old and New Testaments to tutor his conscience. Truth lay in private judgment. This had the effect of leading to religious as well as social individualism. The Catholic Church following the Council of Trent became an authoritative and highly structured church in which truth lay in the authority of the Church. The schism resulted in a religious war. While each of the two great arms of the Church were at the other's throat, the artistic, intellectual, and social movement of the Renaissance would challenge the Christian faith with a denial of the understanding of the fallen nature of man (the human condition), denial of Christian teachings, and a glorification of the pleasures of the flesh.[198] Thus, the European Enlightenment may be said to be the child of the European Renaissance and the religious wars following the Reformation.

The articulation of the new social order was made by the Enlightenment philosophers of the era, particularly those of France. Ancestors of the modern "intellectual", these enlightened philosophers held a common outlook and critical stance and were not scholars that specialized in the mental pursuit of philosophical studies. The capstone of Enlightenment thought lay in the *Encyclopedia,* the twenty-one volume repository of knowledge and propaganda of the French philosophers with publication beginning in 1751-1752. Through this enlightened philosophy was to be found the "…improvement of the lot of mankind by the manipulation of nature and the unfolding to man of the truths which reason had written in his heart." But there were obstacles to be conquered: ignorance, intolerance, and parochialism. Once these hindrances were removed, "…the unimpeded operations of the laws of nature, uncovered by reason, would promote the reform of society in everyone's interest except that of those wedded to the past by their blindness or their enjoyment of indefensible privilege."[199]

The closing years of the 1600s and all of the 1700s are considered to be the period of Enlightenment in which mathematical philosophies and scientific discoveries were applied to moral and social concerns. The Age of Enlightenment was a period of a particularly strong intellectual propensity with regard to the doctrines of progress, rationality, secularism, and political reform. The whole of Western Europe, Russia, and the British Isles were inundated with Enlightenment thought, but France was its center. The French *Encyclopedia* was, "Boldly anti-Christian, contemptuous of the Middle Ages, dedicated to speedy intellectual and social change, developing their own dogmas of the perfectibility of man and society…expected the swift transformation of civilization on purely rational principles…[and had] an enormous confidence in the reason of the individual human being."[200]

At the heart of the Enlightenment was the questioning of authority, "…the generalizing of the critical attitude." Everything was to be scrutinized; ultimately nothing was to be considered sacred. Through the Enlightenment came the notion that there were no moral values that arose from fixed ideas of right and wrong. Rather, moral values were the product of the mind as one experienced pleasure and pain. The enormous consequences of this concept on civilization were incalculable and have had a dominating influence on theories about education, economics, and other disciplines. The sciences grew rapidly and relied on the observation of the senses and promised a method to advance knowledge. Such knowledge would provide a utilitarian efficiency in making possible improvement of the men's lives and the world. Men became optimists and believed that the world was getting better and better. From such optimism arose the seventeenth century idea of progress. The tools by which this knowledge would be obtained and progress achieved were science and reason, an understanding of nature and the intellect of man.[201] J. M. Roberts wrote in his *History of the World*,

> In 'enlightened' thought there seemed to be small room for the divine and the theological. It was not just that educated Europeans no longer felt hell gaping about them. The world was becoming less mysterious; it also promised to be less tragic. More and more troubles seemed not inseparable from being, but man-made.[202]

The ideal society was to be achieved through science and reason. The human race was perfectible. Therefore, the mantra of Enlightenment thinkers was that progress toward the ideal society was to be achieved through education, and "So long as men continue to accumulate knowledge, progress will be inevitable as the growth of a tree; nor is there any reason to look for its cessation."[203] By the middle of the eighteenth century, the ancients were rejected by the scientists of the day. By the end of the century, French Revolutionist Condorcet summarized the hopes of the age by predicting that the principles of the Revolution, that is, eighteenth century faith in reason, would spread over the entire earth to include a strengthening of "…a real economic and social and intellectual equality."[204]

Chapter 7

The Renaissance and Enlightenment: Progress and Perfection – Science and Reason

As Christianity was sorting through the disruptions and distractions brought by the conflict between Catholics and the revolting Protestants, the champions of the Renaissance and Enlightenment sharpened their weapons for an attack on faith. Initially, the weapons of attack are chosen by the aggressors. Thus, Christianity must defend itself against attempts to use science and reason as a wedge to split asunder the foundations upon which it rests.

Science was the first tool in the hands of Enlightenment philosophers to be used to achieve the ideal society. The new science sought power over nature for the service of man and in the process broke with the Middle Ages. The new science exploded in the nineteenth century and would challenge one of the basic underpinnings of Christianity—faith in the Creator who created man in his own image. Swinging the gauntlet in the face of the ancients and their Creator, Charles Darwin would say otherwise. *The Origin of Species* published in 1859 followed by his *Descent of Man* in 1871 would undermine the authority of the Scripture. On the monumental influence of Darwin, John Dewey wrote:

> In laying hands upon the sacred ark of absolute permanency, in treating the forms that had been regarded as types of fixity and perfection as originating and passing away, the "Origin of Species" introduced a mode of thinking that in the end was bound to transform the logic of knowledge, and hence the treatment of morals, politics, and religion.[205]

Natural science challenged the understanding of the cosmos, planet earth, and now physical man. Science became the ultimate tool by which to manipulate nature. Science expressed itself to the average man through technology as it had a positive impact on the lives of people. Beginning with the first great advances in physics during the seventeenth century, science began its domination of society as scientists were highly revered and educational and other institutions were created to further its ascendance. The average man understood the growing control of the environment and improvement of life provided by science, and "This was what made the nineteenth century the first in which science truly became an object of religion—perhaps of idolatry."[206]

As evolutionary biology became the humanistic means to understand and explain his origins, the rise of psychology—the study of the mind—would soon follow to explain the mechanics of human nature. The father of modern psychology is considered to be the German physician Wilhelm Wundt who in 1879 founded the first laboratory dedicated to psychological research. In 1890 American philosopher and psychologist William James wrote *Principles of Psychology*, a seminal work in the systemization of experimental psychology. However, James and others would abandon some of his concepts of consciousness described in the book.[207] Initially, James and other early humanistic psychologists were somewhat tolerant of religion as long as it remained meekly in its place. He wrote, "…no scientist will ever try actively to interfere with our religious faith, provided we enjoy it quietly with our friends and do not make a public nuisance of it in the market-place."[208] However, James' assurance of a lack of interference with religion would soon ring hollow.

Beginning in the 1890s until his death in 1939, Sigmund Freud developed the field of psychoanalysis, a method of psychotherapy. Building on Darwin's retreat from the ancients in the area of biology and geology, Freud challenged the ancients' understanding of human nature. Whereas Darwin was initially tentative in his attack, Freud (as noted earlier) would blast religious doctrines as "…illusions and insusceptible of proof. No one can be compelled to think them true, to believe in them. Some of them are so improbable, so incompatible with everything we have laboriously discovered about the reality of the world, that we may compare them…to delusions."[209] Freud equated religion with mental illness, calling it "…the universal human obsessional neurosis…"[210] For

Freud, a thoroughgoing Darwinian, the reality of human nature was evolutionary and reduced humans to complex animals without notions of moral responsibility. Sin, soul, and conscience were replaced by instincts, drives, and other scientific terms. Freud's id or primitive impulses belonged to the oldest or animal portion of the brain. The ego or rational mind developed from the more highly evolved cerebral cortex. Things that a society labels "bad" merely originate from the animal or more primitive part of the brain; therefore, bad cannot be considered evil.[211]

Freud was aggressively at war with religion, and the heart of his argument was that science and religion were incompatible—the essence of nineteenth century anti-clerical thought. The warfare began in the eighteenth century and has become pervasive in the twenty-first century.[212] Humanists continue to hold the incompatibility of science and religion as axiomatic truth even in the face of numerous defeats, and the average man continues to render unquestioning allegiance to the erring scientists. Why is this so?

To answer this question, we must first separate science from Enlightenment thought and its embedded humanism. There *is* a war between Christianity and Enlightenment thought that challenges Christianity, universal truths, and the revelation of those truths. One must be true, the other false—they cannot co-exist in spite of efforts in some quarters in modern times. But, with regard to a Christian view of science and religion, there is not a war. The Christian sees no conflict with science when he or she believes that God created the universe and put the universal truths in place. Colson wrote that, "…it was Christianity that made science possible…the scientific method, and all it has accomplished, is a great apologetic argument for the truth of Christianity." The fallacy that the rise of science caused the demise of religion began with the first modern historians who were Enlightenment rationalists. The resulting histories of Western civilization by historians such as Voltaire and Gibbon portrayed religion as the antithesis of science.[213] The conflict between science and religion escalated at the end of the nineteenth century through the efforts of scientists and educational leaders in order to wrest control of their institutions from the Church. Therefore, the division between science and religion was manufactured and not an intellectual separation. Thus, the creation of the division by scientists and educators was a strategy executed to achieve cultural power.[214] And, the popular media, scientific journals, and textbooks continue to promote the myth of a conflict between science and Christianity, that science has won the battle, and that the ascendancy of science beginning in the seventeen century caused of the demise of religion.

Isaac Newton is considered one of the greatest of the early scientists. He was a devout Christian and believed that scientific work would reveal the God who created the world. Newton believed that, although the world operated on mechanical causes, "...science shows what is the first cause, what power he has over us, and what benefits we received from him. Our duty toward him, as well as towards one another, will appear to us by the light of nature." Newton believed that the business of science was to show causes from effects and that "as we trace them back, we deduce the first cause must be an intelligent and rational being."[215] Yet, humanistic philosophers, scientists, and historians, while exalting Newton as one of the greatest scientists of the ages, present Newton's work in a totally different light than Newton had intended. Newton was far from being alone in his belief that his scientific discoveries were supportive of Christianity. Most of the great scientists of the era were Christians and their discoveries were considered by them to support the Christian worldview. In reality, their discoveries describe the workings of God's creation, and the scientists often described their work in terms that supported a Christian worldview. Unfortunately, church authorities that represented the Christian doctrine did not accept the truth of their scientific work. When church authorities rejected the scientific discoveries that reflected a new understanding of the world and the universe, those authorities were discredited and by association the doctrines of the Church (creation, fall, restoration). Again, it was authorities within the Church that were in error as to the workings of nature, not the revelation of God. The humanists' of the Renaissance and Enlightenment quickly capitalized on the errors of Church authorities by substituting the revelation of God as being the major point of error rather than church authority and thereby abandoned the first cause. Such humanist thinkers and philosophers readily accepted Newton's light that was shed on the workings of the world and universe but carefully shielded that light from shining on the first cause and the consequent duties owed to the Creator.

The second reason humanists have succeeded in creating the chasm between science and Christian doctrine is the belief that science has disproved Christianity. To adequately challenge this belief, one must first look at what science does and how it does it. In the first place, most dictionaries include several meanings for the word "science": systematized knowledge, knowledge covering general truths or the operation of general laws especially as obtained and tested through scientific method, based upon scientific principles. Out of these descriptions of science arise the perception of fact, objectivity, truth, the source of all knowledge, and even invulnerability. Science and scientific pronouncements have become the gold standard, the thing by which all things are measured. Religion is presumed to be subjective, emotional, or a fantasy and therefore must defer to science. Originally, science was a study of the natural world, but it has evolved into a philosophy sometimes called scientism or scientific naturalism.[216] However, when conducting a scientific investigation, scientists must still deal only with things that can be known and measured. Consequently, scientific naturalism concludes, incorrectly, that if science can't test for supernatural causes, then the supernatural cannot exist. Timothy Keller wrote, "It is one thing to say that science is only equipped to test for natural causes and cannot speak to any others. It is quite another to insist that science proves that no other causes could possibly exist."[217] To deny that the supernatural exists, as does scientific naturalism, is also to deny God. For without the supernatural, how can there be God?

    An analogy may be helpful in demonstrating the fallacy of denying the supernatural (including God) because the supernatural can't be tested and therefore can't exist. How does science deal with the occurrence of love between a man and woman? Generally, they would do so in terms of evolutionary development, the desire for pleasure, animal instinct, or some other explanation divorced from anything other than a sensory attraction. Certainly, physical attraction and desire play a role on the level of Eros love, but love can be far more than sensual. In my case I had watched the young woman for several months. I was almost twenty-six, and she had just turned nineteen when I summoned the courage to ask her for a date. Three months later we were engaged. What did I know about this young woman that would cause me to commit a lifetime to her? My knowledge came from observation and interaction with her, not unlike the methods of a scientist—except my analysis was conducted with a little more passion. She was as advertised—attractive, vivacious, and had a winning personality. Not long into the courtship (an old fashioned word but an apt description) I discovered another factor in her favor—that 'something' a scientist cannot quantify, measure, or define—that thing called love. The decision to ask her to marry me was based on limited knowledge and a measure of present . Thirty-eight years later I still can't say that I really knew her after only three months of courtship. My knowledge of her has grown over the years, and I can now truly say that I know her exceptionally well. I also know that I love her immensely, and I know that the feeling is mutual. The scientist may ask, "Is that love real?" If I say that it is, he may ask, "How do you know that it is real? Can it be measured or proven?" Well, it can't be proven in a laboratory, but it is reality as evidenced by words, actions, and attitudes. To a small degree, even these can be measured and offered as proof to the scientists. Not only does our love transcend the sensual and measurable, it also transcends the noumenal realm in which something that is unknowable by the senses is conceivable by reason. Here our love rises to the third level of reality—a *knowing* that transcends both the senses (physical and material) and understanding (reason). After thirty-eight years of marriage, my heart knowledge (the knowing) of the reality of our love is far greater and stronger than my sensory perceptions and head knowledge. Here we enter into a realm akin to faith for faith is a belief, a knowing. Such knowing or faith does not rest upon but transcends the senses, desires, emotions, measurement, scientists' feeble attempts at proof, and even reason itself. Through faith we enter into the reality of the supernatural.

  Man's knowledge and abilities are and always will be insufficient to prove there is or is not a God. First, we are not God but created by Him. To prove the existence of God would require that we be not only extra-terrestrial but also extra-universe and assume the qualities and powers of God. However, we can know there is a God and discern what kind of a God he is. Keller presents in his book an interesting chapter entitled "The Clues of God."[218] For the Christian, knowing God is more reassuring than proofs of God. Proof of God speaks to man's rational limits. Knowing God rests on faith supported by right reason, the revelation, and observation of the workings of universal truths that consistently allow man to conform to God's plan and thereby reap the beneficial consequences in this life but more importantly in the next. Such beneficial consequences may or may not include the material and will include much that is not understood or viewed by the humanist as being something that is beneficial. In fact, in many parts of the world, knowing and loving God may call for the ultimate sacrifice of one's life.

The third reason humanists have succeeded in creating the perceived conflict between science and Christianity is that humanists have successfully diverted attention from their own failures and inconsistencies. This diversion is accomplished through both substitution and attack. Substitution occurs when humanistic scientific theories and dicta (that contradict or challenge the truth of Christianity and its doctrines) are found to be false. They quickly replace the false suppositions with new theories that continue to support their humanistic worldview. The mistakes are merely viewed as steps on a path to new knowledge in man's ever-progressing march towards perfection. Past errors become the foundation for new truths much as the often told story of Edison's thousands of failures before finding the right filament to create the light bulb, i.e., failure leads to knowledge that leads to progress. However, this rationale will never lead to success (truth) if the basic assumptions and presuppositions upon which the theories are based are false or flawed. In the modern world the erring humanists are not discredited nor held accountable. Freud and his work are an excellent example. The intellectual force of Freudianism was substantially spent by the end of the twentieth century.[219] But even during Freud's lifetime, his theories were under considerable attack. During the early part of the twentieth century, John Herman Randall, Jr., a thoroughgoing humanist and no friend of Christianity, nevertheless wrote a scathing attack on Freud's theories:

> ...these ideas have been projected against a conception of mind and a set of theories that, logically inconsistent, necessarily hypothetical and unverifiable, often deliberately involved and fantastic, and in conflict with much that is definitely established...The faults of the instinct theory are multiplied...Freud's theory contains such sweeping, dogmatic, and wholly hypothetical elements as to have provoked dissent from most of his own followers; and his readiness to apply it in fields like anthropology where he was patently ignorant has not heightened his prestige among the scientifically minded.[220]

Yet, ever the good humanist protecting one of his own, Randall would soften his critique by stating that it "...contains elements of truth that, interpreted in more objective and experimental terms, will do much to clarify the integration of human personality."[221] Even though most of his theories, ideas, and practices have been discredited, Freud's stature, reputation, and influence remain substantial in the twenty-first century.

Diversion of attention from the failures of scientific tenets of humanism is also achieved through attacking those who question or criticize those failures, falsities, and inconsistencies. In other words, for the humanists, a good offense is the best defense. Therefore, exceptional hostility and vitriol are directed toward those of a Christian worldview by institutions that have vested interests in the humanistic worldview (media, education, government, science, sociology, and the arts). The wagons are circled and a counter offensive is mounted against those of the Christian worldview who have the audacity to question humanistic science. Rather than receive answers to their questions or criticisms, those with the Christian worldview are labeled as neurotic, ignorant, bigoted, or whatever appears to be the most effective means of diverting attention from the fact that Emperor Humanist has no clothes.

With the universals of the ancients cast off from the natural science, biology, and psychology, Enlightenment philosophers sought to conform not only the individual but society as a whole to the canons of humanistic thinking. Beginning with the French revolution at the end of the eighteenth century, radical ideas with regard to organizing and administering society would fuse with other Enlightenment ideas of progress, perfectibility of man, and the dismissal of concepts of right and wrong. The science of society would be named sociology during the nineteenth century, and scientism's methods were applied to sociology and politics.[222]

Karl Marx was to sociology what Darwin was to biology.[223] Marx was a German social theorist and philosopher and in his writings and philosophy developed a concept based on a humanistic worldview. Written in 1848, the influence of *The Communist Manifesto* would expand over the next sixty-five years under the banner of socialist labor parties.[224] Western civilization's humanist admirers of Enlightenment philosophy would conduct a love affair with communism during the twentieth century, particularly in its first half. For an example of such devotion, one may again return to John Herman Randall, Jr., a signor of the *Humanist Manifesto I* in 1933. In *The Making of the Modern Mind*, published in 1926 and updated in 1940, Randall wrote:

> Communism stands for the socialist ideal of a planned economy and a classless society, *the great objectives that have emerged out of industrial society*. The achievements of the Soviet Union in its fervent devotion to these ideals are impressive and enlightening; they deserve the *warmest sympathy and most careful study*.[225] (emphasis added)

Thus, the compatible and intimate relationship between Marxism and humanism is readily apparent in Randall's praise. In point of fact, Marx's ideology of mechanistic social planning had its roots in the eighteenth century Enlightenment philosophy of optimism, materialism, and humanitarianism.[226] The compatibility of humanistic science and sociology is further confirmed by the friendship between Marx and Charles Darwin and the mutual admiration of their respective ideas.[227] Yet, Marx's ideas presented in *The Communist Manifesto* ultimately were responsible for the enslavement of a third of humanity for three-fourths of the twentieth century, the consequences of which were death and misery unparalleled in the history of mankind.

As has been stated, the ideal society of Enlightenment thinkers and philosophers was to be achieved through the never-ending progress of man and society, and the tools of progress were science and reason. We have briefly discussed the humanistic theories of science. Now, we turn to reason—the power of comprehending, inferring, or thinking.

Naturalism imagines that scientific laws are adequate to account for all phenomena and denies the supernatural. Naturalism also contends that action, desires, or thought is based only on natural desires and instincts. If nature is all there is, then rational thought (reason and understanding) must have come into existence through an evolutionary process and the consequent gradual disappearance of those less fitted to survive. In other words, the naturalist contends that natural selection, which must preserve and increase useful behavior, somehow turns sub-rational thought into rational, inferential thinking that reaches truth.[228]

As previously noted, the principles and hopes of the philosophers of the French Revolution were based on an eighteenth century faith in reason which would spread over the entire earth and result in real economic, social, and intellectual equality.[229] The heart of the spirit of the French Revolution was captured by Condorcet in his *History of the Progress of the Human Spirit* as he writes of the progress of reason:

> The result of my work will be to show, by reasoning and by facts, that there is no limit set to the perfecting of the powers of man; that human perfectibility is in reality indefinite; that the progress of this perfectibility, henceforth independent of any power that might wish to stop it, has no other limit than the duration of the globe upon which nature has placed us...What a picture of the human race, freed from its chains, removed from the empire of chance as from that of the enemies of its progress, and advancing with a firm and sure step on the pathway of truth, of virtue and of happiness, is presented to the philosopher to console him for the errors, the crimes, and the injustices with which the earth still soiled and of which he is often the victim! It is in contemplating this vision he receives the reward of his efforts for the progress of reason, for the defense of liberty.[230]

Condorcet, knowing he would be consumed by the very forces he vigorously supported, hid in the back room of a meeting house and eventually escaped the guillotine by taking his own life.[231]

A contrarian but still secular view of reason was given by eighteenth century philosopher David Hume, the father of modern secularism. For Hume, reason is only the servant of one's passion, not to identify what is rational or should be wanted. Reason is merely a means to an end—the end being to obtain what people want. Therefore, reason's purpose is only to assist man in attaining his desires.[232]

Whatever the view of reason by Enlightenment philosophers, all would sever the cords of reason from a transcendent God and His permanent things. As with the humanists' depiction of a battle between science and religion, they also depict a battle between reason and faith. By faith is meant religion (especially Christianity in America), the supernatural, a transcendent God, and eternal laws for mankind. Unfortunately, many Christians have come to view faith as the opposite of reason. They shouldn't.

C. S. Lewis wrote that man's rationality or reason is the "little tell-tale rift in Nature" through which it was revealed that there was something beyond or behind her (mindless nature). For Christianity, Divine reason is older than nature, and from Divine reason comes nature in all of its orderliness. Because of this orderliness of nature, mankind may know her. Man was created with the ability to reason, and that ability is not part of the system of nature but something apart. Man's reason is not a "thing" but an ability to comprehend, infer, and think—something we do.[233] When man reasons, his reasoning may be faulty or he may have correct or right reasoning. In one sense God gave man a helping hand in finding right reason. First, man was created in his image, and thus there is something of God's nature in us—something of a homing instinct for the Divine. Second, God gave us road signs in the form of universals that serve as guides to our reasoning. Lastly, He gave us revelation through the books written by the inspired Hebrews and first century Christians. By these standards, all of life should be measured.

As humanists attempt to distance reason and hard factual evidence of science from faith, they fail to see the supporting evidence is at the core of Christianity. "Reason and revelation are not the same thing, but the stand closer together in the Christian faith than any other." The faith of other major religions of the world (e.g., Islam) are based on the assertions of a person long dead. In other words, the revelation of that person must be followed without any evidence or evidential apologetics. As we see the evidential connection between the attributes of the God of the Bible and the universals (the way life works), our faith increases.[234]

If reason is a slave to desires and passions, as Hume believed, there is an implicit denial of free choice or free will. If one acts on reasons that are not subservient to passions and external forces, that is free choice. If one can act only upon the impetus of internal passions and desires or external forces, then reason is powerless to restrain those passions, desires, or external forces. Therefore, man does not have free choice and consequently cannot be held accountable for right or wrong behavior. However, Christianity holds that man can be held accountable for right and wrong behaviors. For a man to be rightly ordered, reason must control passion. But for the humanist there are no absolutes and therefore no restraints on passions to rule reason. Slave reason only produces rationalizations for morally wrong thoughts and behavior.[235] The enigma is that reason given free choice makes possible a restraint of passions, but enslavement of reason comes from giving unrestrained liberty to passions.

Ultimately, reason is used to discover truth, and the end product of our reasoning results in one of two outcomes: presumed truth or confusion and chaos. If we reach a presumed truth, that truth will be examined and tested from time to time as a result of our own doubts or through external sources. The more tests the truth withstands, the more we rest on or rely on that truth and the more it becomes a part of our worldview. Lewis denied the supposed battle between faith and reason, "It is not reason that is taking away my faith: on the contrary, my faith is based on reason. It is my imagination and emotions that attacks faith. The battle is between faith and reason on one side and emotion and imagination on the other."[236]

Faith is an ally of reason. Our reasoning has led us to belief, that is, belief in the truth of Christianity and all upon which it rests. That belief has been derived from our observation and reasoning abilities. That belief has been tested and found to be truth. In the sense used here, faith "…is the art of holding on to things your reason has once accepted, in spite of your changing moods." It is not blind faith but a faith that was introduced by our reasoning ability and from something within—that knowing, that Divine connection—for we are created in His image. In time faith grows to be more important to our belief in the truth than our reasoning ability. Through faith, we can withstand changes in our moods, our failures, our doubts, our circumstances, or any other of life's challenges.[237]

There is a second sense in which one may view faith, perhaps a higher sense. Here this higher sense somewhat departs from reason but yet rests upon its foundation. Faith in this sense leaves it to God to make us like Him. We must repent of our failings (sinful nature and sins). And, we do our part to banish the evil impulse and corral our fallen nature, but we continually fail. Ultimately, we realize we can do nothing except continue trying to be like Him. It is at this point when we despair, but our faith in Christ saves us. That faith in Christ causes us to realize that we can't succeed in our own efforts but at the same time causes us to realize we don't have to. Christ works in us for we are not alone. A Christian "leaves it to God...[when] he trusts that Christ will somehow share with him the perfect human obedience which He carried out from His birth to His crucifixion: that Christ will make the man more like Himself and, in a sense, make good his deficiencies." But, leaving it to God does not mean that we can stop trying.[238] Here our earthly reason quietly bows to the Divine.* Leaving it in God's hands is more than knowing, it is a matter of trust also. And the roots of this knowing and trusting can be traced to the early work of reason.

An excellent discussion of the relationship between reason and faith was made by Professor George. He quotes the late Pope John Paul II's writings in his encyclical letter *Fides et Ratio* (Faith and Reason). The Pope stated that, "Faith and reason are like two wings on which the human spirit rises to the contemplation of truth." George hurries to confirm that there are not two truths but a unity of truth, i.e., a truth of faith is also historically and scientifically a truth as well, and those truths are known in various ways: by revelation and others by philosophy, science, and historical inquiry.[239] George wrote:

> Those (truths) known by revelation are often, however, fully understandable, or their implications fully knowable, only by rational inquiry. And often the full human and cosmic significance of those knowable by philosophical, scientific, and historical inquiry only becomes evident in the light of faith. And then there is the category of truths, particularly in the moral domain, knowable, in principle, at least, by

---

*Seventeenth century mathematician Blaise Pascal wrote of reason in his *Les Pensée*, "Reason's last step is the recognition that there are an infinite number of things which are beyond it. It is merely feeble if it does not go as far as to realize that." [*Les Pensée 188*. Quoted by Malcolm Muggeridge, *The End of Christendom*, (Grand Rapids, Michigan: William B. Eerdmans Publishing Company, 1980), p. x.]

philosophical inquiry but also revealed. Here revelation illuminates the truths of natural law, bringing into focus their precise contours, and making apparent to people of faith their supernatural significance.[240]

George is described by one writer as having "...a Roman Catholic philosophy based on Aristotle, who posited the existence of an objective moral order graspable by human reason and obtainable through free will. As George puts it, 'In a well-ordered soul, reason's got the whip hand over emotion'."[241]

It was not until the twelfth century that the classical philosophies of the Greeks including Aristotle were translated into Latin and therefore became available to European scholars. Because of its pagan origins, Aristotelian thought was initially banned from the universities by the Roman church.[242] This changed with the teaching of Thomas Aquinas (1225-1274), proclaimed by many as the greatest teacher in the history of the Catholic Church. Aquinas sought to reconcile the classical and Christian accounts of the world.[243] Aquinas was an ardent defender of Aristotle and constructed a system of thought that became a great unified system of understanding of the Christian revelation as a whole. According to Aquinas, this understanding came through faith enlightened by reason and was based on the Bible, the church fathers, and Aristotelian reasoning.[244] Francis Schaffer contends that it was Aquinas's teachings that brought about "...the real birth of the humanistic Renaissance." Schaeffer credited Aquinas with the view that, "...the will of man was fallen but the intellect was not.* From this incomplete view of the

---

* Schaeffer's contentions of the influence of Greek humanistic thought are supported by Aquinas's *Summa Theologica*. Aquinas believed the intellect (reason) to be incorruptible. Aquinas wrote that "...the will is not subject to the passions in such a way as necessarily to follow their enticement, but on the contrary has it in its power to repress passion by the judgment of the reason...It retains free judgment either to follow or to resist their attractions, as may seem to it expedient. Only the wise act thus; the masses follow the lead of bodily passions and urgings, for they are wanting in wisdom and virtue...man was so constituted that, unless his reason was subservient to God, his body could not be made subject to the beck of the soul, nor could his sense powers be brought under the rule of reason." [Thomas Aquinas,

biblical Fall flowed all subsequent difficulties. Man's intellect became autonomous. In one realm man was now independent, autonomous." The freeing of man's intellect (reason) also freed philosophy (including the philosophy of humanism) from the constraints of revelation. Through the autonomy of the intellect from revelation Aquinas hoped to find a unity between the heavenly things and earthly things, that is, the supernatural and natural (nature). However, nature freed from revelation is destructive as it focused on particulars (diversity) as opposed to universals. "Where do you find a unity when diversity is set free?" The loss of unity sprang from the growing humanism in the Catholic Church and the doctrine of an incomplete Fall as put forth by Aquinas. Thus, the Roman Catholic view of salvation involves a humanistic element. It is a divided work, "...Christ died for our salvation, but man had to merit the merit of Christ..."[245]

The unintended consequences of the integration of Christian and classical thought in the thirteenth century made possible the revival of humanistic letters of the fourteenth to sixteenth centuries. In the end the essence of the effort to merge the Christian and classical worldviews resulted in a complete break with the world of Aquinas.[246]

Ironically, the answer to this loss of unity between the intellect and revelation was found in the schism of the Reformation in which the whole man was seen as fallen, including his will and intellect.

> The Reformers said that there is nothing man can do; no autonomous or humanistic, religious or moral effort of man can help. One is saved only on the basis of the finished work of Christ...the only way to be saved is to lift the empty hands of faith...[247]

In other words, the evangelical Protestant's understanding of reason differs with regard to the route to free choice, and that route is "...being born again through Christ: Reason by itself, diseased as it is, will not get us there."[248] Blackstone's understanding of reason

---

Aquinas's Shorter Summa, (Manchester, New Hampshire: Sophia Institute Press, 1993, 2002), pp. 79, 143-144, 218.]

concurs, as previously shown, in that our first ancestor transgressed or failed to conform his actions to those eternal laws of human nature. Therefore, his reason and that of subsequent generations were impaired, flawed, unclear, clouded, or an unreliable in finding the laws of human nature from whence one may successfully guide his life.[249] For the evangelical Protestant, the war between reason and emotion was won at Calvary through the Blood of Jesus and the Cross. Watchman Nee[*] provided an excellent discourse on the finished work of Calvary. The two-fold mission first involved Christ shedding his blood for "...our justification through 'the remission of sins'." To put it another way, the Blood covers or disposes of our sins. Second, we are united with Christ in his death, burial, and resurrection by the work of the Cross that "...strikes at the root of our capacity to sin." "Through the one man's disobedience, the many were made sinners."(Romans 3:23 KJV) In other words we were made sinners by our constitution or nature (original sin). Because of our nature, we are inclined to sin. When one is born again, he resides in Christ. Because he is in Christ, he died, was buried, and was resurrected with Him and is no longer slave to sin as long as he abides in Christ.[250]

    Nee also gives an excellent picture of the soul and reason's place therein when he wrote, "...the fruit of the tree of knowledge

---

[*] Watchman Nee was born in 1903 as Ni Shu-tsu (Henry Nee) on the southwestern coast of China. With a heritage that included a grandfather that was a Congregational minister and a harsh mother who was spiritually transformed through a Methodist revival, Watchman (his baptismal name) Nee devoted himself to a study of the Word and became a writer and minister of the Gospel following his conversion in 1920. After the Communists gained control of China in 1949, they began to infiltrate the Church. Nee was arrested in 1952 and held without word from him until 1956 when he was put on trial. Found guilty of charges ranging from "...espionage and counterrevolutionary activities to licentious dissolution...," he was sentenced to fifteen or twenty years in prison (the sources are not clear). Having served almost twenty years and nearing release, he died of unknown causes in 1972 while still in prison. Throughout his years of imprisonment his writings, comprised mostly of his previous sermons and lectures, gained prominence in the western world. [From the Preface to the Hendrickson Christian Classics Edition (Third Printing 2008) of *The Normal Christian Life*, (Peabody, Massachusetts: Hendrickson Publishers, 1961), pp. vii-viii, xi-xii.]

made the first man *over-developed in his soul.* (emphasis in original) The emotion was touched, because the fruit was pleasant to the eyes, making him 'desire'; the mind with its reasoning power was developed, for he was 'made wise'; and the will was strengthened, so that in future he could always decide which way he would go."[251]

Although the Catholic Church tentatively opened the doors for humanistic philosophies in thirteenth century Christendom, mainline American Protestant denominations boldly flung the doors wide for humanistic thought in the late nineteenth and early twentieth centuries. This is discussed in Chapter 18 of Part III.

In the war of worldviews, Catholics and evangelical Protestants must remain allies. Protestants and Catholics share a common general worldview of Creation, the Fall, and Redemption. Differences over the workings of reason and other doctrinal issues must not hinder their unity as the two stand as the bulwark against secularism and humanism in Western civilization. Recognition of secular humanism as the common enemy of both Catholics and Protestants can be found in the words of Pope Benedict XVI. "The great challenge, in his view, is the 'dictatorship of relativism,' which denies the existence of an objective moral order and objective truth."[252] With this evangelical Christians readily agree. However, this unity must not be based on organization or compromise as is often the case with ecumenical efforts and organizations such as the World Council of Churches. Rather, it must be a spiritual unity as taught by the New Testament—something created by God and only preserved by man. As one writer puts it, "It is an organic unity, a unity of life, a unity of the Spirit that vitalizes the body."[253]

As faulty as it may be in fallen man, reason is not banished by Blackstone or the evangelical Protestant. In one sense reason takes us to the door of Christianity, but faith invites us in and holds our hand as we continue the faith journey. However, reason was not left at the door. As we move along the faith journey, we encounter life—all sorts of thoughts, ideas, things, situations, difficulties, trials, struggles, disappointments, opportunities, and so forth. Thus, everyone must examine life and filter it through his or her worldview. Because of our Christian worldview we should examine life in comparison to the universals (the permanent things), the revelation given to the Hebrews (the Bible), and divine guidance (through prayer). And reason is a tool we have to assist in these areas. At this point reason only assists and guides within the framework of truths we hold and have incorporated into our Christian worldview. In one sense, reason helps us to accept the unreasonable (from a humanistic viewpoint) as we search the Bible, pray for Divine guidance, and work out our own salvation.

Christianity and its tenets are intricately associated with faith, and this faith is multifaceted. However, it is beyond the scope of this book to explore all the ramifications of faith and its operation. We shall leave the subject with a reaffirmation of Lewis's view: there is not a battle between faith and reason. Such a view exists in the minds of those who have developed a worldview wherein there is no God or who have limited Him in a worldview where God is not intricately involved with this world or its inhabitants. These two worldviews are defeated by the slavery of reason to imaginations and emotions.

This slavery of reason to imaginations and emotion was evident in the writings of Randall in the early part of the twentieth century. Regarding the Enlightenment of the eighteenth century and science of the nineteenth as the two revolutions that broke the bonds of the medieval world, Randall wrote:

> Man was alone, quite alone, in a vast and complex cosmic machine. Gone were the angelic hosts, gone the devils and their pranks, gone the daily miracles of supernatural intervention, gone was man's imploring cry of prayer…Of all that medieval world, one thing alone was left for those who entered whole-heartedly into this great cold universe—the faith in a Creator in whose image man was made, in a wise and loving Father who had built all this vast machinery for the good of man…This last fond remnant of the Christian epic it was left for the nineteenth century, not indeed to refute, for faith can never be disproved, but to make, for many at least irrelevant and unimportant. For them, man too became a mere part of this vast machine; its finest flower, perhaps—perhaps a cosmic accident and mistake.[254]

Eighty years later, one must ask if faith has proven irrelevant and unimportant as Randall and other secular humanists pronounced. One can imagine that the first and second century Romans seated in the Coliseum had the same thoughts as Randall of the irrelevance and unimportance of faith as Christians were devoured by the lions. They too did not understand the lesson taught by the Son of God who walked the arid hills of Galilee and Judea as a simple carpenter's son in the backwaters of the Roman Empire—"My kingdom is not of this world..."[255]

As we have discussed, much of Western civilization has bought into the dichotomy created by humanists that science and reason are not compatible with Christianity because science is based on fact and religion in general and Christianity in particular are unscientific, not rational, and therefore cannot have a voice in a pluralistic society. However, the bankruptcy of the Renaissance and Enlightenment philosophies that gained ascendancy in the eighteenth and nineteenth centuries became evident as the events of the twentieth century unfolded. The denial of the fallen nature of man for the sophistry of the perpetual effort to perfect man was refuted by the horrors of two world wars, the enslavement of a third of mankind lasting through the end of the cold war, and the general decline of social and moral behavior. However, the war continues to rage between Christianity and those promoting a secular society based upon humanistic principles. We see it in every facet of life, and there can be no truce, no peaceful co-existence, and no détente' between the combatants.

Chapter 8

Colonial American Heritage

In the last two chapters we have briefly chronicled the beginnings of Christianity, its growth in the Roman Empire, its dispersion to the relatively primitive peoples of Western Europe and the British Isles, the growth of Western Christendom in the Middle ages, the challenges brought by the Renaissance and Enlightenment philosophers, the Reformation, and the scientific advances of the nineteenth century that further weakened Christendom. The purpose of this chapter is to overlay that history on the American experience in the colonial period and chart the impact on the founding of the United States. All of this is necessary to give meaning to subsequent discussions and to the central theme of this book as previously noted.

The Founders had two significant pillars on which they created the American government. One was the moral pillar of the Judeo-Christian tradition and the other was the political pillar of English history and law with elements from the ancient Greeks and Romans. The colonial history of America dates from 1607 and continues to the beginning of the Revolutionary War in 1776. However, to adequately explain the colonists' worldview and reasons for being in the New World, it is necessary to look once again at the events and circumstances of Europe in general and Britain in particular in the four centuries prior to the appearance of the first permanent European settlers on the eastern fringe of the continent.

The heritage of America is that of liberty, and that is what the colonists brought with them from Britain. The origins of liberty were medieval and not of the Renaissance or Enlightenment. The British system of law relied on tradition rather than theoretical schemes of abstract reason. The central focus of this tradition was the common law that had existed from "time immemorial." The common law, built up slowly through the ages, was combined with a host of precedents of unwritten custom, judicial decisions, decrees of parliament, and grants and agreements by the kings.[256]

Moderns almost universally depict the Middle Ages as being a time of superstition, autocracy, ignorance, intellectual stagnation, and a night-time of human progress when compared to the Renaissance and Age of Enlightenment. However, it was during the Middle Ages that the foundations of free government were established as opposed to the ideas of ancient Greek and Roman cultures. The rejection of medieval doctrines during the Renaissance endangered Western liberties and has led to autocracies and despotic regimes of the modern era. The central document of the Middle Ages upon which modern liberties of Western societies flow is that of the Magna Carta and its concepts of freedom. It is a remarkable document that limited the power of the state, something previously unknown in the ancient world. The limitations on the power of the state sprang from the biblical religion as it relates to its distinctive views of God, nature, man, and governance. Out of this limit to state power (the kings of the Middle Ages) arose the concept of constitutionalism in the English speaking world.[257]

These views of freedom through constitutionalism saturated the minds of populace of Western Christendom, and two medieval institutions were primarily responsible. The Catholic Church consistently challenged the kings of the Middle Ages just as the Hebrew prophets of old did when kings transgressed the laws of God. In all of Western history, no other institution did more to advance constitutional forms of government. The feudal barons also stood with the church in contravention of the power of the monarchy. As Roman power waned, Europe became a mixture of tribes and races. Out of a lack of central authority and the resulting frequent wars arose the feudal system in which individual barons and their armies created a patchwork of defense centers across Europe. Under the feudal system people grouped themselves together for protection under individual barons and thus became his armed retainers. Irrespective of the faults and failings of the feudal system, the decentralized nature of the powers and military forces that arose contributed substantially to the cause of freedom. King John signed the Magna Carta because he could not defeat the feudal barons and their well-armed followers. Not only military forces were dispersed but wealth also. Thus, the king was forced to negotiate with the feudal barons and clergy for resources. In exchange for the safeguarding their liberties, both legal and economic, the clergy and feudal barons would provide resources (taxes) to the crown. Each time the king needed money he had to negotiate and barter with his subjects. By the early fourteenth century the king added the burgesses (wealthy tradesmen of the towns and cities) to the lords and clergy as sources of funds, and all of these groups became the Parliament. When called, the burgesses, lesser barons, and country gentry segments of the Parliament gathered in the "commons." From this account we discern the source of English freedoms such as the growth of Parliament, safeguards for property, legal privilege, taxation by consent, and other concessions and guarantees that were expressed through the English common law tradition. And without question the source of these freedoms that became the bedrock of the American system of government was medieval Christendom.[258] A factual, clear-eyed account of medieval history provides a different view than that of modern histories and is a far cry from the suppositions of the humanists and other adherents to Renaissance and Enlightenment thought as regards the origins of America's founding and its freedoms.

The traditions of English law and constitutionalism that had grown over a thousand years saw challenges from the English kings that would severely test the medieval advances toward freedom. It was the English kings' reliance on pagan doctrines of the Renaissance that promoted Roman legal theories of the absolutist nature of royal power. A number of political currents in the sixteenth century led to the impetus for such absolutist theories which further led to stresses on the hard won freedoms of the English people over the previous millennium. Parliament was weakened by disunity and conflicts among the various elements of the feudal power bases, the development of a court party within the Parliament, and other changes that weakened the system of restraints on royal power. However, the most damaging blow came during the reign of Henry VIII when he broke with the Catholic Church and vastly increased his power and wealth through confiscation of the property of the Church and replacement of the vigilant priests with clerics of compromise that supported his church. But zealous Protestants would have none of it. Henry's church was "reformed" only in that Henry was now in charge and not the Pope. To the Protestants, the church was still Roman

Catholic and many of the objectionable beliefs and ceremonies remained.[259]

Henry separated from the Roman Catholic Church completely by 1534. Henry's son, Edward VI, ruled for only six years but was heavily influenced by Protestant noblemen. This influence ended for a brief five years as Henry's Catholic daughter reigned. Henry's Protestant daughter Elizabeth would wrest the throne from Mary. During her long reign and that of her successor, James I, Protestantism began its ascension again. However, the church that evolved was neither truly Protestant nor Catholic. The Church of England followed a middle path affirming the primacy of the Bible but insisting that church tradition should be respected if not inconsistent with Scripture. The rancor between the Tudor kings of the 1500s and Parliament continued into reign of the Stuart kings. From 1603 until 1688, the House of Stuart would rule both England and Scotland (briefly interrupted by Cromwell's Commonwealth). The Glorious Revolution of 1688 saw the fall of James II when Parliament asserted its right to choose whomever it pleased as the reigning monarch.[260]

During the period from the beginning of the Protestant Revolution in 1517 until the Glorious Revolution in 1688, there was an almost continual conflict between the English kings and Parliament. The defense of English law and constitutionalism against the designs of the absolutist kings of England was indelibly imprinted on the minds of the American immigrants of the early 1600s. This understanding was retained and greatly influenced the Founders in their design of the new American government 150 years later.[261] Tens of thousands would flee the continental Europe and England in the middle of the unrest at the beginning of the 1600s. In 1607 the first permanent English settlement was established at Jamestown, Virginia. Twelve of the thirteen colonies were established up and down the Atlantic Seaboard between 1620 and 1681 with Georgia being the last established in 1733.[262] Who were these immigrants, and what caused them to cross the treacherous and unpredictable Atlantic and settle in a primitive wilderness among hostile Indians?

Religious liberty was the fundamental principle upon which substantially all of the thirteen colonies were founded. In Pennsylvania it was the Quakers. In Maryland it was the Catholics. Other colonies sheltered French Huguenots, Scotch-Irish

Presbyterians, Swiss Pietists, Baptists, German Lutherans, and Quakers.[263]

The men and women that came to the early American colonies considered themselves Englishmen and were in agreement with much of English law, politics, and social customs. What caused them to leave were their differences concerning the nature of the Christian doctrine. The notion of consulting the Scriptures as opposed to the practices of the English clergy was expounded by a small group of separatists in the north of England. This small group who joined together in voluntary fashion believed in the authority of the congregation in the choice of ministers, i.e., self-government. They disdained the papacy, the Church of England, and also the Puritans of southern England (whom they believed had compromised their faith). In attempting to separate themselves from the world, they defied King James I efforts to make all worshipers to conform to the practices of the Church of England. Persecuted and arrested, the separatists eventually escaped to Holland in 1607 where they lived under severe hardship for thirteen years prior to leaving for the English colony of Virginia in 1620. While crossing the Atlantic on the tiny Mayflower and fearing anarchy because of the larger number of non-separatists, they formed themselves into a political body similar to their church covenant. The Mayflower Compact established a government by consent, similar to their church covenant, with governing authority lying in the entire adult male body with no distinctions as to class, wealth, or church membership. Thus, the compact representing one-third separatists and two-thirds of the voyagers from London with other motives was signed by all adult male members including four servants. The separatists landed at Plymouth, Massachusetts, in November, far north of their Virginia destination, and became known as the Pilgrims. Years of harsh existence lay before them, but they were free to "establish once more on earth the Church of Christ in its pristine purity."[264]

The Puritans of southern England and subsequently Massachusetts Bay established themselves alongside the Pilgrims of Plymouth. The Puritans known as Congregationalists had attempted to remain in England and reform Anglican practices from within. However, King Charles shut down Parliament from 1629 to 1640 and ruled with an iron hand while attempting to suppress dissent of the clergy. During this eleven-year period, over twenty thousand Puritans fled from England to America. This was an extraordinary number in comparison to the various small settlements that preceded this invasion. If there was doubt about the survival of the English experiment in the colonies, the large number of Puritan immigrants, whose leaders were primarily Oxford or Cambridge educated ministers, assured that the American colonies would be permanent and substantial.[265] The Puritans who left England for the American colonies were prosperous and influential Calvinists. The Massachusetts Bay Colony was established as a theocracy in Boston, Salem, and other communities surrounding the bay. The Puritans arose in 1560 within the Anglican Church while seeking "a pure and stainless church." During the early years of the colony, Puritanism "was the finest expression of spiritual life that Britain or America or Continental Europe had at that time."[266] The religious fervor of the newly arrived colonists of the early seventeenth century had settled down into a moralistic Christian routine by the end of that century and into the early eighteenth century.[267]

As has been discussed in an earlier chapter, two camps warring for the soul of man emerged in the eighteenth century. Enlightenment thought heavily reliant on nature, science, and reason was the religion of the intellectuals while pietism and evangelism was the path of the common people. These would develop almost simultaneously in Britain, America, France, and Germany.[268] Deism made inroads into Christianity during the first half of the eighteenth century. Deism grew out of eighteenth and nineteenth century scientific speculation. Although professing belief in a single supreme being, the Deists rejected much of Christian doctrine. To Deists of the era, the Supreme Being was the creator of the universe but uninvolved in its operation and direction. For the Deists, Jesus was a great moral teacher but not the redeemer. Nature and rationalism were man's guides, not revelation. The Deists and Unitarians ascended about the same time and contradicted Christianity by declaring man was intrinsically good and must be liberated from superstition, fear, and belief in the corrupt nature of man.[269]

However, America was filled with ordinary people. These were the same people who were persecuted for their religious beliefs and practices in their mother countries, and the persecution and denial of religious liberty ultimately led to escape westward across the Atlantic. In America, the concepts and suppositions of the

Enlightenment were felt far less than in England and on the European Continent. The Americans were a practical people and often skeptical of abstract concepts such as the perfectibility of man and society; the dismissal of religion as mere superstition; over-reliance on reason; and speedy intellectual, political, and social change. The doctrines of the Enlightenment fell on stony ground in the colonies. A "moderate deism" was the extent of the penetration of Enlightenment theories in America, and that penetration affected only a small minority.[270] In their efforts to marginalize Christianity, humanists ascribe a pervasive deism to the Founders, their motives, and finished work in creating a nation and its government, but their depiction of pervasive seventeenth century deism in America is incorrect.

Humanists are also incorrect in defining seventeenth century deism in America as essentially the same as deism in the eighteenth and nineteenth centuries. There were significant differences. The theological deism of the eighteenth century in the American colonies purported that upon rational grounds God existed, that He should be worshipped, that repentance and a moral life were required, and a future existence beyond this life in which there would be rewards and punishments. Later, this theological deism would become a philosophical deism that attacked the Scripture, granted liberty of conscience, and reliance on reason alone as the path to judge and acquire truth.[271]

The marginalization of Christianity is not a new concept existing only in the twentieth and twenty-first centuries. Writing 170 years ago, Alexis de Tocqueville recognized this tendency in America and its falsity.[*]

---

[*] With all of his keen insights into America obtained during his travels, Tocqueville did not understand the real basis for the power of religion in America. Tocqueville was impressed by the religious atmosphere in America and believed that religion's strength arose from the "opinions, feelings, and emotions which are found to recur in the same form in every period of history." Writing of the main causes for the powerful position of religion in America, Tocqueville challenged the eighteenth century philosophers' beliefs that religion must decrease as freedom and education increase. Yet, Tocqueville also wrote glowingly of the idea of the perfectibility of man and stated that it was "one of the main ideas conceived by the intelligence and formulates an important philosophic theory whose consequences are ever obvious in the conduct of human affairs." The perfectibility of man (as

> The eighteenth century philosophers had a quite simple explanation for the gradual weakening of beliefs. They would say that religious zeal had to burn itself out as freedom and education increased. *How vexing that the facts are in conflict with this theory.*[272] (emphasis added)

Nevertheless, modern history texts penned by humanists present the Founders and framers of the Constitution as being in sympathy with the French philosophers of the Enlightenment in an effort to diminish the influence of religion and create a secular republic. They are presented as Deists, skeptics, or secularists. However, the great majority of the framers of the Constitution were church-going Christians as evidenced by their affiliations: nineteen Episcopalians, eight Congregationalists, seven Presbyterians, two Roman Catholics, two Quakers, one Dutch Reformed, and one Methodist. The framers were not only church going members but held strong religious convictions and were "overwhelmingly believers in the revealed religion of the Bible."[273]

Speculation that George Washington was a Deist is undermined by his devout public and private demeanor and official pronouncements and actions that were overtly Christian. George Mason may have been a Deist but was an Episcopal vestryman. In his will he professed to be a Christian. One acknowledged Deist was Edmund Randolph, but he had been converted to Christianity by his wife prior to the time of the Constitutional Convention. The claim that James Madison was a Deist is contrary to an examination of his life. Madison was a protégé of Calvinist John Witherspoon at Princeton. For four years before the Declaration of Independence,

---

opposed to the Judeo-Christian belief in the fallen nature of man) is one of the linchpin beliefs of the eighteenth century philosophers that he chastised. Tocqueville failed to see that the strength of the Christian religion was its truth and that it was not based on opinions, feelings, and emotions found in every period of history. The truth of the Judeo-Christian ethic is reflected in the permanent things which are universal to all of mankind for all periods of history. Ultimately, the revelation of God through the Bible gave clarity and detail to God's plan for mankind. [Alexis de Tocqueville, *Democracy in America*, translated by Gerald E. Bevan, (New York: Penguin Books, 2003), pp. 344-345, 348, 521, 522.]

Madison studied the Scripture extensively. Madison conducted family prayers at Montpelier and wrote a booklet on *The Necessary Duty of Family Prayer; with; Prayers for Their Use*. Benjamin Franklin has been described as a "fellow traveler of the Enlightenment." Yet, it was Franklin who during a difficult period in the writing of the Constitution proposed that the framers go to prayer. In doing so Franklin, the oldest member of the assembly, asserted "…that the longer I live, the more convincing proof I see of this truth—that God governs the affairs of men."[274] Most of the Founders and framers of the Constitution were born in the first half of the eighteenth century. As the century progressed, the great majority of the Founders and framers would agree with Franklin's assessment regarding God's intervention in the affairs of men. The truth is that any inroads made by deism and Enlightenment thought in the early part of the eighteenth century colonial American declined during the last two-thirds of that century. Several forces were responsible for this decline.

The first force that diminished deism and Enlightenment thought as a relatively inconsequential foundation for the Revolution and founding of the United States was the *experiences of the colonists*. The trauma of the break with England and all the events that led up to the victory at Yorktown focused the patriots on that deep well of faith and perseverance that had sustained them and their ancestors on the American continent. The practical Americans knew the realities of life in the wilderness were far removed from the intellectual speculations and theories of the Renaissance and Enlightenment built upon the myths and failures of societies and institutions long gone. Driven from Europe to escape persecution and obtain religious freedom, they struggled through 150 years of hardship and deprivations in the wilderness and built a society based on English traditions, customs, laws, and patrimony that emerged from the Middle Ages. As the radical new ideas of the English crown and Parliament were imposed on the colonists, they resorted to their faith that had sustained them from the moment their ancestors had first stepped foot on the American Continent.

A second force that rolled back the inroads of the Enlightenment thinking and ideas was the *spiritual renewal* (revival) that arose almost simultaneously with the incursion of Enlightenment thinking. The momentum of the Great Awakening beginning in the

1730s continued to influence the Founders' worldview up to and through the Revolution.

In 1740, one hundred and ten years after the arrival of the Puritans at Massachusetts Bay, evangelist George Whitefield wrote, "Boston is very wealthy. It has the form but has lost much of the power of religion. Ministers and people are too much conformed to the world. There is an external observance of the Sabbath. Many rest in a head knowledge, and are close Pharisees."[275] Whitefield's remarks could have been applied to the entirety of the American colonies to varying degrees. The decline in religious fervor that had enveloped the American colonies reached its nadir by the early part of the eighteenth century. This decline was reversed by the spiritual renewal called the Great Awakening.

America became the land of evangelical revivals beginning early in the eighteenth century, and fervent revivals repeatedly swept over every colony during almost all of the century and continued with periodic renewals into the twentieth century. Early revival stirrings occurred with George Fox and his evangelistic meetings in the colonies during 1671-1672. Sporadic revivals occurred very early in the 1700s and included the Dutch Reformed in the 1720s and Presbyterian evangelist Gilbert Tennent. Revival in New England was sparked by the preaching of Jonathan Edwards. A brilliant and gifted child, he entered Yale at age thirteen already with the ability to read Greek, Latin, and Hebrew. At Yale he studied science, philosophy, and theology. He served as a pastor in New York City, followed by a period as an instructor at Yale. In 1727, at age twenty-four, he was called to an important New England pulpit in Northampton, Massachusetts. Six years later, his preaching led to revival throughout New England. Revival in Georgia was sparked by the preaching of John Wesley in 1736-1737. Other evangelists whose preaching lead to revivals throughout the colonies included the Moravian and Lutheran minister Count Nikolaus von Zinzendorf and David Brainerd who eventually became a missionary to the Indians. George Whitefield visited the colonies seven times between 1739 and 1769. Whitefield, who had been influenced by Wesley while at Oxford, had a powerful voice and preached to as many as twenty thousand at one time. A highly effective evangelist, he often faced persecution and opposition to his message and methods. Sherwood Eddy, writing seventy years ago, called Whitefield the most gifted, popular, and powerful evangelist of modern times. From these revivals sprang rapid growth of many new and popular churches, the movement for popular education, a new emphasis on political democracy, and in the end substantially enhanced the attitudes and efforts of the colonists as they sought independence from a dictatorial and capricious English crown and Parliament during the last third of the century.[276]

A third force that stemmed the tide of Enlightenment thinking was that the Founders' *realization that freedom would not be possible under the onerous English laws and limitations* placed on them. Initially, the Church of England made no demands to dictate to the colonists regarding their spiritual affairs. To a pervasive religious liberty that arose during America's colonial days, we must add growing political and economic freedoms. At the beginning and throughout most of the colonial period, the thirteen colonies were of relatively little importance to England whose political and economic power was growing throughout the world. Thus, the American colonists enjoyed for a time the best of both worlds—England's protection without significant interference from their protector. The British Parliament seldom intervened in America's colonial affairs and demanded no taxes until the reign of George III. In spite of the mother country's benign neglect, the colonists considered themselves Englishmen and all that such a mindset entailed—acceptance of English ideas, art, literature, law, customs, and when needed, protection. But something happened to them during the century and a half since their first arrival on the continent's hostile shores. While retaining their English culture, the colonists developed a unique character and a public order of their own. To the colonists, the freedoms they had experienced were based on the ideas of English constitutionalism and law and must not be lightly regarded or tread upon.[277]

When the boots of the English Redcoats stepped ashore to subdue the colonists who rejected the intrusion of the monarchy and Parliament, the worst fears of the colonists began to be realized. The coming break with England was not so much a revolution or casting aside of tradition but more of a defense of liberty.[278] The 1760s saw the end of the French and Indian War and a new king, George III. These and other changes placed the colonists in a new relationship with their parent country that would bring conflict and ultimately independence. The crown and Parliament began exerting new controls on the heretofore brash and independent-minded Americans. The changes involved the basic freedoms in religion, politics, and commerce that colonists had come to enjoy. To rein in the unruly Americans, the imperial program implemented severe restraints on trade, enacted three major tax bills, imposed procedures for trying cases without juries, suspended colonial legislative powers, prohibited immigration to Western lands from coastal regions, and installed an Anglican Bishopric in Puritan New England. Initially, the anxious child did not want to leave the recalcitrant parent. The colonists continually appealed to their common heritage with the mother country. They spoke of its traditionalism and the 150 years of experience of the colonies under British law. Radical changes by the mother country were now being imposed in direct contravention to British law and traditionalism built up over the centuries.[279] But the protests fell upon deaf ears.

The colonists' problem was twofold: one was to achieve freedom and the other was to create a government that would sustain that freedom. In the Founders' efforts to create such a government, they delved deeply into the historical records of various societies. And in spite of humanists' efforts at revision, the substantial weight of history shows that the Founders understood the ever failing human condition and created a government based on eternal truths and the revelation of God to the Hebrew people and the first century Christians. Such a foundation would ensure the American government would be based on those laws and not man-created law in contravention of those eternal truths and revelation. In the formation of American government, Enlightenment and Renaissance influences were peripheral at best.

Sherwood Eddy captures best the importance of the American religious experience during the eighteenth century upon the Revolution and the writing of the Constitution:

> Throughout the Revolution and the framing of the Constitution, the religious and the secular life of America could not be separated. The very ideals of political freedom had grown out of the principle of religious liberty of the Reformation and out of the experience of the Pilgrims, Puritans, and protesting colonists. It was in the churches of Boston and Virginia that revolutionary meetings were held.

The clergy of the free, dissenting, and popular churches were preaching liberty as a religious principle. The pulpit inspired the Revolution and summoned the faithful to patriotic service and to the realization of the American Dream.[280]

The colonists who had considered themselves Englishmen above all else now would wear the title of Founders of a new nation. It was a title they accepted with reluctance but not with fear. Who were these Founders, what did they believe, and what did they create?

Chapter 9

The American Founders and Their Beliefs

Who were the Founders? Our first question may seem unnecessary for we know of Washington, Adams, Jefferson, Madison, Franklin, and their contemporaries from the smatterings of history on the founding of the United States yet to be found in modern textbooks. However, most of what we know of the Founders comes from the Revolutionary War period and is often presented in caricature. We must delve deeper. Also, we must realize that the Founders included the remainder of American colonial society, the common people. For they were Founders also—the soldiers, shopkeepers, farmers, and others that made up the bulk of the colonial population and who suffered the brutal winter at Valley Forge, lived in the cities and towns under the oppression of British occupation, or lived in the countryside and maintained a meager and uncertain subsistence amidst the marching armies of Great Britain.

A distinctive feature of the American colonial society was the absence of a significant hierarchy of classes. There were no marked class lines such as existed in England. In one sense the English hierarchy of noblemen, lesser gentry, and great merchants was comparable in America to one broad upper group comprised of working capitalists, merchants, entrepreneurs, planters, and land speculators. The ordinary freeholding farmers, small planters, some tenant farmers, master artisans, and shopkeepers formed a large middle group. The difference between this group and the great merchants and planters was a matter of degree of success and not type or kind of background or heritage. Yet, being Englishmen at heart, the colonists were deferential and respectful of rank and took seriously the privileges and responsibilities that rank must carry. The bottom ranks of colonial society included poor, landless individuals; freed servants that had completed their period of indenture; squatters and poor whites; the unfortunate, old, indigent, debilitated, insane, widows, and paupers; and the sons of ordinary men not yet established as artisans or farmers in their own right. Additionally, when compared to England and Europe, the colonists exhibited a relative equality of possessions that ranged from a decent subsistence to modest wealth. The composition of the various groups exhibited a certain fluidity that made possible movement from one group to another by hard work and a bit of luck. In America, there were no uncrossable class lines to crush the hope of bettering one's self and one's family. In summary, colonial society had an upper band of no great wealth or heritage and a lower band made up of a disparate group of individuals of little means or living under onerous circumstances. Between the upper and lower bands was the great middle class composed of various kinds of assorted tradesmen, farmers, shopkeepers, and others. Rowland Berthoff concluded that, "…colonial Americans belonged to a fairly level structure with relatively great opportunity for the propertyless young man to improve his condition and status." Indentured servants and slaves did not form a single laboring class that was an institutional component of colonial society. Rather, they were an appendage to colonial society, and served as a discomfiting supplement to the pool of laborers; although, the slave population played a significant role in the economics of the southern colonies. The institutions of indentured servanthood and slavery would continue to afflict the continent for several decades. Indentured labor would melt away but the cancer of slavery would continue for decades before being exorcised from society at great cost and suffering.[281]

We have seen that the American colonists ventured from England and the European shores in search of religious liberty. For the common man that formed the substantial middle group in colonial society, this religious liberty resulted in the rise of popular churches whose adherents exhibited a fervent, lively, evangelical attitude. America was primarily Protestant, and this Protestantism encompassed various persuasions. They remained Englishmen at heart and looked to the traditions of English law, politics, and social customs. However, the declaration that the colonies would assert in their quest for independence from the mother country resulted from England's radical departure from the same traditions and laws the colonists brought with them to America. The Declaration of

Independence that chronicled the sins of the crown also forced the colonists to examine what they believed and why they believed it.

    What did the Founders believe? What we know of a particular period of history generally comes from the written record of the era. With regard to religion preceding and during the Revolutionary War and to the end of the century, that record has proven to be very misleading and is responsible for much of the debate in modern America with regard to religion's role and place in society. Many if not almost all of the early historians of the revolution gave little place to religion's role. Expanding on that assumption, many present-day historians generally believe that religion was displaced by politics as lawyers replaced the clergy as leaders which effectively "...secularized the intellectual character of the culture." However, it was natural that publications devoted to religious matters would be reduced considerably during the Revolutionary years as the pressing discourse on political matters and the war would take precedence and therefore gave an appearance that religious interest and fervor had subsided. With the decline of religion in the public arena during the revolution, historians have leaped to the conclusion that the American people were significantly less religious. This is a blatant misreading of the tenor and temper of Americans in the Revolutionary period. Protestantism in whatever form it took remained the principle means by which Americans perceived and explained the world and ordered their lives. [282] The American religious impulse was just as strong when Washington's army escaped across the East River in New York, during the bitter winter at Valley Forge, and at the final victory at Yorktown.

    A look at a longer time frame does not support the contentions of both early and modern historians that Americans had lost its spiritual vitality experienced in earlier times. The Revolutionary period was bracketed by huge levels of religious fervor—the Great Awakening and the Second Great Awakening at the end of the century. Rather than a time of religious recession, the religious impulse during the Revolution was not diminished or displaced but transformed just as the political order was being transformed. Church membership levels during the era are not indicative of religious apathy because the American religious experience was dependent upon one's conversion experience, not a matter of the church into which one was born.[283] As noted elsewhere in this book, the state-oriented churches (Anglican, Congregational, and Presbyterian), declined precipitously during the 1760-1790 period. Anglican and Puritan churches accounted for more than forty percent of all American congregations in 1760 but declined to less than twenty-five percent by 1790. However, the new denominations (Methodists, Baptists, and others) were alive and well. The Baptists grew from ninety-four congregations in 1760 to 858 by 1790. During the same time period the Methodists grew from no adherents to over seven hundred congregations. Gordon Wood wrote of this period, "The revolution released more religious energy and fragmented Christendom to a greater degree than had been seen since the upheavals of seventeenth century England or perhaps since the Reformation." Others would call the period a "...Revolutionary Revival."[284] However, by 1790 all denominations began to feel the belated effects of the long period of political and social upheaval that caused the new nation to fall into a downward spiral of immorality. Yet, the last decade of the eighteenth century also saw the planting of seeds destined to flower as the Second Great Awakening.

In answer to our second question, the Founders believed that the fingerprints of God were etched on the heart of man from the moment of his creation. Because of the manner of his creation, man has had the ability, the freedom to walk a path of independence from God. But in God's creation, man is happiest when he functions in accord with God's grand design for man, the world, and the laws that govern the universe. However, the freedom to test those limits, to step outside of the boundaries, is within the nature of man. That is what the Founders believed—that the nature of man was corruptible, and the design of any government must account for the human condition.

Fidel Castro in a speech given in January 1961 on the second anniversary of the overthrow of the Cuban dictator Batista said, "A revolution is not a bed of roses. It is the struggle to the death between the future and the past." So, too, was the French Revolution (1789-1799) in its break with the past. Quoting Russell Kirk, "...the French revolutionaries, hoping to transform utterly human society and even human nature, broke with the past, defied history, embraced theoretic dogmas, and so fell under the cruel domination of Giant Ideology."[285] The French Revolution sought to crush the societal framework of the past upon which the fabric of civil order had been stretched. By contrast, the American Revolution was not so much a revolution but a defense of their existing order against the external interference therewith. The colonial society in America was a society of rising expectations. They considered themselves Englishmen with the same rights and privileges as those in the mother country. The great majority of Americans were satisfied with the colonial society that had grown up over 150 years on the North American continent. The colonists took up arms only when the British government asserted the right of the king and Parliament to levy certain taxes if they so chose without the consent of the colonial assemblies. The Americans wished to preserve the institutions of representative government and private rights that were based on English traditions and chartered rights.[286] Edmund Burke has been called the dominant political thinker in England during the last quarter of the eighteenth century. In comparing the two revolutions, Burke saw the French revolutionaries destroying order that could have been changed peaceably while in America the colonials were merely asserting the rights of Englishmen arising from old charters—creating a political separation from England and not a social revolution.[287]

    Castro's "…struggle to the death between the future and the past" was not the path of the colonial patriots 185 years earlier. The Founders did not destroy the past but preserved a society that was rooted in the Judeo-Christian tradition of morality and a civic social order that had grown over the centuries of Western Christendom. The American Revolution was not born in some witches' brew concocted in the hovels of want and despair, in the lust for power and privilege in cloistered castles, or in the ideology of a deranged madman's fevered brain. The American Revolution and the American order that was established was not an ideology nor a "thing" created for the moment. Rather, it had grown over millennia based on the sound principles of moral and civil social order arising from eternal truths and the revelation of God to the Hebrews and the first century Christians. It was established on these eternal truths and the revelation in which the Founders believed, and upon these pillars they built a nation.

We arrive at our third question as to what the Founders created. The Founders formed a government based on constitutionalism, and the Constitution created by the founders reflected their belief that the nature of man was corruptible.

Even before the yoke of arbitrary English rule had been broken at Cornwallis's surrender at Yorktown, the colonists attempted a weak form of government through ratification of the Articles of Confederation in 1781. Sherwood Eddy wrote of the Continental Congress created by the Articles, "The Revolution had created thirteen new nations whose 'Congress' was little more than a council of diplomatic agents in loose league of friendship and rivalry." With no provision for a president, no means to pay its debts, and no authority to draft soldiers, the struggling nation faced imminent failure.[288] Recognizing the weaknesses of the system and resulting perils to the newly independent nation, the Founders met in Philadelphia in the summer of 1787 much as they had done eleven years earlier when drafting the Declaration of Independence. From May to September the delegates to the Constitutional Convention labored to create a new form of government based on a written constitution. In considering the type of political system desired, the Founders recognized the two extremes of the continuum of political power or control. Anarchy on the one end provided no law, no government, and no systematic control. Tyranny on the other end imposed too much government, too much control, and too much oppression. Under the one system there was no law; under the other was ruler's law. What the Founders' desired was a people's law with "…enough government to maintain security, justice, and good order, but not enough government to abuse the people." People's law would reside at the center of the continuum between anarchy and ruler's law. The Founders began their task with an understanding of history and the difficulties presented by human nature—the tendency to swing from one extreme (tyranny) to the other (anarchy) and back.[289] This human tendency would soon be demonstrated once again during the French Revolution as that nation would go from monarchy to anarchy to dictatorship in the space of a decade.

In writing the Constitution for the United States, the Founders knew they were constructing a framework for a government that would address the reality of human nature, a nature that has remained unchanged through the ages. It was not custom built for one age or economy but to stand the tests of time and to address unchanging human nature.[290] James Madison, writing in the Federalist Papers concerning the dissension between the states, recognized the true nature of mankind.

> To presume a want of motives for such contests as an argument against their existence would be to forget that men are ambitious, vindictive, and rapacious. To look for a continuation of harmony between a number of independent, unconnected sovereignties situated in the same neighborhood would be to disregard the uniform course of human events, and to set at defiance the accumulated wisdom of the ages...[291]

Writing about the Union as a safeguard against domestic faction and insurrection, Alexander Hamilton reiterated Madison's thoughts regarding the nature of man.

> The latent causes of faction are thus sown in the nature of man; and we see them everywhere brought into different degrees of activity, according to the different circumstances of civil society. A zeal for different opinions concerning religion, concerning government, and many other points, as well as speculation as of practice; an attachment to different leaders ambitiously contending for pre-eminence and power; or to persons of other descriptions whose fortunes have been interesting to the human passions, have, in turn, divided mankind into parties, inflamed them with mutual animosity, and rendered them much more disposed to vex and oppress each other than to co-operate for their common good. So strong is this propensity of mankind to fall in to mutual animosities that where no substantial occasion presents itself the most frivolous and fanciful distinctions have been sufficient to kindle their unfriendly passions and excite their most violent conflicts.[292]

In their struggle to perfect a document that would address the corruption and foibles of human nature, none of the Founders appeared happy with the final result including Hamilton and

Madison.²⁹³ However, it was the best that could be accomplished during the summer of 1787. Afterward, the Founders began the task of convincing their respective states to adopt the document. In time, the uniqueness of this remarkable document would be recognized. John Adams called the Constitution "...the greatest single effort of national deliberation that the world has ever seen." Benjamin Rush was said to have, "...deduced it [the Constitution] from heaven, asserting that he as much believed the hand of God was employed in this work as that God had divided the Red Sea to give passage to the children of Israel, or had fulminated the Ten Commandments from Mount Sinai." James Madison said of the Constitution, "It is impossible for the man of pious reflection not to perceive in it a finger of that Almighty hand which has been so frequently and signally extended to our relief in the critical stages of revolution."²⁹⁴

Irrespective of the singular success of the American Constitution in the history of the world and in spite of the intent of the Founders when writing this constitution, the popular mantra for most of the twentieth century and the beginning of the twenty-first century is that the Constitution is a "living document" that must be modified or bent to address the modern age and problems never foreseen by the Founders. By living document, the Constitutional liberals believe that its meaning and intent should be an instrument for enlightened social change to meet the needs of the hour. Thoughtful interpretation of the law is thrown aside in favor of passion and expediency that are employed to make law. Thus, human nature, through its passions, appetites, and desires of the moment, is released from the proscriptions of history, custom, convention, and tradition.²⁹⁵ However, this was not the intent of the Founders. Sherwood Eddy wrote of Jefferson that he "...stood for a strict interpretation of the conservative Constitution to prevent ever-threatened encroachments upon the rights of the people, the legislature, and the states."²⁹⁶ Russell Kirk confirms Eddy's view of Jefferson's opinion of the Constitution, "Thomas Jefferson, rationalist though he was, declared that in matters of political power, one must not trust the alleged goodness of man, but 'bind him down with the chains of the Constitution'."²⁹⁷ The efforts of the modern liberal-progressive to imbue (read into or interpret) the Constitution with new rights and doctrines to meet or address the changes of a modern world travel the same slippery path as those of the French Revolution who based their changes on some ethereal, imaginary, or invented "rights of man" that attempted to address the failings of human nature.

The battle with regard to the Constitution is only one of the skirmishes fought for the soul of the West. For the humanist, there can be no détente. For those of the Judeo-Christian persuasion, there can be no compromise with the heathen. If James Kurth is correct that the clash is really a clash between those holding the Judeo-Christian worldview and those who reject this worldview in favor of humanist orthodoxy, then we must realize that the forces of the humanists are winning the battle and the survival of West is in question. To understand the consequences of the denigration or denial of those proscriptions of history, custom, convention, and tradition brings us to the words of the Bishop of Chartres, as paraphrased by Russell Kirk.* Considering himself and his contemporaries as moderns, Fulbert recognized that his generation ten centuries ago was susceptible, as we are in the twenty-first century, to the opinion that "...wisdom was born with our generation." Fulbert argued that, "...we are no better than dwarfs mounted upon the shoulders of giants...our ancestors, upon whose shoulders we stand...Our civilization is an immense continuity and essence...[and] if we ignore or disdain those ancestral giants who uphold us in our modern vainglory, we tumble down into the ditch of unreason."[298]

---

* Kirk attributed the famous and much used aphorism to Fulbert, Bishop of Chartres (952/970?-1028). Others attribute the aphorism to Bernard of Chartres (b. unknown-d.1126?) a century later. Many others have used the saying including Isaac Newton, Samuel Taylor Coleridge, John Stuart Mill, Friedrich Engels, and Sigmund Freud. [Robert K. Merton. *On the Shoulders of Giants*. Chicago: University of Chicago Press, 1965.]

Chapter 10

The Roots and Rise of Modern Humanism

We have traced the Judeo-Christian tradition and its reliance on a transcendent God, His eternal truths, the revelation of God to the Hebrews, and those proscriptions of history, custom, convention, and tradition based thereon. We now turn our attention to humanism, from its beginning to the force it has become in the twenty-first century.

As has been previously stated, humanism is man's second oldest faith—the great alternative faith of mankind—man without God. Tenets of that faith were operative as early as the third chapter of Genesis. In the eleventh century BC, King David wrote, "The fool hath said in his heart: there is no god."[299] But it was the Greeks of the fourth through sixth centuries BC that gave form and body to the man-made philosophy of humanism that would impact the world second only to Jesus Christ.

It was in the eighth century BC that the first hints of a Greek civilization began to be discernable around the Aegean Sea, and contact with the East was the catalyst for this civilization. Religion was a major foundation for the Greek identity. Their religion consisted of a mass of myths that arose over a wide area and at different times. Some were local myths and legends while others were imported from Asia and elsewhere. A distinctive feature of their religion was that all of the Greek gods and goddesses were remarkably human in spite of their supernatural standing and powers and would give rise to the notion that men could be godlike. The greatest age of Greek history began with the defeat of the Persians at Plataea and Mycale in 481 BC. The war with the Persians would continue for another thirty years before peace with Persia occurred in 449 BC. At that time over 150 Greek states were paying tribute to Athens. In time, the Athenian penchant for intervention in the internal affairs of the states, taxation of the states, and outright aggression resulted in a war between Athens and a coalition of states beginning in 460 BC. After another fifteen years of peace, the great internal struggle known as the Peloponnesian War began in 431 BC. Peace followed interspersed with periodic wars and expeditions and ultimately destruction of the Athenian fleet, blockade, and starvation. Athens made peace in 404 BC. Yet for all the wars and tragedies of the fifth century in this small country, its mark on the world was pervasive and looms large even in the modern world. The Greek fifth century "...has an objective unity because it saw a special heightening and intensification of Greek civilization, even if that civilization were ineradicably tied to the past, ran on into the future and spilled out over all the Greek world." Although the beauty of their art, sculpture, and architecture has been the world's standard for two millennia, they are remembered as poets and philosophers.[300]

J. M. Roberts called the Greek poets' and philosophers' challenge to irrationality in social and intellectual activity the greatest single achievement that has flowed from that pre-eminent civilization. Writing of the ancient Greeks in *History of the World*, Roberts said,

> ...there is a salient theme which emerges in it: a growing confidence in rational, conscious enquiry. If civilization is advance towards the control of mentality and environment by reason, then the Greeks did more for it than any of their predecessors. They invented the philosophical question as part and parcel of one of the great intuitions of all time, that a coherent and logical explanation of things could be found, that the world did not ultimately rest upon the meaningless and arbitrary fiat of gods or demons...the liberating effect of this emphasis was felt again and again for thousands of years. It was the greatest single Greek achievement.[301]

This theme, that rational, conscious inquiry for the explanation of things apart from God, was evident well before the coming of the fifth century Greek philosophers. The Greeks of the time had many gods and a multitude of religious practices, but there came a questioning of their existence. Thales (630/20-546/535 BC) said all existence was based on water while Anaximander wrote *On Nature* and claimed a naturalistic view that all was based on matter in which the spirit played no role. From these first questionings came a succession of philosophers that built the foundations of modern humanism. Protagoras (481/411 BC) in his *Of the Gods* claimed that man could not know whether gods existed or not, and in all cases such were not relevant to man. He would famously define man as "... the measure of all things, of the reality of those which are, and the unreality of those which are not."[302] Protagoras and his followers were sophists, men who were expert and wise teachers of rhetoric, philosophy, and the art of successful living, and noted for their adroit, subtle, specious, and fallacious reasoning.[303]

Roberts paints the picture of the humanistic beliefs of the brilliant Greek intellects of the age with too broad a brush. The greatest influence on Western civilization came from Plato and Aristotle in their understanding of the human condition, but this influence did not carry over into their writings and prescriptions on types and forms of government.[304]

We know of Socrates through Plato, his pupil. Socrates (469-399 BC) saw a divine order in the universe. However, he used dialogue for philosophical exploration, and this method of inquiry became the standard by which humanists question the world around them.[305] A man of great virtue and wisdom, his teachings to restore public and private morality were misunderstood and resulted in his death following conviction by an Athenian jury.[306]

Like his teacher, Plato was not a humanist. For Platonism saw the senses (the body) as ever-changing, transitory, and lacking permanence whereas the mind (the spirit) is viewed as everlasting and eternal. Human life achieves significance by forsaking the realm of the senses and seeking immortality by "rising to the realm of imperishable things and dwelling with them in eternity." Man must choose between the senses and perish into nothingness or he can look to "the spiritual beauty of God's mind and find eternal life."[307] The doctrine of the soul was the central truth of Plato's writings. Righteous order comes through disciplined harmony of the soul, and such disciplined harmony makes all things fitting and reasonable for man. Speaking in symbols and parables, Plato reveals his fundamental beliefs—the immortality of the soul, the existence of divine moral laws, that the soul should be cleansed from false desires and appetites that degrade the soul so that we may conform to the divine law, and that the soul is separate from the body and eternal. While writing his last dialogue, Plato would counter Protagoras of the previous century when he said, "It is God who is, for you and me, the measure of all things."[308]

Aristotle (384-322 BC) was a pupil of Plato, but unlike his teacher, Aristotle had little concern for Plato's immortality of the soul and treated it as little more than a faculty. Like Plato, he believed there was not a real separation between ethics and politics. Focusing on politics, Aristotle emphasized that harmony could be achieved through the avoidance of excesses and extremes. Elements of humanistic thought can be seen in Aristotle's description of a truly happy life as being one of goodness and "…secure from poverty, sickness, and restrictions."[309] Corliss Lamont called Aristotle the first great naturalist (naturalistic humanism, naturalism) in the history of philosophy, but "…marred the purity of his naturalism" by referring to an abstract, non-personal *God* as the Prime Mover, justification of slavery, and belief in the natural inferiority of women.[310] (emphasis in original)

The civilization of ancient Greece has fascinated mankind for 2,500 years. Philosophy, politics, much of arithmetic and geometry, and several categories of Western art were invented in an amazingly short four centuries by the Hellenes, the ancient Greeks.[311] In the early sciences, rhetoric, warfare, and grace of manners, the Greeks far excelled all civilized peoples who came before. Yet, Greek society was powerfully marked by "…class conflict, disunity, internecine violence, private and public arrogance and selfishness, imperial vainglory, and civic collapse." The inventor of politics created a political system that was short lived in spite of their incessant political writings and debates. Throughout their history disharmony and enmity caused by a "…fierce local pride, a ruthless lust for power, and an arrogant individuality…" would stain Greek society.[312] Their political confusion was a result of the weakness of the Greek religion because, "Men must be spiritually free before they can co-operate on the highest terms."[313] Thus, the Greek religion did not provide for the order of the soul. Plato sought to deepen Greek society's religious understanding and thereby renew its vitality. He sought for the recovery of order in both the soul and society. But, "…it was the clever relativism of the Sophists, not the mystical insights of Plato or Aristotle's Supreme Good, which dominated the classical Greeks in their decadence." Four centuries later, Plato's insights into the eternal truths would intersect with the revelation received by the Hebrews and that of the life and words of Jesus of Nazareth and his followers.[314]

The once unifying force of Greek religion that rested on respect for the Homeric gods and goddesses came under the assault of the fifth century BC rationalism. By the first century BC, the slide into irrationalism (the humanist epithet for religion) would force a retreat of fourth century Greek rationalism as its force was spent. As rationalism declined, it was not Greek religion that would be reinstated but the adoption of new creeds and faiths including a host of pagan crazes and mysticism such as raising altars to dead philosophers. The Olympian gods had been replaced by the god of Man the measure, but the new measure did not provide comfort from the buffets and strains of daily life as the Greeks increasingly came under the influence and onus of other societies.[315]

It was with Epicurus (341-271 BC) that Greek thought finally arrived at an unadulterated denial of God. He was the most important of the Greek philosophers from the humanists' viewpoint. Epicurus believed man should search for the contented human life, pursue peace of mind, and awaken to a happy life. His influence in the following centuries was monumental.[316] The Epicurean spirit is the cry of the modern age. As Randall wrote, "In a sense, all our modern philosophies, from Socialism to the worship of business success, are but elaborations of the means for eating, drinking, and being merry in the most satisfactory way."[317] With the decline of the Greek world, personal concerns became preeminent, and man became preoccupied with self. Epicurus epitomized this transition. For him, good was a private experience of pleasure achieved through mental contentment and absence of pain. Yet, Epicurus meant something more austere than blatant hedonism as would be assumed by moderns.[318]

Another means by which the Greeks dealt with a changing world was of renunciation and detachment. Through this philosophy, the Cynics renounced convention and dependence on the material world. Zeno was one of the Cynics and developed the doctrine of Stoicism which held that man could not control life and must accept what happened as his fate because there was a rational order running through the universe decreed by a divine will. Stoicism gave the individual an ethical confidence that replaced their failed state and religion. The Stoic's belief in a disciplined common sense applied to all mankind and erased the distinction between Greek and all others whom the Greeks considered as barbarians. This disciplined common sense would lead to virtue whose value lay intrinsically and not in its consequences. This ethical universalism was widely held in the Hellenistic world and welcomed in the ascending Roman world.[319] Although Greek society fell back on personal concerns, the study of philosophy was still strong in the first century AD.

    The Apostle Paul's encounter with the Greek philosophers at Mars' Hill, recorded by Luke in the seventeenth chapter of the Acts of the Apostles, is one of the most remarkable and unique windows into the history of mankind. Driven from Berea by persecution, Paul escaped to Athens. Four hundred years ago Matthew Henry wrote of the Athenians, "The greatest pretenders to reason were slaves to idols; so necessary was it that there should be a divine revelation, and that centering in Christ." What better man than Paul to deliver the words of the revelation to these highly educated and proud Athenians. Paul was himself highly educated and articulate. Upon arrival in Athens, he went to the synagogues of the Jews who, although in opposition to idols, were enemies of Christ. His conversations regarding Christ were also conducted in the marketplace. Ignored by most, his words eventually attracted the attention of the philosophers, most notably the Epicureans "who thought God altogether one such as themselves" and denied that God made the world or governed it. The second group of philosophers was the Stoics who counted virtuous man (including themselves) as good as God. Those worldviews stood in sharp contrast to that of Paul's which elevated Christ as our ultimate source and debased any confidence we may have in ourselves. Always intent on telling or hearing of some new philosophy, the Athenians and others who came to Athens were interested in those "strange things" Paul brought to their ears, not because of their goodness but because of their newness. In all of the Athenian quests for new doctrines, it appears that they did not know of the books of Moses and the prophets or at least did not heed them for much of what Paul presented to those gathered at the Areopagus was contained in those books. First they called Paul a "babbler" or "scatterer of words", whose thoughts were idle and disconnected. Although not presented as such, the Athenians thought Paul a "setter of strange gods" and therefore saw Jesus as a new god and the resurrection a new goddess. Feeling that he should have a better hearing to give a fuller account of the things they had never heard before, they invited Paul to Areopagus, translated as Mars' Hill, the townhouse of the city where magistrates met to conduct public business and learned men presented their ideas.[320]

When Paul preached to the Jews and Gentiles who were worshippers of the true God, he presented Jesus as the Christ. Paul called them to have faith in the Redeemer and led them through prophecies and miracles. However, when Paul spoke to the heathens at Mars' Hill who worshipped false gods, he led them to knowledge of the Creator by common works of providence, i.e., human destiny sustained and guided through divine power. First, Paul presented the Creator to the Athenians as "...the God that made the world and all things therein...therefore Lord of heaven and earth...He made of one blood all nations of men...He giveth to all life, and breath, and all things...He is the sovereign disposer of all the affairs of the children of men...He is not far from every one of us...In him we live, and move, and have our being...and are God's offspring." Next, Paul challenged their idolatry and rejected the notions that God could be presented as an image, dwelled in temples made with hands, or was "...worshipped with men's hands, as though he needed anything." Lastly, Paul calls the Athenians to repentance for their idolatry. He explained that before the gospel was available to the Gentiles, they were grossly ignorant. "The times of this ignorance God winked at."* With the coming of the gospel, they were held accountable, and "He now commandeth all men everywhere to repent..." Paul was a scholar and by man's standards his discourse was brilliant. Paul's arguments cut at the hearts of the Epicurean and Stoic beliefs. Yet, in the heart of Athenian humanistic hubris, the gospel had little effect. They listened patiently. Some mocked and scorned him, and others would consider Paul's admonitions but would not commit. A few would believe and convert including Dionysius the Areopagite, one of the high court who sat in the Areopagus.[321]

In addition to widespread persecution, the infant Christian faith faced doctrinal obstacles from the Gnostics on the one side and the danger of severing Christianity from its Jewish roots on the other side. The Gnosticism of the first and second centuries differed from

---

*"The times of ignorance God overlooked, but now he commands all men everywhere to repent." [Acts 17:30 RSV.]

what became canonical Christianity in regards to its attitudes toward creation and the nature of man. For Gnostics, creation was not the work of an all-powerful and benevolent creator but rather a Demiurge, that is, a subordinate deity of limited power who left creation finite and incomplete. From this belief came a dualism of good and evil in which man was good and the world partly evil. Man, being superior to the created universe, was charged with its improvement. Some Gnostics saw Christ as one who rescued men from Yahweh's error rather than one who confirmed and renewed the Jewish covenant with God. On the other side was the danger of a complete break of Christianity from its Jewish roots. To the Jews, Christianity was heresy. To Christians, Christ was the fulfillment of Jewish prophecy and consummation of God's plan of the redemption of man (both Jew and Gentile) through the death, burial, and resurrection of Jesus Christ. Had not the early Christians held to those beliefs, they may have become merely a heretical Jewish sect. Had they cut their Jewish connection at its roots, the early Christians may have slid into the mystery cults of the Hellenistic world or the despair of the Gnostics.[322] But it was through the providence of God that a handful of early Christians planted and nurtured the seeds of Christianity until it blossomed and became the dominant worldview of Western civilization. Speaking of Christianity's impact, Roberts wrote, "Christianity's greatest contribution to a later Western civilization would be its stubbornly prophetic and individualist assertion that life should be regulated with reference to a moral guidance independent not only of government but of any other merely human authority."[323] However, Roberts errs in limiting Christianity's greatest contribution only to Western civilization for it was and is the hope of all humanity.

Much has been written of the significant influence of the Hellenistic thought and culture on the newly arrived Christian faith. Randall, writing from a humanist's perspective, stated that Christianity came of age in the Hellenistic world and was essentially a *product of* Platonic thought.[324] Although one may accept the importance of Greek cultural influences on early Christianity (the New Testament was written in Greek), Christians vigorously defend the source for Christian tradition and doctrine as being the revealed word of God to the Hebrews and later to the Apostles and *not* that of the Greeks. Kirk wrote, "...Hellenic thought had been woven inextricably into the fabric of Christian teaching, so that it was next to impossible to distinguish Judaic threads from Greek..."[325] More correctly stated, it was elements of Platonic thought *rightly perceived* that intersected and were consistent with Christian teaching and doctrine that led to an aura of integration between the two, *not* the philosophies of the humanistic Greeks that were diametrically opposed to the revelation of God to the Hebrews and doctrines of the church as shown by Paul's sermon on Mars' Hill.

There were common elements within Christianity and Platonic thought that resulted in somewhat of symbiotic relationship between the Christian and Hellenistic world. Christianity would use that relationship to survive and flourish. Platonic thought, having lost the early battles to salvage Greek society from its adversaries, "began to ferment, long after Plato's death, among peoples far beyond the confines of the Greek world."[326] The fruits of Platonic thought were the insights into timeless, eternal truths that were etched by God into the foundations of the universe and its operations. Plato taught "...that there exist divine moral laws, not easy to apprehend, but operating upon all mankind," and "Man must order his soul in conformity with divine laws...only thus can order in society be obtained."[327] Plato's thought and philosophy are certainly *not* a mirror of the Judeo-Christian ethic, but through profound meditation Plato glimpsed, as though through a glass darkly, those divine truths. But it was the revelation, initially to the Hebrews and continuing through the inspired writings of the Apostles and first century Christians that gave clarity and foundation to those truths that mankind had struggled to apprehend. Because of the revelation given by God, those truths discerned by Plato and others, having been long neglected, found new meaning and acceptance as Christianity began spreading around the Mediterranean basin.

Our eyewitness account of that meeting on Mars' Hill must rank in importance if not supersede that of being present at such monumental events as the signing of the Magna Carta or standing at a ship's rail beside those Europeans who first cast eyes on the New World. However, that meeting on an Athenian hill two thousand years ago did not mark the beginning of a new war of worldviews for that war commenced shortly after the creation of man. But God's plan for man's redemption from his fallen state was consummated at the cross and introduced the church age. It was the first recorded encounter of the two worldviews at Mars' Hill that gave clarity and stark definition to the battle between humanism and Christianity. Those worldviews would influence and dominate the course of human history more than any others.

The rationalistic humanism of Ancient Greece had waned with the advent of the new millennium. But eleven centuries later European scholars once again discovered the classical Greek philosophy as Greek was translated into Latin. Within a hundred years of its arrival in Europe, two thirteenth century men, Albertus Magnus and his pupil Thomas Aquinas, would attempt to reconcile the classical and Christian explanations of the world. As previously discussed, Aquinas's *Summa Theologica* attempted to explain all phenomena but without observation and experiment. So it was that Christendom incorporated the classical Greek heritage with the view that the classical world was the forerunner of the Christian era.[328] It was through this incorporation that made way for the birth of the humanistic Renaissance.[329] With Christendom's embrace of the classical came a revival of humanistic letters in the fourteenth through sixteenth centuries.[330] Once again humanism would raise its voice of opposition to Christianity during the Renaissance and Age of Enlightenment as well as opposition through the humanistic Gnostic heresies regarding man and creation, latent since the first and second centuries.

We have given brief accounts of emerging humanistic thought and influence during the Renaissance and Enlightenment in Chapters 6 and 7. In Part III, we shall further examine the connections between twentieth and twenty-first century humanism with the institutions of American society. However, it is worthwhile to add to our foundation for understanding modern humanism by more specifically examining its principles and some of the more significant branches of modern humanism.

One of the most comprehensive articulations of the principles of humanism was made by Dr. Corliss Lamont in *The Philosophy of Humanism*, written in 1949 with the eighth addition published posthumously in 1997. It is considered the standard text on humanism in the United States. Dr. Lamont was a contemporary of other notable proponents of humanism during the first half of the twentieth century including Columbia University associates such as Joseph Blau, John H. Randall, Jr., and John Dewey (under whom Lamont studied).

According to Lamont, humanism is a man-made theory in which the main purpose of human life is to advance the happiness of man through the enjoyment, development, and availability to all of the abundant material, cultural and spiritual goods of this natural world. Humanism has many varieties and beliefs and means different things to people. However, Lamont states that in its greatest sense it is "…a philosophy of which man is the center and sanction." More specifically, humanism is "…a philosophy of joyous service for the greater good of all humanity in this natural world and advocating methods of reason, science, and democracy." In other words, humanism posits that the ultimate moral ideal is service to one's fellowmen, i.e., an individual's highest good is working for the good of all. Humanism rejects the notion that humans are directed merely by self-interest and that authentic altruism is one of the moving forces of mankind.[331]

Lamont proposes that the philosophy of humanism gives a specific and straightforward explanation of the universe, man's nature, and treatment of human problems and suggests ten central propositions in support of this philosophy. In summary, the propositions state that all forms of the supernatural are myths and that Nature is the totality of being and exists independently of any mind or consciousness. Man is the evolutionary product of Nature, and his mind is inextricably joined with the functioning of his brain. Therefore, there is no conscious survival after death due to the unity of body and personality. Through reason and the scientific method, man can solve his own problems. Humans are masters of their own destiny and have freedom of choice and action but recognize that there is some conditioning by the past. Human values are grounded in this-earthy experiences and relationships. Happiness, freedom, and progress in this world are the highest goals of all mankind. Life is harmonious when personal satisfactions and continuous self-development are joined with work and activities that support community welfare. Extensive development of art and an awareness of beauty promote an esthetic experience that can become a pervasive reality in the lives of men. Extensive social programs are necessary for the establishment of democracy, peace, a high standard of living, and a thriving economic order. Freedom of expression and civil liberties in all areas of life through democratic procedures and parliamentary governments come from the complete social implementation of reason and the scientific method. Finally, humanism rests on the *unending questioning of basic assumptions and convictions* including those assumptions and convictions upon which humanism itself rests.[332] (emphasis added) Some of these propositions have been briefly compared to the Judeo-Christian ethic in prior chapters; however, a more extensive comparison and examination is made in Part III and summarized in Part IV.

Although in error in calling the Judeo-Christian ethic a philosophy in the sense that philosophy is man-made as is humanism, Lamont agrees that all worldviews attempt to answer life's basic questions when he writes of the "…perennial need of human beings to find significance in their lives, to integrate their personalities around some clear, consistent, and compelling view of existence, and to seek definite and reliable methods in the solution of their problems."[333] He is very close to calling for answers to the same questions Colson and Pearcey posed earlier: "Where did we come from, and who are we? What has gone wrong with the world? What can we do to fix it?" As we have stated, worldview is "…the comprehensive framework of one's basic *beliefs* about *things*." But life tends toward chaos and disorder and at the same time attempts to fractionalize and disintegrate one's worldview which brings pain. When that worldview lacks order, one seeks to assemble the disparate building blocks to ease the pain…that is to integrate the parts to make sense of life. Thus, humanists and Christians both agree that answers to life's basic questions are paramount.

Just as there are several branches within the Judeo-Christian ethic, so too are there branches of humanist philosophy with the two main branches being secular humanists and religious humanists. Various adjectives are affixed to the term "humanism" to describe its various denominations such as Greek humanism, ethical humanism, scientific humanism, religious humanism, rationalist humanism, and humanistic Judaism.[334] However, Lamont narrows the field by outlining the major branches of humanist thought, ethics, and worldview that exist in modern-day America and Europe. All such branches fall under the "leading Naturalisms and Materialisms." Lamont defines naturalism as follows:

> Naturalism considers that human beings, the earth, and the unending universe of space and time are all parts of one great

Nature. The whole of existence is equivalent to Nature and outside of Nature noting exists. This metaphysics has no place for the supernatural, no room for superphysical beings or a supermaterial God, whether Christian or non-Christian in character, from whom we can obtain favors through prayer or guidance through revelation. But the adherents of Naturalism recognize and indeed rejoice in our affinity with the mighty Nature that brought us forth...[335]

Many humanists consider Benedict Spinoza of seventeenth century Holland as one of the greatest modern philosophers. Following a brief popularity under Spinoza, Naturalism declined once again until receiving new life upon the publication of Darwin's *The Origin of Species* in 1859. The revival of Naturalism occurred primarily in the United States and more specifically under Professors John Dewey and Frederick J. E. Woodbridge and their colleagues at Columbia University. Dewey refined the philosophy of pragmatism which was the work of Harvard's William James. Dewey's brand of pragmatism promoted "...reliance on experimental intelligence as the most dependable way to solve the problems that face the individual and society...and that we should apply that method to every sector of our lives and that the most profound need of our day is to extend scientific thinking from the natural sciences to the broad field of social, economic, and political affairs."[336]

Materialism is a close cousin of Naturalism except that Materialism tends to lump the "...behavior of living creatures and human beings to the operation of the same laws that apply to inanimate existence." Seventeenth century foundations for Materialism were laid by Thomas Hobbes, but the greatest resurgence came with the French Encyclopedists such as Diderot. Materialism's particularly virulent anti-religious stance is evident in Diderot's statement that, "Men will never be free until the last king is strangled in the entrails of the last priest!" The widely held Materialist philosophy in France may explain the violent ferocity of the French Revolution. Materialist philosophy in the nineteenth century was centered in Germany and included such men as Ludwig Feuerback, Karl Marx, and Frederick Engels. Feuerbach's contention that traditional religion resulted from the unfulfilled longings, needs, and feelings of humans had a profound influence on Marx and Engels whose Dialectical Materialism would become the most influential branch of Materialism and the official philosophy of Communist governments and parties around the world.[337]

To give clarity to our understanding of the meaning of humanism, we must address "secular humanism", a term that came into vogue during the last thirty years of the twentieth century. Secular humanism describes a general characteristic of substantially all humanist philosophies and is not a particular branch or philosophy thereof. In one sense, the two words used together are somewhat redundant. Secular infers an indifference to or rejection or an exclusion of religion and religious considerations. In the context of a philosophy, humanism implies an emphasis on secular concerns and generally rejects supernaturalism.[338] As has been previously discussed, Lamont's first proposition in describing a philosophy of humanism is that all forms of the supernatural are myths. Furthermore, secular humanism should not be seen as an opposite of religious humanism for all forms of humanism must reject all forms of religious mythological allusions, i.e., belief in a supernatural God.[339] Rather, religious humanism is a religion in a naturalistic sense (as opposed to a supernatural religion) that, like other religions, pursues the ideal or quest for the good life. Such pursuit involves faith, aspiration, commitment, loyalty, hope, and love in an effort for man to be better than he is.[340] Lastly, religious humanism should not be confused with those religions that have incorporated considerable amounts of humanist doctrines and teachings within their church organizations but still cling to remnants of the supernatural fabric that once covered them.

Should one gather a couple of dozen humanists in a room and assign to them the task of defining humanism, you will get as many definitions as there are humanists in the room. Figuratively speaking, that is what Paul Kurtz did when editing *The Humanist Alternative: some definitions of Humanism*. At the end, in an attempt to bridge all of the disagreements and divergent definitions proposed, Kurtz begins with what humanism is not. First, he states that the term "humanist" cannot apply to anyone who still believes that the source and creator of the universe is God. Kurtz wrote,

> Humanism as a philosophy is opposed to all forms of mythological illusions (religious or ideological) about man

and his place in the universe. This means that Humanism involves some scientific view of nature and of man. Any theistic interpretation of the universe and any eschatological drama about divine beginnings and ends is rejected because it is logically meaningless and empirically unverified.[341]

In this categorical opposition to any and all forms of the supernatural, Kurtz has violated one of Lamont's propositions that humanism rests on an unending questioning of basic assumptions and convictions. In other words, one must question the basic assumptions and convictions of everything *except* when it comes to humanism's denial of the supernatural.

In his attempt to bridge all of the proposed definitions, Kurtz claims the term "humanism" has no fixed meaning but is proscriptive rather than descriptive and expresses a normative ideal to guide and direct conduct. It is a description of what ought to be—how we treat human beings, interpret social institutions, and a model for the future. Also, Kurtz states that humanism cannot be defined as a specific political program or a vague, emotional humanitarianism. Kurtz spends several pages writing about what is fundamental to humanism, what it is committed to, and what it defends. However, Kurtz does not give a clear, convincing, or coherent definition of humanism other than a gossamer, platitudinous statement that all humanists share "…a set of moral ideals which are committed to saving and enhancing the qualities of human experience, but primarily a commitment to the use of critical intelligence." Even if one is able to mine from his discourse solid nuggets of moral ideals, Kurtz cautions that these moral ideals provide focus and direction and are "…at best general, and not specific in character." Kurtz warns that even though there is danger that humanistic principles are not enumerated with some specificity and placed in practice and thus become "…empty rhetoric and glib generalizations", he still believes that it is difficult to "say what is the true or authentic 'Humanist' position." Yet, when Kurtz states that "…it is difficult to say exactly what is and is not humanistic", his words succumb to the danger about which he warns—empty rhetoric and glib generalizations that do not give necessary answers to the basic questions of life.[342] However, the lack of a specific and practical definition does not prohibit a description of humanism's tenets of faith as Lamont accomplished in his ten propositions.

  Kurtz believes that humanists must be prepared to abandon or modify certain humanist stances as "liberal humanist clichés" become apparent. His examples include the growth of science and technology, presumed to be the key to improving mankind, which must now recognize that technology can dehumanize and depersonalize man and destroy the ecology. Democracy as the hope of mankind now must be tempered because uncritical participatory democracy can debase learning and destroy standards of excellence. Humanists must recognize that sexual liberation has a dark side—bestialization, dehumanization of sex, and pornographic and economic exploitation. While humanists are sympathetic to socialism and see it as the wave of the future, humanists must see also that changing conditions of ownership of the means of production may not reduce the inequities of life, the denial of basic human rights and the oppression of the human spirit. Kurtz also states that humanists must understand that not all injustice has a cultural basis and social remedy. Some injustice derives from biological and genetic sources. Lastly, Kurtz continues to support working for progressive improvement, but he admits to the fallacy of Progress that was supposed to rest in the "womb of nature" and that there is "an inevitable march of human history." Kurtz effectively defines humanism's dilemma, "Humanism, if it is too general is empty sermon; if too concrete, it runs the risk of degenerating into a sect or cult or political ideology." His solution is to add to the above list of ideals the essential defining characteristic of humanism, "...the centrality *of the ideal of free thought.*" (emphasis in original) Kurtz demands that humanism be committed to free inquiry and the use of critical intelligence, but he demurs that humanism cannot be expected to provide "...a specific economic or political theory, or a specific social or technological solution to every problem. Nor should it be expected to offer a total world view which will answer all the questions people raise, or offer it as the salvation of mankind."[343] Essentially, Kurtz is saying that humanism doesn't have all the answers but also denies that others do. It is apparent that humanism, as a worldview, does not provide a comprehensive framework for one's basic *beliefs* about *things.* In other words, humanism is a house of cards built upon a foundation of shifting sand lying above earthquake-prone continental fault lines.

This modern proud boastful humanist worldview of the twenty-first century is the same as Fulbert's modern vainglory of ten centuries ago, and those espousing this modern humanist worldview continue to wallow in the same ditch of unreason.

Chapter 11

The "Why" – Worldviews of Humanism and Christianity

In prior chapters we have briefly examined the competing worldviews of humanism and Christianity and have outlined the tenets of each. In those chapters we have answered the "what" about each. Now we look more closely at the "why" behind each of the worldviews and our basis for belief in one or the other as these beliefs have a bearing on a thorough understanding of the combatants and their positions in modern society. For those holding the Judeo-Christian position, the origins of creation and all that it contains is God. For the humanist, creation resulted by operation of nature and the evolution thereof without benefit of the supernatural.

The Judeo-Christian ethic holds that God existed prior to the beginning of the universe and that He created the universe. Why did God create the universe and ultimately mankind? We can only speculate, but such speculation is aided and guided by what we know of God from a reading of the revelation to the Hebrews, from the inspired New Testament writings, and an examination of those universal truths evident in various societies throughout history. The Bible is filled with descriptions of God including his attributes, glory, love, characters, holiness, knowledge, power, and presence. And there is another clue to help us gain a picture of God, and that is man for "…God said, Let us make man in our image, after our likeness…"[344] By looking at man we may see elements that reflect God.

One of the fundamental needs of mankind is to dwell together, in other words, a need for relationships. For the Christian, the importance of human relationships is a reflection of the Trinitarian relationship, a picture of His fundamental being. God's being is shown by the Father-Son relationship and the relationship of Christ with the Church of which He is the head and we are the body.

For mankind, the relational pattern is present in various entities—marriage, family, community, nations, and the Kingdom of God. As Wilfred McClay wrote, "…we shape our relationships, but we are more fundamentally shaped by the need for them, and we cannot understand ourselves without reference to them…we are made by, through, and for relationship with one another."[345]

First of all, it is not necessary to know why God created the universe and all therein to know that he did. However, the question as to why God created the universe and ultimately man leads to mediation and reflection on the greatness of God and his special relationship with man. God did not create man out of need. Rather, it was a will to love, an expression of the very character of God, to share the inner life of the Trinity. Man's chief end is to glorify God by communing with God forever. Being God, he knew the course and cost of His creation. By creating man with a free will meant the possibility of rejection of God and His love. In other words free will and the potential for rejection of God was the penalty for the possibility of love. So it is on the earthly plane, to risk love is to risk rejection. Rejection was not a surprise to an omniscient God. Before creation, God knew the cost would be the death of his son, and this is hinted at in Revelation 13:8, "…Lamb slain from the foundation of the world." God's infinite love exceeded the cost of that love at Calvary.[346]

Man's rejection of God created a broken relationship and thus separated himself and his family from God. Although God's love and plan for mankind never wavered, yet the gulf separating man from God was un-crossable. For man, the emptiness caused by his broken relationship and separation from his creator tormented his soul. Man desperately sought to restore to that relationship, but he knew not how. Faint hints from the past stirred vague memories imprinted in his being. Those hints were the permanent things, universal truths that pointed to the laws which guided the universe, nature, and human nature. These perceived truths also pointed to that special relationship man once had with God, the way it was and ought to be. As man struggled to understand and appropriate the message of those distant voices from the past, chaos diminished, life was better, and hope grew.

Although discussed in a prior chapter, we must reiterate that the universe was made in accordance with certain hidden but discernable laws. Following these laws result in certain outcomes which are oriented to God. These outcomes, "...when rightly ordered, flow and move and act in ways pleasing to Him." However, free will allows man to flow or move in ways not pleasing to Him which creates disorder in the soul, in relationships, and everything around him.[347]

What are these universal truths, the rules of the road so to speak, that bring order or orientation to one's life? These universal truths are found in many cultures and are not confined to the Judeo-Christian writings. Examples of these universal truths include "...special duties to parents and elders, special duties to my wife and child, duties of good faith and veracity, duties to the weak, the poor and the desolate."[348] These norms provide "...a common human law of action which can over-arch rulers and ruled alike."[349] Before the revelation man still struggled, as if in a fog, searching for his way home but endlessly wandering in the mists, occasionally grasping the nearest lamp post with its dim circle of light spread at his feet in which he sees only his miserable and lost self. These lamp posts of universal truth bring a faint measure of light to which one attempts to orient oneself on this earth. They do nothing to bridge the gulf between God and man. The revelation to the Hebrews brought clarity, definition, and focus to those truths by which man must live. More importantly, the revelation pointed to the Savior who would act as that bridge between man and God. Jesus Christ is God's son and became the advocate for man and a means of man's redemption from his sin. The inspired New Testament writings confirmed the prophecies of the Old Testament and pointed toward a time of eternal communion with God for those who accept His invitation. However, man is still a creature with a free will, and by his free will and the drawing of the Holy Spirit he must approach God with repentance for sin or face an eternity of nightmarish loneliness and separation.

As we have said, elements of various universal truths and reliance thereon are found in many cultures and are not confined to the Judeo-Christian writings. One of the most important of these that contained elements of universal truths was the code of King Hammurabi. Apart from bits and pieces from other cultures discovered by archeologists, the code of Hammurabi is the oldest to survive as it was cut in stone and displayed in temple courtyards for the people to consult. Hammurabi became king (1792 BC?) of a new empire in Mesopotamia centered on the city of Babylon. At its height the empire stretched from the Persian Gulf northward to Assyria, seven hundred miles long and one hundred miles wide. The Hammurabic code was of extensive length and well-ordered in presentation. In some 282 articles, the code addressed many questions such as wages, divorce, and fees for medical attention and generally dealt with family, land, and commerce. Importantly, these directives were *not legislation but an assemblage of rules already observed*. In effect it was a body of "common law" assembled over a long period of time.[350]

Humanists often point to numerous ancient laws conceived by various peoples and point to elements of those laws that are common to more than one group or religion. Through this comparison they attempt to deny divine inspiration of the scriptures. To the contrary, commonality of certain laws between peoples is a strong testimony in favor of universal truths. We have already noted that all religions contain some hint of truth. These universals point to a particular manner of life that, if followed, improves man's sojourn on this planet. Those universals, eventually made known to man in their fullness through the revelation of God to the Hebrews and first century Christians, gave clarity as to how man ought to order his life. If the Bible were just an assemblage of universal truths recorded by numerous authors living as a nomadic people that spent much of its pre-Christian history in captivity, bondage, or exile over a sixteen hundred year period, it would be a remarkable feat to the point of being explained only through divine inspiration and guidance. However, the Bible is much more than a guide for living life on this earth. Through the Bible, God pointed the way for man's reunification with God, and He chose the Hebrews to carry His message to humankind.

Why did God create the universe and choose man as a repository for his love? We can only look at who He is as described in the Bible and look at His image created in man. From this we see His unfathomable love for man by creating him, giving him a free will, and when he failed, providing a means of redemption at the cost of His son at Calvary. That may not answer the "why" of creation, but could man hope for any better explanation other than the supreme love of God?

Now we turn our attention to humanism. As we have seen, humanism denies a supreme being that existed before the creation of the universe. So where do we begin our humanist journey through the eons? First of all, humanists attempt to discredit Christianity by pointing at the "...staggering immensity of the universe...During the twentieth century the astronomers ...have shown that our galactic system is only one out of billions upon billions of similar galaxies scattered throughout the universe." Pointing to the insignificance of the earth as "...a mere microscopic blur upon the unimaginably vast canopy of heavens...," Lamont mocks belief in an "omnipotent, benevolent, and personal God" who made human beings as his major concern.[351] Humanists are incorrect when they state that *only* moderns recognize that the earth is infinitesimally small in relation to the entirety of space. The tens of thousands of stars visible to the ancients had as much impact on their understanding of the immensity of space as the impact on the modern astronomer when peering into the vast reaches of space with the most powerful telescope. Contrary to humanists' assertions that modern science has radically altered the primitive picture of things that encourage the Christian religious view, earth's insignificance in relation to the vastness of space, whether seen or unseen, is neither a modern concept nor a legitimate argument against Christianity.[352]

Humanists also point to the enormous time spans of the cosmos as evidence that speaks against Christianity. For many humanists, including Corliss Lamont, it is more sensible to believe the universe is eternal as opposed to having a beginning initiated by a Creator or First Mover. Humanists claim that creative matter, the stuff of the universe, does not need a Prime Mover to jump start the universe and keep it going. On the contrary, it is claimed that the universe is auto-dynamic in its existence, operation, development, and continuation. Humanists point to geologists who now put the age of the earth at least four billion years, and therefore modern science has completely blown away the world view of "old-time religion." Given its age and dynamic nature, many humanists call the universe an eternally existing reality and assert that it is not logically necessary to accept the conclusion that there is a beginning in time and, by extension, a supernatural God as Creator or First Cause.[353]

Yet, science and scientists, the presumed allies of humanism, says otherwise. Stephen Hawking wrote *A Brief History of Time* as an effort to make sense of what we see around us. As man attempts to develop his "world picture", certain questions arise as to the nature of the universe, where did it and man come from, man's place in it, and why is it this way. A former professor at Cambridge University for forty years, Hawking attempts to give some answers to those questions. Scientists depict the universe in terms of two partial theories. The general theory of relativity describes the large-scale structure of the universe and the force of gravity. The other partial theory called quantum mechanics explains phenomena on an extremely small scale such as an infinitesimal fraction of the head of a pin. However, the two theories are inconsistent with each other, and therefore at least one of the theories must be incorrect. Hawking explains that if the universe is governed by definite laws, the two theories must be combined into a complete unified theory to describe and explain everything in the universe. In writing of man's quest for this unified theory Hawking said that, "...since the dawn of civilization, people have not been content to see events as unconnected and inexplicable. They have craved an understanding of the underlying order in the world. Today we still yearn to know why we are here and where we came from."[354]

Hawking states that before 1915 space and time were thought of as being fixed, i.e., that space and time continued forever. However, Hawking and his associate, Roger Penrose, "...showed that Einstein's general theory of relativity implied that the universe must have a beginning and, possibly, an end." The general theory of relativity proposes that an infinite state of density existed at some point in the past. When this dense mass exploded in what is known as the "Big Bang", it was effectively the beginning of time. Therefore, it is meaningless to consider any influence of space and time outside of the universe. With the Big Bang the idea of an unchanging universe was replaced by a dynamic, expanding universe that had a beginning and possibly an ending (the big crunch). All the laws would have broken down at the moment of the Big Bang, and "...God would still have had complete freedom to choose what happened and how the universe began."[355]

Although not a believer in God, at least in the Judeo-Christian God of the Bible, Hawking has an exceptional ability to frame the basic questions of life regarding the universe. Hawking observes that even in making the assumption that it was possible to develop a unified theory of the universe, it would be just a set of rules and equations and does not answer the "why" there should be a universe. "What breathes fire into the equations and makes a universe for them to describe?...Why does the universe go to all the bother of existing? Is the unified theory so compelling that it brings about its own existence? Or does it need a creator, and if so, does he have any other effect on the universe? And who created him?" As to the question of why it is that we and the universe exist, he states, "If we find the answer to that, it would be the ultimate triumph of human reason—for then we should know the mind of God."[356] Of course Hawking is speaking metaphorically rather than theologically. However for Christians, such statements have theological implications. To believe that if by reason alone man should presume to know the mind of God brings to mind the confusion that fell upon those who defied His authority and instruction at Babel on the plain of Shinar several millennia ago. Perhaps with God at the center of the scientific equation, He may permit man to have a clearer glimpse into the workings of His mind.

The Christian contends that there was a beginning to time, and science seems to confirm that contention. But in fairness, that contention alone does not mean that there is a God. Let's examine another area of scientific knowledge that speaks not only to his existence but his purposeful design of this world for man. Keller states that the conditions necessary for the development of intelligent life on earth are present in very limited areas throughout the universe. The necessary conditions are dictated by fifteen constants. These constants, or fundamental numbers as Hawking called them, appear to have been very precisely adjusted to make possible the universe as we see it. Keller wrote that these constants (e.g., gravitational constant, strong and weak nuclear force) have precise values. Keller quoted Francis Collins from his book, *The Language of God*, "If any one of those constants was off by even one part in a million, or in some cases, by one part in a million million, the universe could not have actually come to the point where we see it. Matter would not have been able to coalesce, there would have been no galaxy, stars, planets, or people." This is called the Fine-Tuning Argument or anthropic principle.[357] Paul Davis, a professor of theoretical physics, wrote:

> The really amazing thing is not that life on Earth is balanced on a knife-edge, but that the entire universe is balanced on a knife-edge, and would be total chaos if any of the natural "constants" were off even slightly...the universe seems unreasonably suited to the existence of life—almost contrived, a put-up job.[358]

Earth's knife-edge balancing act is connected to the conditions present at the moment of the Big Bang. Although virtually all cosmologists accept the Big Bang theory as the beginning of the cosmos, the theory still does not explain certain aspects of the universe. These problems occur because the scientists' Big Bang model is unstable. To explain the Big Bang as scientists understand it today requires very unlikely initial conditions at the instant of the bang. It appears that those initial conditions seem contrived as thought they were "put in by hand." Should tiny deviations have occurred in those initial conditions, the universe as it is known now would not exist (it would have met an early death). An answer was proposed in 1987 by Allen Guth, an MIT physicist to remove this unsatisfactory state of events. Guth's theory of inflation speculates that at the moment of the Big Bang, the universe expanded (inflated) at an unimaginably faster rate that it does today. The inflation theory would remove some of the cosmological problems related to the Big Bang, but inflation theory remains scientific speculation as there is no experimental proof. Even if proven, inflation theory still does answer all of the cosmological problems.[359]

Proponents of a strong anthropic principle claim the universe was prepared for human beings. Those supporting the weak anthropic principle are humanists such as Richard Dawkins who claim it is inevitable that, given the trillions of universes and enormous amounts of space and time, life as we know it would have occurred in some of those universes through the slow process of biological evolution and without a supernatural Creator. But Hawking casts doubt on Dawkins' assertions, "The odds against a universe like ours emerging out of something like the Big Bang are enormous. I think there are clearly religious implications...It would be very difficult to explain why the universe would have begun in just this way except as the act of a God who intended to create beings like us."[360] Certainly Hawking and other scientists continue to look for the Holy Grail of science, a unified theory of the universe, but his statements apparently reflect an honest assessment of the accumulated scientific knowledge of the universe at the end of the twentieth century. Given the weight of the Fine-Tuning Argument and its scientific underpinnings, one may add to Hawkins comments by saying that if God did design the earth for life on a small planet on the backside of the universe, it is also safe to assume that the design was specifically intended for the flower of His creation—humankind.

It is interesting that one humanist writer counts the Big Bang theory as support for humanism[361] while at the same time Lamont in *The Philosophy of Humanism* states that "…no logical necessity forces us to the conclusion that there is a beginning in time…"[362] The disagreement among humanists is further evident from Hawking's statement that much of the opposition to his theory of the big bang beginning of the universe came from the Russian humanists, the Marxist who defended their humanistic doctrine of scientific determination which believes that human cognition, behavior, decision, and action, is *causally* determined by an *unbroken chain of prior occurrences*. Even Einstein was initially convinced that the universe had to be static when he formulated his general theory of relativity in 1915.[363] With regard to the question of time, space, and the universe, perhaps the humanists should not be so ready to consign the Bible to the library shelves marked "fiction" because of its phrases "In the beginning…" from Genesis and "…there should be time no longer…" from the Book of Revelation.

Now we turn our humanists' attentions from the extra-terrestrial to the terrestrial and the origins of man. One humanist writer dates the origin of the "human family" at about seven million years ago. The enlarged brain occurred in man's evolution at two and a half million years ago with the latest version of man, Homo sapiens, appearing only 35,000 years ago. The process by which all this was supposed to have come about was set forth by Charles Darwin's *The Origin of Species* in 1859. Jim Herrick calls evolution as proposed by Darwin one of the two key scientific theories upon which humanism rests, the other being the theory of cosmic origins in a big bang as noted above.[364] Darwin's three fundamental propositions regarding evolution are inter-related. First, new species have appeared through "descent with modification" throughout earth's history. Second, the diversity of all life on earth can be accounted for because living things descended from a very small group of common ancestors. The third proposition states that the species were crafted for survival by natural selection or "survival of the fittest" as opposed to the guidance of a creator.[365]

If man evolved from simple life forms to be what he is today, what of the mind? Lamont calls the connection between the physical body and the personality (in which he includes every aspect of the mind) as the most important problem with respect to nature and the destiny of mankind. Humanists hold to the monistic theory which sees such a close and fundamental connection of body and personality (including all aspects of the mind) that it results in an indissoluble unity. Implicit in this theory is that the personality is not immortal and that man's earthly existence is all there is. Christians and certain other religions adhere to a dualistic view that the soul (will, intellect, emotions) is separate and independent from the body and that the soul survives the body's death. From this seminal difference flow enormous consequences for man in the areas of knowledge, ethics, education, and individual freedom. These conflicts and consequences are evident in the schooling of our children, making of our laws, moral choices, and in almost every other aspect of our lives. Humanists believe "biology has conclusively shown" that humans and other life forms are the product of an infinitely long process of evolution that exceeds three billion years. The body was primary and basic but with its increasing complexity came development and integration of animal behavior and control. This integration culminated with Homo sapiens and the "phenomenon of the mind" or man as we know him today. Speech arose from man's social nature and developed from "...elementary movements, grunts, and cries..." Moral standards were not sent down from a divine creator but were rather a social product that evolved through human association. Lamont called the monistic view of body and personality one of the greatest achievements in the history of science. He claims that science and "simple common sense" have shown that the monistic relationship between body and personality "...provide(s) a satisfactory account of the complex human organism...and makes untenable any theory of a worthwhile personal survival after death." As we shall see in Part III, science and "simple common sense" will *not* give the comfort and assurance to humanist theories as Lamont so smugly claims.[366]

Humanists have a worldview that accounts for the universe and the evolution of life on earth to the twenty-first century, but what of the future? Christians foresee an eternity spent with their Creator. Humanists believe that changing the social and economic systems in much of the world would assure everyone a socially significant life that is secure and abundant in resources. "A more cooperative form of society would discourage present tendencies towards selfish individualism and expansion of ego that foster the urge for everlasting self-perpetuation...[and] the belief in a hereafter...would tend to disappear." [367] As we shall later see, Lamont's "more cooperative form of society" is socialism. What is the humanist nirvana and vision for mankind? Lamont obliges,

> ...we can find plenty of scope and meaning in our lives through freely enjoying the rich and varied potentialities of this luxuriant earth; through preserving, extending, and adding to the values of civilization; through contributing to the progress and happiness of humankind during billions and billions of years; or through helping to evolve a new species surpassing Homo sapiens.[368]

> Through eliminating the more pressing evils of present day society, and through putting into general effect already known measures of health and education, humankind can improve considerably both physically and intellectually...For a scientifically induced mutation in humans may well bring into existence a more advanced species, call it *Superhuman* (emphasis in original)...In any case infinite possibilities remain of further triumphs for human beings in various realms, including, above all the winning of adequate control over human nature itself.[369]

These comments by one of the recognized leaders of the humanist philosophy in the twentieth century bring to mind a number of images of this future humanist utopia: socialism (putting into effect already known measures of health and education), ever onward and upward progress (progress and happiness of mankind), creation of a new super race (scientifically induced mutation in humans), imposition of the "right" values (preserving, extending, adding to the values of civilization), and subjugating people who are not in agreement with those "right" values (winning adequate control over human nature itself). Regarding the winning of adequate control over human nature itself, one must wonder what this apparently aberrant form of human nature is if it too is also a product of evolution. All of Lamont's utopian imageries call to remembrance other images from the not too distant past when many of these same goals with similar sounding euphemistic names were imposed on large masses of people with disastrous consequences.

Most humanists believe that the they have won the battle as reflected by statements such as Herrick's who said, "The theory of evolution is now almost completely accepted—apart from the kick-back of a number of Creationists, particularly in the U.S." This is one of the tactics of the humanists—to present the conflict of Christians and humanists regarding evolution as a war between science and religion. We shall address the battle involving evolution as well as the supposed war between science and religion in more detail in Part III.

Part III – Humanism in American Institutions

In Part I we examined the Baby Boom generation and their general worldview. In Part II we described the historical background of the conflicting worldviews of humanism and Christianity, their respective tenets of faith, and the course of battle since the arrival of the Europeans in North America. In Part III, we shall describe and examine the impact of the conflict of worldviews on American institutions—religion, government and politics, family, academia, economics, art and culture, and society in general.

Christian Smith called the profound changes in American society that began about 1870 a secular revolution that represented a displacement of the dominant Protestant power and authority and secularism's capture and transformation of culture and institutions that govern the nation's public life. Smith identified a number of institutions affected: Science and the production of new knowledge in which religion was considered irrelevant and an obstruction to true knowledge; higher education that favored an "…a-religious and irreligious pursuit and transmission of knowledge and credentializing of new professions"; transformation of an overarching Christian public culture through liberal political theories "…that privatized and made religion irrelevant in public deliberations"; diminution of religion as an important part of jurisprudence through the erection of a "wall of separation" between church and state; transformation of the Protestant concepts of spiritual and moral "care of souls" to a "…naturalistic, psychologized model of human personhood"; and the displacement of diverse religion-friendly venues of public discourse by a relatively few centrally-owned print and broadcast media whose reporting practices marginalized religion in the name of neutrality and objectivism.[370] In summary, this secularization process is the separation of "…historic religious organization and authority from public institutions and relegating them to private life."[371]

Books are written to give a measure of permanency to their contents as opposed to the disposable immediacy of most periodicals, cyber-space, and broadcast media that deal with current events and personalities. Yet, current events and personalities must be included in any description of "the workings of contemporary institutions."[372] Therefore, the difficulty in writing Part III is a fear of being too topical—that is, to be too immersed in the words and sound bites of the issues of the moment. Most of those issues are symptomatic of societal dysfunction and fail to recognize or address root causes, that is, the bigger picture. Many books are written to address important issues of the moment but after passage of a period of time seem dated and irrelevant to the new problems that dominate our attention. Yet, the issues of the moment added to many other issues of the moment create a mosaic that reveals a better picture of the root causes of societal dysfunction, perhaps better described as a loss of order. That is the purpose of including such topical issues and examples in our examination of the conflict of worldviews. If we are successful, future editions of this book will require only updated examples, and the original picture created by the mosaic will remain unchanged.

A second challenge in writing about the conflict of worldviews as they impact each of the major institutions of American life is the difficulty of adequately addressing all of the issues pertinent to each of those institutions. Books can be and have written about the conflict within each of these institutions. Yet, space limitations and a limit to the readers' patience and/or attention span must be considered. Hopefully, the discussions will give an adequate if incomplete picture of the conflicts surrounding the institutions under analysis. Additionally, the conflicts between the worldviews are not clearly compartmentalized or segregated within each American institution. In fact, most of the issues discussed will involve more than one of the major American institutions. For example, when writing about religion, such considerations will likely involve governance and politics. When writing of modern culture, religious considerations will arise for religion is part of culture. Regardless of the difficulties aforementioned, at the end of Part III the reader should have an integrated picture and understanding of the conflicts and the causes of disorder in American society and humanism's central role in creation of that disorder.

Chapter 12

Religion – The Power of Religion in American History

In their efforts to discredit man's belief in a transcendent God, humanists ascribe the ills of mankind to religion and its attendant divisiveness throughout history. The offered solution is to embrace secular humanism and retreat from all religions including those resting upon Judeo-Christian ethic. In America, this means substantially eliminating secular humanism's greatest obstacle in achieving its goal—Christianity. However, if all religion brings divisiveness, then humanism must pronounced its own self guilty as well. Not only has the Supreme Court held that humanism is a religion, *Humanist Manifesto I* calls humanism a religion.[373] Whether humanism is a religion or a philosophy may be a moot point, but what is not arguable is the enormous impact on America through humanism's attack on the Judeo-Christian ethic upon which the nation was founded.

Let us return to two major questions raised by humanism: Is religion the root source of human conflict and misery? and the larger question, Can religion effectively and permanently be banished from mankind? We shall address the second question first.

Richard Weaver's *Visions of Order*, the third book in his trilogy on the decline of the West, describes man as a special creature with two selves. The first is his animal being, "…an organism living in an environment." What makes man different or special is the second half of his being. This second half involves man's understanding of the picture of himself that is derived from his spirit. This image or picture is the subjective part of man's being and is comprised of his wishes, hopes, imaginations, and desire to see things beyond himself. In effect, man must fit this picture of himself into a relationship with all other things. There is an urge to bring this image into focus and harmony with the surrounding world, and this urge is recorded on ancient walls, whether cave or hut, as well as the most modern shrine, temple, or other edifice. Weaver wrote:

> Without the picturization, man feels an unendurable nakedness in the face of his environment and before the questions of life. From such poverty he rescues himself through projections that include the natural environment and whatever is suggested by his spirit regarding the mystery that broods over creation. Look beneath the surface of the most brilliant cultures of history, and you find a hunger and a wonderment, reaching even to a kind of melancholia…This great yearning of man to be *something* in the imaginative sense, that is, to be something more than he is in the simple existential way or the reductionist formula of materialism is both universal and proper to him…This is the point at which he departs from the purely utilitarian course and makes of himself a being with significance. It is a refutation of all simplistic histories and psychologies, but it is one of the most verifiable facts about man.[374] (emphasis in original)

Imagine the most remote tribe in the remotest of jungles without outside contact or influence for thousands of years. As they sit huddled around a campfire while gazing at the star-filled sky above, the gray-headed patriarch patiently explains to the wide-eyed young children the mysteries of this world and the unseen world; the way things work, what one must do and not do to live—the basic questions of life. The aged patriarch is transferring a system of beliefs held with ardor and faith by which he attempts to cover his "unendurable nakedness." It is endemic to all of mankind, in every age and every people group. It is religion.

In characterizing the of power of religion in America as he saw it 120 years before Weaver's *Visions of Order,* Tocqueville wrote:

> …the imperfect joys of this world will never satisfy his heart. Man alone of all created beings shows a natural disgust for existence and an immense longing to exist; he despises life and fears annihilation. These different feelings constantly

drive his soul toward the contemplation of another world and religion it is which directs him there. Religion is thus one particular form of hope as natural to the human heart as hope itself. Men cannot detach themselves from religious beliefs except by some wrong-headed thinking and by a sort of moral violence inflicted upon their true nature; they are drawn back by an irresistible inclination. Unbelief is an accident; faith is the only permanent state of mankind.[375]

In other words, the power of religion grows because it is not linked to human experiment, invention, or ideologies but to the permanent things or first principles. Man as a created being, man's soul seeking the afterlife, and man's search for and reliance on those permanent things that recur in every period of history also speak to Tocqueville's belief that in early America religion meant Christianity.

In the humanist world man is not to be directed by religion. For the humanist, religion is an entirely human social construction whose function is merely to draw people to gather and give meaning to their lives. There is no room for any worldview in which supernaturalism is a part. Religion is merely a form of human experience and values, and such experience and values are empty and meaningless if it "…substitutes a dead God for a living ideal of human justice."[376] Humanists deny the dualism that divide the universe into two separate realms—the material and the spiritual.[377] This denial is not supported by science itself. Charles Colson quoted Harvard professor Herbert Benson, a non-believer, who admitted that believing in an infinite and absolute [God] was part of the human genetic blueprint in which man is "…wired for God…"[378] In modern America humanists wielding Ockham's Razor* may have some

---

* William of Ockham (1285-1349) was a fourteenth century philosopher who became identified with the principle of parsimony, a concept in which any scientific explanation of natural phenomena should be based on the fewest assumptions or hypotheses possible to give an explanation to the facts involved. Any explanation not supported by facts or observation should be rejected. This concept was called Ockham's Razor and remains a basic premise of the scientific method. Because of this reliance on facts and observation, reason was powerless in matters of faith. Ockham's nominalism denied the existence of universals and thus separated religion from philosophy. [Lawrence T. McHargue, "The Christian and Natural

temporal success in separating the religious from the secular in their attempts to answer the basic questions of life and give order to society, but they shall never pare the religious impulse from the mind of man. Man must seek answers to life's basic questions, and religion is the means whereby he seeks those answers. But many religions give false or inadequate pictures of life and thus fail to give man satisfaction. Through these religions man's picture of himself becomes distorted and out of focus which results in a disorder of the soul as the questions of life remain unanswered.

We now return to our first question: Is religion the root source of human conflict and misery? The humanist quickly agrees. Those who believe in a supernatural transcendent God will also agree that there have been considerable conflicts based on different religious beliefs. However, religious conflicts are symptoms and not the causes of the discord, and humanists attempt to exorcise the symptom without addressing the root causes. The root causes are defective worldviews, and this presupposes that there are right and wrong answers to the basic questions of life. Therefore, we must return to the conflict of worldviews.

In the conflict between the Christian and humanistic worldviews, we should understand the weapons of war with which Christians fight. Humanists use science and reason in their efforts to undermine Christianity. However, Christianity does not surrender those weapons to the humanists. Properly understood, reason and science support the Judeo-Christian ethic. The battle is not to be won with reason and science but reliance on God's Word as recorded in the Bible. Humanists such as Herrick will have us believe that science has already defeated the claims of the Bible, but distraught Christian warriors do not understand the power of their weapon and that of their Commander-in-Chief.

For Humanists, man writes his own story. The story is written in continually changing theories, hypotheses, explanations derived from human reason, scientific investigations, speculation, suppositions, and ultimately imagination. By imagination is meant,

---

Science," *Elements of a Christian Worldview*, comp. and ed. by Michael D. Palmer, (Springfield, Missouri: Logion Press, 1998), p. 154; Russell Kirk, *The Roots of American Order*, (Washington, D.C.: Regnery Gateway, 1991), pp. 207, 209.]

"...the act or power of forming a mental image of something not present to the senses or never before wholly perceived in reality."[379]
The story of evolution is an excellent example of the use of imagination. We say imagination not in the sense that it is true or false but in the sense that it is a story or image by which evolutionists attempt to explain the development of mankind and ultimately a portion of the evolutionists' worldview. Based on observations, study, and the work of others, an evolutionist perceives the historical events in the story of man's development and attempts to explain what he perceives to be natural phenomena that occurred over millions of years.

In a discussion of the power and necessity of imagination, Russell Kirk wrote, "All great systems, ethical or political, attain their ascendancy over the minds of men by virtue of their appeal to the imagination; and when they cease to touch the chords of wonder and mystery and hope, their power is lost, and men look elsewhere for some set of principles by which they may be guided." Certainly, the humanistic worldview does not touch the chords of wonder and mystery and hope despite its grandiloquent claims of achievement of progress and happiness of humankind through time and the adoption of a humanistic belief system. Its appeal to the imagination fails because its principles by which men may be guided fail. Yet, evolution is almost universally touted as scientific fact while belief in a supernatural Creator is myth in the sense that the basis of such belief is false. In support of the humanists' flawed assumptions, they point to numerous perceived falsities and inconsistencies in the Bible as evidence by making it something it was not intended to be or claimed to be.

Christians believe that God wrote man's story, and this story is recorded in the Bible. Humanists attempt to pull the Bible into the arena of science and scientific investigation to prove its falsity. We must remember that the Bible is not a science book, but it is also not anti-science. However, as we have seen, a favorite tactic of humanists is to portray a war between science and religion, and Christian theologians have been partially responsible for this perception. Stephen Toulmin, quoted by Craig M. Gay, states that,

> Twice already, Christian theologians have committed themselves enthusiastically to the detailed ideas of particular

systems of scientific theory. This happened, firstly, when the medieval church naturalized Aristotle, and gave his views about nature an authority beyond their true strength: secondly, when, from the 1680s up to the late nineteenth century, Protestant thinkers (especially in Britain) based a new religious cosmology on mechanical ideas about nature borrowed from Descartes and Newton...Having plunged too deeply in their original scientific commitments, the theologians concerned failed to foresee the possibility that Aristotle's and Newton's principles might not forever be the last word; and when radical changes took place in the natural sciences, they were unprepared to deal with them.[380]

Science has provided a great understanding of the natural world. However, the non-material things that are just as real in our human experience lie outside the capabilities of science to decipher. Such things include justice, love, fairness, morality, righteousness, charity, and mercy. One must consider to whom the biblical account was initially revealed and the purpose of that revelation. It was not God's purpose for the Bible to instruct the Hebrews and early Christians in the science of the natural world.

Suppose for a moment that you are God. You have watched man since the Fall and his misery and "...groping toward divine love and wisdom—implanted in a people's consciousness, before the dawn of history."[381] It is now time to give direction through revelation and point to a savior whose death, burial, and resurrection will make possible the reunification of man with God. What would you say and how would you give this message to man? First, you must decide if you will reveal the message to all of mankind at one time or select an earthly messenger to spread the message? Christians believe that God chose a particular people to carry his message to the world. Next, you must reveal your message in words that would be intelligible for that people in that particular era. The message must be true and consistent with the nature of God and those universal truths that man sought and dimly perceived through the ages. This is what God did through his revelation as recorded in the Bible. The Bible is a book of history, poetry, prophecy, parable, and allegory. These are the tools whereby God painted the mural of man's true story from his creation to his eternal destiny.

The Bible is inerrant and, as such, may be counted to stand as the Christian's authority in all matters regarding the questions of life. Humanists such as Herrick misapprehend the meaning of inerrant and literal when they refer to Christians "...calling every word of the Bible true—an approach known as the inerrancy of the Bible. Such people believe in the literal account of the creation and the fall of Adam and Eve."[382] Regarding inerrancy, renowned theologian J. I. Packer wrote:

> If the words of Scripture are God breathed, it is almost blasphemy to deny that it is free from error in that which it is intended to teach and infallible in the guidance it gives. Inerrancy and infallibility cannot be proved (nor, let us note, disproved) by argument. Both are articles of faith.[383]

Humanists and others inappropriately interchange the usage of literal and inerrant. The meaning of "literal" implies a concern mainly with facts, and for the humanist that means facts that can be scientifically validated. But as we have said, the Bible is a book of history, poetry, prophecy, parable, and allegory. All are part of the word picture God used, and it is an inerrant picture of God and man and their relationship. Many humanists must agree that even they believe certain historical accounts in the Bible are literally true. And Christians agree that Jesus used parables or short fictitious stories to illustrate a moral or religious principle. The point is that humanists attempt to force the inerrancy of the Bible into a laboratory test tube, but as previously stated the Bible deals with the non-material things that are outside the capabilities of science to decipher and are just as real in our human experience as any scientifically proven hypothesis.

Because the humanist denies the supernatural, he also denies the possibility of miracles. A miracle is an extraordinary occurrence resulting from a supernatural work of God and may involve the suspension of natural laws. For the Christian, the initiation of a miracle is within the power and prerogative of God. For the humanist, it is an impossibility. A Christian may believe that the earth was created in six days, each of twenty-four hours length.* Alternatively,

---

*Joao Magueijo, a professor of theoretical physics at Imperial College, London, and other scientists have challenged the most fundamental rule of

he or she may believe that God created the earth and its inhabitants over a much longer period and that the words of Genesis are descriptive of that creation in a metaphorical or symbolic manner. Others believe that the earth is of great age, but fully formed and functional man was of recent creation. All are miracles and none of the creative techniques are greater or lesser miracles than the others, and none of the beliefs undermine the inerrancy of the Bible. The important thing to remember is that the Bible reveals the truth that God created the earth and its inhabitants, and in doing so He revealed His creation in a manner that could be understood by man. A miraculous event need not, and indeed cannot, fit into the confines of science or scientific investigation. In the presence of a miracle, scientific investigation is relegated to a recognition that something happened outside of its ability to explain, describe, or measure.

An illustration of the reality or truth of something that cannot be seen or measured by science will be helpful. The Hubel Space Telescope was launched in 1990 and orbits the earth while peering into deep space. Isaac Newton built the first reflecting telescope in 1669. Three hundred years later scientists were building the space telescope based on most of the same principles as Newton used. Newton's reflective telescope uses a different method of viewing than that of refractor telescopes such as used by Galileo. Refractor telescopes have a single lens together with eyepiece that brings the image directly to the eye, and such are now mainly the province of

---

modern physics which states that the speed of light is the only aspect of the universe that is unchanging. The challenge comes from the "varying speed of light" theory (VSL) which is presented as solving some of the cosmological inconsistencies and paradoxes that exist within the present understanding of the universe's creation and operation. From VSL's emergence in the 1990s, there has been a growing interest in the theory and its ramifications as to our understanding of the cosmos. From research and recent discoveries sparked by VSL, scientists are considering the possibility that the speed of light has been slowing significantly over the years. In other words, the speed of light was much faster in earlier ages. The implication is that the earth and universe may be much *younger* than presently thought. VSL remains highly speculative (as are some of the more accepted explanations of the universe) and controversial and may be proven wrong. However, VSL is a fascinating concept which is vigorously opposed by many in the scientific community. [Joao Magueijo, *Faster Than the Speed of Light*, Cambridge, Massachusetts: Perseus Publishing, 2003.]

the young backyard astronomer. Reflective telescopes are light gatherers and use two mirrors to produce focused images that can be viewed through an eyepiece. Modern astronomers at the great observatories rarely look through the eyepiece but capture the information on photographic plates. However, the Hubel telescope captures the data on an electronic version of the photographic plate. The Hubel light detectors convert the data to radio waves that are transmitted to earth. Scientists not only locate distant galaxies and stars within, they are able to determine the composition of those celestial bodies through the use of a spectroscope. Celestial bodies emit white light which contain a spectrum of colors. Different substances emit light of different colors. Comparing the colors emitted by the celestial bodies with the colors in a laboratory spectra of earthly substances allow the scientist to identify a celestial body's fingerprint or, in other words, to identify the presence of various substances on a distant star.[384]

    Humanists may claim that the data gathered by the Hubel is solid scientific fact without the least hint of the supernatural. But there is a large element of faith in the humanists' suppositions. First of all, scientists see only images of light from deep space. The light is captured by mirrors, converted into data transmitted by radio waves to earth, and then converted into images on computer monitors which may ultimately be transferred to the printed page. The scientists have not "seen" the distant stars but have faith in their equipment and that they are seeing an accurate representation or reflected image of those distant stars. The scientists also have faith that the substances on the distant objects will produce the same colors in the light spectrum as like substances on earth and thereby identify the star's composition. Likewise, Christians believe in the existence of a Creator that loves mankind and is intimately involved with his destiny and whose image is captured by the inerrant Bible. Similar to the Hubel space telescope, the Bible reflects the image of God and his creation including mankind. This reflection of God is given to mankind through history, poetry, prophecy, parable, and allegory. We observe man and his fallen condition. We observe the biblical prescriptions for life, both earthly and eternal, and find they work to bring order to our souls and society. Like the colors displayed by a spectrograph, the eternal truths that were present throughout the universe at its creation are still true today on this earth. We see the fingerprints of God in creation and see His fingerprints in our daily lives. And, much like the scientists, we have faith in what we see.

As we noted earlier, the infallibility of the Bible is derived from the belief that the words of the Scripture are God breathed, i.e., written by human hands but under the inspiration of God. With regard to the authority of the Bible, Packer asks the question, "Where is the supreme court for the Christian? Is it the Bible acknowledged as the Word of God (evangelicalism), the church's canons and traditions (traditionalism) or some faculty lodged within humanity itself (subjectivism, liberalism)?" Packer answers that "Jesus and the apostles, followed by the early church, stand unambiguously for the authority of the Word." The manner in which Christ and the apostles quoted, used, and viewed the Old Testament was an affirmation of its divine authority, and through the "control of divine providence that the New Testament was written."[385] However, humanists often attempt to undermine the authority of the Scripture by pointing to the numerous translations of the Bible through the centuries, and therefore claim the Bible can't be accurate as that of the original versions. Some Christians fall into this trap when they use such phrases as "the divine inspiration and infallibility of Holy Scripture *as originally given*." (emphasis in original) Implied is that later translations are less than infallible, consequently suspect, and therefore not reliable. However, as the people of God of every age have pointed to the inerrancy of the Scripture, so too do they point to God's "providential preservation of the Scriptures." To seek the original form of the biblical text is worthwhile, but if we believe God gave great care to reveal his will and intent by causing inspired or God-breathed Scripture to be given to mankind, is it also reasonable to believe that God would not allow his Word to be corrupted. The Christian can rely on God's providential care in sustaining the accuracy of his revelation through the centuries, and we can confidently use standard and long accepted translations such as the Vulgate and King James versions as well as faithful modern translations.[386]

Chapter 13

Religion in the Public Arena – Mention Jesus Christ and "...all hell breaks loose"*

We continue our discussion of Christianity in America with a one of those topical moments, of great debate at the time but which will be forgotten within a year by most unless reminded. However, by the accumulation of such moments we give face to a culture and thereby better understand that society within which one resides. The issue at hand is archetypal in that it clearly defines the conflicts surrounding the appearance of religious faith in the public arena. In this instance we have Brit Hume, a Fox News commentator, appearing with Bill O'Reilly on *Fox News Sunday*. Mr. Hume commented on the recently disclosed and highly publicized serial marital infidelity of golfer Tiger Woods. Hume suggested to O'Reilly and the television audience that, "My message to Tiger would be: Tiger, turn to the Christian faith and you can make a total recovery and be a great example to the world"...and that Woods' professed Buddhism "doesn't offer the kind of forgiveness and redemption that is offered by the Christian faith." Hume's statements were widely reported and roundly criticized by the mainstream secular media and even some self-described Christians. One viewer's response best characterizes the mindset of those objecting to Hume's audacity in mentioning Jesus as the solution to Woods' problem, "Religion is such a deeply personal issue, and it is wrong to discuss what another person should believe. Mr. Hume should have contacted Tiger Woods privately instead of taking it public." O'Reilly defended Hume but questioned, "How many of us want to be told how to achieve forgiveness in a public forum?"[387]

---

* Brit Hume's comment to Bill O'Reilly on *Fox News Sunday*. [Quoted by Joel Belz, *World*, January 10, 2010, page 4.]

Several responses may be made to the viewer and others criticizing Hume. Our first response is to Christians. Christians that are faithful to Christ and his direction for living in this world must recognize the importance of sharing the Christian faith. According to Scripture (Matthew 28:19-20), one must make disciples or Christians of all nations. That does not mean that one is a Christian because of being a citizen of a nation considered Christian. To be a Christian means to have a personal relationship with Jesus Christ through repentance and acceptance of him as one's personal Lord and Savior. As the viewer stated, "It is a "…deeply personal issue…Mr. Hume should have contacted Tiger Woods privately instead of taking it public." The viewer is correct in that faith is a personal matter (as in individual faith rather than group faith), but that does not make it a private matter. For Christians, sharing the gospel is not optional. The Scripture does not distinguish between a public broadcast and a private conversation in sharing the Christian message with people. Woods' fame is worldwide, and his predicament attracted a firestorm of media coverage that lasted for weeks as the facts and circumstances unfolded. There was much speculation in secular media of what Woods must do to redeem himself in the eyes of the public and to recover his golfing career. Hume's comments were just one of hundreds of public statements made regarding a solution to Woods' troubles. Christ's example should be our guide. The manner in which Christ presented his message ranged from a gentle approach to men and women on a private level (the woman at the well) to harsh and highly public castigation for wrong doing (driving the money changers from the Temple). But this response, addressed to Christians, will not satisfy non-Christians.

The reaction of the major media was huge, severe, and stinging. But the reaction is also exceptionally enlightening regarding the major media's hatred of Christians and Christianity. Joel Belz wrote in *World* Magazine of the incident.

> If media critics wanted to be transparent about their scorn for Christianity in the public square, they succeeded after the broadcast. Comedy Central's Jon Stewart lampooned Hume in a four-minute segment. MSNBC's David Shuster called Hume's remarks "truly embarrassing." Washington Post critic asked: "Who did he sound more like—Mary Poppins on

the joys of a tidy room, or Ron Popeil on the glories of some amazing potato peeler?"...Hume['s]... hope for Woods strikes Shales as "looniness."[388]

The lesson is clear. Speak ill of Mohammed or Buddha and you will be accused by the media of intolerance, insensitivity, or bigotry. Speak ill of Jesus Christ or Christians and, like Saul at the stoning of Stephen, the media will guard the coats of those throwing the stones.

For the secularists and humanists, Mr. Hume's *sin* was not only that he publicly discussed another's faith or lack thereof, but he had the audacity to even approach another person about his faith because, in the viewer's words, "...it is wrong to discuss what another person should believe." For the Christian we have given an answer. For the secularist and humanist, we counter with a question, "Why not discuss with someone what they should believe, either publicly or privately?" Who made the rule that we shouldn't? The airwaves are filled with thousands of people discussing their most intimate and private lives before millions of people. Some will counter that discussions of religion and faith is just not done in polite society. However, is it a matter of etiquette to not offer a solution and solace to those in pain or despair? If one were in a dire, life-threatening situation and the secularist or humanist held the means of escape, would he or she hesitate to offer assistance? Of course they wouldn't. Likewise, Christians are not imposing their views on anyone but sharing "...the difference Jesus has made in their lives and they care enough about others to want to share His (Christ) message in the hope that other lives will be similarly transformed."[389]

Secularists and humanists also chastise Hume for presuming that the Christian faith is superior to other faiths. In America, this is a favorite weapon used to diminish Christianity by claiming all religions lead to the same God. C. S. Lewis addressed this issue in *Mere Christianity*. According to Lewis, this view "...simply says there is a good God in Heaven and everything is all right—leaving out all the difficult and terrible doctrines about sin and hell and the devil, and the redemption."[390] However, all faiths are not the same (as Hume pointed out), and all faiths do not lead to God. Woods' professed Buddhism is an excellent example. As one editorialist wrote, "Adherents to the key Buddhist doctrine of non-attachment—to things, people, or life itself—argue that we only imagine the difference between war and peace, civilization and savagery: All are illusions."[391] The Buddhist religion cannot, as Hume correctly observed, bring redemption and forgiveness when such beliefs result in the denial of the reality and claim that any distinctions between right and wrong or good and evil are illusory. Christianity is the only worldview that leads to order in one's soul and society.

One may ask why a humanist would want to equate Christianity with all other faiths when the humanist denies a deity in the first place. The answer is that those opponents of Christianity, who wish to destroy or at least drive it from the public square, attempt to erase all distinctions between Christianity and other religions in their demand for a simplistic, non-demanding religion in which all religions lead to the same God. They then indict Christianity for the failures of other religions with false worldviews in bringing answers to life's basic questions.

There are several tactics used by the secular humanists to drive Christianity from the public square. The first of these tactics has its roots in the promotion of the dualism of faith and society. This is not an admission from humanists of the rightness of accepting a private faith as long as it receives no illumination in the public square. On the contrary, for the humanist it is a means whereby faith will be allowed to die a natural death having been successfully driven from the public square and limited in its exposure to following generations. So successful has this tactic been that we are now assumed to be in the post-Christian era. In the promotion of a dualistic mindset regarding faith and the remainder of society, pluralism is the banner flown by humanist in the war to eradicate Christianity from the public square. A pluralistic society is one "…in which members of diverse ethnic, racial, religious, or social groups maintain an *autonomous participation* in and development of their traditional culture or special interest *within the confines of a common civilization.*"[392] (emphasis added) For the secular humanist, pluralism demands all religion be removed from the public square, but this is a different interpretation of pluralism than held by Americans of the Revolutionary era.

From its beginnings America was a pluralistic society in that it did not have a politically established national religion, i.e., one state sponsored denomination or sect. Far from it, the colonists arrived on the shores of the continent in search of religious freedom, independent of the dictates of government. But Europe was

Christendom and so was America by extension. Although exhibiting a form of pluralism that denied government interference with their beliefs, America exhibited an exceptionally strong religious sanction. This sanction was the "...power of Christian teaching over private conscience [that] made possible the American democratic society."[393] Tocqueville concurs as his prescient comments reveal when he spoke of religion and Christianity interchangeably when describing faith in America. He wrote, "...Christianity reigns without obstacles by universal consent...the result is that in the world of morality everything is definite and settled, although the world of politics is given over to debate and human experiment." Upon his arrival in America in the 1830s, it was the religious atmosphere that first struck Tocqueville and where he found the spirit of religion and the spirit of freedom "...intimately linked together in *joint reign* over the same land." (emphasis added) The reason for this he discovered was the separation of church and state.[394] However, the Founders' separation as described by Tocqueville was far different from the impenetrable "wall of separation" as envisioned and portrayed in the twentieth and twenty-first centuries. On closer examination, we see that separation of church and state meant something entirely different to the Founders and other pre-twentieth century Americans when compared to that of the modern secular humanist aberration. When Founders wrote the Constitution, they weren't "fixing" and "insuring" religious freedom but preserving it. They were *not* building a wall to restrain religion and its influence in the public square. To the former colonists, religion in America was separate in that it was the over-arching cover, the center to which one looked in the times of political turmoil, the anchor to which citizens held in times of national peril.

    A proper understanding of the separation of church and state is not enough. Religion, although not dictating a particular faith, is not passive but plays vital role in the republic. According to Tocqueville, the Christian religion in America "...has retained the greatest real power over people's souls and nothing shows better how useful and natural religion is to man...religion governs not only behavior but extends its influence to men's minds." Tocqueville believed that a tyrant state may be able to dispense with religion but freedom cannot. A society cannot avoid destruction if moral ties are not tightened in the face of relaxed political ties. Tocqueville asked, "And what can be done with a nation in control of itself, if it is not subject to God?"³⁹⁵ Therefore, we see the spirit of religion and the spirit of freedom "jointly reigning" over the land. We also see that the modern drive to remove religion from the public square through the application of a distorted conception of plurality in America is ludicrous given religion's importance and place in the creation of this country. For the Americans of the Revolutionary era, separation of church and state was *not* meant to restrain religious influence nor cause it to disappear from the public square.

How do we reconcile Tocqueville's "separation of church and state" with his "reign of the spirit of religion over the land"? Tocqueville explains:

> ...the man who still believes is not afraid to display his faith for all to see. He looks on those who do not share his hopes as unfortunate rather than hostile...He is, therefore, in conflict with no one; since he does not view the society in which he lives as an arena where religion has to struggle constantly against a thousand relentless enemies, he is attached to his fellow men...With unbelievers hiding their incredulity and believers parading their faith, public opinion pronounces its support for religion, which is loved, upheld, and respected.³⁹⁶

Tocqueville's observation may appear quaint and outdated and cause instant apoplexy for the secular humanist of the twenty-first century, but the secular humanist view so widespread in modern America is a distortion and obscures truth.

The Founders stated in the Constitution that the government could not establish a state sponsored religion, i.e., a particular denomination or sect. However, the Founders were anything but ambivalent or hostile to religion in general and Christianity in particular. Traveling through America and speaking with the children of those who fought the revolution and created a nation, Tocqueville succinctly articulated the feelings of the Founding Americans (the majority of Americans of the era, not just the Founding fathers) when he wrote, "Religion, which never interferes directly in the government of Americans, should therefore be regarded as the first of their political institutions, for, if it does not give them the taste for liberty, it enables them to take unusual advantage of it."³⁹⁷ Therefore, on the one hand we have a separation of church and state while one the other we have the moral force of Christianity and Christian teaching that operates on private conscience. This joint reign made possible American democratic society.

Secular humanists now insist that we not only erase Christianity from the public square for purposes of religious freedom and fairness, but we must do so to avoid overt religious warfare due to the great diversity of beliefs. The humanist rhetoric would have us believe that we are on the verge of religious warfare unless we somehow subdue the pervasive religious sanction of Christianity and place all religious belief on a level plain that is devoid of a voice and influence in the public square. In a 2006 speech before he became President, Barak Obama warned that "...the dangers of sectarianism have never been greater. Whatever we once were, we are no longer a Christian nation; we are a Jewish nation, a Buddhist nation, a Hindu nation, and a nation of nonbelievers."[398] If immigration statistics are an indication of diversity of religious belief and practices, President Obama's and secular humanists' fears of sectarian violence through religious differences are wholly unsupported. The percentage of the U.S. population that was foreign born in the five decades ended in 1900 through 1940 was 12.38%. For the five decades ended 1950 through 1990, the average was 6.24% or about one-half of the previous five decades.[399] The percentage of foreign born population had risen to almost 12% by 2004 and almost 13% by 2006. However, approximately one-third of the foreign born were in the country illegally. Removing the illegal immigrants from the calculations reduces the percentage of foreign born to about 8%, not much above the average for the decades ended 1950 through 1990.[400] The implication of these numbers is that the opportunity for sectarian violence in times of high levels of immigration as in the early decades of the twentieth century would be far greater than was the decades ending from 1950 through 1990. If the threat of violence is a reality due to the increase in percentage of foreign born population similar to that of the early twentieth century, it is because of the huge number of illegal aliens in the country and heightened racial and ethnic sensibilities. We are seeing evidence of that violence bleed across the nation's southern border, but that violence is occurring due to reasons other than religion. Therefore, President Obama's claim that "...the dangers of sectarian violence have never been greater..." are bogus, merely an expression of his secular humanist sentiments, and a ploy to suppress dissent from religious conservatives in America.

America flourished during the immigration melting pot years of the last half of the nineteenth century and the first decades of early twentieth century as people from all faiths and backgrounds arrived at Ellis Island and other ports of disembarkation. The overarching religious sanction of Christianity made this possible. Although the times were often brash and chaotic, the new immigrants built a new life, practiced their religions in freedom, and were absorbed into America society. However, fears of ethnic and religious violence in twenty-first century America are of the secular humanists' own making through the imposition of their philosophies, social engineering, and prescriptions for the modern world. It is through the awarding of imaginary rights, imposition of aberrant definitions of equality and pluralism and the means for achieving such, and the focus on differences that are increasing the racial, religious, and economic divisiveness in the public square, not the presence of Christianity and its moral suasion that preserved and stabilized America through the great waves of immigration a century ago. Not only is the cause of religious and racial divisiveness the result of secular humanism's influence, the humanists' means of addressing this divisiveness is in error. The moral suasion of the Christian faith worked through the individual and family to bring stability and unity to the nation as opposed to enforcement by the state. Yet, the modern secular humanist looks to the hammer of the state to preserve and stabilize America through a myriad of divisive policies, edicts, and laws designed to level society in accordance with humanist theory and practice. The cost of such leveling is a loss of unity, purpose, and vision. There is no center to which the nation may look to gain its bearings or anchor to restrain the ship of state as it is beset by the storm of political and human avarice in the conduct of the nation's affairs.

One of these leveling practices is multiculturalism, a humanist doctrine that came into vogue during the late twentieth century. As humanists see it, morality shouldn't be imposed by religions or legislated by governments. Rather, the alternative is to develop civic and moral virtues in accordance with humanist doctrine by means of moral education.[401] Therefore, the multicultural movement in schools is premised on the belief that America is too immersed in Western "Eurocentric" teachings to the detriment of other cultures. Thus, the education curriculum must be redirected to various counterculture teachings (such as Afrocentrism, humanistically defined feminism, and homosexual teachings and radical doctrines such as neoMarxism) that challenge the "white, male-dominated European studies." A closer examination of the humanist multicultural agenda reveals that multiculturalism is not intended to supplement but rather to supplant Western culture that is so steeped in Christianity. The attack on Western civilization comes through a dismissal of American religious values as they intersected with and made possible the rise of the American political system. Alternatively, multiculturalists promote humanistic philosophers and their adherents such as Rousseau, Hobbes, Nietzsche, Freud, Marx, and Dewey, most of whom had little to nothing to do with American liberty.[402]

      Multiculturalism has been called a suicidal ideology, and examples in modern society permeate American intellectual and educational institutions. To see America's multicultural future, one must look only to other Western nations that have traveled farther along the secular humanist road. A British school teacher in Sudan was arrested, tried, and imprisoned while angry Muslim mobs demanded the death penalty. Her crime was accepting the vote of her class to name a teddy bear Mohammed and thereby insulting the prophet. What was the typical multicultural reaction in her home country? Some branded her as being insensitive to the Sudanese culture. The machinations of political correctness demanded by multiculturalism occasionally cause problems for its humanist adherents. In the case of the British school teacher, the National Organization of Women refused to take a stand on her situation. In another example, the humanists' championing of freedom of expression yields to self-censorship in deference to Muslim sensibilities. While creating an obscene depiction of the Virgin Mary in "Transvestite Brides of Christ", the artist does not touch Islam for "…fear that someone will slit my throat" but Christians won't do that and remain fair game for the artist.[403] The artist's fears are well founded. Dutch filmmaker Theo van Gogh was murdered by a Muslim in 2004 for being critical of Islam. An outspoken critic of Islam, Geert Wilders is a Dutch politician and member of the Freedom party who has been tried by the Netherlands Supreme Court for derogatory comments about Islam, banned from travel to England by the British government for allegedly violating laws against inciting religious hatred (overturned), and in the United States faced attempts to block his speeches at two universities. He has received numerous death threats and lives under police protection.[404] Other signs of departure from blind multiculturalism have arisen. Swiss voters approved a ban on the erection of Muslim minarets or mosque towers. The constitutional amendment garnered a fifty-eight percent approval. Supporters of the ban claimed the minaret as "…a sign of political power and demand" and quoted Turkish Prime Minister Recept Tayyip Erdogan who "…compared mosques to Islam's military barracks and called 'the minarets our bayonets'."[405] In America, the State of Maine has taken the opposite track when it fined the Christian Action Network for allegedly sending mailings that contained an "inflammatory anti-Muslim message." The mailing was a fundraising effort that opposed the adoption in Maine of California school curriculum "…that asked students to dress up as Muslims, chant 'Praise to Allah' and learn the five pillars of Islam."[406]

The essence of multiculturalism has its roots in the denial of absolutes, one of the cardinal doctrines of humanism, which translates into a moral relativism. Such a values free approach, according to the humanists, makes it impossible to judge one period or era in relation to another or to say that one culture's ethic is superior to another. Therefore, we must agree that all belief systems are "…coexisting and equally valid." Thus, multiculturalism is merely a subset of the larger humanistic doctrine of cultural relativism and its corollary, Tolerance. In the humanistic worldview, cultural relativism requires a suspension of judgment since all belief systems contain some truth within while no one belief system has all the truth. The humanists' prescription for providing order in such a worldview is toleration, and through toleration comes liberty.[407] According to the humanists, if one accepts a worldview that certain religions that rely on absolutes, such as Christianity, are superior to others in answering the basic questions of life and providing a means to effectively order one's life, then such religions are opposed to liberty and therefore freedom. From these false assumptions, humanists present religion, especially Christianity, as being anti-liberty, repressive, oppressive, antiquated, narrow, arbitrary, bigoted, and intolerant. Pluralism in modern America, as defined by humanists, must presuppose that there are no universals, i.e., no God.

In *The Reason for God*, Timothy Keller gives an excellent answer to humanists' contention as Christianity is a cultural straitjacket that "...forces people from diverse cultures into a single iron mold." Keller states that Christianity far exceeds secularism and many other worldviews in adaptation to diverse cultures. The demographic centers of Islam, Buddhism, Confucianism, and Hinduism all remain in their places of origin. However, Christianity has spread successively from first century domination by the Jews, to the Hellenist Mediterranean, to the barbarians of Northern Europe which evolved into Western Christendom and transference to North America. Yet, Christianity in the twenty-first century is no longer a Western religion for most Christians now live in Latin America, Asia, and Africa. The African continent has grown from a Christian population of nine percent in 1900 to forty-four percent in the first decade of the twenty-first century. The growth in percentage of Africa's Christian population (an increase of thirty-five percent) in one hundred years will be far eclipsed in rapidity by the projection that China's Christian population will grow from a tiny group to thirty percent of its population over the next thirty years.[408]

Why has the growth of the Christian worldview been so successful given that it is supposedly forcing various groups into a cultural straitjacket? The short answer is that Christianity is the truth and therefore provides the answers to life's basic questions and is a worldview that gives order to one's soul. Christians understand that God created all peoples, but those people have developed different cultures and worldviews. But long before the proffering of theories by humanistic philosophers as to man's origin, the Judeo-Christian ethic recognized the common origin of man as described in Genesis of the Old Testament and in the New Testament when Paul spoke to the assembled Athenians of the God of the Hebrews that "...made of one blood all nations of men for to dwell on the face of the earth..."[409] For those who say Christianity forces various cultures and groups into cultural straitjackets ignores the weight of history.

Toleration, cultural relativism's corollary, is much touted by secular humanists, and it is one of Kurtz's supports for humanists' belief in democracy. He states that honest men may and often do disagree, and basic to the idea of freedom is tolerance. Kurtz follows with a claim that no man or group can claim to be infallible with regard to truth and virtue and that "...truth is often the product of the free give and take of conflicting opinions." In other words, truth is a product, i.e., it can be manufactured. That is the humanist stance and a reflection of moral relativism and the antithesis of the beliefs of Christianity and many other religions. Kurtz believes that "...it is a serious mistake to root Western forms of political democracy and the ideals of liberty that it expresses on any religious grounds or to insist that we do so." Yet, he admonishes the believer and nonbeliever, theist and secularist alike, to work cooperatively in defending America against those who would destroy it.[410] Evidence of such a cooperative spirit is strikingly absent among secular humanists when it comes to their almost universal denigration of Christianity in American government, educational institutions, secular media, and cultural life.

Richard Weaver, in his brilliant analysis of culture, describes how it develops, how it operates, and what it must do to survive. Culture is a product of the collective consciousness of a group seeing certain felt needs, "...a complex of values polarized by an image or idea." The group's dissatisfactions with the way things are results in an ordering process, a way of looking at the world as it should be. The very foundation of the cultural concept is unity that presupposes a general commonality of thought and action. As a culture is formed and begins ordering its world to bring the satisfactions for which it was created, directions must be imposed on its members. These directions, limits, and required behaviors radiate through a center of authority with a subtle and pervasive pressure to conform. This pressure may range from cultural peer pressure to moral and legal restraints. Those that do not conform are repelled of necessity. Thus, in any culture there are patterns of inclusion and exclusion. Without such patterns, the culture is unprotected and disintegrates over time. Every culture has a center which commands all things. Weaver calls this center imaginative rather than logical and "...a focus of value, a law of relationships, an inspiring vision...to which the group is oriented." The intrinsic nature of culture compels that it be exclusive rather than all inclusive, a concept of almost heretical proportions for the secular humanist. Cultures fail and disintegrate without the power to reject that which does not adhere to its central force. As noted in the previous chapter, cultures also fail over time if they adopt worldviews that are inadequate to answer life's basic questions.[411]

Just as there is a dynamic tension between freedom and the organizational strictures required by culture, there is also a tension between tolerance and exclusivity demanded by culture. Tolerance suggests acceptance and inclusiveness while exclusivity implies segregation and denial. By segregation is not meant segregation *within* a culture but *between* cultures. On the contrary, the culture that values its central vision welcomes integration of diverse groups that share that common central vision. It becomes a stronger culture. It is in the humanistic definition of pluralism that cultures are prone to failure. By its very essence, culture must discriminate against those outside its boundaries that do not share its central vision. A culture must believe in its uniqueness, worth, and the superiority of its worldview. To attempt to meld together or comingle multiple cultures into one culture with multiple centers of vision is to create a powerless culture with little influence and place it on the road to disintegration. By definition, culture must be an inward-looking vision and resist the alien. Without such is a loss of wholeness, and culture's cohesiveness dissolves into chaos as its various parts drift into orbits of parochial interests and egocentrism.[412]

When one talks of culture and the erosion of its central vision, it is easy to assume those changes occur only over time moving at glacial speed and do not affect society immediately. However, the secular humanists' purging of Christianity from American culture has gained great momentum, and their efforts are filtering down rapidly to what one might call street level. An example of such a street level purge of Christianity from secular society involves the Christian Legal Society (CLS) at the University of California's Hastings Law School. The school denied recognition of the group (and university resources provided to recognized groups such as meeting space, student email network, and student activity fund) due to CLS's requirement that voting members and leaders sign a statement of basic Christian commitments. These commitments included a requirement that members live by Christian standards and not engage in sexual immorality which included homosexuality. The university argued CLS's requirement was discriminatory as it was based on sexual orientation. University policy requires all that clubs accept anyone into membership. The university prevailed in a lawsuit brought by CLS, and the Ninth Circuit Court of Appeals upheld the ruling.[413] In a 5-4 decision, the Supreme Court upheld Hastings Law School's requirement that CLS must effectively open its leadership positions to all students, including those students who disagree with the group's fundamental beliefs and statement of faith.[414] The CLS case is a symptom of a larger erosion of the central vision of American culture and the consequent loss of wholeness and cohesiveness that will lead to disintegration.

There must be a point at which a pluralistic society suspends tolerance and act in opposition to a rival culture. That point is reached and pluralism defended when a rival culture attributes immanence to its forms, i.e., attempts to replace the pre-existing pluralistic society's central vision.[415] Even humanists such as Kurtz recognize the dangers of unlimited tolerance and contend that tolerance is not applicable to all actions. He states that, "...we are tolerant of beliefs and the expression of beliefs, of thought and conscience, and speech. But where belief or speech translates into action a civilized society has the right to regulate conduct and to enact legislation to protect the public good...The principle of tolerance...is not an absolute." He highlights two areas in which he sees the need for society to limit tolerance through regulation and legislation: individual liberty and multiculturalism.[416]

With regard to tolerance and individual liberty, Kurtz believes that those things that ought not to be regulated by society are those things that concern the individual alone. Public sphere issues that can be regulated include guarding individuals from violence, public health, education, taxation to supply public services, and transportation. Areas of private concern which are not subject to regulation and legislation include "...inner thoughts and conscience, religious belief or unbelief, control over one's own body, sexual preference between consenting adults, abortion, reproductive freedom, euthanasia, the right to die with dignity, artistic expression, and so on." As one can readily see from this laundry list, these are the flashpoints of disagreement in the battle between those of the Judeo-Christian ethic and secular humanists that occur daily in legislative bodies, the judiciary, and in broader society. Basic to these disagreements is the determination of what constitutes private action versus action that, although private, has adverse consequences to the public good. One example given in an earlier chapter regarded the recreational use drugs, a private action with public consequences. This determination of what constitutes a private action cannot be answered by logic. The answer will be decided by the dominant worldview in American society. As we have shown, the central vision is image that is the anchor or central picture of American culture that commands society. Kurtz recognizes that freedom is not enough and that genuine moral freedom requires moral education of the young to "...cultivate the best within the young, to guide them so they are morally compassionate and empathetic, and have developed some sort of reflective moral wisdom." So we are back to an argument as to whose morals are best. Kurtz believes that humanists must "...defend moral excellence, nobility, and qualitative standards but not through the regulation of conduct by church or state." Rather, the humanists believe that the development of civic and moral virtues is achieved by means of moral education.[417] Kurtz's stance is disingenuous in that moral education as discussed throughout this book was the derivative of the Judeo-Christian ethic in America from the arrival of the first Europeans to the twentieth century. Kurtz would counter that "moral" means those definitions as dictated by secular humanism. However, as previously stated, it was the moral suasion of Christianity that made possible the founding and survival of the United States.

    The proponent of the Judeo-Christian ethic as the central force or vision for America claims that the moral basis for its worldview rests on a host of intelligible sources such as the permanent things, the universal truths perceived by mankind, the revelation of God to the Hebrews and the world, and the impact of Christ and the apostles—the sum total of man's experiences, both negative and positive, passed down from generation to generation since time immemorial. When the secular humanists talk of "moral excellence, nobility, and qualitative standards", upon what are such based? How can one claim those moral values when it embraces moral relativism? If all morals are relativistic, by what authority do humanists pronounce certain ideas and values worthy of achievement? Most modern humanists have abandoned the doctrinaire defense of subjectivism and relativism regarding humanists' moral claims due to the inconsistency of many of their moral claims. In its place are moralistic and non-relativistic pronouncements that the rights of others are the principle moral constraints upon action. However, one must ask again, from whence do these rights flow? What is the source of the moral wrongness in violating the rights of others? Christian teaching speaks unerringly in defense of the concept of universal human rights and why each is obligated to respect the rights of others.[418] However, humanists believe that because we are social animals morality results from our innate altruism, a moral instinct of selflessness although not equally developed in all humans. The origin of man's morality evolved from his ability to connect value or benefit with behaving well toward others. Human need resulted in a moral code, and "…codes of behavior in society come from our social agreements, our social construct of morals that benefit us all."[419] One must ask which worldview identifies the correct condition of man. Is the evolved innate goodness of mankind evident in the world or is the Christian view of fallen man searching for redemption more descriptive of the human condition? The overwhelming weight of evidence from history supports the Christian worldview.

Kurtz's second limit on tolerance regards multiculturalism. In this regard Kurtz would limit the efforts to undermine university curricula in Western civilization. Although Kurtz believes that students should be exposed to a wide range of cultures and their values, he does not think all values are equal. He defends the "…values of the scientific, rationalist, and democratic outlook implicit in Western civilization…" and disagrees that "…all ethnic outlooks and values ought to be equally expressed and/or supported." Conflict flares when all ethnic differences are tolerated equally, and he believes that ethnicity has reached the stage of being reactionary, oppressive, and divisive. The humanist solution is to recognize that a new planetary society is emerging which goes beyond "chauvinistic ethnicity" to an inclusive ethnicity that recognizes its membership in the world community. This conversion occurs through recognition that states must be secular in nature, that there are concepts and methodologies that transcend individual cultural boundaries, and that an essential part of the new world morality requires adherence to humanist values beginning "…with a recognition of universal human rights" with Kurtz's caution that universal human rights are not to be found in the Bible or Koran. Kurtz also cautions against destroying diversity while at the same time praising as the highest good intermarriage between people of different ethnicities, races, religions, and cultures and thereby "…contributing to the new human species that is emerging on this planet."[420] So what happens to diversity and multiculturalism when the world has a new human species and one humanistic culture? It would appear that the cultural strait jacket supposedly promoted by Christianity and other religions is in reality of humanist "one size fits all" construction and designed for the new human species.

In America the imaginative center of culture was overarched by the religious sanction of Christianity which was of critical importance in the founding and survival of the United States. It was the veil of the Judeo-Christian ethic that both covered and defined the common civilization in America up to the twentieth century. Only in the twentieth century did the secular humanists successfully (the permanency of which is yet to be determined) rip this veil from its masts, this fabric of common civilization covering the public square, and led us into a sterile, hopeless desert where mankind wanders aimlessly and endlessly in search of answers to life's basic questions. These answers (humanistic ideologies, theories, inventions, and solutions—all without God) appear shimmering with promise in the distance but evaporate as does a mirage when embraced.

We have talked of multiculturalism, moral relativism, and tolerance. These concepts intersect with larger issues such democracy, freedom, equality, and justice that will be addressed in a later chapter.

In summary, history reveals that chaos eventually occurs within any society that lacks an overarching worldview that gives order to the soul as well as society. The principles upon which the nation was founded flowed from Christianity and brought order to American society. To drive out Christianity along with all other religions and put in their place humanism, whether a religion or philosophy, is to cause monumental disorder to the soul and American society.

Chapter 14

Government – "...America is not a Christian nation"*

On April 6, 2009, a joint press conference was held at the Cankaya Palace in Ankara, Turkey by President Barack Obama and President Gul of Turkey. In that press conference, President Obama made certain comments that caused a considerable amount of controversy and debate in the United States. During the press conference, Obama stated:

> I think that there – where there's the most promise of building stronger U.S.-Turkish relations is in the recognition that Turkey and the United States can build a model partnership in which a predominantly Muslim nation, a Western nation and a nation that straddles two continents—that we can create a modern international community that is respectful, that is secure, that is prosperous; that there are not tensions, inevitable tensions, between cultures, which I think is extraordinarily important.
>
> That's something that's very important to me. And I've said before that one of the great strengths of the United States is—*although as I mentioned, we have a very large Christian population, we do not consider ourselves a Christian nation or a Jewish nation or a Muslim nation; we consider ourselves a nation of citizens who are bound by ideals and a set of values.* (emphasis added)

---

* From President Barak Obama's comments at a news conference in Ankara, Turkey, April 6, 2009.

I think Turkey was—modern Turkey was founded with a similar set of principles, and yet what *we're seeing is in both countries that promise of a secular country* that is respectful of religious freedom, respectful of the rule of law, respectful of freedom, upholding these values and being willing to stand up for them in the international state. (emphasis added) If we are joined together in delivering that message, East and West, to—to the world, then I think that we can have an extraordinary impact. And I'm very much looking forward to that partnership in the days to come.[421]

Many have risen to defend President Obama's remarks. Some have said that he was making a broader point about the ecumenical nature of his country. Whatever President Obama's intent or motives, his ecumenicalism, if that is what it was intended to be, undermines those ideals and values that he says binds us as a nation. If Judeo-Christian ideals and values are not the ones by which we are bound, what are those ideals and values? In fact, his statements continue the growing denigration of the truth of and respect for the tenets of faith upon which this nation was founded. The United States is a nation founded upon the Judeo-Christian beliefs. We are a nation whose majority professes Christianity. And, in spite of President Obama's assertion, the majority of Americans *believe* that we are a Christian nation.[422] Although a Christian nation, we are a nation that respects the freedom of every individual to worship or not worship as he or she sees fit and guaranteed that freedom in the First Amendment to the Constitution. It is disingenuous to claim that those opposed to his statement are attempting to impose Christianity on the citizens of the United States as so many political pundits and defenders of President Obama have said or implied.

If President Obama believes the United States is not a Christian nation (or not "just" a Christian nation as some defenders attempt to mitigate), then what are we? A much more revealing statement was overlooked by those debating both sides of the President's comments at the Turkish news conference. He stated that, "…we're seeing in both countries that promise of a secular country…" In light of his statement, it is interesting to look at the meaning of the words "secular" and "secularism." The various meanings are illuminating: relating to the worldly or temporal, not overly or specifically religious, not bound by monastic vows or rules, and exclusion of religion and religious considerations.[423] Is that the promise of a secular country—to exclude religion and religious considerations and to be not bound by monastic vows or rules? The secularist would give a quick affirmative answer followed by an admonition that the Founders did not believe in the establishment of a state religion, and therefore, we are not a Christian nation. The politician's response is to explain and mollify.

President Obama could be excused for a slip of the tongue if that was the case, but the Turkish news conference was not the first time he made the statement that America was not a Christian nation. Therefore we must look deeper to determine President Obama's vision for a secular America. In a 2006 speech entitled "Our Future and Vision for America", we catch a glimpse of this vision. Although stating that, "Our law is by definition a codification of morality, much of it grounded in the Judeo-Christian tradition," President Obama undermined this foundation when he said:

> Democracy demands that the religiously motivated translate their concerns into universal, rather than religion-specific, values….I cannot simply point to the teachings of my church or evoke God's will. I have to explain why abortion violates some principle that is accessible to people of all faiths, including those with no faith at all.
>
> Now this is going to be difficult for some who believe in the inerrancy of the Bible, as many evangelicals do. But in a *pluralistic* democracy, we have no choice. Politics depends on our ability to persuade each other of common aims based on a common reality. It involves the compromise. At some fundamental level, religion does not allow for compromise. It's the art of the impossible. If God has spoken, then followers are expected to live up to God's edicts, regardless of the consequences. *To base one's life on such uncompromising commitments may be sublime, but to base our policy making on such commitments would be a dangerous thing…*[424] (emphasis added)

From these statements we see the humanist vision bleed through his protestations of faith and common ground with people of faith. And such statements leave President Obama in an unsupportable position. When he says that "...the religiously motivated must translate their concerns into universal, rather than religion-specific, values," he is at odds with the Judeo-Christian ethic upon which the republic was founded. What are these universal values and from whence do they come? In reality, President Obama's democracy, that demands the religiously motivated subordinate their concerns to universal values, effectively establishes a worldview that transcends all other beliefs—and that belief is humanism. The pragmatic President Obama states we must *not* base our policy making upon uncompromising commitments. Therefore, following his dictum, we must conduct our political enterprises as though nothing is sacred, unchanging, and true. Every facet of every policy and decision is open for debate and negotiation. However, our Founders and millions since our founding have risked their lives and fortunes to maintain certain values and immutable laws that cannot be compromised and upon which our republic was founded. To the humanist these principles are available to be placed on a table as chips for bargaining in the game of politics and expediency. Are there principles that are right, true, noble, and permanent that won't be abandoned in pursuit of policy making? Apparently, President Obama thinks not.

It is true that the Founders did not permit the founding of a state religion. However, humanists have gone far beyond the intent of the Founders in their efforts to ban all religion and religious expression from the public arena. A favorite tool used is to parrot Thomas Jefferson's "wall of separation between church and state" contained in a letter to the Danbury Baptist Association[*] on January 1,

---

[*] The purpose of Jefferson's remarks was to assure the Baptist group that the government would not establish any denomination as the national denomination. Jefferson had borrowed the phrase from Roger Williams, the Baptist's own prominent minister. Williams' wall was to be one way and meant to protect the Church from the government and not the government from the Church. This understanding was evident in a number of Jefferson's addresses and correspondence over the next several years. Jefferson's famous words resurfaced in Reynolds v. United States, 1878, seventy-six years after the Danbury speech. A lengthy excerpt from Jefferson's speech

1802.[425] Yet, it was only two days after Jefferson wrote the Danbury Baptists that he attended one of the church services in the Capitol Building.[426] This wall in the form of the First Amendment states that, "...Congress shall make no law respecting the establishment of religion, or prohibiting the free exercise thereof..." However, the Founders were very explicit in their words and deeds in demonstrating that religion was to play an important and central role in the public affairs of the nation. The First Amendment prohibition dealt with the establishment of a *preferred* religion, a state sponsored religion if you will. It also prohibited the meddling of the federal government into the free exercise thereof.

In their efforts to drive any form of religion or religious expression from government, education, and the halls of business and commerce, the secular humanists have become somewhat akin to a few eminent paleontologists and archeologists who find an ancient bone or tooth and construct a whole species from the artifact. Subsequently, the scientists are embarrassed by the discovery that the hallowed object was merely a swine's tooth or the lower jaw of an orangutan fitted to the upper portion of a human skull. For secularists, Jefferson's "wall of separation", has become that bone upon which all manner of jurisprudence, legislative action, and executive or bureaucratic fiat have been constructed to repair society and (to paraphrase one forgotten writer) keep the hordes of rabid Baptists,

---

was used in the case in which the Mormons claimed that the First Amendment prohibited laws that would prohibit them from the "religious exercise of polygamy." However, while reiterating that the government was prohibited from interfering with opinions on religion between one denomination and another, the government was still responsible for enforcement of "...civil laws according to Christian standards." Effectively, the court was saying that separation of church and state applied to matters between denominations, but *not* to exercise of Christian principles. In this case, polygamy was a violation of Christian principles. Jefferson's speech was used in its *full context* in the 1878 case, but this would not occur in the 1947 Everson case in which the words "a wall of separation between church and state" were extracted and used *out of context* to announce the court's new meaning of separation of church and state. From this point forward, the removal of Christianity from public affairs accelerated with successful challenges to a number of state laws dealing with religious practices in the public arena. [David Barton, *The Myth of Separation*, (Aledo, Texas: WallBuilder Press, 1989), pp. 41-44.]

Presbyterians, and Methodists from roaming the streets in search of hapless victims upon whom they force to listen as they read the New Testament.

A careful and contextual examination of Jefferson's "wall of separation" in relation to the Founders' beliefs, the Founding documents, the Founders' writings, and their governing of the new republic will reveal a startlingly different picture of the Founders' intent with regard to separation of church and state. This picture is contrary to that which secularists would have us believe. Libraries full of books are available to prove the point. In response to President Obama's press conference statements in Turkey, the U.S. House of Representatives approved a strongly worded House Resolution affirming the rich spiritual and religious history of our nation's founding and subsequent history.[427]

Supreme Court Justice William O. Douglas wrote the majority opinion for the Supreme Court in the 1952 Zorach case. This opinion gives strong support to the Founders' intent that the nation was founded on religious principles. Justice Douglas, although known for his liberal stance on most issues, wrote:

> We are a religious people whose institutions presuppose a Supreme Being. We guarantee the freedom to worship as one chooses. We make room for as wide a variety of beliefs and creeds as the spiritual needs of man deem necessary. We sponsor an attitude on the part of government that shows no partiality to any one group and that lets each flourish according to the zeal of its adherents and the appeal of its dogma...To hold that government may not encourage religious instruction would be to find in the Constitution a requirement that the government show a callous indifference to religious groups. That would be preferring those who believe in no religion over those who do believe...We find no constitutional requirement which makes it necessary for government to be hostile to religion and to throw its weight against efforts to widen the effective scope of religious influence.

The ferocity of the debate regarding religion's role, and in particular that of Christianity, in both the founding of the United

States and present day America, is well demonstrated by the response to the President's comments in Turkey. Such debates are occurring with greater frequency as the secular humanist proponents of removing any mention of God and religion from government and society in general have intensified their efforts and attacked long-held religious beliefs and traditions of the nation.

As is often the case in the world of electronic sound bites of information, both sides of the debate miss the point or argue from different perspectives. The President's statement that the United States is not a Christian country is a classic example. The defenders of that viewpoint state that the Constitution prohibits the establishment of a religion and, therefore, the United States is not a Christian nation. Those holding opposing views point to the majority of Americans that profess Christianity and believe that America is a Christian nation. In an attempt to prove their respective points of view the opponents look for specific statements by various Founders or by lifting a phrase or statement from the founding documents. These statements may give some light and direction; however, isolated examples will never give the comfort and assurance sought by either side for no one man's words will supply the definitive answer. The decisive answer to our query is found in more than the isolated words and writings of the Founders.

Nelly Custis, George Washington's step-granddaughter and early biographer, wrote a first-hand account of Washington's religious faith.

> He always arose before the sun, and remained in the library until called for breakfast. I never witnessed his private devotions, I never inquired about them. I should have thought it the greatest heresy to doubt his firm belief in Christianity. His life, his writings, prove that he was a Christian. He was not one of those who act or pray "that they may be seen of men." He communed with his God in secret.[428]

Thomas Jefferson is reputed to have said to the Dey of Tunis that the United States is not a Christian nation.[429] Secularists will also point to Jefferson's statement denouncing "…the 'priestcraft' for converting Christianity into 'an engine for enslaving mankind…into a mere contrivance to filch wealth and power to themselves'."[430] Yet,

Jefferson in his own day tired of others proclaiming his hostility towards religion. This was evidenced by his 1802 letter to Dr. Benjamin Rush regarding Jefferson's views on religion which were "...very different from the anti-Christian system imputed to me by those who know nothing of my opinions." Jefferson also said, "God who gave us life gave us liberty. Can the liberties of a nation be secure when we have removed a conviction that these liberties are the gift of God?" These words were reinforced by Jefferson's actions during his lifetime which demonstrated considerable support for a strong religious presence in the public life of the nation. Examples of Jefferson's support of Christianity in the public arena include his permission to use the United States Capitol building for church services, authorization of federal funds to support a Catholic missionary to the Kaskaskia Indian tribe, and his design of the first plan of education for the District of Columbia which used the Bible and a hymnal as its principal texts. Not only did he authorize the use of the Capitol for church services, he attended regularly during both his terms as vice president and president. James Madison also attended the Capitol church services.[431] Madison, reputed to be the author of the Religion Clauses in the First Amendment, apparently was not opposed to a strong religious presence in the public life of the nation and therefore found no wall of separation between church and state as interpreted by modern liberals and progressives.

  Therefore, the better approach to answer the question "Was the United States founded upon Christian principles?" is to look not only at statements of the Founders but also at the complete history of the lives of the Founders, and their actions, words, and deeds as well as the history of the colonies since Jamestown was established in 1607. It is by a distillation of the history of the entire founding era and the generations of colonists before that one can discern the mosaic of the infant United States. Once that examination is accomplished, it becomes overwhelmingly apparent that Christianity and Christian principles and traditions stand at the center of that mosaic. The nation's Founders were in fact heavily reliant on the Hebraic-Christian tradition and principles and wove those principles throughout the Constitution, Amendments to the Constitution, laws, and other founding documents that govern this land. Therefore, as to the question of whether or not the United States was founded on

Christian principles, the weight of evidence is significant and decisive in yielding an affirmative answer.

Once it is agreed that America was founded upon Christian principles, a second question is raised: Are we bound to be governed by those principles? Again, the question must be answered in the affirmative. Can a government ever be established on certain principles and that same government ignore those principles in the everyday business of governing? Without question, such governments will fail if the dichotomy between words and actions is not corrected. The United States is a case in point. The Declaration of Independence states that "...all men are created equal." That principle, for a time, was ignored with regard to slavery in the United States. As repugnant as slavery was to the substantial majority of the Founders, the principle was ignored for almost nine decades until the disconnection between words and reality almost destroyed the country during the Civil War. Thirty years prior to the war, French philosopher and Alexis de Tocqueville, in his *Democracy in America,* wrote:

> Whatever efforts southern Americans make to preserve slavery, they will not succeed forever. Slavery, which is limited to one point on the globe, which is attacked by Christianity as unjust and by political economy as pernicious and which is placed next to democratic freedom and enlightenment of our times, is not an institution which can last. It will end through the actions of the slave or of the master. In either case, great misfortunes are to be expected."[432]

Yet, in fairness, sometimes the words must come before the actions. If the question of slavery had been addressed during the founding of the United States, it is very likely that the quest for independence would have failed. Although a half-step with regard to ending the cancerous institution of slavery in the body of the American republic, it was a step never-the-less that would eventually bring the promised freedom for the enslaved and reaffirm that all men are created equal.

In further answer to our second questions regarding the obligation to govern the nation by adherence to Christian principles, we must also look to the Supreme Court's view. For most of its history, the Court's view was also patently affirmative. A noted case was *Holy Trinity Church v. United States, 1892*. The heart of the case was Holy Trinity's hiring of an English clergyman which was in violation of an 1885 immigration law enacted by Congress. The Supreme Court held that the application of the law was "absurd" (not the law itself) and that the absurdity arose from its application to the letter of the law but which violated the spirit and intent of the law's framers. The Court concluded that "...No purpose of action against religion can be imputed to any legislation, state or national, because this is a religious people...this is a Christian nation."

The first half of the Court's written ruling dealt with the legal issues. The second half was devoted to numerous examples from Columbus down to the Declaration of Independence and included portions forty-four state constitutions that affirm the religious nature and Christian character of the American people.[433] In summing up the Court's decision, Justice Brewer wrote:

> There is no dissonance in these declarations. There is a universal language pervading them all, having one meaning; they affirm and reaffirm that this is a religious nation. These are not individual sayings, declarations of private persons: they are organic utterances; they speak the voice of the entire people...[citing *Updegraph v. The commonwealth*] 'Christianity, general Christianity, is and always has been, a part of the common law...not Christianity with an established church...but Christianity with liberty of conscience to all men.'...[citing a New York Supreme Court ruling, *The People v. Ruggles*] 'The people of this State, in common with the people of this country, profess the general doctrines of Christianity, as the rule of their faith and practice...we are a Christian people, and the morality of the country is deeply engrafted upon Christianity, and not upon the doctrines or worship of those impostors [other religions].'[434]

The affirmative answer to the second question raises a third question: If we are bound to govern by Christian principles, does this violate the establishment of religion clause? The first amendment to the Constitution states: "Congress shall make no law respecting an establishment of religion, or prohibiting the free exercise thereof..."

In answer to our first question we have affirmed that the United States was founded upon Christian principles, and in answer to our second question we have determined that the principles upon which a government was founded must be followed in the actual governing. Therefore, if in answer to our third question we say that governing by Christian principles does violate the establishment of religion clause, then one must ask by what principles we should be governed. The secularist will argue that the principles upon which we govern should be religion neutral as only a secular worldview can provide, i.e., a safe, religion free alternative. However, as Professor George points out, secularism in itself is another worldview that deserves no special place or role in governance. Secularism is its own faith—a faith that denies God or at the least banishes God to remain behind the closed doors of a silent church or in the muzzled confines of one's heart. More importantly, such a society will be highly disordered and miserable in its existence. This certainly cannot be the intent of the Founders. Therefore, we must agree that governing by Christian principles does *not* violate the establishment clause.

To the avowed secularist, the debate will be won or lost in answering the first question. To admit that the weight of the evidence supports that the founding of the United States was based upon Christian principles is to surrender on questions two and three. Such an admission will not be forthcoming. Therefore the battle will continue.

The secularists, as opposed to their embarrassed paleontologist and archeologist counterparts, know no embarrassment at the error of their ways because their words and concepts have come to mean whatever they want them to mean. They continue to pursue their secularist agenda by dent of volume (say it loudly and continuously) mixed with conviction and a measure of righteous indignation, and soon the masses ignorant of our nation's history will believe America was born a secular nation, and that the public square should be devoid of any religion, particularly the Christian religion. Aleksandr Solzhenitsyn's belief that in the twentieth century men have forgotten God may be inaccurate as it relates to America. For it seems that many of our current government and business leaders, scientists, and cultural elite have chosen to bury God while worshiping at the shrine of secularism and humanism. The remaining majority of our nation, having not the benefit of truthful teaching for two or three generations, has never learned of the influence of Judeo-Christian tradition on our founding. One cannot forget what one has not known. Whether by worshiping the false god of secular humanism or whether by ignorance, the removal of God from America cannot be blamed on loss of memory.

America cannot exclude religion and religious considerations from government and at the same time, as President Obama says, be "...respectful of religious freedom, respectful of the rule of law, respectful of freedom, upholding these values and being willing to stand up for them in the international state." Quite the contrary, a secular humanist society is the breeding ground for divisiveness and tribalism. No overtly secular society in history has been successful in maintaining religious freedom over the long term. The recent immigration of large numbers of those of the Muslim faith into secular Europe and the resulting tensions have dramatically affirmed this fact. The secular humanist will point to many secular nations that have religious elements. Even Communist countries tolerate certain religious entities. But these entities have little to no freedoms, and all will feel the crushing boot of the commissar if their religious values and practices conflict with the policies, laws, or whims of the state. The crushing boots of the secular humanist commissars are rapidly becoming more evident in America.

Unlike our Founders and most of our leaders since then, it is apparent that President Obama sees our promise in being a secular nation and, more specifically, a secular nation that is not a Christian nation. Again, the important distinction is that the United States is not a nation that attempts to impose Christianity on all of its citizens (even though we may be a Christian nation by heritage, belief, and numbers), but rather it is a nation founded upon on Judeo-Christian principles that should be adhered to in the governing of the nation.

To paraphrase President Obama, to base one's life on God directed commitments is a dangerous thing when making policy. That is the fundamental flaw in the President's reasoning—a secular humanist society's requirement that man place adherence to man's law above adherence to God's law. On the contrary, all of a society's laws must be subject to the authority of a higher law. This was the belief of our Founders, and this belief is evident in their actions, words, writings, and documents that define us as a nation. The Founders' beliefs agreed with those of William Blackstone, the eminent English jurist of the eighteenth-century, when he wrote, "This law of nature...directed by God Himself...is binding in all the globe, in all countries, and at all times: no human laws are of any validity, if contrary to this; and such of them as are valid derive all their force and all their authority, mediately or immediately, from this original."[435] Upon the authority of this higher law was this nation founded. Statements to the contrary are made through ignorance, heresy, or political expediency.

Chapter 15

Government – Liberalism and Progressivism in America

If we are to understand the origins of the pervasive humanism and secularization that blankets modern America, particularly as it affects government, we must examine the origins and rise of liberalism. The political legacy of the Enlightenment was liberalism and its concepts of freedom to which it would adhere. Such freedom was more practical than idealistic. This freedom proposed that man should be happy on this earth, a new concept invented in the eighteenth century.[436] Out of the Enlightenment came the attack on the Church and eventually religion itself. The difference between liberalism spawned by the Enlightenment and the Judeo-Christian ethic revolves around a disagreement on the end purpose of man. As Paris Reidhead has stated, "Christianity says, 'The end of all being is the glory of God.' Humanism says, 'The end of all being is the happiness of man'."[437]

Liberalism as we know it came of age in the nineteenth century. The Enlightenment was a skeptical and revolutionary cultural tradition that emanated from eighteenth century Western Europe and "…promoted the belief that critical and autonomous human reason held the power to discover the truth about life and the world, and to progressively liberate humanity from the ignorance and injustices of the past." The two European philosophers that had the greatest impact in the movement to secularize America were Auguste Comte, a Frenchman (1798-1857) and Herbert Spencer (1820-1903), an Englishman. Their philosophies contained a common thread that limited human knowledge to the phenomenal or physical world in order to provide a purely naturalistic understanding of the way things were. In their denial of the supernatural, they directly attacked the intellectual legitimacy of Christianity. As the powerful moral forces of Enlightenment liberalism rolled across the Atlantic from Western Europe, the Protestant establishment and the nation experienced significant inroads of secularization between 1870 and 1930. From that developed a tenuous compromise between evangelical Protestant Christianity and Enlightenment liberalism. The American Christian church, already divided by denomination, region, race, ethnicity, and class, would split again into fundamentalists and modernists between the late nineteenth century and the mid-1920s. Amid the rising skepticism, positivism, and Darwinism emanating from Enlightenment liberalism, the new liberal and modernists Protestant leaders chose survival through accommodation with the adversary and their doctrines of Science, Progress, Reason, and Liberation. But this compromise would only forestall the approaching "…final dominance of Enlightenment moral order in the public square and the relegation of Christian and other religious concerns to private life" that has gained increasing momentum since the 1930s.[438]

Modern concepts of liberalism fit well with Enlightenment ideas of progress, rationality, secularism, and the denigration of the divine, the eternal, and the afterlife. For the liberal the senses rule, and this world is all that counts. The inculcation of liberalism in the institutions of American society including much of the church is almost universal and a testimony to the power of that philosophical and political legacy. However, we must distinguish between the liberalism of the founding of the United States and the creation of its Constitution and that of contemporary liberalism. In the manner with which liberalism was associated with the founding, such liberalism was based on beliefs in "…religious freedom, political equality, constitutional democracy, the rule of law, limited government, private property, the market economy, and human rights." However, contemporary liberals champion vast government-run programs involving health, education, and welfare; affirmative action programs for minorities and women; prohibition of discrimination based on sexual orientation; legalization of same-sex marriages, legalized abortion and government funding of abortion for women with inadequate financial means, and opposition to the death penalty. In summary, the platform upon which the contemporary liberal stands rests on two supports. The first support is an activist government that proactively identifies real or perceived economic or social injustice and designs and implements programs to attack the various forms of injustice. The second support of contemporary liberalism is the advancement of a "personal liberationist's" agenda that rejects traditional norms of morality (generally dealing with sexuality, life, and death) and laws that enforce or promote those traditional norms.[439] As can be seen in the daily newspaper or on the evening news broadcasts, these are the flash points in the war of worldviews in the United States. Unlike the overarching moral suasion of Christianity and Christian principles under which our nation was founded and made possible religious freedom for all faiths, the thrust of modern liberalism is coercive at the least and provocatively repressive of religious freedom in the broader sense.

The litany of liberal values often includes an exaltation of the individual through phrases such as the dignity of the individual, freedom of speech, and equal rights before the law. These are secularized by-products of the Judeo-Christian ethic, but humanists have seized these concepts and defend them by reason alone. However, liberalism's concern for the individual is a fallacy for the liberal's free will is divorced from tradition and religion and consequently is shackled by the power of the state and results in the devaluation of the individual.[440] Can anyone honestly deny the course of a growing humanistic society's march over the last one hundred years with regard to growth of the all-powerful, all-knowing, and ever-present state and the consequent dehumanization of the individual?

Liberalism is an ideology which includes several almost universal postulates. Kirk lists four. One is the affectation of change. The liberal's chant for change is a matter of principle and reflects a doctrinaire hatred for permanence. A second article of faith for the liberal is the exaltation of the individual with a resulting self-centeredness; hence, selfishness becomes virtue. For the liberal, community is secondary to a pervasive individualism where individual, personal rights are supreme. Duty and obligation to clan and community are consigned to the dustbin of a foolish and irrelevant past. Third, liberals envision themselves with a mandate to remake the world by discarding tradition and destroying the foundations upon which such traditions rest. Such a remaking of the world must dispense with constraints of justice and order. Fourth, Kirk lists the liberal's idea of progress in which mankind, with no aid from a supernatural God, is getting better and better. Through enlightened self-interest and private judgment the present is presumed to be far superior to the past, and the future will be better still. One need only compare Corliss Lamont's ten propositions of humanism with the list of liberal postulates to see how nicely the glove of liberalism fits the hand of humanism.[441]

But what is the liberal's answer as change upon change only compounds the lack of rootedness? Change requires movement, but movement doesn't always mean progression. The promises of progress ring hollow in light of rising social disorder. The individual finds no solace in self, only an increasing sense of loneliness and lack of purpose. Self-sufficiency deteriorates as reason fails. As the liberal social architects continually remake the world to fit the current dogma or fix the latest problem, man spirals downward into malaise without God and without hope. Without "…variety, individuality, moral improvement…he [man] is willing to settle for an eternal and equalitarian stability." Failing to deliver the promised utopia, liberals answer with an offer of an insipid security. However, the price for that security is high and entails a rapid "…sinking into an uninspired collectivism, which at best could bring society only a dreary monotony." Kirk called it a loss of manhood.[442]

Liberals attempt to define conservatism as opposites of the concepts and ideologies upon which liberalism rests. But unlike liberalism, conservatism is not an ideology encompassing a sociopolitical program of continuously changing assertions, theories, and aims—a thing invented by the mind of man. Rather, conservatism avows that there exists a transcendent moral order in which man and his society ought to conform. Conservatism upholds social continuity which has produced order, justice, and freedom over many centuries. Conservatism relies on the principle of prescription—adherence to things established by immemorial usage including rights and morals. Social institutions and modes of life long established are preferred over the "…narrowing uniformity and deadening egalitarianism of radical systems." Conservatism recognizes the imperfectability of man and therefore the impossibility of creating a perfect social order.[443] The reader should note that none of these concepts are created by conservatism but rather observed.

Another means to contrast liberalism and humanism with conservatism is to look at truth and time. For the conservative, truth is absolute and therefore timeless, i.e., things of the highest value are not affected by the passage of time. Liberals often decry conservatives for being antiquarian, wanting to live in the past, or wishing to turn back the clock to a time from which mankind really wanted to escape. For the liberal mantra is progress, ever onward and upward to a better society, perhaps even a utopia. Progress implies movement, change, and challenge to the status quo. Yet, as the liberal marches boldly into the future, he has become a prisoner of time, perhaps more precisely a prisoner of the moment. Truth becomes relative. Search for an enduring order fails as one's worldview constantly changes bringing disquiet to the soul and society. Progress, being oriented to time, fails to apprehend those timeless truths that bring order to the soul. Conservatives search for those permanent things, those moorings to which one may cling as the river of time sweeps by toward an unattainable infinity.[444]

The humanistic concept of human perfectibility is known as progressivism and arose during the Age of Enlightenment. Liberals hitched their wagon to the Industrial Revolution of the early eighteenth century for progress was to be achieved through the advance of scientific knowledge and the growth of industry. Progress is the foundational element in support for liberalism and ultimately humanism. "And above all the liberals stood for progress…" Liberal philosophies flowed into the nineteenth century middle class who came "…to identify material and political progress with the course of nature and the hand of Providence…No longer was progress something to be effected by human endeavor; strive as men might, it was inevitable."[445]

In his acceptance speech at the Nobel Peace Prize ceremony in Oslo, Norway, on December 10, 2009, Barak Obama eloquently contrasted the incompatibility of religious Holy Wars with that of peace and faith. He stated that the purpose of faith was that we do unto others as we would have them do unto us, and that this concept was at the heart of all great religions. Most revealing are his beliefs as to the perfectibility of the human condition and his faith in human progress.

> Adhering to this law of love has always been the core struggle of human nature. We are fallible. We make mistakes,

and fall victim to the temptations of pride, and power, and sometimes evil. Even those of us with the best intentions will at times fail to right the wrongs before us….But we do not have to think that human nature is perfect for us to still believe that the *human condition can be perfected*. We do not have to live in an idealized world to still reach for those ideals that will make it a better place. The non-violence practiced by men like Gandhi and King may not have been practical or possible in every circumstance, but the love they preached—*their faith in human progress*—must always be the North Star that guides us on our journey.[446] (emphasis added)

President Obama's statements that although man is fallible, we must reach for those ideals that will make the world a better place are important and consistent with biblical imperatives. However, he erroneously equates King's preachments of love with faith in human progress and ultimately the perfectibility of the human condition. An examination of Dr. King's beliefs, but more importantly an examination of the Bible upon which Dr. King based his beliefs, reflects no such linkage between love and faith in human progress that is supposed to lead to perfectibility of the human condition. The North Star for mankind must be the Creator of the universe who is the foundation of the Judeo-Christian ethic and not illusory human progress or belief that the human condition can be perfected. The distinction between love and faith in human progress may seem trivial or unimportant. However, therein lies a major chasm between humanism and Christianity, and belief in one view or the other significantly impacts one's worldview.

President Obama's assertion that man is fallible but the human condition can be perfected may seem a contradiction and thereby mitigate his position with regard to the fallen nature of man. That is not so. With a closer look at progressivism one sees that progress is a top-down affair—society to individual man. Social engineers and planners adjust and tweak society so that man might improve. Progressivism is a child of humanism and places its faith in mankind's ability to solve his own problems. Those solutions will be achieved through far reaching social programs resting upon a complete social implementation of reason and scientific method.[447]

For progressives such as President Obama, the top-down approach is a progressive's statement of the natural order of things. Ignoring his fallibility, man must be molded by the conditioners of society (as C. S. Lewis called them). These conditioners or controllers will choose their own artificial norms in order to perfect the human race.[448] However, the conservative understands that man must achieve order of the soul before society can achieve order. Individual man must return to a right relationship with God, a state of being rather than becoming, and this right relationship brings order to the soul. As man orders his soul, so too will society achieve order.[449]

Progressivism's notion of infinite progress is a flight from reality. The goal of infinite progress can never be achieved outside of the supernatural. The progressive labors on the treadmill of time, always moving but never arriving at his destination for the goals of infinite progress always recede into the future and therefore are never attainable. In fact, the goals of such progress are not even identifiable apart from the pliable platitudes of the current conditioners of society. For the progressive, time and matter are paramount, but such are temporal and pass away. However, the things of the highest value rest with truth, and without eternal truths man becomes purposeless.[450] "What animates every organism, what constitutes its nature, is *purpose*..."[451] (emphasis in original) Without purpose and fearing annihilation, man stares into the dark night of his soul, raises his fist to the heavens, and cries, "I exist," but, to no avail.

The progressive may even equivocate that although the goal of perfectibility of the human condition will never be attained (something not admitted), the process of self-improvement is still worthwhile and thereby mankind will become better and better. However, an understanding of human nature and history defeats this assertion. Civilization is an intermittent process with some cultures descending "...from a high state of organization to dissolution." History is replete with societies that achieved great stature in past eras only to fall to ruin—Greece, Venice, and Germany to name a few. These and other examples contradict the Whig theory of history which states that the most advanced point in time is the point of its highest development. However, humanism's pillars of reason, material success, and scientific advancement failed to sustain its promise of infinite progress. Those with a conservative or Christian worldview are not unprogressive because they oppose the humanist's progressivism.[452] They do not deny the value of improvement. Conservatives only assert that the source of those improvements must initially and fundamentally flow from God and not man. For those that look to first principles, those universal truths, in ordering their world, they move to the center. They focus on the eternal beyond time—not regressing nor progressing in an ever frustrating march to some unknown, unknowable, and unattainable destination.

We began this chapter with the liberal view of the purpose of man as happiness, the liberal values and attributes ascribed to the individual, and the idea of continuous change that is embedded in the concept of progress. We also examined the progressive's faith in the perfectibility of man. We continue with a discussion of the opposing humanistic and Judeo-Christian concepts of the individual.

Forty years after *Humanist Manifesto I* (1933), a group of men and women developed *Humanist Manifesto II* to present an updated humanist vision to "…serve present-day needs and guide humankind toward the future." The Manifesto's fifth principle dealt with the individual.

> The *preciousness and dignity of the individual person* is a central humanist value. Individuals should be encouraged to realize their own creative talents and desires. We reject all religious, ideological, or moral codes that denigrate the individual, suppress freedom, dull intellect, and dehumanize personality. We believe in a maximum individual autonomy consonant with social responsibility. Although science can account for the cause of behavior, the possibilities of individual *freedom of choice* exist in human life and should be increased. (emphasis in original)[453]

Humanists wax eloquent when talking of the individual, his dignity, his worth, and his freedom to choose. Paul Kurtz wrote that "…the defense of individual freedom thus is an essential condition for social good…Any humanism that does not cherish the individual…is neither humanistic nor humanitarian."[454] However, a close reading of the literature of the leading proponents of humanism reveal a different picture of the individual's dignity, worth, and freedom. Kurtz also wrote:

> Most contemporary humanists have a commitment to some form of the greatest-happiness-for-the-greatest-number principle; they consider that the *highest moral obligation is to humanity as a whole*. This involves the view that since all men are members of the same human family, it is our obligation to further the welfare of mankind.[455] (emphasis added)

Corliss Lamont's writing echoes Kurtz, "To define twentieth century humanism briefly, I would say that it is a philosophy of joyous service for the *greater good of all humanity* in this natural world..." (emphasis added) He follows this with his sixth principle proposition of the humanist philosophy, "...the individual attains the good life by harmoniously combining personal satisfactions and continuous self-development with significant work and other activities that *contribute to the welfare of the community*.[456] (emphasis added)

The humanist's clarion call is for individual freedom. Yet, there appears a fundamental conflict in the statements of humanists with regard to the individual and the larger society, and such conflict cannot be hidden by fuzzy and euphemistic definitions extolling the dignity of the man and the cherishing of the individual. Under the humanist philosophy it is evident that the individual must be subordinate to the good of all humanity, and it is the leaders of the state that determine the definition of what is good. This subordination of the individual is confirmed by terms such as "greater good of all humanity", "obligation to humanity as a whole", and "contribute to the welfare of the community." Ultimately the conditioners of society rule as they see fit and do so without regard to the individual. All reflect a top-down form of viewing and organizing society with the individual being the down portion of the equation. For seven decades Marxist-socialist Russia was a classic example of rulers subordinating the individual for the "welfare of the community."

As to the individual, humanists promise a freedom from the mores, norms, tradition, and distant voices of the past by which humanity has achieved a measure of civilization. The freedom espoused by the humanist is a freedom that gives unbridled control to the self and senses and ultimately leads to bondage. For all of man's time on this earth this personal license has been the path toward disaster. To believe that such personal freedom will lead to the greater good of mankind is folly for man is a fallen creature, and he cannot lift himself by pulling at his own bootstraps.

Humanism remains an ancient pagan concept with man ruling man, whether by kings or dictators of state or the conditioners of the one-world humanist utopia. It was the Judeo-Christian ethic that reduced the power of the state and simultaneously raised the individual. For man is God's creation, but man's specialness lies in his inherent *individual* worth because he was created in God's image, possesses an immortal soul, and journeys on the path of redemption that will lead to an eternal relationship with his creator. Thus, man's allegiance is to God and transcends the bonds of earth and time. We speak no more of mass man but of the human person who God loves. Biblical individualism presented a new limit to earthly powers. Religious, political, and philosophical systems threatened with a loss of power, allegiance, and dominion assault biblical individualism through humanistic doctrines. Christianity is attacked for its "individualism" by humanist philosophers who claim that man's direct link to a divine power isolates him from humanity to his detriment.[457] The humanists' argument ignores the teachings of Christ and the resulting order of one's soul that derives from following Christ. It also ignores history's lessons that lack of order in one's soul translates into a lack of order in society. Contrary to humanist assertions, the order of the individual's soul is the prerequisite of order in society.

The attack on biblical individualism was an attack on man's dignity or worth. Although espousing great reverence for the dignity of the individual, the humanist philosophy speaks to the contrary. Richard Weaver in his *Visions of Order* presented three steps in the progressive demotion of man which are fundamental to the humanist philosophy. First, astronomers in the last half millennium have discovered that the earth is but a mere speck on the fringes of a vast universe. Because the earth is physically "insignificant" in relation to the totality, it is implied that man is also insignificant. As reasoning goes, the creator must have little concern for insignificant man. Nevertheless, Weaver points out the fallacy that importance is based on size or location. Value is imputed by the creator, not his creation, and the value of man is enormous when one considers the cost of his redemption. Darwin's theory of the descent of man was the second means of depreciating the worth of man. No longer the center of creation, he was robbed of his special origins, the divine spark snuffed out, and was now counted among the animal kingdom sharing a common ancestry with other creatures that struggled out of the primeval ooze and late of the anthropoid clan. Weaver briefly points to several difficulties of Darwin's theory of evolution. The question-begging fallacy requires acceptance of the doctrine of naturalism before explanation is offered. Other difficulties include inadequate explanations by evolutionists of the theory of mutation, natural selection, and the mystery of the origin of language. The third assault on biblical individualism occurred when man was robbed of his free will, and his actions are now explained by material causality. He is now brute beast, a slave to animal passions, and those actions can be predicted and explained (or will be at some future point after enough study) by materialistic determinism. Man only reacts to material, physical stimuli the same as might a laboratory rat or Pavlov's dog. Therefore, mechanistic man has no spirit, but this denial runs contrary to the intuitive consensus of all mankind that he does have a free will, and this consensus holds true whether it comes from the most advanced and modern civilization or the most remote pockets of primitive peoples on the planet.[458]

The struggle between humanist and Christian worldviews regarding the status of the individual centers on his freedom. As M. Stanton Evans succinctly wrote, "If we want to find the sources of our freedom, we first need to know what freedom is."[459] In modern times and under the assault of those proposing a "new freedom", the meaning of freedom, like the meaning of the word "love", has attained a loose, ephemeral quality and has attached to it a range of emotions, meanings, and synonyms (e.g., liberty and license). Perhaps a better way of describing freedom is to describe its opposite or what freedom is not. Coerce means to "…restrain or dominate by nullifying individual will, to compel to an act or choice, to enforce by force or threat."[460] Thus, freedom is an absence of restraint or domination of the individual. Freedom operates where the individual is free to act or choose and not subject to force or threat. However, freedom is akin to fire in the sense that unbridled freedom or licentiousness allows irresponsibility and destroys. In other words, one's personal liberty must not become oppression or harm to another. At the other end of the continuum is bondage in which freedom dies. However, man desires order and organizes himself in society to achieve a measure of freedom. To achieve order and therefore make possible a measure of freedom, he must surrender some of his freedom and this surrender involves control of his appetites and passions. Various societies choose different political vehicles by which this freedom is voluntarily limited. However, it is in those societies where the definition of freedom is joined to something else which corrupts the meaning of freedom and thereby pushes that society from freedom to one end or the other of the anarchy-totalitarian continuum. Yet, there are societies and worldviews which operate wonderfully under governing systems that respect the non-coercive definition of freedom. But those societies must also have a compelling central vision by which it operates.

Let us examine the humanist and Christian worldviews as it relates to the definitions given in the previous paragraph. A close reading of the New Testament yields an incontrovertible picture of Christianity as a non-coercive presentation of the gospel of Jesus Christ, and Christ instructs his followers to share the good news through evangelism. But for the secular humanist, this public profession and sharing of Christian faith violates the secularist dogma that religion is a private matter, and consequently Christianity is labeled as a repressive and tyrannical doctrine. Secular humanists wrongly perceive the sharing of the good news of Jesus Christ as being coercive, but such coercion is contrary to the theme of the entire Bible and contrary to the Judeo-Christian doctrine of free will. As has been noted previously, the overarching moral suasion (influence or persuasion) of Christian principles under which our nation was founded made possible religious freedom for all faiths. Such moral suasion of Christian principles is not coercive as humanists would have us believe. The moral suasion of Christian principles provided the nation with a central vision and resulted in stability and unity by working through the individual as he voluntarily chooses the manner in which he orders his soul.

To better understand the differences in the humanist and Judeo-Christian worldviews, we must examine the concepts of order, freedom, equality, and justice as they impact the individual. The need for order in both the individual and society has been examined in an earlier chapter. In the remainder of this chapter we will examine the individual as he relates to the concepts of freedom, equality, and justice. These are not abstract and arcane subjects only for discussion and debate by ivory tower philosophers and sociologists who attempt to dissect, analyze, and interpret for the masses what is already known by the common man and attested by history. The individual and his relation to these concepts are intricately and intimately a part of the jostle of everyday life as the conflict of worldviews plays out in modern society.

In spite of their protestations, humanistic concepts vest the primacy of freedom with the group, not the individual. The importance of the group as opposed to the individual is confirmed by a re-reading of the excerpts from *Humanist Manifesto I* and *II* previously quoted. In the humanist philosophy, freedom is not a state of being but rather something that is created and fastened to the so-called *greater good of all humanity* and thus has become adulterated. Under humanists' assault, freedom has lost its meaning and becomes a tool for the conditioners to mold society by group coercion as opposed to individual choice. The thrust of secular humanism is coercive to individual freedom in the least and forcefully repressive of religious freedom in the broader sense. And the humanist worldview cannot provide a unity that requires a general commonality of thought and action, i.e., the central vision of a culture. Without such unity filtering up from individuals, there can be no order to the soul or society, and without such order society deteriorates over time and eventually disintegrates. America was created and survived not because of force of state but through unity and stability brought about by the influence and persuasion of Christian principles operating on and through the individual.

In support of this last statement, one needs look only to the history of free peoples. Freedom, its concepts and institutions, are of European origin. It is found in the United States, the United Kingdom, and Europe. This freedom has been transplanted to a few other places on the globe—pockets in Africa, the Pacific Rim, and

South America—while the great bulk of the world's population remains locked in the confines of statist, dictatorial, or totalitarian regimes. Evans asked the question as to why freedom is of an almost totally of European origin. The answer revolves around religion in that every culture reflects the influence exerted by its religious precepts. For Western civilization, that meant Christendom. Buddhism, Hinduism, Islam, and Confucianism have been and continue to be associated with societies that deny freedom. For centuries Christianity and the Church were the only universal institutions and supplied the unity to a European society comprised of multiple languages, customs, ethnic groups, and ambitions. Through Christianity came a "common consciousness and sense of cultural and spiritual unity…religion that suffused the whole with a common outlook and gave to Europe its distinctive view of statecraft." Out of this came the foundation and superstructure of free societies in the Western world. The strong association of Christianity with political freedoms and remarkable advancement of Western civilization is an overwhelming denial of the humanists' claims that Christianity is repressive and an enemy of freedom. Rather, "…biblical teaching was the formative influence in the creation of Europe, and…was the nursery of freedom as we know it." Through the influence of Christendom came an elevation of the individual and limits on state compulsion.[461]

Before we leave the subject of freedom, we must address "democracy." Often defined in error as a synonym for freedom, democracy is merely a method of voting. In fact, democracy can be a great threat to freedom. Our Founding Fathers recognized this threat and spent considerable effort to reign in democracy to insure it would not become an "elective despotism."[462]

Democracy is often placed on the shelf next to freedom, liberty, order, and justice as icons to be worshipped. Nevertheless, democracy is not an end but a means and can be fallible and uncertain. F. A. Hayek calls democracy a device for safeguarding internal peace and individual freedom, but when it fails to guarantee individual freedom, democracy may persist in some aberrant form under totalitarian rule. Where democracy is not guided by fixed rules (e.g., the Constitution), it becomes arbitrary. Many mistakenly view democracy as the ultimate source of power, i.e., the will of the majority expressed. But if democracy is the source of power, it can become corrupt and arbitrary. It is the limitation of power that prevents democracy from becoming arbitrary.[463] Rather than a source of power, democracy is a tool to be carefully maintained and used to safeguard internal peace and individual freedom.

Recognizing the utility of "democracy" in furthering their philosophy, humanists have appropriated the term, redefined its meaning, and employed it in precisely the manner warned against by Hayek—as a tool to arbitrarily consolidate power and limit individual freedom with a resulting deterioration of internal peace. For the humanist, democracy has evolved into a thing of vast proportions and meaning. Kurtz imbues it with ethical dimensions in his *Defense of Secular Humanism*. To Kurtz, democracy expresses certain moral principles including a commitment to the principles of liberty and equality, is concerned for the worth and dignity of the individual, recognizes the individual's right to do what he wishes and limits undue interference with his individual choice and action, provides opportunity for growth and personal realization, is tolerant of diversity, and enlarges our discovery and insight. Additionally, Kurtz states that democracy "…is based on the idea of freely given consent…[but] consent is never enough. We should always seek to enlist real participation in the affairs of the state, the sharing of power and responsibility at all levels." Finally, Kurtz ends, "In recognizing that no individual or group may possess all the truth, democracy leaves open the possibilities for the clash of competing views and thrives on heresy and nonconformity."[464] Having been transformed from a tool or form of governing, Kurtz has endowed democracy with moral principles—something of value in and of itself. Many of Kurtz's moral principles of democracy echo much of his humanist philosophy and that of Corliss Lamont. Consequently, according to Kurtz's moral principles of democracy, if one opposes abortion or euthanasia, one opposes democracy in that it is undue interference with individual choice and action. If one believes the Bible is the source of unchanging and God-given truth, one opposes democracy for Kurtz's moral principles of democracy states that no individual or group may possess all the truth.

Likewise, Lamont embroiders democracy with all sorts of embellishments in support of the humanist credo. It is method and a goal; a means and an end. Lamont believes that democracy is more than political machinations and civil liberties and should be broadened to include the "...functioning of nongovernmental agencies and organizations and in extra-political fields such as those of economics, cultural activity, and race relations." To that end he sees ten different types of democracy: political, civil liberties, racial or ethnic, economic, organizational, social, cultural and educational, democracy in religion and philosophy, equality between the sexes, and international democracy. As with Kurtz, Lamont's humanism also "...welcomes differences and disagreements and cherishes, as a creative force in society, minority criticisms of existing customs and prevailing patterns of thought...[and] the constant challenges to basic assumptions."[465]

Humanists have effectively idealized democracy and given it meanings that conforms it to humanist philosophy. Having captured the moral high ground through false definitions, bogus assumptions, and effective promotion regarding humanist ideas of democracy, humanists attack all competing worldviews and in particular Christianity in the humanists' effort to alienate and purge the Judeo-Christian ethic from the institutions of American society. With that accomplished, the humanist conditioners will continue their efforts to transform society into the humanist utopia in which adequate control over human nature will be attained on the way to creating Lamont's "...more advanced species, call it *superhuman* or what you will, that will be as superior to us in brain power as we are to the anthropoid ape."[466] (emphasis in original)

Christianity does not denigrate or minimize the importance of democracy. On the contrary, it was the product of Christendom. But it must be viewed as a means to achieve those values and conditions under which the individual achieves true freedom, not an icon to be worshipped and imbued with false qualities or moral imperatives as humanists would have us believe. At the same time, we must carefully handle fragile democracy to prevent it from becoming the tool of a tyrant majority or state and thereby destroy those purposes and values for which democracy is properly employed.

Equality is another term much abused and misunderstood term in modern America. Since the middle 1960s the civil rights movement charted a new course in which the crusade for racial equality was divorced from racial harmony and brotherhood. From that point forward, racial harmony and brotherhood was left in the dust and is given only infrequent lip service. Fifteen years before the emergence of the civil rights movement of the early 1960s, Richard Weaver wrote of the folly of seeking equality in lieu of the larger ideal of fraternity in his *Ideas Have Consequences*.

> The comity of peoples in groups large or small rests not upon this chimerical notion of equality but upon fraternity, a concept which long antedates it (equality) in history because it (fraternity) goes immeasurably deeper in human sentiment. The ancient feeling of brotherhood carries obligations of which equality knows nothing. It calls for respect and protection, for brotherhood is status in family, and family is by nature hierarchical. It demands patience with little brother, and it may sternly exact duty of big brother. It places people in a network of sentiment, not of rights—that *hortus siccus* (dry garden) of modern vainglory.[467] (emphasis in original)

Weaver's network of sentiment looks toward a central vision that a viable culture must have. The network of sentiment implies feelings toward that central vision resulting in an adherence to the common body of beliefs of the group. Culture must reside on the foundation of fraternity which is other-directed and implies common purpose. Equality is self-directed whereas fraternity is unifying and smoothes the way in preservation of culture. Unsentimental equality is fragmentary and divisive in its futile attempts at a mechanistic leveling of the elements of culture and leads to disintegration.

The usual defense of the pursuit of the humanist ideal of equality is that social harmony will be achieved because the nation is moving closer to the ideals upon which it was founded. However, such pursuit has the opposite effect. The pursuit of equality has resulted in the identification of an ever expanding array of social problems demanding governmental attention. Such attention is demanded because of the creation of "illusory rights" supposedly on par with the original Bill of Rights. Samuelson points out that these so-called rights involve social problems that deny equal outcomes whereas the Bill of Rights as enumerated by the founders belongs to almost everyone on comparable terms. The many new "synthetic" rights do not belong to everyone. In the quest for equality, these new rights must be addressed by a redistribution of social, political, and economic power that not only raises some but pushes others down. According to Samuelson the quest for ever greater equality fails as the result of two problems. The first is a problem of magnitude. Government cannot fix everything due to limited resources. Also, the mere intervention of government often results in unintended consequences that cause even greater social problems than the one upon which it was called to remedy. One example is the overdependence on welfare that results in an intergenerational institutionalization of poverty. A second reason for the failure in the push for equality is public opinion. Americans favor equality and fairness, and they also believe in assistance to the less fortunate. However, the relentless quest to level society requires the extension of preferential treatment to various aggrieved groups. Americans see this preferential treatment of certain groups as unfairly impinging on other individuals. It is the awarding of such preferential treatment that Americans find disquieting and somehow contrary to tenets upon which the nation was founded. As more and more synthetic rights are discovered/awarded and government attempts to redress the perceived violation of those rights, the greater the conflict and contention in American society. Ultimately, government disappoints those seeking new levels of equality because it cannot fulfill the multiplying demands while at the same time government alienates the remainder of society who perceives it as acting unfairly in awarding preferential treatment. Government that attempts to guard equality over-commits itself because the well of want is bottomless. When commitments are not met, there is an erosion of public trust and consent that is required by a functioning democracy.[468] Weaver called equality a "disorganizing heresy...creating a reservoir of poisonous envy. How much of the frustration of the modern world proceeds from starting with the assumption that all are equal, finding that it cannot be so, and then having to realize that one can no longer fall back on the bond of fraternity!"[469]

How did America arrive at this predicament? We begin with a return to the eighteenth century French who developed the democratic ideas of human equality. The idea of human equality flowed from the humanistic assumption of the perfectibility of man. For what men are comes from experience. Therefore, men are equal at birth and differences and inequalities arise due to environment. The solution is education that will result in an ideal democratic society.[470] These ideas of human goodness were advanced by the philosophies of the rationalistic Enlightenment. The French revolutionaries adopted the optimistic doctrine of human goodness as opposed to the American founders' reliance on a biblical view of man. Thus in constructing the foundation for revolution, the French relied on the insubstantial timber of equality inserted between the planks of liberty and fraternity whereas the Americans relied on order that rested upon "a respect for prescriptive rights and customs." The leveling theories of French radicalism led to the Terror and autocracy while the biblical view of man led to the Constitution of 1787.[471]

These sentiments are echoes of John Adams words when he wrote:

> That all men are born to equal rights is clear. Every being has a right to his own, as moral, as sacred, as any other has…But to teach that all men are born with equal powers and faculties, to equal influence in society, to equal property and advantages through life, is as gross a fraud, as glaring an imposition on the credulity of people as ever was practiced by monks, by Druids, by Brahmins, by priests of the immortal Lama, or by the self-styled philosophers of the French Revolution…
>
> But what are we to understand here by equality? Are the citizens to be all of the same age, sex, size, strength, stature, activity, courage, hardiness, industry, patience, ingenuity, wealth, knowledge, fame, wit, temperance, constancy, and wisdom? The equality of nature is *moral and political only*, and means that all men are independent. (emphasis added) But a physical inequality, an intellectual inequality, of the most serious kind, is established unchangeably by the Author of nature; and society has a right to establish any other inequalities it may judge necessary for its good. The precept however, *do as you would be done by*, implies an equality which is the real equality of nature and Christianity… (emphasis in original)[472]

As to political equality, "No society can rightly offer less than equality *before the law*." [473] (emphasis added) However, undefined equalitarianism is the most insidious force used to destroy a culture.[474] Adams definition strikes at the heart of what equality really means—a moral and political equality only—equality before God and before the law.

Equality of a sort *other* than that proposed by Adams would arise as the influence of the Enlightenment and humanism grew during the nineteenth century, the idea that equality meant more than equality before God and the law began to emerge again. However, this was contrary to the beliefs of James Madison and other Founders. In defending the new Constitution in the *Federalist Papers* Madison wrote, "Theoretic politicians, who have patronized this species of government (pure democracy), have *erroneously* supposed that by reducing mankind to a perfect equality in their political rights, they would at the same time be perfectly equalized and assimilated in their possessions, their opinions, and their passions."[475] (emphasis added)

Having realized the failure of political equality in providing equality of outcome, the levelers demanded economic democracy.[476] In the quest for a new economic democracy we move from equality of *opportunity* to equality of *condition*. With the growing recognition of synthetic rights coupled with broad but non-specific egalitarian ideals, political choice becomes limited. People are guaranteed certain outcomes and political equality suffers. As government responds to inequalities, it imposes equality, and here the American concept of equality becomes muddled. The definition of equality shifted and became one of outcome and condition to assure equality of opportunity. Samuelson presents three reasons for this shift of definition. First, the racial inequalities that precipitated the civil rights movement of the 1960s evolved into a morality tale. As documented in an earlier part of this book, television played a major part in involving all Americans in the struggle. Political remedies for discrimination were enacted, but the end of discrimination did not result in equality for blacks. The inability of blacks to gain equality even without discrimination gave rise for second reason for the change of definition of equality to mean equality of outcome. Inferior social conditions (housing, education, medical care) were used to explain the failure of blacks to achieve equality. Individual effort was devalued as social conditions became the dominant determinant of success in society. Thus was born the assignment of preferences to "remedy" inequality. The third reason for a defining equality in terms of outcome or condition arose through the court system. If legislation was not forthcoming, aggrieved groups approached the bench, and courts increasingly became arbiters of social policy.[477] As a consequence, the claimed synthetic rights achieved permanency as they became legal rights. However, forced equality of condition can never result in racial harmony and brotherhood in a civil society.

Economic democracy is the ideal and goal of humanist levelers of society. Economic democracy is the antithesis of freedom. It is not a natural human motivation and therefore requires enforcement. Ultimately, economic equality must lead to an ever increasingly despotic regime. The political-economic framework for such a regime is socialism and will be discussed in the next chapter.

It is fitting that we follow equality with our final concept as it relates to the individual—justice. As we have seen from the previous discussion, the humanistic definition of equality does great injury to the ideals of fairness, impartiality, and right action. These ideals are the stuff of justice, "...the principle or process by which every man and woman in society are accorded the things that are rightfully their own: their lives, their dignity, their property, their station in life." Kirk believed justice one of the "...three fundamental virtues that forms the bond that unites American society, the other two being order and freedom." Order is the first need of a society. As a society recognizes certain principles of a tolerable civil order, justice is possible and enforceable. Therefore, we see justice as the critical link between indispensable order and the elixir of freedom. From justice come laws that quell violence and make freedom possible. A just society requires a standard of judgment by which fairness, impartiality, and right action is measured, and this standard of judgment must be above the temper of the moment. This standard of judgment is the law which follows established principles and is no respecter of rank or station. For America those established principles flowed from the English common law that arose over centuries of judicial decisions and was derived from the "...experience of people living in community and settling their differences by legal means over a very long period of time." Much of common law flowed from natural law (discussed in an earlier chapter), a set of norms that derive from an authority above the state and "…pertains to a people's culture across the whole of life, not to matters of law merely." Statutory law developed later to address situations in which common law was viewed as inadequate. It is through the convolutions and inventions of statutory law by liberals and progressives that great damage has been done to the restraining standards of the common law heritage of the United States.[478] Ignoring corruptible man, the levelers of society admonish Justice to peak beneath her blindfold and act arbitrarily and capriciously to impose the latest standards dictated by the passions of the moment. Prescriptions of fairness, impartiality, and right action derived from an authority above the state and built up over the centuries are now considered quaint, failing to keep up with modern times, or just plain wrong-headed. In other words, the definition of justice has been changed by the humanists to fit their worldview. But, like order and freedom, justice is not of human construction, and no amount of humanist tinkering will change the heart of man with regard to a right understanding of fairness, impartiality, and right action in a civil society. Societies that ignore the true meaning of justice do so at their peril as respect for law and its rule are diminished.

Justice for the humanist derives *not* from the long centuries of human interaction that created standards of fairness, impartiality, and right action. Rather, humanists construct a definition of justice to fit their worldview. For the humanist, man is an economic being. Herrick quotes John Rawls who wrote in *A Theory of Justice* that, "All social values – liberty and opportunity, income and wealth, and the bases of self-respect – are to be distributed equally unless an unequal distribution of any, or all of these values is to everyone's advantage." Herrick continues, "The legitimacy for such a society is not a god, or the rule of a king, or even the rule of a powerful clique. It is as if *we construct* society according to an imaginary contract that *all rational citizens* could have made. Justice means that there is a fair measure of economic distribution."[479] (emphasis added) Numerous objections and questions arise to Rawls' and Herrick's admonitions. Why is it fair to take one man's property and give it to another? By whose authority does Rawls dictate an equal distribution of income and wealth? He says such authority flows not from a god or king. For Herrick, that authority lies with all rational citizens that would grant mental assent to such a society constructed from the imagination. Thus, when Herrick says "we construct", he means those rational citizens who are the conditioners of society—those who decide what and how income and wealth will be distributed.   One wonders if Herrick would categorize all citizens who object to such a societal construct as irrational and therefore without authority.

The concept of justice is a universal truth, a thing of permanence that transcends the whole of man's time on this planet and pertains to all cultures. Weaver defines such a concept as having "status" or permanence as opposed to "function" or change. When a culture "... by ignorant popular attitudes or by social derangements" imposes a political concept that creates a different principle of ordering society contrary to universal truths, dissatisfactions arise because society has tampered with the "nature of things."[480] No longer having status or permanence, justice has moved to the realm of function in a political concept used to order society into an image consistent with the humanist worldview. That political concept is socialism.

Chapter 16

Government – Humanism and the Rise of Socialism

As we saw in the last chapter the concepts order, freedom, equality, and justice as it relates to the individual have strikingly different meanings depending on one's worldview— humanist or Christian. The political framework for the imposition of the humanists' version of these concepts is socialism.

The strong bonds between socialistic forms of government and the humanist philosophy have existed since the eighteenth century, grew mightily in the nineteenth century, and became a global menace in the twentieth century. The bond or linkage between humanism and socialism is well illustrated by an examination of *Humanist Manifesto I* and *II*. The Fourteenth affirmation of *Humanist Manifesto I* reads as follows:

> The humanists are firmly convinced that exiting acquisitive and profit-motivated society has shown itself to be inadequate and a radical change in methods, controls, and motives must be instituted. A *socialized and cooperative economic order must be established* to the end that the equitable distribution of the means of life be possible. The goal of humanism is a free and universal society in which people voluntarily and intelligently cooperate for the common good. Humanists demand a shared life in a shared world.[481] (emphasis added)

Humanist Manifesto II broadened the reach of humanism's philosophy as regards government and economic controls:

> Tenth: Humane societies should evaluate economic systems not by rhetoric or ideology, but by whether or not they

increase economic well-being for all individuals and groups, minimize poverty and hardship, increase the sum of human satisfaction, and enhance the quality of life. Hence, the door is open to alternative economic systems. We need to democratize the economy and judge it by its responsiveness to human needs, testing results in terms of the common good. (emphasis in original)

Fourteenth: The world community must engage in *cooperative planning* concerning the use of rapidly depleting resources. The planet must be considered a single ecosystem. Ecological damage, resource depletion, and excessive population growth must be checked by international concord. The cultivation and conservation of nature is a moral value; we should perceive ourselves as integral to the sources of our being in nature. We must free our world from needless pollution and waste, responsibly guarding and creating wealth, both natural and human. Exploitation of natural resources, uncurbed by social conscience, must end. (emphasis in original)

Fifteenth: The problems of economic *growth and development* can no longer be resolved by one nation alone; they are worldwide in scope. It is the moral obligation of the developed nations to provide—through an international authority that safeguards human rights—massive technical, agricultural, medical, and economic assistance, including birth control techniques, to the developing portions of the globe. World poverty must cease. Hence extreme *disproportions in wealth, income, and economic growth should be reduced* on a worldwide basis.[482] (emphasis in original)

The seeds from which socialism sprang were planted in French soil during the eighteenth century Enlightenment by Jean Jacques Rousseau (1712-1778). Although Rousseau opposed much of the French Enlightenment establishment, his vision and theory were idealized and implemented during the French Revolution and became the foundation for modern collectivist governments. Rousseau saw man as good but capable of evil. To change this propensity for evil, man's environment and education must be made right. The new education and environment would be accomplished by a proper ordering of government that granted liberty to the middle class. Rousseau's liberty meant obedience to the law but that law was one to which the individual freely subscribes. Under his Social Contract, all men must consent and be bound to the will of the majority. Rousseau defined two types of will: the will of the people as reflected by popular vote and the general will, an ideal of what is really best for every member of society. When men are properly educated, they will know what is best for them, and consequently the majority's will aligns with what it really wants and is best for them.[483] However, Rousseau's basic fallacy in his Social Contract theory rests upon his belief in the goodness of man as opposed to his fallen nature. Lacking safeguards for the man's intrinsically corrupt nature, the freedom of individuals and minorities are trounced by the despotic majority.

Edmund Burke (1729-1797) was an English politician, a formidable intellect, and brilliant interpreter of the European political scene in the last quarter of the eighteenth century. He published *Reflections on the Revolution* in November 1790 near the beginning of the French Revolution. It was cautionary endeavor to warn his British homeland of the dangers arising in France. His ideas and assessments were immediately excoriated on both sides of the channel including members of his own party. But Burke recognized the fatal flaw in the Revolution that eventually became evident in the Terror of 1792-1794. To Burke's mind, the French view of man was one-dimensional, and to govern on that basis was to invite chaos and instability. The French philosophers and revolutionaries began with an invented virtue for man who was endowed with and aware of his abstract rights which society owed him. He was also clear about duties that welded him to society—liberty, equality, and fraternity. Effectively, the French had started with the ideal and descended to the practical. Calling them experimenters in morality, Burke accused the French of failing to consider history and traditions of the past as well as the corrupt nature of man. The French following Rousseau's lead rushed

> ...to find a substitute for all the principles which hitherto have been employed to regulate the human will and

action...They have therefore chosen a selfish, flattering, seductive, ostentatious vice, in the place of plain duty. True humility, the basis of the Christian system, is the low, but deep and firm foundation of all real virtue. But this, as very painful in the practice, and little imposing in the appearance, they have totally discarded. Their object is to merge all natural and all social sentiment in inordinate vanity.[484]

The basic differences between Burke and Rousseau's vision of man, government, and society have changed little as the clash of worldviews continues in the modern twenty-first century civilization of the West.

Following Rousseau, French nobleman Claude Saint-Simon's seminal writings in the early nineteenth century reflected a belief that scientific and technological advance required planned organization of the economy. In the new planned economy intellectual and economic elites would replace the traditional aristocratic and rural ruling classes as society's economic rulers. His ideas influenced many French thinkers and others during the 1830s.

Economic hardship, famine, food shortages, and widespread unemployment plagued Europe in the 1840s. In 1848 numerous revolutionary uprisings occurred amongst various peoples of Europe including the French, Austrians, Italians, Hungarians, and Czechs—many wanting national independence rather than a constitutional government.[485]

Karl Marx and Frederich Engels joined the League of the Just in the spring of 1847. Reorganized as the League of Communists during that summer, the group committed itself to the overthrow of the bourgeoisie, rule by the proletariat, and the eventual establishment of a society without classes or private property. The League met in London in November-December 1847 and requested Marx and Engels draft the League's goals and policies. The twenty-three page document, apparently written with some haste, was published in February 1848 only a week or two before the revolutions of 1848 began. Although a summation of the ideas of both Marx and Engels, the final draft of the *Manifesto of the Communist Party,* generally known as *The Communist Manifesto* since 1872, was written by Marx. Some call the Manifesto the single most important writing on politics since *the Declaration of the Rights of Man and Citizen* that came out of the French Revolution six decades earlier. During the 1850s and 1860s, the Manifesto was republished only a couple of times and three or four translations made. Interest in the Manifesto was revived as Marx's rise in the International Working Men's Association grew along with the growth of two working-class political parties in Germany. However, two events propelled the Manifesto and Marxist influence over the next forty years. The first involved the Paris Commune and the second the trial of three German-Social Democrats. At that trial, the Manifesto was read and became a part of the court record and thereby received a now legal and large printing.[486]

The Paris Commune arose in 1871 when a wide range of popular reformers and radicals captured control of the city. The Commune did little more than produce considerable left-wing rhetoric and become the symbol of social revolution. After a few weeks of quite, the French government assembled its forces and recaptured the city in slightly over a week of bloody street-fighting but at a loss of life comparable to that of the Terror of 1793-1794. Although crushed, the heroism and martyrdom of the defenders of the Paris Commune would insure that the revolutionary myth would survive and produce a new force to be reckoned—a reinvigorated socialism.[487] The Socialist labor parties grew rapidly beginning in the 1880s until the Russian Revolution of 1917 when the movement returned to its original title—the Communist Party. The influence of the *Communist Manifesto* from the 1880s to the time of the Russian Revolution is illustrated by its publication in hundreds of editions and translation into over thirty languages.[488]

The essence of the Manifesto appears in Section II and calls for the abolition of private property, the family, and ultimately countries and nationalities. The proletarians, wage laborers who have no means of production of their own, would rule. Once in power, the national differences and antagonisms between people would vanish through united action leaving only good government or administration. Marx declared that old social orders would fall through implementation of ten measures: abolition of private property, heavy progressive income tax, abolition of the right of inheritance, confiscation of property of immigrants and rebels, state control of credit, state control of communication and transportation, state control of the instruments of production, equal liability of all to labor, combination of agriculture and industry resulting in a more equitable distribution of population over the country, and free education for children.[489]

To the Western mind of the modern socialist, the Manifesto's goals may seem excessive or even draconian. However, the differences are of degree and not kind. One may look at socialism from three perspectives: goals, means, and ends. For those quick to point out that the socialist goals are ends or the desired outcomes such as justice, equality, and security, we must point to the history of socialistic societies and declare that such is never the end result. The altruistic and lofty goals of socialism become somewhat tarnished when one examines a society under the growing influence of socialism: freedom becomes slavery, prosperity erodes to poverty, equality descends to mediocrity, and security dissolves into ennui.

By its intrinsic nature, socialism has little in common with democracy except with regard to equality, but that commonality is in name only and not by definition. Equality in a democracy is a matter of liberty while under socialism it is a matter of "restraint and servitude." Given a choice between liberty and bondage, men choose liberty, and from time immemorial freedom has meant freedom from the impositions of other men. So what is the socialist to do? How do the levelers sell socialism when it implicitly requires a limit on the strongest political motive—the urge for freedom? With a subtle shift of meaning the socialist promises a "new freedom." Hayek described the shift of meaning.

> To the great apostles of political freedom the word had meant freedom from coercion, freedom from the arbitrary power of other men, release from the ties which left the individual no choice but obedience to the orders of a superior to whom he was attached. The new freedom promised, however, was to be a freedom from necessity, release from the compulsion of the circumstances which inevitably limit the range of choice of all of us, although for some very much more than others. Before man could be truly free, the "despotism of physical want" had to be broken, the "restraints of the economic system relaxed."[490]

The new freedom is merely another name for leveling society through an equal distribution of wealth. Rather than expanding the range of choice, leveling results in a greater limitation on choice, and that limitation is the ultimate outcome of all socialistic systems.

In practical terms, socialism "means the elimination of private enterprise, of private ownership of the means of production, and the creation of a system of 'planned economy' in which the entrepreneur working for profit is replaced by a central planning body." Socialist reform (i.e., the current version of social justice as defined by the socialist) is achieved through centralized economic planning. However, centralized economic planning intrudes into all areas of man's life. One need only to look at the former Soviet Union or today's China for examples of economic planning pervasively affecting all of one's life: lack of choice of profession, number of children one may have, whether one works or not, care of one's children, and determinations as to where one lives. Although all governments are coercive to some degree, in a democracy power is limited "...to creating conditions under which the knowledge and initiative of the individuals are given the best scope so *they* can plan most successfully..." In a socialist system "...a rational utilization of our resources requires *central* direction and organization of all our activities according to some consciously constructed 'blueprint'."[491] (emphasis in original) Socialism in its beginnings was truly authoritarian. As has been noted, Claude Saint-Simon was the first of the modern socialist central planners. Those that chose to defy his proposed boards of planners would be "treated as cattle." Whether a democratic socialism (a phrase that tends toward the oxymoronic) or a crushing totalitarian communism, the governing process is not a matter of type but degree; both restrict individual freedom where man is an agent of society. Tocqueville called democracy "...an essentially individualist institution [and] stood in an irreconcilable conflict with socialism."[492]

As the socialist labor parties spread rapidly across the European landscape during the last two decades of the nineteenth century, the age of reform was birthed in the United States. The leaders of the reform movement sprang from the intellectuals of the 1880s who saw man as inherently perfectible but held back from that perfect state by his environment. Almost all came from families of wealth and privilege, having never experienced privation or hardship.

Many of the intellectuals came from mainstream Christian religions of the era that were of a secular leaning such as the Unitarians. Virtually none came from the Baptists, traditional Methodists, or others holding fundamental biblical doctrines. With wealth, position, and time, the social gospelers focused on reforming the perceived ills of society, and there were many inviting targets. This was the beginning of the era of the social gospel, and it had strong ties with socialism and humanism. The teachings and beliefs of Christianity are uniquely compatible with some of the ends of socialism. The social gospeler successfully appropriated the role filled by the Christian church for centuries and then quickly marginalized if not entirely eliminated its core beliefs and teachings as the process became secularized. The social gospel movement, headed primarily by mainstream Protestant ministers, switched the emphasis from perfecting the inner man to social justice.[493]

Following the period of reconstruction after the Civil War, the nation was focused on the settlement of the West, growth of large cities, and the formation of huge business enterprises. Political corruption and scandals, legislative vote buying by large businesses, and abuses of the spoils system were added to the rapid pace of change, and a sense of disquiet arose in America. A large influx of immigrants, the "Negro problem" (as it was labeled following the Civil War), Indian policy, decline of the family farm, and rise of the factory system of economic organization added to the stress of Americans. In this boisterous, churning age, the reformers cast large-scale businesses in the role of villain and sought legislation that regulated business. The reformers (eastern intellectuals, upper class philanthropists, and middle class women) were joined by the Agrarians who saw themselves as victims of abuse from large businesses, railroads, banks, and other moneyed interests, all aided by government policies. The two groups had little in common apart from their pursuit of widespread social and economic changes in which they saw government as the means to achieve their goals.[494]

At the beginning of the twentieth century, the reformers found their champion. Theodore Roosevelt held the progressive view "…that government should reside in the hands of 'true men' and trusted reformers who could focus their 'battle-instinct' on the social issues of the day." "He became the most activist president since Andrew Jackson…" Roosevelt's beliefs included that of the progressive principle of human advance. Typical of that era of reformers, he came from wealth and privilege, but it would be any foe's mistake to underestimate Roosevelt. Brilliant, extremely well read, and a bundle of energy, his one weakness was a lack of understanding of capitalism, private enterprise, and the nature of modern industry in America. This weakness coupled with his intense reformist spirit did "...more to impede business than any president since Old Hickory." Although proving to be a disappointment to Roosevelt, William Howard Taft was as progressive as his predecessor. Progressivism would continue if not accelerate as it reached its peak during the Wilson administration. According to Schweikart and Allen, the imposition of an income tax and reform of the national banking system did more to change the order of American economic life than even the dramatic changes imposed during the New Deal of the 1930s or the Great Society of the 1960s. Under Wilson's banner of progressive idealism, "...he advocated a 'middle ground' between individuals and socialism. Wilson argued that 'all combinations which leads to monopoly must be under the direct or indirect control of society." Following World War I, America cast off the much of progressivism's economic constraints of "...exorbitant tax rates, large government debt, and price fixing..."[495]

With government restraint considerably reduced, America's economic engine was unleashed in the 1920s, and due to an eight year period of manufacturing and innovation it produced one of the most prosperous eras in American history.[496] However, progressivism's reach would again accelerate during Herbert Hoover's administration and explode under Franklin Roosevelt's New Deal to levels that would have been unimaginable by the Founders and most Americans since the Revolution.

Following Franklin Roosevelt's administration, we once again encounter the children of the Greatest Generation. We began this book with a description of the impact of the humanist doctrine on that generation and their institutions. Without a doubt, the continued socialization of the American economy continues into the twentieth-first century and is accelerating at speeds not seen since the 1930s.

Experiments with socialism as a means of organizing society occurred well before its incorporation into humanist doctrine by

Enlightenment philosophers. Two occurred at the very beginning of European arrival on the American continent. Jamestown was founded in 1607 and became the first permanent settlement in the New World. For the first few years the colony was operated on a communal basis. Settlers were forced into labor gangs and whipped or hanged for shirking work. However, the communal storehouse would be open as a last resort for those with insufficient work habits but in danger of starving. Realizing that personal incentives were superior to threats of force and violence, private ownership of land was permitted. Private enterprise and the introduction of tobacco saved the colony.[497] Eddy wrote of the Jamestown early years:

> The plan of communism upon which the first Virginia colonies were founded was a complete failure, as it promoted laziness and inefficiency. One-fifth of the members did all of the work while most of the rest were drones. Learning from their mistakes, each member was later given three acres of his own to cultivate. Under this system industry and thrift replaced idleness and there were no more famines.[498]

A recent nationally circulated newspaper article claimed that conservative politicians and pundits were attempting to rewrite history. An example of this purported rewriting was Former House Majority Leader Dick Armey's speech at the National Press Club in which he stated that the Jamestown founding was a socialist venture. The writer stated that Armey's claim of Jamestown's socialism was not true and countered that the "Jamestown settlement was a capitalist venture financed by the Virginia Company of London—a joint stock corporation—to make a profit."[499] However, Sherwood Eddy's account was written seven decades ago and can hardly be said to be a modern revision of the Jamestown history. The real revisions of history began in the early part of the twentieth century as the secular humanists began capturing the institutions of American society, particularly academia. Then as now, when the facts of history don't support humanist theory, doctrine, or conceptions of mankind, the technique for revision is to obfuscate and/or ignore the offending facts. In the case of Jamestown's founding, the writer fails to distinguish between the capitalistic financing and purpose of the Virginia Company and the on-site operation of the colony which was socialistic. It is the operation of a society rather than the source of its financing that determines whether or not a society is socialistic. Three hundred years of history prior to the advent of the twentieth century support Eddy's and Armey's conclusion that the Jamestown colony nearly failed due to its early socialistic attributes. These attributes included a lack of private enterprise, a lack of private ownership of the means of production, and centralized planning.

Thirteen years after the founding of Jamestown, the Pilgrims arrived on the Massachusetts shore and founded Plymouth colony. Although they had bound themselves to the London Company of Adventurers for seven years labor without compensation, the Pilgrims came "…to realize the principles of God in the wilderness of the new world." Like their Jamestown counterparts, the Pilgrims experimented with a collective or communistic organization, but after four years of bitter poverty, starvation, hardship, and many deaths, the communal effort was abandoned and each family was given an acre of land and later a hundred acres to own and cultivate. William Bradford, an original member and early historian of the colony, wrote of the folly of communism. Although the experiment was tried for several years by "Godly and sober men", Bradford pointed to the vanity and conceit of Plato's writing that "…the taking away of propertie and bringing communitie into a commonwealth would make them happy and flourishing; as if they were wiser than God."[500]

Because of their isolation from the civilized world, Jamestown and the Plymouth Colony stand as great laboratory experiments on the validity and worthiness of socialistic principles. Communism of an almost pure variety, in an isolated and controlled environment of the New World, failed miserably as laziness and inefficiency trumped thrift and industry. Human nature exposed the soft and rotten underbelly of the tenets of the socialistic and humanistic faith in mankind and their commitment to the principle of the greatest-happiness-for-the-greatest-number which humanists consider to be the highest moral obligation for humanity as a whole.

The central conflict between socialism and capitalism is the status of private property and personal income. We begin with a quote from an address by Abraham Lincoln to the New York Workingmen's Democratic Republican Association.

Property is the fruit of labor. Property is desirable, is a positive good in the world. That some should be rich shows that others may become rich, and hence is just encouragement to industry and enterprise. Let not him who is houseless pull down the house of another; but let him labor diligently and build one for himself, thus by example assuring that his own shall be safe from violence...I take it that it is best for all to leave each man free to acquire property as fast as he can. Some will get wealthy. I don't believe in a law to prevent a man from getting rich; it would do more harm than good.[501]

Lincoln's short homily on the value of property as a positive good and an encourager to industry and enterprise is important but not sufficient. Property is more than something valuable that can be weighed in the balances against some competing thing. Weaver writes that, "Almost every trend of the day points to an identification of right with the purpose of the state and that, in turn, with the utilitarian greatest material happiness for the greatest number." Weaver argues that private property is the last metaphysical right remaining because it does not depend on some measure of social usefulness that can be bent to the greatest good for the greatest number. State control of the material elements of a society positions it to allow the denial of freedom, but private property and personal income stands as a bulwark and provides a "...sanctuary against pagan statism."[502] The biblical worldview through its imposition of boundaries on the power of the state consequentially supports and encourages economic freedom and subsequently free-market economies because the power of government to dictate or interfere with private transactions is limited.[503]

The Founders were very aware of the need to limit the power of the state with regard to private property. Efforts of the English Crown to take colonists' property were considered a violation of English common law. John Adams wrote, "The moment the idea is admitted into society that property is not as sacred as the laws of God, and that there is not a force of law and public justice to protect it, anarchy and tyranny commence. Property must be secured or liberty cannot exist." James Madison would echo Adams' sentiments when he wrote that it was the duty of government to protect property of every sort and that it was not a just government "... where the property which a man has in his personal safety and personal liberty is violated by arbitrary seizures of one class of citizens for the service of the rest." Prior to 1936, the Supreme Court held that:

> The preservation of property…is a primary object of the social compact…The legislature, therefore, had no authority to make an act divesting one citizen of his freehold, and vesting it in another, without a just compensation. It is inconsistent with the principles of reason, justice and moral rectitude, it is incompatible with the comfort, peace and happiness of mankind; it is contrary to the principles of social alliance in every free government; and lastly, it is contrary to the letter and spirit of the Constitution.[504]

Beginning in 1936, the Supreme Court's liberal interpretations of the "general welfare" clause of the Constitution have dramatically enlarged the powers of the federal government and encroached on fundamental property rights through its welfare programs.[505] This liberal interpretation significantly expanded what the legislature could do with regard to providing for the "general welfare" of the United States. The debate as to the meaning of the "general welfare" clause began with Jefferson and Hamilton and continues today. Rather than continue the argument, let us evaluate the outcome of the distortion of the meaning of the "general welfare" clause. The results of the liberal interpretation of the "general welfare" clause is an unprecedented assault on right of private property through imminent domain laws, a diminution of the right of contract and obligations there under, an oppressive income tax system, and the onerous limitations on the possession and use of property through regulation.

Eminent domain is the right of government to take private property for public use. The Fifth Amendment to the Constitution states that no person shall "…be deprived of life, liberty, or property, without due process of law; nor shall private property be taken for public use, without just compensation."[506] The problem arises in definition of what constitutes public use. Recent times have seen the tendency to count any reason given by a governmental body for taking private property as justifiable public use. Public use once meant use for a highway, a park, a school, and other facilities used by the public, or to facilitate broad public purposes. In a 2005 ruling, the Supreme Court with a narrow 5-4 margin upheld a verdict in which the "...New London, Connecticut city government condemned the property of middle-class homeowners in an unblighted neighborhood for the purpose of getting the property into the hands of commercial interests that would pay more taxes."[507] One may argue that increasing taxes facilitates broad public purposes. If that is the case, the right of private property becomes meaningless as it bows to the whim of the planner who has a vision or purpose that will raise taxes to fill the government coffers to be used for the greater good of all. Apologists will argue that the Constitution's Fifth Amendment has protected the property owner because he received just compensation. Could not such an argument be made in the case of a young women who was gang raped but received a five dollar bill from each participant. It can be argued that her property (her body) was taken for the greater good of all, and she received compensation. Not happy with that outcome, her subsequent due process hearing becomes *not* a matter of her rights having been violated but whether she received just compensation for her property. In this analogy as well as in the abuse of eminent domain by the state, private property rights have been prostituted—that is, what was once private is now public to anyone with a desire to take and the dollars to pay. Such is hardly a Bill of Rights guarantee of fair treatment.

A second area of assault on private property comes with the attack on right of contract. A brief explanation is necessary with regard to the right of contract, its connection to property, and its centrality to the economic philosophy of western civilization. The concept of property is the motive for economic activity, and communal or private property can only exist in an ordered society. The disposition of property depends on the social and economic structures adopted by a society. In a communistic society, individual interests are subordinate to the interests of the group, and communal property dominates. In an individualistic society, group interests are subordinate to the individual, and private property dominates. In Western civilization, private property and right of contract form the basis of its dominant individualistic societies. Basic common law that arose over the centuries had as its primary function the security of personal liberty and private property. Thus, property was not just things but rights created by contract. "Contract rights—enforceable promises—became valuable and represented wealth. Thus, the contract in the free enterprise system was the effective instrument by which property was created." Property is meaningless unless associated with individuals, and such association is expressed as "ownership, title, and possession."[508] Thus, it can be seen that with the curtailment or damage to the right of contract comes a loss of property rights.

  A stunning example of governmental bullying and abuse of power with regard to the right of contract and private property occurred during the 2009 governmental bailout of the auto industry. In the spring of 2009, Chrysler Corporation was facing bankruptcy, and the Obama administration was attempting to engineer a bailout. Four entities were involved: the federal government's Troubled Asset Relief Program (TARP), the United Auto Workers Union (UAW) that donated $5 million to the Obama election campaign, big banks (JP Morgan Chase, Citigroup, Morgan Stanley, and Goldman Sachs) who were the recipients of up to $100 billion in federal government bailout funds, and a group of lenders who had never taken TARP funds. The deal proposed by the administration was that the senior lenders would receive about twenty-eight cents on the dollar invested in Chrysler while the UAW would get forty-three cents on the dollar and fifty-five percent ownership of the surviving company. Non-TARP lenders refused to go along because their contract claims were superior to others lenders who were receiving a greater percentage than the non-TARP lenders. Non-TARP lenders' claims were a matter of contract and were superior to the claims of shareholders and employees. In spite of the non-TARP lenders' superior claims, Michigan Congressman John Dingell called the non-TARP lenders "vultures." President Obama called them "speculators." In a bullying tactic, he publicly ridiculed the non-TARP lenders by accusing them of holding out for "...the prospect of an *unjustified* taxpayer-funded bailout"...as opposed to "...to those stakeholders who made sacrifices and worked constructively..."[509] (emphasis added) Although non-TARP lenders had superior claims through right of contract, it would appear that President Obama believes that such individual claims are inferior to the group's desires. Such beliefs that rights deriving from contract and therefore private property are inferior to the greater good of all are reminiscent of socialistic societies as described above. As government gains greater and greater control over the "general welfare" of individuals through the control of organizations and means of production, the freedoms of the individual will decline correspondingly. A leader in the Russian Revolution of 1917, Leon Trotsky said, "In a country where the sole employer is the State, opposition means death by slow starvation."[510] He spoke prophetically with regard to millions enslaved in Soviet Russia and its satellite communist regimes, and it appears his admonition may have application to America in the twenty-first century.

The third assault on private property is through oppressive taxation. The purpose of taxation is to fund the operation of government and meet its obligations, but what are government's obligations? Jefferson wrote in the Declaration of Independence that government was instituted to secure certain unalienable rights endowed by their Creator, "...that among these are Life, Liberty and the pursuit of Happiness." It should be noted that Jefferson spoke of the "pursuit" of happiness rather than a provision or guarantee of happiness. John Adams words were less judicious in describing the "...happiness of society is the end of government" and in error when he said that "...all divines and moral philosophers will agree the happiness of the individual is the end of man." Regardless of intent, the happiness that Adams wrote of did not imply a large national government bent on addressing every whim or supplying every morsel necessary for a happy populous. Rather, for Adams happiness derived from representative government and the attendant civil society as opposed to government that ruled by fear which was the norm for mankind. But contained in Adams words were the ingredients for mischief and "created latent obligations for government."[511]

The Founders held a biblical understanding of the corruptible nature of man and a belief that government was untrustworthy due to its corruptibility. Traditional ideas of limited government prevailed until the occurrences of the Great Depression and World War II during the first half of the twentieth century. Americans still distrusted government, but through the growing influence of the humanistic worldview, they saw government as a mechanism for dealing with societal problems. Politicians happily acquiesced and more and more "problems" were discovered requiring appropriate governmental response. Growing social and political demands were increasingly added to the realm of being in the public interest. However, funding government and the growing list of wants, rights, and wishes of the populous has become problematic for government cannot do everything for everybody. Samuelson calls this "the politics of overpromise…the systematic and routine tendency of government to make more commitments than can reasonably be fulfilled.[512]

Government is now viewed as the provider or guarantor of happiness as opposed to making possible the pursuit thereof. After decades of an ever increasing institutionalization of synthetic rights purported to be due to the great majority of the populous, progressive politicians and bureaucrats must find someone to pay for the costs associated with a benefactor government. Yet Americans retain a tolerance for taxes far lower than their wants require. What is the progressive to do? The solution increasingly relies on writing Congressional tax legislation such that a minority is taxed for the support of the majority. In this way the voting majority keeps their benefits and doesn't have to pay for them or pays proportionately less than the value received. Theoretically, every American that earns income pays taxes on a progressive scale ranging from ten percent to thirty-five percent.[513] Nevertheless, through writing the rules of taxation Congress has chosen to deliver social benefits through a myriad of tax credits which do not offend taxpayer sensibilities that he or she is receiving government welfare. Effectively, what one hand takes away, the other gives. For 2009, the net effect of the redistributive efforts of Congress was that forty-seven percent of all taxpayers and fifty-five percent of the elderly and families with children paid no federal income taxes. A third of all taxpayers paid payroll taxes but not income taxes, but these taxes are withheld before receipt of a paycheck and therefore appear less onerous to the average American worker.[514] Additionally, many families and individuals receive a larger tax refund than the amount paid in. With more and more citizens on the receiving end of government's generosity, the nation is near a tipping point at which a majority will be completely disconnected from the cost of government. That accomplished, what incentive is there for the voting majority to reign in excessive government or to restrain themselves from voting themselves greater and greater benefits funded by the taxed minority?

Writing in the Federalist Papers in defense of the new Constitution, Alexander Hamilton stated:

> There is no part of the administration of government that requires extensive information and a thorough understanding of the principles of political economy so much as the business of taxation. The man who understands those principles best will be least likely to resort to *oppressive expedients*, or to *sacrifice any particular class of citizens* to the procurement of revenue. It might be demonstrated that the most productive system of finance will always be the least burdensome. There can be no doubt that in order to a judicious exercise of the power of taxation, it is necessary that the person in whose hands it is should be acquainted with the general genius, habits, and modes of thinking of the people at large, and with the resources of the country. And this is all that can be reasonably meant by a knowledge of the interests and feelings of the people. In any other sense the proposition has either no meaning, or an absurd one.[515] (emphasis added)

Contrary to Hamilton's cautions and with the reins of government increasingly in the hands of the levelers of society ignorant of political economy, progressives have resorted to oppressive expedients and have sacrificed particular classes of citizens in their rush to fund the bloated programs that attempt to satisfy the ever expanding public interest. Such redistributive efforts do great harm to the idea of private property which is fundamental to the maintenance of freedom.

The fourth assault on private property is accomplished through excessive governmental regulation. Humanism is intrinsically socialistic. A socialistic government allows its humanist elite to level society by their attempts to parcel out the greatest material happiness for the greatest number. This is accomplished through the regulatory process which is the skeletal structure of all socialistic governments. One example with regard to the environment comes from a reading of *Humanist Manifesto II*.

> ...the door is open to alternative economic systems...The world community must engage in *cooperative planning*

concerning the use of rapidly depleting resources. The planet earth must be considered a single ecosystem. Ecological damage, resource depletion, and excessive population growth must be checked by international concord.[516] (emphasis in original)

Yet, at the same time, the Manifesto self-righteously states that, "...bureaucratic structures should be held to a minimum. People are more important than...regulations." In spite of these platitudes, calls for minimal regulations are disingenuous for humanists know that *cooperative planning* is code for regulation, and socialistically-oriented societies require massive amounts of regulation. In this section we are limiting our discussion to property and its loss through regulation. Regulation not only limits use of private property (which is in effect a taking of private property under increasingly socialistic regimes) but devalues private property through excessive regulation. Examples are numerous including imposition of blanket environmental regulations of massive over-reach and questionable value. Andrée Seu humorously wrote (of the type "If I don't laugh, I'll cry" variety) of her conversation with John the handyman. Fortunately for Ms. Seu, John was only installing her new electric dryer. Being a handyman, John did other things like paint. After the implementation of new federal regulations in 2010, John's painting jobs consisted of a lot more than just throwing down a drop cloth, opening his can of paint, and climbing his ladder.[517] The source of the new regulations is found in a federal government Executive Order.

> Executive Order 12898, Federal Actions to Address Environmental *Justice* in *Minority* Populations and *Low-Income* Populations: Establish as Federal Executive Policy on Environmental *Justice*. Its main provisions directs federal agencies *to the greatest extent practicable and permitted by law* to make environmental *justice* part of their *mission*...[518] (emphasis added)

This new Executive Order applies to thirty-eight million homes in the United States which were built on or before a certain date. For those homeowners or business owners that fall under the regulation and wishing John to do some painting for them, John would first read to the owner from a "...pamphlet entitled 'Renovate Right: Important Lead Hazard Information for Families.' He would then have to cordon off the 'contaminated' area, put out 'Lead Hazard Area' signs, and laid plastic (not drop cloths) six feet in every direction from the work site (10 feet, if outside)." When John completed all of these tasks, he would get into his protective gear—his little suit, mask, boots, gloves, and hood. If he forgot a tool in his truck or has to go to the bathroom, he must get undressed and place his suit, boots, gloves, hood, and mask in a contractor's trash bag. Into this bag also goes any hasmat sheeting used during the day. At some point all of this material in the contractor's bags (filled to not more than two-thirds full) must be transported it to a landfill. John spent eight weeks in a mandatory EPA course to become certified. The course costs were not John's only expense. In addition to the protective clothing and sheeting, John had to purchase a new $1,100 HEPA vacuum that uses $70 filters and $12 bags. According to John, should Ms. Seu want her bathroom remodeled, the new regulations would add $1000 to her costs. John was very careful to follow the rules to the letter. The penalty for failure is $37,000 per day per violation.[519] In all of this environmental caution, all of the thirty-eight million homes are *presumed* to have been contaminated. This is regulatory overkill at a massive cost to the nation's homeowners not only in cost of renovation and repair but in losses to property values. A close reading of the title reflects the real intent of the regulations—to impose a humanistic definition of justice and equality.

Socialism appears to have many striking parallels with the infamous Kudzu vine that covers much of the southeastern United States. A native of Japan and southeastern China, the twisting, coiling, and fast growing vine spreads by runners that root at the nodes. It may also spread by seeds which can lay dormant at a site for several years and then reappear after it was thought eradicated. Kudzu made its appearance in the United States at the Philadelphia Centennial Exposition in 1876 and was planted by the Civilian Conservation Corps during the Great Depression years. It was promoted by the government between 1935 and the early 1950s for environmental purposes to control soil erosion. Once the aggressive and overpowering nature of the plant became obvious, it was named a pest weed by the Department of Agriculture in 1953. In spite of efforts to control the vine, it has naturalized into approximately eight thousand to twelve thousand square miles in the southeastern United States and costs a half billion dollars in lost crops and control efforts. However, control efforts are failing as the vine covers an additional 150,000 acres each year at an additional cost of six million dollars. Once promoted for environmental purposes, the weed has and is producing devastating environmental damage.[520]

Apart from a few failed attempts in the early colonial period, socialism is not native to America or the governmental sentiments of the Founders of the United States. Nevertheless, socialism took root during the late 1800s as liberals began using government as a tool for progressive social action. The growth of government, like Kudzu, was highly promoted beginning in the early 1930s and touted as the answer for the ills of society. In spite of repeated efforts to cut back and control the ever expanding growth, Americans have seen the tentacles of government spread into almost every aspect of their lives—strangling initiative, appropriating an ever larger share of one's productive efforts, and generally demoralizing the spirit with an insidious and coercive invasion into the living of one's life. The weed of Kudzu-like socialism is producing devastating damage to the American order upon which the nation was founded.

The American government as we know it in the twenty-first century has come to mean massive government involvement in almost every aspect of the individual's "general welfare." The general welfare of the individual is not just encouraged, it is now supported. A striking example of the difference between encouraging and supporting the general welfare of society was given by Charles Murray. Murray states that the totality of life, the "stuff of life" as he calls it, revolves around four institutions: family, community, vocation, and faith. In his lecture titled "The Happiness of the People," he noted that personal success in one or more of these areas results in personal satisfaction, that is, a measure of happiness. He further stated that as America encouraged personal success in each of these areas, the nation thrived. The past American *encouragement* of success in each of these institutions was contrasted with the European *support* that each of these same institutions received over years through advanced socialism. The support given by European socialism has undermined those institutions. Faith is supported by providing and maintaining church buildings that remain empty. Generous childcare and maternity benefits are provided to the family, yet the birth rate has plummeted. Vocation is supported through workplace regulation but has led to low job satisfaction. Community is supported by creation of a "European Brand", but in place of unity has come a growing cynicism in France, Germany, Spain, and Sweden. In effect, socialism has usurped the responsibilities formerly in the province of the individual and consequently "…sapped much of the energy, drive, and satisfaction from living."[521]

Chapter 17

Science – Naturalistic Evolution

Naturalism was briefly discussed in Chapter 10. To summarize, humanism's gospel is naturalism, and its tenets of faith insist that human beings, the earth, and the unending universe of space and time are all parts of one great Nature. Existence and Nature are one and the same, and apart from Nature nothing exists. An explanation of everything that exists can be obtained through observation of the forces of nature. In the naturalistic explanation, the universe was an endless and unbroken series of causes and effects through time. However, naturalism is a philosophy and not scientific fact for naturalism's premises cannot be tested empirically. In fact, new discoveries in the twentieth century point to a beginning of the universe and time (the Big Bang) and is a near lethal blow to naturalism's philosophy of an unbroken and endless sequence of cause and effect. In light of this discovery, those who espouse naturalism now suppose the universe resulted from purposeless chance over eons of time.[522] If there was a finite beginning of the universe, then for naturalism the specter of a possible creator of that universe arises and with a creator comes the potential for design or purpose in that creation. Design and purpose chases away naturalism's basic tenet that the universe was created only by purposeless chance over eons of time. The stakes were high. The naturalistic worldview and the belief that science is the only source of knowledge were in danger of falling from their positions of dominance. Therefore, God must not have anything to do with creation. Humanism's gospel of naturalism must have its own creation story, and that story was evolution.

Standing head and shoulders above all others in the move of nineteenth century science away from the supernatural was Charles Darwin. Born into a wealthy family on February 12, 1809 in Shrewsbury, England, Charles Darwin was the son and grandson of doctors. His mother, daughter of Josiah Wedgwood (famous for pottery manufacture), died when Charles was eight years old. In 1825 he began medical training at Edinburgh University but after two years transferred to Cambridge to study for the ministry. Indications were that he chose the ministry to allow himself the free time necessary to pursue his real passions which included hunting (although he could not stand the site of blood and was the reason he left medical school), natural history, and scientific experimentation. Through the influence of a botany professor, Reverend John Henslow, Darwin's interest in zoology and geography grew to the point that he accepted a position as a naturalist on a British Navy survey vessel, the *HMS Beagle,* in 1831. The planned two year voyage lasted five years and included extensive explorations of South America and many islands in the Pacific Ocean. Returning to England in 1836, he established a reputation as a skilled naturalist. In 1839, Darwin published his journal of the voyage of the *Beagle.* He married Emma Wedgwood, his cousin, that same year.[523]

The concepts that became the basis for Darwin's *On the Origin of Species* were developed during his voyage on the *Beagle*. Descent with modification by natural selection was formed in his mind by 1838, but it was eighteen years later in 1856 that he began writing *On the Origin of Species* which he completed and published in 1859. Darwin's religious convictions also evolved over time. He began with "the firm conviction of the existence of God, and of the immortality of the soul." While studying for the ministry at Cambridge, he "did not then in the least doubt the strict and literal truth of every word in the Bible" and that God was an intelligent first cause. During his voyage on the Beagle, God changed to a "revengeful tyrant" when Darwin could not reconcile how a loving, beneficent God could allow such suffering and inhumanity in the world. Fifteen years later the death of his 10 year old daughter destroyed all of his remaining doubts about the non-existence of a loving God. A year after the publication of *On the Origin of Species* Darwin still believed that God was the ultimate Lawgiver, but as he developed his theory of origins by natural processes, he would eventually deny belief in the Bible as divine revelation and that Jesus Christ was the Son of God. Eventually confessing to agnosticism but never atheism, he believed that the religious instinct had evolved with society.[524]

In Darwin's theory of evolution, humanists had found a weapon to not only sever the natural from the supernatural but to destroy the supernatural altogether. Naturalism and Darwinian evolution was a symbiotic relationship for the naturalistic worldview in explaining creation and was of critical importance for Darwinism. The first deals with the concept of descent with modification. Darwin proposed that the species were not immutable. Rather, species were capable of or susceptible to change over time, and new species have appeared by the process of descent with modification over long periods during the earth's history. The second proposition states that all life descended from one or just a few common ancestors. The third proposition states that the diversity of life flowing from the common ancestors was not haphazard or erratic but guided by a force called natural selection, more popularly known as "survival of the fittest."[525]

Even for the evolutionist there was a point when through some mysterious circumstance that non-life became life (abiogenesis- the origination of living from lifeless matter). In fact, evolutionists believe in creation, but it was creation through naturalism's chance, undirected spark of life, not directed by an intelligence with a purpose to create, i.e., a creator. Here we enter the realm of mathematics and probabilities. Donald E. Johnson wrote a small, highly technical book entitled *Probability's Nature and Nature's Probability-A Call to Scientific Integrity*. A double PhD in Chemistry and Computer and Information Sciences, Johnson cites numerous sources regarding the probabilities of the occurrence of the undirected origin of life. Johnson, referring to Harold Morowitz's estimates, states that, "...the probability for the chance formation of the smallest, simplest form of living organism known is one in $10^{340,000,000}$. Johnson also quotes Ilya Prigogine, a two-time Nobel Prize winner, "The statistical probability that organic structures and the most precisely harmonized reactions that typify living organisms would be generated by accident, is zero."[526] Missing in the discussion of extreme improbability of life *beginning* through undirected natural causes are the further improbabilities of *survival* of that random spark where life arose from non-life.

There are only two mechanisms for life to exist—either life occurred through a deliberate act of creation or life arose from undirected natural causes. For the evolutionist, "...the only allowable mechanism is undirected and natural." Therefore for life to exist

"...it must have occurred that way, despite the improbability." Such a proposition is self-proving and is called a tautology.[527] However, such self-proving statements do not pass muster with regard to the humanist's hallowed scientific method. If Darwinism is not supported by scientific fact, why is it so dominant today? Its supremacy is a result of its support of the humanistic worldview.

In an effort to bridge these two opposing views, some have adopted the approach of theistic evolution in which the natural world is perceived to be God-governed but yet attempts to remain compatible with Darwinian evolution on scientific matters.[528] C. S. Lewis identified this as the In-between view, a blend of materialist and religious views. More explicitly he called it "Creative Evolution or Emergent Evolution", which says that "...the small variations by which life on this planet 'evolved' from the lowest forms to Man were not due to chance but to the 'striving' or 'purposiveness' of a Life-Force." Lewis equates Life-Force as something that must be with or without a mind. Either is fatal to the In-between view. On the one hand, if the force is without a mind, it is cannot strive or have purpose. If it has a mind by which that life arose and moves to perfection, then the mind is really a God which is at odds with the Darwinian view.[529]

Proponents of the theory of intelligent design believe that "...certain features of the universe and living things are best explained by an intelligent cause, not an undirected process such as natural selection." Rather than accept the religious view of who that designer is, some intelligent design proponents believe that the identity of the designer must be sought through the study of present-day causes that are overlaid on the "...historical record in order to infer the best explanation for the origin of the natural phenomena being studied." Although much of intelligent design is compatible with many theological views, intelligent design researchers for the most part attempt to detect "apparent design" in nature and make no claims as to the identity of the cause of the "empirically detectable marks of intelligence." The identity or cause of design falls in the realm of theology and philosophy and beyond the dominion of empirical science.[530]

In Ray Comfort's words, "Darwin theorized that all living things evolved from simpler life forms through an undirected process of mutations and natural selection. If a mutation...occurred in the genes, and it provided the creature some survival advantage, this benefit would be passed on to its offspring through the process of natural selection." But we must distinguish between microevolution in which small-scale variations occur within a kind and macroevolution upon which Darwin's theory of evolution is based. Few disagree that microevolution occurs to cause a species to change over time. These small-scale changes arise from adaptability and natural selection, but such changes occur within a kind and does not create something new.[531] Examples are prevalent. Dairy cattle are bred for greater milk production, and beef cattle are bred for meat production. Race horses are bred for speed. As much of the world moved beyond subsistence agriculture, humans adapted by becoming taller and heavier. Naturalistic evolutionists attempt to use microevolution as proof of macroevolution and endeavor to blanket the two with an elastic all-encompassing definition. They submit arbitrary philosophical principles that the many small micro evolutionary changes result in a new species but fail to provide scientific proof—the proverbial missing links.[532]

It is not the purpose of this book to present an extensive or complete examination of Darwinian evolution and its modern variants and their failures. However, naturalism and Darwinian evolution are critical supports upon which the dominant humanist worldview rests. It is upon these supports that the humanist philosophy has become the dominant doctrine of the various institutions of American society and their protectors including government, biological and social sciences, media, and education. Therefore, it is important for the reader to understand the considerable flaws and weaknesses in Darwin's theory as well as those of Neo-Darwinists.[*] Several of these flaws and weaknesses are summarized in the following paragraphs.

We begin with the fossil record. Under Darwin's theory the great diversity of life present on the earth evolved from one or at most a few ancestors. As one species evolved to another, there would be transitional forms, e.g., half ape and half man. These transitional forms would provide a measure of proof for the Darwinian

---

[*]There are many new books and a wealth of relevant historical resources available to examine Darwinian evolution's claims and counterclaims. The reader is encouraged to investigate these sources including those listed in the bibliography.

evolutionary process. The source of that proof is found only in the fossil record, the province of paleontology, the science of the study of fossils.[533] However, the fossil record poses a problem for Darwinian evolution, and Darwin recognized this in *On the Origin of Species*, Chapter VI – Difficulties on Theory.

> Firstly, why, if species have descended from other species by insensibly find gradations, do we not everywhere see innumerable transitional forms? Why is not all nature in confusion instead of the species being, as we see them, well defined?[534]

Darwin's explanation centers on a logical extension of "survival of the fittest," i.e., parents and transitional varieties will generally have been continually and gradually exterminated by the new and improved species. However, the transitional types are not only missing from the present world but also missing from the fossil record. Darwin argued that the fossil record is extremely imperfect and should be looked upon as not a continuous record but snapshots of relatively short periods of time separated by exceptionally long periods; hence, the gradual transitions are missing from the fossil record. Although Darwin reasonably suggests gaps in the fossil record, he fills in these gaps with imagined evolutionary processes.[535]

Two features of the fossil record appear particularly inconsistent with evolution's necessary ingredient of gradualism of specie change. The fossil record reflects fully-formed sudden appearances of species as opposed to gradual, steady transformation. Once appearing fully formed, the fossil record reflects specie stasis, i.e., most species exhibit very little morphological change and if such change is present, it is usually limited and directionless.[536]

Should Darwin's theory of gradual evolutionary change be correct, the pattern of species extinction should also reflect an even greater degree of gradualism as better adapted descendants arose. Darwin wrote, "The extinction of species and whole groups of species…almost invariably follows on the principle of natural selection; for old forms will be supplanted by new and improved forms." However, the record of extinctions appears far more the responsibility of catastrophic global events than the gradual disappearance of obsolete species.[537]

A few evolutionists have attempted to address these objections to evolution with a theory called punctuated equilibrium. Under this theory the failure to find a clear path of evolutionary progress lay in alternating periods of evolutionary progress coupled with arbitrary catastrophic extinction.

> The most important concept of evolution by punctuated equilibrium...is that speciation (the formation of new species) occurs rapidly, and in small groups which are isolated on the periphery of geographical areas occupied by the ancestral species. Selective pressures might be particularly intense where members of the species are just barely able to survive, and favorable variations could spread relatively quickly through a small, isolated population. By this means, a new species might arise in the peripheral area without leaving fossil evidence. Because fossils are mostly derived from large, central populations, a new species would appear suddenly in the fossil record following its migration into the central area of ancestral range.[538]

In other words, Darwin's gradualism is replaced by an evolutionary process (punctuated equilibrium) that happened in a short period of time, was caused by sudden changes in the environment, and was too quick to be reflected in the fossil record. These spurts of evolution would be followed by relatively long periods of stability.[539]

However, most neo-Darwinists generally reject punctuated equilibrium and attribute sudden appearance of species to the gap theory in fossil records. To explain stasis or lack of change over long periods of time, neo-Darwinists have developed the concept of "mosaic evolution" in which that the soft body parts may have evolved while the body parts normally fossilized stayed the same. A second explanation for the lack of evolutionary progress in the fossil record is attributed to "stabilizing selection." Under stabilizing selection, change is prevented by eliminating all the innovations through natural selection. This prevention of change may last for millions of years and continue through changing environmental conditions that would normally encourage adaptation.[540]

The weakness, inconsistency, and shear mental gymnastics required of the theories and arguments in support of naturalistic evolution of whatever stripe are revealed by such explanations. When the fossil records do not support Darwin's "insensibly find gradations", punctuated equilibrium is presented. Others suggest mosaic evolution in which soft body parts evolved and the parts subject to fossilization did not evolve. Finally, although the guiding force of natural selection is presented as the engine of change resulting in the proliferation of species and is the critical component of naturalistic evolution, under stabilizing selection, natural selection is a preventer of change. In other words, natural selection is the guiding force for change, but when the fossil record does not support evolutionary change, natural selection was the preventer of change.

Support for naturalistic evolution from the fossil record continues to erode when one looks at what paleontologists have labeled as the Cambrian Explosion. Known as "The Biological Big Bang," the majority of complex life forms "…appear for the first time in the fossil record already fully evolved with most of their characteristic features present…" According to one writer, if life on earth was the equivalent of a twenty-four hour day, the Cambrian period would account for only two minutes of that day.[541] Paleontologist and evolutionist Robert Carroll, author of *Patterns and Processes of Vertebrate Evolution*, wrote:

> Although an almost incomprehensible number of species inhabit Earth today, they do not form a continuous spectrum of barely distinguishable intermediates. Instead, nearly all species can be recognized as belonging to a relatively limited number of clearly distinct major groups, with very few illustrating intermediate structures or ways of life.[542]

Even Darwin recognized that, "If numerous species, belonging to the same genera or families, have really started into life at once, the fact would be fatal to the theory of evolution through natural selection."[543]

The discovery of the "missing link" in mankind's evolutionary history is the naturalistic evolutionist's equivalent of the quest for the Holy Grail. However, man is not the only species with a missing link. Darwin wrote:

> On the doctrine of the extermination of an infinitude of connecting links, between the living and extinct inhabitants of

the world, and at each successive period between the extinct and still older species, why is not every geological formation charged with such links? Why does not every collection of fossil remains afford plain evidence of the gradation and mutation of the forms of life? We meet with no such evidence, and this is the most obvious and forcible of the many objections which may be urged against my theory. Why, again, do whole groups of allied species appear, though *certainly* they often falsely appear, to have come in suddenly on the several geological stages? Why do we not find great piles of strata beneath the Silurian system, stored with the remains of progenitors of Silurian groups of fossils? For *certainly* on my theory such strata *must* somewhere have been deposited at these ancient and utterly unknown epochs in the world's history. I can answer these questions and grave objections only on the *supposition* that the geological record is far more imperfect than most geologists believe.[544] (emphasis added)

Darwin admits that the fossil record does not support his theory. However, he blames the failure of support for his theory on the imperfections of the sister scientific discipline of geology and its practitioners for failing to recognize those imperfections.

In spite of the certainties, musts, suppositions, and hopes of Darwin and his followers, the fossil record appears very much as it did 150 years ago when *On the Origin of Species* was first published. Noted naturalistic evolution critic Phillip Johnson summarizes the fossil record's evidential verdict, "The outstanding characteristic of the fossil record is the absence of evidence for evolution."[545]

During the first half of the twentieth century, various fields of biology such as comparative anatomy, genetics, and embryology began developing their respective definitions of what evolution was. Thus, evolutionary theory began to mean different things to different scientific disciplines. Through a series of interdisciplinary meetings as mid-century approached, the leaders of the various fields attempted to develop a coherent theory of Darwinian evolution based on Darwin's principles. This "evolutionary synthesis" became the basis of modern evolutionary thought and was called neo-Darwinism. Neo-Darwinism was essentially non-molecular and did not account for modern biochemistry whose beginnings came after the neo-Darwinian synthesis was launched. In *Darwin's Black Box*, Michael Behe wrote, "...for the Darwinian theory of evolution to be true, it has to account for the molecular structure of life." Behe effectively demonstrates in his book that it does not.[546]

Neo-Darwinists rely on random mutation and natural selection as the primary mechanism for evolution. A mutation results from an error in the copying commands of DNA's genetic code. Generally, mutations are at the very least harmful and can be fatal. An accumulation of these mutations leads to degeneration or retrograde evolution. But neo-Darwinists require that many thousands of rare but helpful or beneficial mutations must occur in a single organism and result in a new organ or structure. Here we enter into the realm of fantastically large mathematical improbabilities.[547]

Not only must thousands of rare but helpful mutations occur, Darwinists believe favorable mutations occur because their environments "demand" such and therefore mutations are "directed" to provide a fix. However, mutations are random and are not related to the usefulness of that mutation.[548] In one sense, the humanists' environments that demand favorable mutations have become the intelligent designer, the concept to which they so vehemently object.

For naturalistic evolutionists, mutations have the ability to create new structures while in reality mutations can only modify or eliminate existing structures. Under macroevolution, additional genetic information must be created for the new structures, but "Scientists have yet to find even a single mutation that *increases* genetic information."[549] (emphasis in original)

The everyday reality of mutations is that they cause change to details of existing structures rather than create new ones. This was illustrated by an experiment with sugar beets that began in 1800. To increase the sugar content of beets selective breeding initially produced rapid and significant results from six percent to seventeen percent over a seventy-five year period. However, continued attempts to increase sugar content over the next fifty years failed as the content never increased above seventeen percent. Not only are there limits to the change that selective breeding can achieve, there is a tendency for organisms revert to its original type when the pressures of selective breeding are removed. Luther Burbank, arguably the most famous botanist and horticulturalist of all time, called this tendency a natural law which he named Reversion to the Average. Breeding only deals with existing genes and does not add any new genes to the gene pool. As selective breeding pressure is maintained, disease and sterility increase which places the breeding subject at risk of death and extinction.[550]

Darwin's first of principles was that species were capable of or susceptible to change over time, and new species have appeared by the process of descent with modification over long periods during the earth's history. Darwin discussed the eye as one of the most difficult examples with which to defend his theories.

> Although the belief that an organ so perfect as the eye could have been formed by natural selection, [it] is more than enough to stagger anyone; yet in case of any organ, if we know of a long series of gradations in complexity, each good for its possessor, then, under changing conditions of life, there is no logical impossibility in the acquirement of any conceivable degree of perfection through natural selection… we may confidently believe that many modifications, wholly due to the laws of growth, and at first in no way advantageous to a species, have been subsequently taken advantage of by the still further modified descendants of this species.[551]

Thus, for Darwin, simple organisms evolved into complex organisms. However, the concept of irreducible complexity poses significant problems for Darwinian theory, and those problems have not been addressed with any degree of merit by evolution's defenders. Something that is irreducibly complex is described as follows:

> …a single system composed of several well-matched, interacting parts that contribute to basic function, wherein the removal of any one of the parts causes the system to effectively cease functioning. An irreducibly complex system cannot be produced directly (that is, by continuously improving the initial function, which continues to work by the same mechanism) by slight, successive modifications of a precursor system, because any precursor to an irreducibly complex system that is missing a part is by definition non-functional.[552]

For a complex organ to have irreducible complexity, all components required for operation must be present *and* operate together to perform the specified function. Not only must the parts be present and operate together, they must achieve minimal function to accomplish the specified function or purpose of the complex system. Remember Darwin's own words that, "If...any complex organ existed which could not possibly have been formed by numerous, successive, slight modifications, my theory would absolutely break down." Natural selection merely chooses systems that are already working.[553] Thus, Darwinian evolution must account for the addition of complex organs in their entirety, not piecemeal through a long series of gradations in complexity. The evolution of complex systems through countless gradations of change won't work.

When Darwin wrote of complex organs, he was referring to systems that were visible to the eye, and he could not have imagined the immense complexity of the unseen molecular world. However, modern biochemistry has revealed an astounding array of complex systems residing in the simplest cells "... an interwoven meshwork of systems", and almost every cell is capable of "...synthesis, degradation, energy generation, replication, maintenance of cell architecture, mobility, regulation, repair, and communication...and each function itself requires interaction of numerous parts." The intricate and interdependent machinery of the molecular world dramatically multiplies Darwinian evolution's difficulty in defending gradualism.[554]

The genetic code, sometimes called the DNA code, is the latest battleground between Darwinian evolutionists and those that see the hand of a designer in the creation of life. The DNA code communicates information to the cell and "...is exquisitely complex, and extremely precise." Each one of the one hundred trillion cells in the human body contains enough genetic information to fill one thousand encyclopedia-size books.[555] In an effort to account for the molecular structure of life, neo-Darwinian evolutionists have proposed various theories such as junk DNA, the non-coding part of DNA. The junk DNA theory proposes that, "In every generation, natural selection removes the less successful genes from the gene pool, so the remaining gene poll is a narrower subset...what is the information about? It is about how to survive."[556] However, Donald

E. Johnson, quoting Lee Spetner's *Not By Chance*, refutes the neo-Darwinists' assertions.

> There is no evidence that genetic information can build up through a series of small steps of microevolution...Mutations reduce the information in the gene by making a protein less specific. They add no information, and they add no new molecular capability...None of them can serve as an example of a mutation that can lead to the large changes of macroevolution...The failure to observe even one mutation that adds information is more than just a failure to find support for the theory. It is evidence against the...neo-Darwinian theory.[557]

A number of challenges to the theory of naturalistic evolution have been listed; some identified by Darwin himself and others of recent origin. The list of challenges include the fossil record and its lack of transitional forms, catastrophic annihilations as opposed to extinction by Darwinian gradualism, the degenerative nature of mutations, sudden appearance of species followed by stasis, limits to change within a species as shown by breeding experiments, tendency to revert to type (Reversion to Average), irreducible complexity in the development of complex organ systems, and the origin of the genetic code. The weight of evidence that undermines the theory of naturalistic evolution continues to mount with each passing year as do the evolutionists' contortions in attempting to answer the challenges and prop up a discredited theory.

Some of the strongest challenges to Darwinian theory have come from supporters of intelligent design based on an examination of life at the molecular level. A number of those who support intelligent design of the universe and life on earth do not support the Judeo-Christian model of creation. However, it is interesting to note the strong if not almost rabid resistance of evolutionists to any consideration of intelligent design in explanations of the universe and life on earth. The reasons for this are suggested by Michael Behe. Behe notes that the cumulative efforts to discover the secrets of the cell unambiguously and significantly support the concept of design, but the scientific community addresses the "stark complexity" of the cell with embarrassed silence. He then asks the question, "Why does the scientific community not greedily embrace its startling discovery?" Behe points to the scientific community's dilemma and calls it an elephant. One side of the elephant is labeled intelligent design, but what the scientists fear most is that the other side might be labeled God.[558] Behe continues:

> Many people, including many important and well-respected scientists, just don't want there to be anything beyond nature. They don't want a supernatural being to affect nature, no matter how brief or constructive the interaction may have been...they bring an a priori philosophical commitment to their science that restricts what kinds of explanations they will accept about the physical world.[559]

Given the mounting difficulties in the defense of naturalistic evolution, why is there such massive and fierce defense of naturalistic evolution as "accepted fact"? Why is it tantamount to heresy for one to even question the supports upon which the theory of evolution rests?

It was the first day of biology class in my sophomore year in the fall semester of 1964. With a stern, no nonsense, expression on his face, the professor began with a warning that the class would be based on the accepted fact of evolution and that the validity or truth of the subject would not be argued or debated. I complied with his instruction, dissected my share of frogs, and earned a respectable B. Even at that young age, I had enough wisdom to pick my battles, especially when it involved an almost nineteen year old college student versus a PhD in biological sciences. In reality, my reticence most likely was not so much a matter of wisdom but of self-interest for I had to successfully complete a number of core curriculum courses that included biology if I was to receive a business degree. Little did I realize that my professor's stern, don't question the "accepted fact" admonition was the modus operandi for naturalistic evolutionists and their supporters.

For the scientist, the litmus test for truth is the scientific method which Paul Davies in his book *The Mind of God* calls "...an immensely powerful procedure for helping us to understand the complex universe in which we live." But the method's rigorous demands of experimentation, observation, deduction, hypothesis, and falsification can only go so far. At some point there is an end to the "explanatory chain" where scientific explanations must "have certain starting assumptions built in." Ultimately, the deep questions of existence "...will always lie beyond the scope of empirical science..."[560] Where the explanatory chain ends, faith begins, and the scientist must leave science and its experiments, analyses, and hypotheses behind. For the humanist that faith begins with naturalism, and naturalism preaches that apart from nature nothing exists including a supernatural creator. It is a given, an accepted fact, but not provable by science. Without faith in the accepted fact of naturalism, evolution would not have a foundation. Thus, evolution too must rest on the humanist faith in naturalism.

Evolution's road from theory to "accepted fact" began with Charles Darwin himself. In the closing chapter of *On the Origin of Species,* he wrote:

> That many and grave objections may be advanced against the theory of descent with modification through natural selection, I do not deny...Nothing can appear more difficult to believe than that the more complex organs and instincts should have been perfected...by the accumulation of innumerable slight variations, each good for the individual possessor... Nevertheless, this difficulty, though appearing to our imagination insuperably great, cannot be considered real *if we admit the following propositions,* namely,—that gradations in the perfection of any organ or instinct, which we may consider, either do now exist or could have existed, each good of its kind,—that all organs and instincts are, in ever so slight a degree, variable,—and , lastly, that there is a struggle for existence leading to the preservation of each profitable deviation of structure or instinct. *The truth of these propositions cannot, I think, be disputed.*[561] (emphasis added)

In essence, what Darwin said is that he recognized the difficulty of belief in the theory of evolution. However, he believed that those difficulties disappear if we believe in the truth of the propositions that are critical to the acceptance of his theory of descent with modification through natural selection. In other words, the following are accepted facts: organs and instincts are perfected through a long process of gradations; that all organs and instincts are variable, in ever so slight a degree; and that each profitable deviation of structure or instinct are preserved through the struggle for existence. Further, he claimed those propositions cannot be disputed. Therefore, if his propositions are beyond dispute (and by inference beyond examination), they sweep away any objections to his theories.

Herrick wrote, "The theory of evolution is now almost completely accepted—apart from the kick-back of a number of Creationists, particularly in the US. There is querying and debating of the mechanism of evolution and continuing data adds to the picture which Darwin originally put forward."[562] Let us compare Darwin's and Herrick's statements. Notice that if one accepts Darwin's details as accepted fact, then his general theory must be believed. For modern day evolutionists such as Herrick, the theory of evolution is accepted fact, and it is the details (mechanism and the appearance of new data) that must be worked out. In other words, for Darwin truth was in the details that supported belief in the general theory. When those undisputable details proved fallible, latter-day evolutionists point to the accepted fact of evolution with the promise that supporting details will be discovered. Malcolm Muggeridge believed that evolution "…will be one of the great jokes in the history books in the future. Posterity will marvel that so very flimsy and dubious an hypothesis could be accepted with the incredible credulity it has."[563]

With sardonic yet insightful humor, C. S. Lewis charts the humanist's version of man's evolutionary journey through space, time, and the primordial soup to his arrival at comfortable positions of power in the ivory towers and centers of influence and opinion.

> The drama proper is preceded…by the most austere of all preludes; the infinite void and matter endlessly, aimlessly moving to bring forth it knows not what. Then by some millionth, millionth chance…the conditions at one point in space and time bubble up into that tiny fermentation which we call organic life. At first everything seems to be against the infant hero of our drama…But life somehow wins through. With incalculable sufferings… against all but insuperable obstacles, it spreads, it breeds, it complicates

itself; from the amoeba up to the reptile, up to the mammal...amidst the beasts that are far larger and stronger than he, there comes forth a little naked, shivering, cowering biped, shuffling, not yet fully erect, promising nothing: the product of another millionth, millionth chance. His name in this Myth is Man...He thrives. He begins killing the giants. He becomes the Cave Man...a brute yet somehow able to invent art, pottery, language, weapons, cookery, and nearly everything else...dragging his screaming mate by her hair...cowering before the terrible gods who he has invented in his own image. But these were only growing pains. In the next act he has become true Man. He learns to master Nature. Science arises and dissipates the superstitions of his infancy...See him in his last act, though not the last scene of this great mystery. A race of demi-gods now rule the planet...Eugenics have made certain that only demi-gods will now be born: psychoanalysis that none of them shall lose or smirch his divinity: economics that they shall have to hand all that demi-gods require. Man has ascended his throne. Man has become God. All is a blaze of glory. And now, mark well the final stroke of mythopoeic genius...Sun will cool...the whole universe will run down. Life...will be banished without hope of return...All ends in nothingness. Universal darkness covers all.[564]

Chapter 18

Human Sciences and the Secularization of America

"What makes real people?" This question was asked by Billie, the young daughter of migrant workers during the Great Depression. In response to her father's abrupt and dismissive response, she attempted to explain. "People that live in houses. People that stay together in towns." Billie was the oldest child in a family that grew to nine children, two of which she watched die before her own eyes. Knowing little but poverty and rootless drifting punctuated by brief stays in one of the one-room migrant shacks or tents pitched at the edge of fields, Billie knew she, her family, and the families of other migrant workers were different. That difference was reinforced when they were called "gypsies," "migratory workers," "fruit tramps," "farm labor," "transients," and "oakies." To Billie, the separation was so obvious that she began to think of the townspeople as *"real people."* Eventually, she understood that there was a different life where there existed a measure of stability and permanency.[565] (emphasis in original)

> I asked "What makes real people?" because I had sensed, probably more deeply and quickly than most children, the vital concepts of being and belonging. My way of life caused me to have what students of society describe as a marginal experience. I moved in various worlds and could see contrasts that were hidden to those whose lives were more ordered and predictable. I wondered why I was different from the town kids and how people joined together in towns. I was driven to voice as a guileless minor what philosophers and theologians have always pondered: Why am I like I am? Who Am I? Why am I here? Do I belong anywhere? How do I relate to

others? What is a person? Out of attempts to answer questions like these grew the studies, discoveries, and theories of psychology and sociology.[566]

Every person has some understanding of human nature. This understanding or perspective of human nature helps shape our worldview and comes from personal experience and media. Formal knowledge of human nature, that is the study of human nature, comes from the fields of psychology and sociology. The histories of these disciplines have been marked by attempts to avoid philosophical and theological assumptions that recognize the person as "…a whole being, having inner qualities that precise scientific theories cannot explain." This is why the two disciplines tend to reflect such little progress. New theories are constantly proposed to replace out-of-fashion fads and discredited theories. The disciplines will continue to go in circles and cycles until the subjects of personhood, human behavior, and relationships are looked upon from a biblical perspective and are not based on the assumptions put forth by social Darwinism.[567]

Writing almost prophetically in the last few paragraphs of *On the Origin of Species*, Darwin accurately foresaw the application of naturalistic evolution theories in the human sciences. "Psychology will be based on a new foundation, that of the necessary acquirement of each mental power and capacity by gradation. Light will be thrown on man and his history."[568] Darwin's prediction should not be surprising in that his theory of evolution operated on both structure and instinct. Darwin's theory not only invaded psychology but virtually all of the social sciences. Herbert Hovenkamp, quoted by Bradley C. S. Watson, stated:

> Only a few ideas in intellectual history have been so powerful and captivating that they have overflowed the brim of the discipline from which they came and spilled over into everything else. The theory of evolution is unquestionably one of these…It was a model…that infected everything, and one that appeared to answer every question worth asking, no matter the subject.[569]

Between 1870 and 1930, American institutions were remarkably changed through the secularization of American public life.[570] The political conception of what the American Founders had understood and implemented with regard to the limitations of politics was being discarded. Additionally, the secularization of American thought and the dethronement of the authority of religion in favor of science were well under way. In religion's place arose social Darwinism whose doctrines and philosophical assumptions soon dominated American intellectualism. Beginning in the last three decades of the nineteenth century, social Darwinism first captured academia and then secularized much of mainstream religion through the social gospel movement.[571] As previously noted, the teachings and beliefs of Christianity are uniquely compatible with *some* of the ends of socialism. This tenuous compatibility enabled the ascending leadership of the liberal Protestant denominations to successfully promote the social gospel, but secularizing forces ultimately appropriated the role filled by the Christian church for centuries. The secularization process quickly marginalized if not entirely eliminated Christianity's core beliefs and teachings as the social gospel movement, headed primarily by mainstream Protestant ministers, switched the emphasis from perfecting the inner man to social justice.[572] However, social Darwinists were not content with marginalizing or eliminating Christianity from the social gospel movement. They sought to remake religion in their own image, and that would be achieved through the human sciences.

For social Darwinists, natural selection was the tool chosen to elevate human science to the level of natural science. This new human science could be applied to a host of human problems through the application of organic, genetic, and experimental logic. Having freed life from the static bonds of morals and permanency, "…'genetic' and 'experimental' processes and methods can guide our inquiries into the human things." For the social Darwinian, "Good" would be defined as change, which is identified with "…organic adaptation, survival, and growth." In such a definition of good, philosophy concerns itself with processes rather than origins or ends. Without the absolute or permanent to guide or constrain, morals, politics, and religion are open to "…maximally experimental social arrangements."[573]

The human sciences encompassed by social Darwinism were psychology—the study of an individual's mental process and behavior, and sociology—the study of society, social institutions, and social relationships. The great champion of Darwin in the human sciences was John Dewey. For Dewey and other social Darwinists, there were no differences in the physical and human sciences. Integration of the doctrines and philosophies of physical and human sciences is made and applied as a single empirical, naturalistic scientific approach in addressing the needs of individuals and society.[574] However, the social Darwinist construction of human sciences has proven defective. It has left out the element that makes humans uniquely human. That element is God.

Psychology was not always the province of the social Darwinists. Before psychology was thought to be a science in the late nineteenth century, its various aspects could be detected in literature, medicine, physiology, philosophy, and theology. However, in his landmark 1890 *The Principles of Psychology,* William James had redefined psychology as the empirical science of the mind. Under a distinctively American brand, James and others rationalized religion through scientifically-based psychological explanations. As psychology wrenched the moral authority from religion, it also became the standard by which religious truth was measured.[575] Christian Smith saw this as a transformation from the Protestant concepts of spiritual and moral "care of souls" to a "…naturalistic, psychologized model of human personhood."[576]

As we have stated, psychology was originally approached from a variety of disciplines with primary emphasis given to theology and philosophy. In the early nineteenth century, the work of German philosopher Johann Friedrich Herbart (1776-1841) would be credited for directing later psychologists away from the philosophical approach of studying human psychology. Herbart proposed an empirical approach that emphasized experience and objective observation as opposed to the philosophers' analysis of thoughts and feelings. Therefore, experience and objective observation are applied to psychology's two major concepts. The first is mental processes that deal with "…reasoning, thinking, feeling, and perceiving. The second is behavior and is related to physiology and studies behavior as a function of the nervous system." With one foot in the realm of philosophy (mental processes) and the other foot in the realm of physiology, psychology had to balance the "...rigid prescriptions of scientific investigation with the dynamics of humanity." And the dynamics of humanity include such questions as "...the meaning and purpose of human existence." Three methodological approaches arose within psychology to address the mental-physical dichotomy. Experimental psychology deals with the development of a method for studying conscious awareness. Clinical psychology is a subcategory in the field and emphasizes counseling techniques and therapy primarily for dealing with emotional problems. Under clinical psychology, Freud developed psychoanalysis to treat patients. Humanistic psychology promoted "freedom of the individual to choose what to do and become." Under this method, the importance of people realizing their own potential or self-actualization is stressed.[577]

Having lost its moral authority to science and having allowed secularization of the social gospel, the survival of mainline American Protestantism as an important influence on American society was in doubt at the beginning of the twentieth century. However, mainline Protestantism chose not to fight but to compromise, accommodate, and acquiesce to the secularizing aspects of social Darwinism. Keith Meador described this process.

> In the 1920s, mainline Protestant seminaries began teaching the concept of "self-realization," which conceived of the self as an entity whose fulfillment and full potentiation were paramount within the spiritual life. As a result, helping people "adjust" and "adapt" in service of the self became the goal of pastoral care and counseling.[578]

One of the great leaders in mainline Protestantism's embrace of secular human sciences was Charles Clayton Morrison, publisher of the journal *Christian Century*. Morrison was prepared for the pulpit by his Disciples of Christ minister father and attended Drake, a Disciples of Christ college in Des Moines, Iowa. Morrison was heavily influenced by H. O. Breeden, another Disciples pastor that supported evolution and biblical criticism. Subsequently, Morrison began graduate studies in philosophy and psychology at the

University of Chicago as opposed to theology because he believed the "...problems of theology originated in philosophy." His teachers included John Dewey and others of the functionalist school of psychology. Morrison wrote of his education under Dewey and others in Chicago.

> When I left [the University], I was thoroughly immunized against every form of rationalism, apriorism, or speculation of any kind based on dogmatic or authoritarian ideas. Ideas, I saw, arise in experience, they are conditioned by experience, they refer to experience...In a word, ideas are functional for experience.[579]

While blending theology with psychology, the *Christian Century* became the most influential Protestant journal during the half century following the publication of James' *The Principles of Psychology* in 1890. The journal began life in 1884 as the *Christian Oracle*, a liberal voice for Disciples of Christ pastors and laity. With a name change to *Christian Century* in January 1900, the editors of the journal optimistically wrote of the forthcoming century in which "...its Christian character" would dramatically expand through "a 'progressive' and 'constructive' vision, an 'optimistic' and hopeful, tolerant and liberal' Christianity." For the editors this meant that the journal would "... embrace psychology as a progressive science of the mind..." and they heartily promoted the William James and John Dewey school of functionalism in the application of psychology to religion and education. The publication was strongly supportive of evolutionary theory and preached that a new era of Christian unity would be achieved through science. But the struggling journal continued to be plagued by low readership and financial difficulties. It bankrupted three times between 1900 and 1908. It was at a sheriff's sale resulting from the last bankruptcy in 1908 that Charles Clayton Morrison (1874-1966), an occasional contributor, purchased the small publication for $1500. By 1917, Morrison had declared that the *Christian Century* would no longer be a journal just for the Disciples of Christ but for all Protestant Christians with national and international coverage. With the reorganization, the journal achieved rapid success through increased readership and rising cultural prominence, and it became the standard bearer for the renewed social gospel movement after World War I.[580]

Under Morrison's editorship, the *Christian Century's* commitment to liberal theology strengthened. Darwin was "hailed as the most important figure of the nineteenth century…and that evolution does not contradict but affirms the Christian account of creation." For Morrison and his liberal colleagues, theology was about God, sociology dealt with the outer life, and psychology dealt with the inner-self life, and psychologists were the experts for the inner-self life, not theologians. Through psychology, religion became a science. In addition to the *Christian Century's* focus on the inner life through psychology, the social gospel was another plank in the liberal platform "…where modern social theories are breaking up the crust of established custom and introducing principles of reconstruction which…are bound to give us a plan of living together far happier and more just than the social scheme to which long ages have grown accustomed." Liberal Protestantism was profoundly affected by the promotion of psychology through Sunday school teachers training courses, promotion of books on psychology, pastoral care and counseling, seminary training, and Sunday school classes. By the 1920s, psychology was fully accepted as a part of American life, and this acceptance was fully supported by the *Christian Century* to the extent that the journal had begun publishing articles about psychology without mention of religion. Consistent with the mantra of psychology, sin was defined as "…living under the influence of subconscious instincts, desires and habits when the time has come to pass under the higher rule of reason and conscience…" Jesus was referred to as "…a supreme psychologist, in that he sought to liberate and sublimate the native powers of man and use their energy for higher ends—forging passion into power, and the cunning of greed into the strategy of righteousness."[581]

By 1938, Morrison had been the editor of the *Christian Century* for thirty years. In that time the journal had attained great cultural prominence but at the loss of much of its Christian character. Although indistinguishable from many of its secular peers, the journal was recognized as the preeminent voice of mainstream American Protestantism. One year later, Morrison shockingly wrote "How My Mind Has Changed" in which he described the secularizing consequences of the publication on American Protestantism in which he and his staff "...introduced and popularized psychology with a language of instinct and personality, which displaced the Christian theological language of morality and grace."[582]

> I had baptized the whole Christian tradition in the waters of psychological empiricism, and was vaguely awakening to the fact that, after this procedure, what I had left was hardly more than a moralistic ghost of the distinctive Christian reality. It was as if the baptismal waters of the empirical stream had been mixed with some acid which ate away the historical significance, the objectivity and the particularity of the Christian revelation, and left me in complete subjectivity to work out my own salvation in terms of social service and an "integrated personality."[583]

Belatedly, and at great cost to the Christian faith, Morrison realized modern culture was not moving toward Christian goals and that, in reality, modern culture defined by liberalism was the enemy of Protestantism. For decades Morrison and his liberal colleagues believed that liberalism reflected a "...radical criticism of culture in light of Christian faith." But for Morrison at the end of his career, liberalism was unmasked and revealed science and contemporary education's "...radical criticism of the Christian faith in light of modern culture." The deception was perpetrated through modern culture's secular goal of "progress" which was prescribed as the answer to a faith cluttered with Christian tradition.[584]

For well over one hundred years, naturalistic and humanistic psychologists have attempted to squeeze psychology into the mold of natural science and have rejected religious explanations of human nature. But without God in the equation, secular psychologists distort a clear understanding of human nature because science explores only natural processes and ignores "human realities" and questions of "...human meaning, purpose, and spiritual conditions." We have stated that the Bible is not a science textbook. We can also say the Bible is not a psychology textbook, but many of the principles of psychology have their origins in the Bible. There is a consistency between many valid psychological concepts and Biblical truth. "Christian psychologists note that every basic finding in scientific studies of human behavior reflects some biblical or theological truth...There are striking parallels between what researchers are concluding and what Christians believe."[585] It must be remembered that the religious moorings of psychology came from early American humanistic psychologists, of whom many were sons of Protestant clergy and began their academic careers in preparation for the ministry.[586] Elements of biblical truth, however repainted, mixed, or repackaged for the secular audience, still linger in secular psychology.

    Sociology generally encompasses fields of study involving family, government, education, economy, and religion, and some of which have been dealt with in earlier chapters. Psychology deals with the individual. Sociology deals with the patterns of relationships by which people are connected in society, social institutions, and social relationships. As people form relationships, sociology concerns itself with the structure and processes of those relationships. For secular humanists, two concepts for finding answers for questions of human nature and the essential qualities of society are *naturalistic* (sometimes called *positivistic*) sociology and *humanistic* sociology. Naturalistic sociologists generally follow the work of Auguste Comte (1798-1857) and Emile Durkheim (1859-1917), both French philosophers, who believed society was a thing itself. Under naturalistic sociology, the behavior of human beings is believed to be subject to certain laws similar to natural physical properties and interactions. The socially determined actions of persons occur in response to the demands and expectations of society. Humanistic sociologists believe that persons are not passive objects of social force. People have choice and therefore investigating social problems is paramount as opposed to patterns of natural science. Humanistic sociologists generally follow the work of Karl Marx (1818-1883), German social philosopher and revolutionary and Max Weber (1864-1920), who believed that "...society is composed of interacting persons in a complex dynamic relationship."[587]
    Both the naturalistic and humanistic sociologies fail to adequately explain human behavior and deal with social problems. Billie Davis wrote of the two concepts and the relationship of each with the Christian worldview.

> Naturalistic assumptions are compatible with the concept of original sin but not with the doctrines of creation and free will. Humanistic assumptions are compatible with the view of creative humanity but not with the truth of fallen nature and the inability of humans to provide their own salvation...[588]

The disunity among the various camps within humanistic psychology and sociology continues to grow wider. There appears to be little hope that a single theory will be developed to answer the questions of human nature and behavior with regard to the "biological aspects of mental processes and human introspection, emotions, and motivations." This conflict between the various theories and specializations results because behavioral and social sciences fail to deal with the purpose for which God created man. "That purpose is to glorify God, to love and be loved by Him, and to enjoy forever interacting with Him and His creation." We must recognize that we were created in His image and must develop those "*image of God* qualities" to be in harmony with God's purpose. (emphasis in original) Recall that we have said that the ultimate purpose of God's creation of man was for relationship with the Trinity, and relationship implies membership and belonging—"...the natural state of human beings." This relational image of God also applies to our relationships with each other, and this is the business of sociology. Davis quotes Russell Heddendorf from his book *Hidden Threads*, "...essential truths about persons and society are to be found in the Bible. Sociologists discover some of this truth. Usually unconscious of its original source, they try to explain it in human terms. So...we can find 'hidden threads' of scripture as we study sociology." As we have stated, the Bible is not a psychology textbook nor is it a sociology textbook. However, studies in the behavioral sciences, properly founded on a biblical worldview, can address the questions of cultural influence not specifically addressed by the Bible because "...relationships among people are determined more by customs and socially constructed attitudes than by human nature or individual personality traits."[589]

To consider humans as the children of God is abhorrent to social Darwinists. Denying this truth and spurred by belief in the perfectibility of man, scientists seek to know man himself and society. Perhaps it was inevitable that the methods used in the natural and biological sciences would be confidently extended to the affairs of mankind. If the universe is a vast machine run by natural laws, then those laws would operate with regard to man and society. Thus, scientism—the rational application of scientific theories and methods of the natural sciences to society and politics—would allow mankind to sweep away the ills of society including ignorance, poverty, war, hatred, and crime. Scientism took its cue from evolutionary biology and viewed man as an animal that evolved over the ages. Man and society could be studied, understood, manipulated, and improved. Man would no longer be limited by imaginary concepts of right and wrong as he is merely a bundle of instincts and urges. Learned responses were responsible for flaws in human nature, not moral corruption. No longer would the barometer of conscience be allowed to guide and restrain. Without a conscience, could there be a need for moral reasoning and moral responsibility? And of the soul, enlightened man has no need. But then again, the promise of this brave new world comes with a price. We may be a little less human, the malaise of life a little greater, but we shall have bread, security, imposed structure, and…boredom. However, we can rest assured that the social scientists, technocrats, and bureaucrats will do their very best for us as we are being perfected.[590] As previously noted, C. S. Lewis called these men "conditioners" or controllers who will choose the artificial norms "they will, for their own good reasons, produce in the Human race. They are the motivators, the creators of motives. But how are they going to be motivated themselves?"[591]

At the age of seven Billie Davis learned what it meant to be a real person…a whole being, and her understanding did not come through the explanation of precise scientific theories.

> Somewhere as we followed the migrant stream to another crop we pitched our tent beside a river…In the morning I saw children passing on the bridge. "Where are they going, all dressed up?" Real people. Incredible as it sounds to modern middle-class persons, I was more curious than afraid…I followed them, all the way to a small church at the edge of the village, and finally into a Sunday school class. It was there I heard the first direct answer to the question in my

heart. "You are the children of God," the teacher said, facing us all with a small inclusive gesture. It was as though she reached out, like a fairy with a wand, and granted me identity. I was a child of God…After 60 years of study, research, and teaching in the behavioral sciences, I know the first answer I received was the pivotal one, the one all other truth about human nature depends on.[592]

Chapter 19

American Education

One must make a distinction between instruction and education. A body of knowledge may be known by simple instruction, that is, the transmission of facts and principles. However, education encompasses a far broader mission. Education not only may contain instruction but is training for a way of life. Training for life must involve recognition of the central authority—the central vision—the collective consciousness in which the world is viewed. For a culture to survive, its adherents must see its implicit and unique worth. In most societies, the educator presents the social and political constitutions that support the preservation of that culture and consequentially that culture's educational system. When points of view contrary to the reigning cultural worldview are presented and promoted by educators and gain critical mass, conflicts or, in the modern vernacular, culture wars result. For almost one hundred years, a major conflict has grown between the dominant American culture including the beliefs and values upon which the nation was founded and the ascendant progressive theory of education and its proponents. This conflict arose because of a systematic attempt by a radical minority of educators and their allies to undermine through the educational system American society's traditions and beliefs. Of all American institutions under assault, the subversion of American culture through the humanistic educational establishment's progressive movement represents the greatest single threat to that culture.[593]

In *Visions of Order*, Richard Weaver listed a number of assumptions and tenets of the progressive movement's educational objectives. The striking differences and conflicts between the aims of progressive education and the core teachings and traditions of Western civilization as defined by the Judeo-Christian heritage are readily apparent. First, under progressive education's worldview, there is no permanency to a body of knowledge. The truth or falsity of such knowledge applied to concrete situations is judged only in light of the needs of the individual. Therefore, since the essence of the world is change, there are no fixed truths or final knowledge. Today's truth may be tomorrow's falsehood. All depends on the needs of the hour. Second, the focus of education is to teach students as opposed to teaching knowledge. Teaching students implies adaptation to the student. As adaptation occurs, ideals and standards by which to measure students lose value and respect and tend to fragment and crumble. Third, with such principles instilled in students and the educational process, the students' desires dictate what subjects to study and the aspects thereof as well as the amount of time and timing of that study. Fourth, the teacher relinquishes his/her role as the authority (generally viewed as bad) and becomes a leader whose purpose is to "…synchronize and cooperate with the work of the group." Fifth, competition and grades are considered injurious and prejudicial because they promote feelings of superiority and inferiority which are "undemocratic." Competition and grades may produce fear which should never be present in a school setting. Sixth, democracy requires sensory or activist (hands on) learning and must be on a level with intellectual learning. Therefore, things of the mind should never be exalted over the senses. The feelings of the mentally deficient, slow, less bright, and lazy must never be injured even if it means damage to the entire tradition of intellectual education. Seventh, progressive education emphasizes the greater use of hands on, concrete objects as opposed to education through symbols such as language and mathematics. Eighth, through a progressive education, students will adjust themselves to the existing society specifically and to a society conceived as social democracy generally. Weaver believed these tenets and assumptions were not all inclusive but representative of only a portion of progressive educational theory.[594]

    With an understanding of the basic tenets of progressive education and its goals, we now look at its origins and development. The roots of higher education in North America were an unequivocally Christian enterprise. The churches were the principal founders of the first colleges and universities in the colonies and whose purpose was for the training of pastors. During the eighteenth and nineteenth centuries, colleges and universities expanded their academic portfolios, and the cultural ties between the Church and higher education gradually weakened. However, the weakening ties generated little cultural controversy because explicitly Christian and generally conservative ends were understood by the great majority of Americans. However, as the end of the nineteenth century approached, "...the breach separating the universities and the churches widened suddenly, and culminated in the extraordinarily rapid and dramatic 'disestablishment' of conservative Protestantism from North American academic life between roughly 1890 and 1930."[595]

    The progressive reform era that arose between the 1870s and about 1930 was discussed in the last chapter. We also noted the progressive's usurpation of moral authority from religion through the human sciences and the social gospel. By the 1870s, the stage was also set for reform of the ideology, organization, and practice of education. Politicians, educators, and ordinary citizens were calling for modernization in education as a result of pressures caused by the growing problems of an emerging industrialized society. "Progressives were confident that they could use science to discover the kind of individual needed for the new industrial democracy, and then apply to schools scientifically proven tools for creating that individual." Over the course of the next half century progressive intellectuals seized the reigns of public education and effectively marginalized religious discourse and influence which ultimately resulted in "...a secularized educational ideology and bureaucratized public school system..." except for a smattering of local religious practices. But early progressive era accommodation of a mild religious synthesis quickly evaporated and became explicitly anti-religious and aggressive in the promotion of naturalism following World War I. In the battle with theologians, progressives' strategies and tactics allowed them to define the assumptions upon which the debate would occur. Under these assumptions, educational theory, administration, and the teaching profession were couched in terms of scientific natural processes. Scientific knowledge and pragmatic principles were woven into educational theory and administration. Additionally, teaching was professionalized in accordance with progressive standards, principles, and practices. The newly minted professionals became the expert authorities and monopolized the repositories of "...specified practices and the abstract knowledge associated with them." Through these strategies and tactics that supplanted the religious tradition in education with scientific naturalism, progressives "...thoroughly secularized national educational ideology, marginalizing historic, 'supernatural,' religious discourse among elite educators." Yet, however much they controlled the national educational agenda, American education was still accomplished at the local level.[596]

It was at the level of the local superintendency that progressives interfaced with the local schools and thereby spread the progressive educational agenda. Superintendents had to balance the pressures for modernization and efficiency with local pressures and politics. In this tug of war, progressives had a powerful ally in the form of psychology which independently and scientifically legitimized the progressive agenda. A second ally was the research university at which abstract knowledge was constructed and education professionalized. Thus, there was a growing and powerful cabal of intellectuals in a variety of academic disciplines that developed and supported various symbiotic relationships in education, psychology, and the natural sciences. By early in the twentieth century, the constant pressure from distant, degreed professionals who had become the awe inspiring national scientific experts in education and human sciences had effectively "...excluded religious articulations from their discourse." In response to the national educators' displacement of religious influences and the infusion of the scientific natural process into education, Protestants were limited to fighting to preserve certain symbolic practices in schools such as Bible reading and prayer while Catholics sought to gain public monies for sectarian schools. Through national legal and political pressures, progressives effectively used the conflicting goals of Protestants and Catholics to eventually rout both branches of Christianity from public education with the loss of initial hard won compromises permitting certain local religious practices in the educational process.[597]

The secular revolution in American education progressed in stages. From 1876 until the close of the century, various movements professing progressive themes began networking and building infrastructure around the unifying theme that scientific knowledge should be the basis of institutions in solving social problems and building a new society. From the turn of the century through the end of World War I various progressive movements organized themselves within national associations, universities, and political parties all supportive of the common agenda in which scientific discourse became codified. Following World War I, progressivism reached its zenith and vigorously implemented and expanded programs, refined techniques in practice, populated the expanding educational bureaucracies with like-minded progressives, founded professional associations, and "...elaborated more radical theories." The national education movement was the product of a relatively small group of individuals that usually held university positions. This elite group of educators fell within one of two movements. The first group comprised the administrative reformers who favored scientific administration and business efficiency and gained substantial power within urban education settings. The second group was the teaching practices/curriculum reformers that used psychology to promote "child-centered" teaching methods and curricula. This group of educational intellectuals became strongly networked through relationships established in graduate school, in academic positions, at professional meetings and conferences, publishing reports and textbooks, placement of students in key jobs, and involvement with foundations in obtaining research support. This group became the progressives' educational priesthood in which education was a "...religious calling to dispense the saving grace of knowledge, and the missionaries were the teachers, trained and sent out by the schools of education." The gospel was "child-centeredness" and psychology based on nature and science as opposed to God and religion.[598]

Child-centeredness in education fully embraces the humanistic worldview. Under the child-centeredness approach, education is based on "child nature" and focuses on the interests, abilities, and needs of a child. This is well stated by the authors of *Reforming Education, Transforming Religion*.

> In the enlightenment tradition...Progressives saw human nature as essentially good or neutral, rejecting the view of original sin...The child, in this view, develops naturally through reason and experience. Child-centeredness thus locates the source of authority in the self and human nature, rather than in God and the Supernatural. Because human nature is good and because the child is innately programmed to develop naturally, education must nurture the intrinsic

development and expression of child nature rather than break it or submit it to authority. This conception lies at the basis of modern primary education.[599]

The progressive educational agenda was framed by child-centeredness and psychology. Children were taught that an understanding of morality flowed from reason based on experience and that there was no one morality good for all societies. Reason through science became the determinant of what was good for society and replaced character education as modeled by Judeo-Christian morality. Science was the new morality, and progressives often cast their higher calling in religious tones such as "…the intrinsic spirituality of child (human) nature and human society." John Dewey wrote, "The religious is emancipated from religion by transferring the object of our 'idealizing imagination' from the supernatural to 'natural human relations' or the 'comprehensive community'." In Dewey's religious framework, value and meaning exist in humanity and does not flow from a transcendent God. Dewey's religion focuses on humanity rather than God, and the goal of that religion is not a relationship with God but individual and collective self-realization through civilization.[600]

Craig Gay presents a penetrating analysis of the reasons for the rapid and comprehensive secularization of American education at the beginning of the twentieth century. First, insurgent secular-humanist ideology displaced the reigning conservative Protestantism at colleges and universities in North America. In the growing secular culture, conservative Protestant educators feared appearing illiberal or sectarian to those political and industrial power bases whose support was necessary. Additionally, conservative Protestant educators allowed the progressives to frame the arguments and methodologies for establishing biblical truth. Effectively surrendering the moral high ground, conservative Protestant educators were swept aside by the rising tide of secularism and cultural pluralism. Gay credits the rise of the modern research university with multiple scientific disciplines and specialties, each with their corresponding commitments to their own logic and methodology, as a second cause of the rapid secularization of life at North American colleges and universities. Within the confines of such institutions arose a number of secularizing factors. Gay notes the "… modern intellectual habits of criticism, analysis, redefinition, and rearticulation, and even of simplification..." promotes agnostic tendencies and threaten "...belief in an eternal and unchanging truth."[601] In conjunction with the innate secular logic of science and the ideology of secular humanism, Gay points to a number of other structural features of the modern research university that are intrinsically secularizing.

> ...the academic commitment to plurality and to the due consideration of all points of view, a consideration that requires the protracted suspension of judgment until "all of the facts are in," as it were; the tendency toward ever increasing specialization of knowledge, a tendency which, as we have seen, has rendered the task of integrating disciplines more and more difficult; the professionalization of academic standing, a process in which performance is no longer measured against any kind of authoritative standard of character or belief, but is instead evaluated solely on the basis of professional competence as measured chiefly by a record of increasingly specialized publications; the relentless pressures to publish and the tacit valuation of innovation and experimentation this kind of pressure presupposes.[602]

We have reviewed progressive education's core tenets and assumptions and examined the history of the takeover of education by the progressives. How is this stranglehold on education perpetuated in spite of opposition of a majority of Americans who hold opposing beliefs and cultural worldview?

The perpetuation of progressive education's core tenets and assumptions at the primary and secondary educational levels pale in comparison with their influence within colleges and universities. That influence began with academe, and its power is illustrated by a classic case of liberal and progressive thuggery in higher education.

Texas is generally considered to be one of the more conservative states of the Union. Some may be surprised that the University of Texas is a liberal enclave of liberal indoctrination as are most public and private universities in the United States. The University of Texas System has over 200,000 students and 7,600 tenured or tenure-track faculty on nine university campuses and six health institutions. The 2010 System's budgeted revenues were $12.2 billion (estimated to exceed the Gross Domestic Product of each of the bottom thirty-five percent of the nations of the world) with budgeted expenditures of $11.9 billion which includes sixteen percent or $1.9 billion for research.[603]

Rob Koons was born in 1957 in St. Paul, Minnesota where his father was completing a PhD in chemistry. He grew up in Tulsa, Oklahoma and suburban Houston, Texas. Following a degree in philosophy at Michigan State University, he won a Marshall Scholarship and spent two years studying philosophy and theology at Oxford University. This was followed by studies in logic and philosophical theology at UCLA where he completed requirements for his doctoral degree in 1987 with a dissertation on logical paradoxes of truth and rationality. In the fall following graduation, he became an assistant professor at the University of Texas in Austin. In 1994 he was named an associate professor and continues as a philosophy professor on the Austin campus.[604] Koons is a Christian and member of a local Lutheran church.

In 2002, Koons and three other professors began work on the creation of a program in Western Civilization and American Institutions that would offer to all undergraduate students a sequence of Great Books seminars to address the general lack of required courses, structure, and systematic order in meeting core course requirements for liberal arts studies. The Western Civilization and American Institutions program as originally proposed would countermand the reigning rationale that that students should "accumulate courses that meet a 'distribution' standard, a smattering of courses scattered among many categories...," which is also becoming a trend within majors. Students would have been allowed to obtain a concentration in Western Civilization and American Institutions (although not a major) and satisfy eighteen of the forty-two hours of general education requirements by taking the sequence of courses proposed by Koons and his associates. Koons and his associates spent six years in design, implementation, and operation of a successful program that threatened the progressive leviathan and offended the leftist/liberal/progressive purveyors of intellectual conformity, political correctness, and general humanistic worldview. The success of the program was demonstrated by the establishment of a new field of study on the campus, program designation as an area of "concentration", hiring of four postdoctoral teaching fellows, and receipt of over $1 million in financial support. In December 2008, in spite of the program's success, Koons was fired as director of the program. The following spring, the administration and faculty redesigned the program and called it Core Texts and Ideas without a list or criteria for such "core texts" and without the required sequence. Effectively, Koons program was ravished of the intended content and structure that represented the heart of its value.[605]

Barbara Moeller's essay titled "The Texas Mugging of Western Civ" captures the internecine efforts against Koons personally and against the Western Civilization and American Institutions program by the administration and faculty of the College of Liberal Arts and their co-conspirators. After four years of work by Koons and his associates, the Faculty Council approved Western Civilization and American Institutions that allowed the program an official university website and credibility in its promotional efforts. The program's conception centered on the classic educational tradition of a liberal education built on a foundation of great books (with the term "liberal" meaning an education with a broad foundation as opposed to a political position or the multicultural smorgasbord of unrelated coursework). The speaker series during the last two years of Koons' directorship were exceptionally popular and won plaudits from both the public and the academic community. Speakers were recruited from a broad range of disciplines and political orientations.[606]

Randy Diehl was appointed as the new dean of the College of Liberal Arts in the spring of 2007. He inherited a soured relationship between the College and the Liberal Arts Advisory Council, an official University of Texas group of alumni that raised money for the College. The rift occurred because of the monies donated under his predecessor's administration were used for purposes other than what donors intended. With considerable help from Koons, Diehl was able to assuage the problems with the Liberal Arts Advisory Council. In Koons debt, Diehl was vocal about his "wholehearted" support of Koons' program. However, there was a "systematic undermining" of Koons' program that originated in the Dean's office. Dr. Koons found himself immersed in a bureaucratic fog of rules, regulations, and red tape for which others in his position had been trained to deal with but which he had not. A second and much more serious challenge to the viability of the program occurred when Assistant Dean Richard Flores refused to allow Koons' program courses to fulfill the General Culture course requirements for graduation from the College of Liberal Arts. Therefore, all of Koons' program courses became "super electives" meaning none of the courses would fulfill graduation requirements. The third level of bureaucratic harassment came from the meetings with chairs of other departments. The meetings were initially called by Flores and later Diehl supposedly to obtain everyone's views but, as Barbara Moeller described them in her essay, amounted to "browbeating 'truth' sessions" in which the heads of other departments expressed their dislike of Koons' program and its name. The consensus of the departments of English, Religious Studies, History, and American Studies was that "American" in the Koon's program title was "taken" and that much of Koons' program coursework in Western civilization was already being taught but without the politically incorrect words attached. Additionally, the other department heads considered Koons' program to be "triumphalist" in that it would reignite the culture wars that began back in 1968, the outcome of which had been decided.[607]

In spite of the opposition from the College of Liberal Arts, the Western Civilization and American Institutions program received "field of study" status, and in September 2008 a major celebration was held. In attendance were a host of dignitaries including the president and interim Chancellor of the University of Texas, legislative representatives, and various heads from the schools of law, business, and engineering. The guest of honor was Anthony Kronman who had written a book regarding his analysis of the state of liberal arts and a defense of the core curriculum tradition. Conspicuously absent were the assistant deans in the College of Liberal Arts. Three weeks later a *New York Times* article titled "Conservatives Try a New Tack on Campus." Moeller wrote, "In any other paper, it would have been considered a great plug for the UT Program. In the *New York Times*, it served as a clarion call to the Left to eradicate the scourge of conservatism from the academy." It appears that Dean Diehl immediately came under a great deal of anger and pressure from numerous sources. Several professors serving on the program's steering committee resigned due to political pressure. Diehl met with Dr. Koons and expressed shock to find out from the article that funding for the program raised by Koons had come from conservative foundations irrespective of the fact that all checks had gone through the Dean's office. Diehl informed Koons that this was a breach of trust and that he was withdrawing his support for the program, a move that would kill it for all practical purposes. Koons and his associates believed that due to the program's considerable national attention and favorable reception by influential alumni, cancellation would be a significant embarrassment to the university. Using this as an indirect means to save the program, Koons asked for a meeting with Diehl that occurred on November 17, 2008. Koons informed Diehl that without the Dean's support he had no choice but to discontinue the program. Diehl was livid and with a flurry of foul language fired Koons as the program director.[608]

    Diehl attempted to keep the firing secret from the entire Dallas area alumni group as he did not want to endanger a promised large donation. Diehl's reasons for firing Koons were varied, illogical, and without merit. To the program's steering committee, he accused Koons of financial malfeasance, citing the Witherspoon Institute's presumed financial arrangement as a "slush fund." There is no record of this reason ever being mentioned again. Pressed by questions from donors and faculty about Koons firing, he responded that Koons was insubordinate for complaining about his firing to President Powers. In other words, Koons was fired for something that could not have happened until after he was fired. Scrambling amidst numerous meetings and exchanges between Diehl and the chairman of the Board of Regents the president, and the provost, Diehl enlisted Tom and Lorraine Pangle as interim Director and Assistant Director. However, the program experienced a greatly expanded steering committee and a name change to the Jefferson Center for the Study of Core Texts and Ideas. Gone from the program were the junior fellows program and the graduate seminar. Events sponsored by the reconstituted program were poorly attended, but in Moeller's words, "...the faculty advising committee became swelled with faculty happy to sign on to a new center whose name did not include the banned words: Western, Civilization, American." Subsequently, a bill was introduced in the Texas Legislature that would create a School of Ethics, Western Civilization and American Traditions in the College of Liberal Arts. The Pangles testified against the bill during the legislative hearings. Tom Pangle asserted that his major objection to the bill was the proposed name of the new school and later told a reporter for the *Daily Texan* that "…these words, American, Western, and Civilization were just too 'right wing'."[609]

In addition to progressivist faculty hostility to the courses and fields of study that examine the traditional roots of Western civilization and American institutions, Koons identifies a second reason for faculty opposition: the threat to what Koons calls the Uncurriculum that prevails at most universities. Such an approach to curriculum design usually exhibits a general lack of required courses, structure, and systematic order in meeting core course requirements for liberal arts studies. Rather, such a structure allows an accumulation of a group of unconnected courses that meet a 'distribution' standard. An unstructured, smorgasbord approach to curriculum offerings gives students the allusion of choice, but the choice is among courses the faculty wishes to teach (generally related to their specialties) as opposed to required core courses. Therefore, faculty members can concentrate on research and publication from whence flow promotions, salary increases, prestige, and tenure. Their self-interests are defended through a chant of post-modern and multicultural ideals.[610]

Standing in opposition to the scattershot approach of the Uncurriculum is that of a liberal education which, in Koons' words, "…encourages students to think through the great questions of life in a systematic manner, with the great minds of the Western tradition as their guides and interlocutors."[611] Put another way, a liberal education means "…an ordering and integrating of knowledge for the benefit of the free person—as contrasted with technical or professional schooling…" According to James Russell Lowell, a liberal education "…is intended to free us from captivity to time and place: to enable us to take long views, to understand what it is to be fully human—and to be able to pass on to generations yet unborn our common patrimony of culture."[612] Russell Kirk wrote, "…[a] liberal education is conservative in this way: it defends order against disorder. In its practical effects, liberal education works for order in the soul, and order in the republic."[613] It is at this juncture that the Uncurriculum fails man and society for it does not provide a means to achieve order for the soul or society.

True education is meant to develop the individual human being, the person, rather than to serve the state. In all our talk about "serving national goals" and "citizenship education"—phrases that originated with John Dewey and his disciples—we tend to ignore the fact that schooling was not originated by the modern nation-state. Formal schooling actually commenced as an endeavor to acquaint the rising generation with religious knowledge: with awareness of the transcendent and with moral truths…to teach what it is to be a true human being. The person has primacy in liberal education.[614]

The true ideal of education is shoved aside and replaced with the acquisition of unrelated details which becomes an end in itself. The abandonment of true education for the Uncurriculum is a form of fragmentation by which is meant fragmentation of worldview. Furthermore, fragmentation causes man to descend from the glorious heights from which one can clearly see truth to a forest of facts and minutia that hide truth and ultimately destroys within men's minds the concept that truth exists. This is called relativism in which selected facts are arranged to fit the desired outcome. When the desired outcome fails to materialize or falls victim to another fad or fashion, old facts are discarded and new facts are marshaled to support the new desired outcome. In the fragmented worldview, facts become truth and particular facts are counted as wisdom.[615]

By necessity society needs its specialists, and professional education must contain certain core courses and assists man in becoming an effective instrument in some chosen field. These fields rightly deal in facts and minutia. However, such specialization (in and of itself inherently fragmentary) does not perfect the man nor does the typical university-required mixture of non-professional course work drawn from the Uncurriculum. These professionals (accountants, economists, doctors, lawyers, teachers, and a host of other "specialists") become unwitting soldiers in the army of the "knowledge class" having been indoctrinated with a humanistic worldview. C. S. Lewis called this class "men without chests."

> It is an outrage that they should be commonly spoken of as Intellectuals. This gives them a chance to say that he who

attacks them attacks Intelligence. It is not so. They are not distinguished from other men by any unusual skill in finding truth…It is not excess of thought but defect of fertile and generous emotion that marks them out. Their heads are no bigger than the ordinary: it is the atrophy of the chest beneath that makes them seem so. All the time…we continue to clamour for those very qualities we are rendering impossible…In a sort of ghastly simplicity we remove the organ and demand the function. We make men without chests and expect of them virtue and enterprise. We laugh at honour and are shocked to find traitors in our midst. We castrate and bid the geldings be fruitful.[616]

Given the multiple generations that have stepped from the secular and humanistic halls of higher education in America without the ability to take the long view, to understand what it is to be fully human, and to be without an awareness of the transcendent and moral truths, can we really be surprised at the ethical failures of leadership at all levels of government, the professions, and in the halls of commerce and industry and the consequential growing disorder so evident in American society?

The Koons affair is but one of many such battles that play out on almost every American university campus. In all of these battles, the bias against evangelical Christians stands at the apex of the academic disdain for other religious viewpoints. The Institute for Jewish and Community Research conducted a scientific survey of almost thirteen hundred faculty members in over seven hundred colleges and universities to determine academic anti-Semitism compared to other religious groups. The percentages of the surveyed group that reflected the holding of unfavorable feelings to various groups were as follows: Jews 3%, Buddhists 4%, non-evangelical Christians 9%, Catholics 13%, atheists 18%, Muslims 22%, Mormons 33%, and evangelical Christians 53%. Leaders from such organizations as the American Association of University Professors did not deny the results of the survey. Rather they stated that the poll reflected "a political and cultural resistance" as opposed to a religious bias and that the anti-evangelical bias would "not likely translate in to acts of classroom discrimination."[617]

Professorial claims of political and cultural resistance instead of bias ring hollow when even a cursory examination is made of the treatment of religious and conservative students on almost every campus in America, and this bias is exercised regularly in both subtle and overt ways. Jennifer Keeton found this bias so severe that she was threatened with expulsion unless she changed her religious views. A graduate student at Augusta State University in Georgia, Ms. Keeton was threatened with dismissal from the master's program in school counseling unless she changed her religious beliefs with regard to lesbian/gay/bisexual/transgender (LGBT) lifestyles. Ms. Keeton believes that homosexuality is a personal choice and results from identity confusion. She voiced her disagreement during classroom discussions and has expressed interest in conversion therapy for those following such lifestyles. The school has argued that she "was failing to conform to professional standards because of her views on lesbian, gay, bisexual and transgender issues." The school required that she "participate in a 'remediation plan' to increase her tolerance of gays and lesbians...The remediation plan...included attendance at three workshops on diversity, a monthly two-page reflection on what she has learned from research into LGBT counseling issues, and increased exposure to gay populations...with the suggestion that she attend Augusta's gay pride parade."[618]

Jennifer Keeton's experience is not isolated or reserved for the university level. A New Hampshire court has ordered a home-schooled girl into a government-run school because "her religious beliefs (Christian) are a bit too sincerely held and must be sifted, tested by, and mixed among other worldviews..." The court agreed that the 10-year-old Christian girl is "social and interactive with her peers" and "intellectually at or superior to grade level..." However, the court found that the girl "appeared to reflect her mother's rigidity on questions of faith" and that her interests "would be best served by exposure to a public school setting" with "different points of view."[619]

Richard Weaver succinctly and superbly describes the consequences of progressive education's revolt against the traditional idea of education.

Knowledge, which has been the traditional reason for instituting schools, does not exist in any absolute or binding sense. The mind, which has always been regarded as the distinguishing possession of the human race, is now viewed as a tyrant which has been denying the rights of the body as a whole. It is to be "democratized" or reduced to an equality with the rest. Discipline, that great shaper of mind and body, is to be discarded because it carries elements of fear and compulsion. The student is to be prepared not to save his soul, or to inherit the wisdom and usages of past civilizations, or even to get ahead in life, but to become a member of a utopia resting on a false view of both nature and man.[620]

Writing over five decades ago, Weaver observed that progressive education's theories and philosophies have been not only taught but enforced as dogma in which the teacher either accepts or is advised to leave the profession.[621] At the beginning of the second decade of the twenty-first century, perhaps even Richard Weaver, if he were alive, would be shocked at the extent to which the secular-humanist tentacles of progressive education have woven their way into every corner and cranny of American education in a fashion similar to that of our analogy of effects of kudzu-like socialism on American life.

Chapter 20

American Family – Marriage and Family

Before we launch into a discussion of the assault on the family unit by humanistic theories and philosophies, let us briefly expand our scope of inquiry to humanistic and Christian worldviews regarding humankind's relationships in the broader sense. Recall that we have said that the Trinitarian relationship is a picture of God's fundamental nature or being. Under Judeo-Christian ethic or beliefs, man was specially created for relationship with God. We are also made for relationship with one another. These Judeo-Christian beliefs are supported by a thoughtful reflection on the history of humankind in which those permanent things and universals stand as unrelenting testimonies of the truth of this special relationship with God and with each other. This history also points to the hierarchical nature of the relationships of God, humankind, and nature.

The distinction between the respective worldviews of humanism and Christianity regarding relationships can be visualized in positional terms, i.e., vertical versus horizontal. For Christians, the primary nature of those relationships is vertical (hierarchical)—God's being is shown by the Father-Son relationship and the relationship of Christ with the Church of which he is the head and we are the body. Because man was created in God's image, the hierarchical pattern of relationships is evident in various entities throughout history—marriage, family, community, nations, and the Kingdom of God. Hierarchy implies authority, superior and subordinate, order, and rank. Furthermore, if society is to be understood, it must have structure, and structure requires hierarchy which implies distinctions. Weaver called the "steady obliteration of those distinctions" the most significant omen of our time. Modern society embraces the humanistic perversion "…that in a just society there are no distinctions", but this leads to a loss of cultural center and ultimately disintegration. And the most dangerous idea of modern society is an undefined equalitarianism which pretends to be the champion of justice but is the opposite.[622] In reality, humanistic equalitarianism is a thief of status, property, patrimony, and ultimately freedom. In such is not found justice.

Codes of behavior upon which cultures and societies must rest rely on fraternity and not equality. Fraternity resonates through history as it is the offspring of the seminal purposes of man—relationship with God and other men. The object of fraternity is other-directed and speaks of duty, congeniality, cooperation, and sense of belonging whereas equality focuses attention on self and results in egotism. Equality, rightly applied, is equality before God and the law. But under the humanistic worldview, equality has become a rapacious egalitarianism that imposes regimentation and leveling of circumstance which results in unnatural social groupings. One senses the relentless gravity of the humanistic worldview pulling society downward from hierarchy into a flat (horizontal) social plain and consequential mediocrity. Such humanistic regimentation and leveling of condition result in loss of a sense of belonging and place which leads to suspicion and resentment. From this we see the humanistic definition of equality as "...a disorganizing concept in so far as human relationships mean order."[623]

If one reflects on the various descriptions of humanism through its definition, philosophy, application, and worldview as given thus far in this book, one can see the emphasis on the horizontal (egalitarian) and the sharp contrasts with the vertical (hierarchical) with regard to relationships in all spheres of family and society. By egalitarian is meant a belief in human equality with special emphasis on "social, political, and economic rights and privileges" and a focus on the removal of any inequalities among humankind.[624] An examination of just a few of humanism's principles will assist in developing this mental picture. Chief among these principles is humanism's insistence on denial of God, a severance that encompasses both time and authority. In other words, God does not now exist nor existed before the appearance of the universe. Creation was a random process of nature; therefore, we are not subject to the authority of some creator. A second example of the horizontal nature of relationships (and denial of hierarchy, rank, and order) in the humanistic worldview regards the nature of man. There are no giants upon whose shoulders we stand. Quite the contrary, contemporary man is the latest and greatest model that evolved from the slime pits of the past. As a product of evolution, humankind cannot be fallen nor have need of redemption. If man is not fallen, then there cannot be right and wrong, only different points of view. Man is his own master and owes nothing to a mythical God or the ancients. Humanism's exaltation of self over family, denial of patrimony, emphasis on the present and the experiential, flexible and interchangeable values, life lived for the moment for there is nothing beyond, and deference to the senses represent a detachment from any hierarchical bonds of duty, obligation, patrimony, and the permanent things. There is no heaven above nor hell below and therefore no hierarchy, only an everlasting march to an unattainable and unknowable horizon that continually recedes into the distance.

In contrast to the humanistic worldview, Weaver described the hierarchical nature of family and its bond with fraternity.

> The ancient feeling of brotherhood carries obligations of which equality knows nothing. It calls for respect and protection, for brotherhood is *status* in family, and family is by nature *hierarchical*...It places people in a network of sentiment, not of rights...[625] (emphasis added)

With this foundation of contrasting worldviews of relationships, we are now able to move into a more specific examination of humanistic and Christian worldviews as applied to marriage and family in the twenty-first century. The following three chapters will deal with modern feminism; the life issues of abortion, suicide, and euthanasia; and homosexuality.

As one reflects on how humans have organized themselves over time, there is and has been a great diversity of societal forms in different cultures and periods of history. However, underlying this variety is a structured order or arrangement that reflects the "creational givens." One of these givens is that the family structure is a societal institution established by the creator. And the family structure consisting of "...a father, mother and children living together in bonds of committed caring is not an arbitrary happenstance; nor is it mere convention that can be dismissed when it has outlived its usefulness." This ordered family structure is a part of the human constitution and is ingrained in man's nature in all of its facets—biological, emotional, social and moral. This structure allows for variety but sets definite boundaries, i.e., lines that cannot be crossed without being in opposition to the structured order of the family.[626]

The ordered family structure flows from God and is described in Genesis 1:27 which states, "God created man in his own image...male and female he created them..." Their characters and roles are distinct, but both are created in His image. Therefore, the roles of husband and wife and father and mother (monogamous married couple living with their children) are not societal constructs from which we are to be liberated. True human fulfillment is attained when men and women are faithful to the foundational principles of family. The outward fabric of the family may vary markedly in various cultures and societies down through the ages, but the divinely ordered family structure is intrinsically a part of the fundamental identity of the family in every society and for all time.[627] The divinely created family structure is one of those universals or permanent things that are imbedded in the foundation of creation. Cultures and societies that violate this ordered structure with impunity disintegrate.

The nuclear family was not born fully formed. Recall Blackstone's excellent description of the course of human history after the Fall. Man's reason and that of subsequent generations were impaired, flawed, unclear, clouded, or an unreliable in finding the laws of human nature from whence one may successfully guide his life.[628] Although reason was impaired, there was within human nature an intrinsic and timeless truth regarding the structure of marriage and family. Imperfectly perceived, man nevertheless began arranging society in accordance with those glimmerings of truth that emanated from within his nature.

One need not adhere to the Judeo-Christian worldview to recognize that marriage is a cultural universal. Kay S. Hymowitz wrote *Marriage and Caste in America* in which describes the post-marital age of separate and unequal families. Ms. Hymowitz does not speak from religious conviction and is a self-described agnostic. However, she recognizes that marriage is a "human universal" which "exists in every known society, no matter how poor or rich..." She describes a widening gap in American social structure in which family breakdown is the driving force behind poverty and other ills of modern society in America. She states, "...there is no way to attack these worrisome economic trends without tackling culture—the system of beliefs, values, and practices that help us define and live a good life."[629]

The highest form of the modern nuclear family is this: marriage is a freely chosen, exclusive, and permanent arrangement between a man and a woman that is a repository of sexual and emotional intimacy, affection, and friendship. Within this institution of monogamous marriage, children are conceived, born, loved, disciplined, nurtured, and raised.[630] This gold standard of marriage and family is a reflection of the relationship God intended between Himself and humankind. God created man for friendship, affection, and intimacy, and the various facets of man's relationships should mimic spiritual love.* It was to be a monogamous relationship..."You shall have no other gods before me."[631] It is a relationship of choice in which man has the right to accept or reject. If accepted, it is to be a permanent (eternal) relationship. We become His children, and as His

---

* As man was made in God's image, so too should man's love reflect the character of God's love. The Bible frequently uses the term "charity" for love. Charity in its true meaning is love of God and selfless love to others. The Apostle Paul in 1 Corinthians 13 describes the true meaning of spiritual love as long suffering, kind, not envious, behaves with courtesy and good will toward men, not selfish, not angry, not malicious or vengeful, does not take pleasure in harm or evil, does not expose the weaknesses or faults of others, patient, believes well of all, and hopes well for others when belief cannot be sustained. Apart from love of God, there are various relational facets of man's love. Although each relationship is different, all must strive to reflect spiritual love. These relationships are marital love, love of family (of which children rest at the pinnacle), and brotherly love (whether arising from familiarity or love owed to a stranger). And we must not forget Eros which in its culmination includes physical sexual love properly confined to the marital bed. But according to C. S. Lewis, Eros encompasses more than mere physical pleasure and sexual activity. It is a state of "being in love" that at some point includes sexual desire. But sexual desire and physical intimacy can be the object sought and occur without Eros. "But Eros wants the Beloved"...not just the act of physical intimacy. [C. S. Lewis, *The Four Loves*, (New York: Harcourt, Brace, Jovanovich, Publishers, 1960, 1988), pp. 91-92, 94.]

children we are loved, disciplined, nurtured, and find our redemption in Him.

As a cultural universal, the concept of the traditional nuclear family was molded and shaped by human experience, economic considerations, accumulated wisdom, and moral enlightenment through revelation in the Old and New Testaments over the course of humankind's existence after the Fall. But this shaping and molding was not haphazard. Rather, as William Bennett puts it, "There has been a tendency of change, change in a certain direction. More: Just as certain characteristics of the family have been malleable, adjusting to times and trends, other aspects, tethered as they are to deep human realities, have remained largely fixed and timeless."[632]

Through the millennia the molding and shaping of marriage and family progressed, not with changes to the basic structure but in the fleshing out of its bones. By our very nature, men and women are a "pair-bonding" species. From such comes reproduction and nurturance. Parents shape the moral understanding, behavior, feeling, and worldview of their children. Most importantly, "The family is where 'socialization'—the generational transmission of moral and cultural values—takes place." The home was the basic organizing unit of humankind—a father, mother, and children living together in bonds of committed caring. The home became part of the extended family, then village, community, and ultimately state. Society arose from the success of the home, and without the stable home society would have been impossible.[633]

The cultural universals of marriage and family provide for the needs of society, and across the millennia economic and political considerations played a major role in selection of marriage partners.[634] Society grew and stabilized through marriage and family and a network of extended family (relatives and friends) in which there are reciprocal expectations, obligations, and responsibilities. In this larger sense, marriage was more than just commitment between two people. It is a ceremonious and formal union in which two families celebrate the marriage and the consequent "entanglement" of the families. Each family rises in status or affinity with the other as well as having reciprocal claims on each other. With status and affinity comes the motivator to right conduct by not bringing dishonor to the family. Another basic need of society is the establishment of rules for sexual conduct. The family supports monogamy between the husband and wife. To such is born children that have status as family. Without monogamy the family tends to dilution and disintegration through "...loss of legitimacy, social identity, legal recognition, cultural tradition, and an estate." In both the nuclear and extended families, marriage provides the best arrangement for the nurture and protection of children, the impartation of respect for the authority of parents, and the recognition of obligations to the elder members of family. And the importance of children rose as "...family is where 'socialization—the generational transmission of moral and cultural values—takes place."[635] More than economic and political concerns, the preservation of moral and cultural values are critical for the preservation of the central vision of a culture. Without a cohesive central vision, a society disintegrates.

    The seedbed of what are considered to be many of the ethical qualities of the modern nuclear family that were critical to its development in Western civilization lay in the tribal society of ancient Israel, but the nuclear family as we know it was not a product of that society. Characteristics of ancient Israel that are in conflict with definition of the modern nuclear family include polygamy and the keeping of concubines among certain classes and the wealthy, arranged marriages (for economic, political, and social reasons), and the lack of legal and property rights and status for women. However, from the Hebrews we received two outstanding contributions to the development of the modern nuclear family: their commitment to family life and making marriage the focus of human sexuality (and opposition to infidelity and homosexuality). Where the Hebrews opened the way, Christianity would continue the moral refinement of marriage and family. As Western civilization was Christendom, we must recognize the importance of Christianity and its inestimable impact on our understanding of marriage and family. In Christianity, the marriage relationship was of such importance that it is described in terms of Christ's relationship with the church (his bride). With the new definition of marriage and family in the New Testament came a remarkable elevation in the status of women. In the first century world, women were of low social standing in virtually all cultures. They were considered inferior to men and responsible for sexual sin. But, Jesus' attitude and example during his earthly ministry became the definitive model for our understanding of male-female relationships, marriage, and family life. Paul's teachings on the relationship of men and women, marriage, and family added texture and detail to Jesus' ministry. Both men and women were held accountable to the same standards of morality. The vows of marriage were meant to be permanent with divorce allowed under very limited circumstances. With Christianity the understanding of the divine concept of marriage and family came into full view. But it would take another 1,500 years before "…permanent, monogamous marriage had triumphed, and home was more comforting and more private."[636] To that we now turn our attention.

Throughout much of history marriage has been a ritualistic and solemn occasion between a man and woman—a highly public profession of commitment to the most private of relationships. The solemnity of the occasion arises from the enormous magnitude and significance of the commitments—to take the marriage partner as wife or husband, to have and to hold, for better or for worse, for richer, for poorer, in sickness and in health, to love and to cherish; from this day forward until death do us part. This ceremonial language resonates with powerful sentiments that link us with prior generations since time immemorial and to an enduring and exclusive commitment to union while facing the uncertainties of life to come. The ritualism symbolically binds the families of the man and woman and attests to the importance of the unbreakable commitments of which God is both witness and participant.

The reasons for such commitments arise from human nature which is rooted in creation—the need to give love and receive love, a deep longing for sexual intimacy and emotional attachment, and a desire for a home and children. The humanist will argue that these things can be attained without requirements of marriage, monogamy, commitment to the permanency of relationship, and God. But such humanistic counterfeits are a weak, unsatisfying, and an imperfect imitation of marriage, "… the honorable estate, instituted by God." Marriage orders the soul whereas sexual intimacy outside of marriage, co-habitation, divorce (apart from infidelity and willful desertion), and homosexuality are illegitimate and therefore not heirs to that honorable estate. History and human nature attest to these assertions for according to researchers, married life as opposed to all other similar social arrangements provides greater financial security, better health and sex, and a longer and better life.[637]

Bennett called marital love that rests upon a foundation of unconditional commitment as "...safer, more enduring, and more empowering that any sentiment yet discovered or any human arrangement yet invented." He credits these attributes to the basic complementarity of man and woman joined together as one in marital love. The complementariness of the relationship is based on the differences, not just the physical but also the emotional and psychological. As the physical differences make sexual union possible, so too do the emotional and psychological differences of the marriage partners complement and complete each other.[638] The union becomes stronger than its parts. Do non-marital heterosexual relationships (homosexuality will be discussed in a later chapter) have the potential to be as strong? No, for such commitments are in conflict with human nature and cultural universals which God formed at man's creation. Such conflicts result in disorder of the soul. However, couples that do not hold the Judeo-Christian worldview but whose marital relationships are based on the cultural universal of monogamy and commitment to the permanency of the marriage relationship between a man and woman will achieve an order of the soul and a better life insofar as it relates to their marital relationship.

Let us examine the mindset of modern marriage partners which typically falls within one of two camps. First, the vast majority view marriage as a contract which is reflective of the humanistic (horizontal or egalitarian) worldview regarding marriage. The contract mindset focuses on marriage as a mutually beneficial relationship and getting as opposed to giving. When the benefits stop flowing or hard times arise, the relationship is easily broken through divorce. The contract mentality in marriage emphasizes the details, e.g., "If you do that for me, I'll do this for you." In other words, the marital ledgers must always be balanced, but marriage partners often have differing views of the value of what is given and received. These differing perceptions in a marriage often result in growing resentment, hurt, anger, and ultimately divorce.[639]

The second view is that marriage is a covenant relationship. Like a contract, a covenant is an agreement between two or more parties, but that is where the similarity ends. The nature of a covenant agreement is very different from that of a contractual agreement, and the key difference is motive. The covenant relationship is the essence of the cultural universal of marriage and is uniquely expressed in Christianity. God is a covenant maker and the importance of covenant relationships is illustrated by His covenants with Moses, Abraham, David, and others throughout the Bible. Jesus Christ fulfilled the old covenant and initiated the new covenant. Rather than to receive something in return, covenants are initiated for the benefit of others, that is, to minister to another person as opposed to manipulating someone to get something. In a covenant marriage, the *motive* is a commitment to the well-being of the spouse. However, it would be naïve to believe that most young couples would possess that motive and level of maturity at the time of the marriage ceremony. Rather, covenant marriages are grown and strengthen through the years. If couples commit to covenant marriages and recognize the covenant relationship requires nurturing during the difficult times, those marriages will far more likely endure than contract marriages based on a cash register/accounts receivable ledger mentality. In a covenant relationship, the promises made are not conditional but open-ended, that is, the promise or commitment is not conditioned on reciprocal behavior. There are no "If…then" clauses in covenant marriage vows.[640]

The ideal of romantic love inextricably linked with individual happiness *devoid* of the covenantal commitment is of recent origin and rests of the tenets of the humanist philosophy and worldview. When one examines the humanist view of marriage, it may surprise many that humanist writings have little to say with regard to marriage for the emphasis is not on a matrimonial bonding of a man and woman but the liberation of the individual. Two of the common principles of *Humanist Manifesto II* clearly elevate the individual as opposed to the two who shall become one flesh. These principles are:

> Fifth: *The preciousness and dignity of the individual person* is a central humanist value. Individuals should be encouraged to realize their own creative talents and desires. We reject all religious, ideological, or moral codes that denigrate the individual, suppress freedom, dull intellect, dehumanize personality. We believe in maximum individual autonomy consonant with social responsibility… (emphasis in original)

Sixth: In the area of sexuality, we believe that intolerant attitudes, often cultivated by orthodox religions and puritanical cultures, unduly repress sexual conduct. The right to birth control, abortion, and divorce should be recognized. While we do not approve of exploitive, denigrating forms of sexual expression, neither do we wish to prohibit, by law or social sanction, sexual behavior between consenting adults. The many varieties of sexual exploration should not in themselves be considered "evil."…individuals should be permitted to express their sexual proclivities and pursue their life styles as they desire…[641]

To the average twenty-first century American, covenant marriage may appear impractical if not impossible amidst the swirl of a humanistic popular culture that idealizes romantic love inextricably linked with individual happiness. Most moderns hope to sail the seas of marital bliss in the flimsy craft built of fleeting emotion and temporal happiness. Marriages based on this false ideal will soon crash on the rocky shores of reality. Rather, covenant relationships are centered on steadfast or spiritual love[*] which is far stronger and deeper than fleeting, emotion-driven romantic love. When the storms of life rage, the deep keel of a covenant marriage will keep the marital ship afloat. Certainly steadfast love contains emotional and romantic elements, but steadfast love is a choice, a way of thinking, a mindset and is best expressed in 1 Corinthians 13:4-8, "Love is patient; love is kind. Love does not envy; is not boastful; is not conceited; does not act improperly; is not selfish; is not provoked; does not keep a record of wrongs; finds no joy in unrighteousness, but rejoices in the truth; bears all things, believes all things, hopes all things, endures all things. Love never ends."

This last phrase brings us to our next point. The covenant marriage is intended to be a permanent relationship. We can enter into a contract with anyone. The contract may involve sex, security, status, or a hundred other clauses and may or may not include love. However, we enter into covenant relationships only with those we love.[642] Therefore, to achieve the fullness of its promise, love must be

---

[*] See footnote earlier in this chapter for a discussion of spiritual love.

an ingredient in the covenant marriage. In Paul's description of love in his letter to the Corinthians the careful reader will note an absence of the words important to proponents of the humanistic worldview—autonomy, independence, growth, and creativity. Faithful adherence to the words of 1 Corinthians 13 bring forth the fruits of a covenant marriage relationship. Such fruit is harvested only after the hard work of planting, weeding, and watering which is all wrapped up in one word—nurturing. Covenant marriages will involve its share of difficulties, trouble, and pain, but the harvest is worth the effort.

For humanists and their feminist fellow travelers, extolling the virtues and provisions of a covenant marriage relationship may elicit howls of contempt. As has been noted, the focus of the humanists is on the "I" and not the "we", a message constantly conveyed and reinforced by media, government policies, the educational establishment, and popular culture. And this prevailing humanist worldview is carried into the great majority of male-female relationships regardless of type—marriage, cohabitation, or sexual promiscuity. We need not belabor these conclusions with additional explanation of the differences that are readily evident between the Judeo-Christian and humanist worldviews regarding marriage and family.

The family and societal carnage that occurred in America during the twentieth century and thereafter as a result of the domination of humanist worldview is monumental and recounted in numerous studies and reports. The statistics reflecting the precipitous decline of the American family are incontrovertible and coincide almost exactly with the emergence of the Boomer generation in the mid-1960s and the rapid and accelerating ascendancy of the humanist worldview. Perhaps the signal statistic in the collapse of the traditional family is the high level of births to unmarried mothers as reported in 2006: 68 percent of all black children, 45 percent of all Hispanic children, and 25 percent of all white children.[643]

The collapse of the traditional family is even more evident when one examines the population of women with and without spouse present. Of particular note is the dramatic twelve-fold percentage increase between 1960 and 1990 of women with children under the age of eighteen who have never married. This accounts for almost a third of all women with children under age 18 with no spouse present. For eighty years between 1880 and 1960, this figure declined from slightly over 12 percent to 2.6 percent in 1960 before the dramatic escalation to 31.6% in 1990. By the end of the first decade of the twenty-first century, four out of every ten births in America are to unwed mothers.[644]

What is also remarkable and further highlights the impact of the humanistic view of marriage is the decline in the percentage of women with children under eighteen who have a spouse present. For eighty years between 1880 and 1960, this figure was very stable at or near 90 percent before dropping to 76 percent in 1990.

The trend in divorce statistics for the period between 1960 and 1990 is also alarming. In 1960, divorces occurred at the rate of 35 per thousand persons married where the spouse was present at time of divorce. By 1990, the rate had increased to 142 divorces per thousand, and by 1995 the rate was 160 divorces per thousand.[645] Cohabitation numbers are much more fluid and difficult to track. However, the consequences of the instability of such arrangements compared to marriage are all too evident. Compared to married couples, the breakup of couples in cohabitation is more likely to occur, last a shorter period of time, pose a greater risk of infidelity, and is more prone to incidences of domestic violence and child abuse. Another troubling sign with regard to the future of marriage is the comparison of married and unmarried couples with regard to multiple partner fertility. Where unmarried couples have a child together, one or the other of the partners will have a child from another relationship in almost 60 percent of the cases as compared to only 20 percent for married couples. In other words, for 80 percent of married couples, neither partner has had a child from another relationship. The ramifications for children of unmarried couples with one or more siblings from another parent include erosion of parental responsibility, conflicts arising over parental authority, and conflicts resulting from past relationships that damage the cohesiveness of the family and the well-being of the children involved.[646]

In 1960 the marriage rate per one thousand unmarried females was 73.5 percent compared to 54.5 percent in 1990 and 50.8 percent in 1995.[647] As marriage declined the number of single parent households headed by females (as a percentage of all households: married couples, headed by single males, and headed by single females) that were below the poverty threshold increased dramatically from 23.7 percent in 1960 compared to 53.1 percent in 1990.[648]

Table 3 United States Women with Children Under Age 18 Presence or Absence of Spouse		
	Spouse Present	No Spouse Present
1880	88.4%	11.6%
1910	90.2%	9.8%
1940	90.1%	9.9%
1960	90.4%	9.6%
1990	76.0%	24.0%

Percentages for Tables 3 and 4 derived from Source data: Marital status of mothers with children, by race: 1880-1990, Table Ae221-244, *Historical Statistics of the United States, Earliest Times to the Present*, Millennial Edition, Vol. One, Part A, Population, (New York: Cambridge University Press, 2006), p. 1-674.

Table 4 United States Women with Children under Age 18 and No Spouse Present Reason for Spousal Absence					
	Never Married	Married, Spouse Absent	Divorced	Widowed	Total
1880	12.4%	17.1%	3.4%	67.1%	100.0%
1910	9.0%	19.7%	6.2%	65.1%	100.0%
1940	5.3%	32.4%	15.0%	47.3%	100.0%
1960	2.6%	43.1%	27.0%	26.2%	100.0%
1990	31.6%	22.0%	40.9%	5.5%	100.0%

Author's calculations based on Source data: See Table 3 footnote.

In other words, there were more single women heads of households below the poverty line than both married couples and those headed by single males combined. These sad statistics show that marriage has proven to be the best antidote for poverty regardless of gender. According to a U.S. Census Bureau, American Community Survey, 2006-2008, unmarried families accounted for 71.2 percent of all *poor* families whereas married families accounted for 74 percent of all *non-poor* families.[649]

Working women with children under six years old increased from 18.6 percent in 1960 to 58.9 percent in 1990 and 63.5 percent in 1995. And the younger the age of the child appeared to make little difference in a woman's participation in the labor force for 55.5 percent of women with children under age three were working mothers in 1990 and 60.9 percent in 1995.[650] As a result of this trend, the use of organized child care facilities grew rapidly from six percent in 1965 to 29 percent in 1995.[651]

In their flight from marriage, humanists promised women emancipation and fulfillment; however, the big lie produced only bondage, drudgery, and exhaustion—poverty, long hours of daily separation from their children, and the drudgery of low-paying jobs in the workforce. The seeds planted by the those promoting the humanist worldview over the decades prior to the 1960s and thereafter have born bitter fruit—illegitimacy, cohabitation, fatherlessness, divorce, and a large number of single parent families with children who are locked in a continuing cycle of neglect and poverty. When compared to homes where children were raised by married parents, children raised in homes by single parents are more likely to encounter emotional and behavioral problems, drink, smoke, use drugs, be physically abused, exhibit poor school performance and drop out, and exhibit aggressive, violent, and criminal behavior.[652] And in such an environment the memory of what once was or might have been is lost, and the transmission of the central vision of American culture to another generation is in peril.

Daniel Patrick Moynihan retired from the United States Senate (Democratic Senator from New York) in 2000. Near the beginning of his career he was an assistant Secretary of Labor in Lyndon Johnson's presidency. At the time of his retirement, the senator was asked to describe the biggest change he had seen in his forty years of government service. Articulate and intellectual, the distinguished public servant, having served both Democratic and Republican presidents, replied, "The biggest change, in my judgment, is that the family structure has come apart all over the North Atlantic world" and had occurred in "an historical instant. Something that was not imaginable forty years ago had happened." Author of the 1965 Moynihan Report officially known as "The Negro Family: The Case for National Action", Moynihan knew that of which he spoke.[653] Enormously controversial at the time of its release, the report continues to be a topic of debate in the twenty-first century. The report characterized the instability of the black families in America and the importance of the family unit in providing that stability.

> At the heart of the deterioration of the fabric of Negro society is the deterioration of the Negro Family. It is the fundamental source of the weakness of the Negro community at the present time…The role of the family in shaping character and ability is so pervasive as to be easily overlooked. The family is the basic social unit of American life; it is the basic socializing unit. By and large, adult conduct in society is learned as a child…the child learns a way of looking at life in his early years through which all later experience is viewed and which profoundly shapes his adult conduct.[654]

Writing shortly after Moynihan's perceptive summation of the condition of the family structure, William Bennett noted the deep concern of Americans with regard to the family. Bennett pointed to the general instability of the American family and the contributing factors such as the decline in the status and centrality of marriage in society, substantially more common out-of-wedlock births, and the significant increase in co-habitation. With the decline of social perception and necessity of matrimony, children are less valued, more neglected, more vulnerable to non-family influences, and have less resources devoted for their care and benefit. Bennett wrote that, "Public attitudes toward marriage, sexual ethics, and child-rearing have radically altered for the worse. In Sum, the family has suffered a blow that has *no historical precedent*—and one that has enormous ramifications for American society." (emphasis added).[655]

Another decade has elapsed since Moynihan's diagnosis of the disintegration of the family unit as the major modern affliction of the Western world and Bennett's reporting of Americans' purported concern for the survival of the family. It is no longer the problem of the black population. The deterioration of the family unit is pervasive and crosses all ethnic, socio-economic, and religious lines although the poor and disadvantaged bear a greater portion of the misery. Yet, there has been no public hue and cry to reverse the decline, no urgency or sense of crisis in dealing with the problem, no new series of government studies explaining the situation, and no investigative reporting or meaningful media attention regarding the most profound change in society that has had no historical precedent. Why is this so? The answer is that the solutions to reverse the decline and devastation of marriage and the family unit stand as polar opposites of the prevailing and pervasive humanistic worldview.

The modern nuclear family is the fabric stretched over the cultural universal of marriage and family structure. This fabric was woven, thread upon thread, over the course of time through the efforts and accumulated wisdom of generations of our ancestors. Bennett wrote of the importance of the modern nuclear family.

> The most important and precious achievements in the realm of marriage and family life have not been the result of mere happenstance. Spurred (or detained) by economic circumstances, they have been primarily the result of trial and error, of accumulated wisdom, and of moral enlightenment—sometimes one, sometimes another, sometimes a combination. Shaped as we are by long human experience, we must be all the more careful not to lose what has required so much time and so much effort to accomplish. The modern nuclear family is a rare construct; we tamper with its essentials at our peril.[656]

Chapter 21

American Family – Feminism and the Roles of Men and Women

In *Marriage, a History*, Stephanie Coontz states that the male breadwinner/full-time housewife marriages that were the standard in 1950s and 1960s America and Western Europe were *not* a brief historical oddity. Rather, she argues that such male-female role characterization was the culmination of a trend that had been growing since the late eighteenth century. For over 150 years there had been continuous movement toward and development of the once radical concept that love should be the basis for marriage and that the marital decision process should be controlled by the couple considering marriage.[657] These dramatic changes began in the eighteenth century and were embraced by both the humanistic and Christian worldviews. However, the meaning and implementation of these changes would become a battleground in the war between the humanistic and Christian worldviews.

First, let's look at the roles of husbands and wives throughout most of history. Typically, men in all cultures and times have been the defenders of and providers for the family whereas women have been the nurturers and care givers for husband and children. From the remotest tribes to upscale suburbia, although similarities through comparisons would be almost unrecognizable, the complementary roles of husbands and wives along the lines just described will be present. Although those roles may not have finite and sharp distinctions (husbands and wives may share most roles in varying degrees), the basic defender-provider/nurturer-care giver dichotomy remains a constant.

For much of history, marriage was *not primarily* about love. Rather, the needs and desires of the man and woman and their children were secondary to the needs of the larger group. Through marital status within the group came adulthood and respectability.[658] In the last chapter we stated that society grew and stabilized through marriage, family, and a network of extended family (relatives and friends) in which there were reciprocal expectations, obligations, and responsibilities. Marriage was economically, politically, and culturally vital to the success and survival of the larger group. Marriage and family were the keystone of society and provided hierarchy and structure and thereby allowed a division of labor and power by gender and age. From this we see the roles of the husbands and wives emerge. Wives were part of the family labor force. She would combine her productive tasks with that of motherhood and domestic chores. In the early barter economies, the household was the center of production. However, as societies moved from barter to wage-based economies, production occurred outside of the home, and it became more difficult for women to perform both roles. The new division of labor found the father and children working outside the home while wives concentrated on domestic activities. These included not only wives' traditional tasks and care of younger children but growing food, cooking, home maintenance, making clothes, and tending to animals—all of which were more valuable to the family than any wages she could make outside of the home. With prosperity, women's roles became less a matter of economic survival but one of homemaking which was viewed as an act of love and a mark of a family's economic status and social success. From this transition developed the new role and identity of wives. Homemaking lost its status as an economic activity. Women were no longer considered work-mates—economic producers and co-providers—but soul mates. From this new way of organizing marital relationships emerged two spheres brought together in a "well-rounded whole."[659]

At the same time marriage was beginning to be viewed as a private relationship between two individuals and not just a "link in a larger system of political and economic alliances." Formerly, the husband was the overseer of the family labor force, but he became the sole provider for the family. The wife, no longer an integral component of that labor force, directed her energies to the emotional and moral aspects of family life. "The husband was the family's economic motor, and the wife its sentimental core." Because of the changes facilitated by the emerging market economy and the spread of wage labor, young people obtained a greater measure of independence from parents. Marriages occurred at younger ages as couples no longer had to wait on dowries, inheritances, or the completion of apprenticeships.[660] These dramatic changes in the roles of husband and wife and relationship with parents were of monumental importance in the making of the modern nuclear family. To contrast the differences between the humanistic and Judeo-Christian worldviews, it is important to again summarize the Judeo-Christian foundation for understanding marriage—a freely chosen, exclusive, and permanent arrangement between a man and a woman hat is a repository of sexual and emotional intimacy, affection, and friendship. Within this institution of monogamous marriage, children are conceived, born, loved, disciplined, nurtured, and raised. Although the structure of the cultural universal of marriage has been present throughout history, the hard-won, fully formed beauty of marriage and family as intended by God and revealed through a careful reading of the Bible, especially the New Testament, has been absent in most societies. Although marriage is freely chosen, the extended family and circle of friends still play a vital and restraining role in marriage and family.

During the age of the Enlightenment and in particular the eighteenth century, advances toward the modern nuclear family would also bring dangers that would threaten its survival. These dangers included a more secular view of marriage and sexual relationships propagated by the tide of humanist thought and influence that swept through the nineteenth century as described earlier in this book. By the 1960s and for the first time in history, the ideal of marriage came under direct attack by social engineers who "...believe a lifelong vow of fidelity is unrealistic or oppressive, especially to women...[and] marriage and family ties were...potential threats to individual fulfillment as a man or woman. The highest forms of human needs, contended proponents of the new psychologies, were *autonomy, independence, growth, and creativity,*" and marriage was considered a hindrance to these human needs.[661] (emphasis added) Whereas the need to give love and receive love, a deep longing for sexual intimacy and emotional attachment, and a desire for a home and children were the foundational bricks in the modern nuclear family, now autonomy, independence, growth, and creativity became the new but insubstantial building materials. For many women, this liberation to focus on self would be found under feminism's over-arching banner of political, economic, and social equality. Certain aspects relating to political and economic equality of women have been and must be championed by the proponents of the modern nuclear family and the Judeo-Christian ethic. However, conflict arises with feminist contentions regarding marriage in general and the relationships and roles of husbands and wives.

In modern Western societies, strains to marital unions have grown significantly through demands of equality in marital relationships, and the denigration of the traditional roles of husbands and wives has resulted in a general decline in the perceived importance and sanctity of the institution of marriage. Demands for equality are a direct attack on the hierarchical nature of the marriage relationship. In the last chapter we noted that the complementariness of the relationship between men and women is based on the differences, not just the physical but also the emotional and psychological. Complementariness in relationship does not imply that men and women are equal for they are not. Rather, complementariness implies greater strength in an area where the other partner is less strong. Some defend equality in marriage as the supreme goal. But to argue that marriage should be a 50-50 proposition implies that each partner must maintain a close accounting so as to make certain he/she gets his/her share of the dividends in the partnership. Some would carry the argument farther by saying that there need not be equal content in giving, merely equal levels of giving. However, the differing perceptions of value of the things given and received become the basis for contention and strife. This quest for equality in marital relationships is a caustic that will eat away at the coveted and sublime self-giving that occurs through unconditional commitment at all levels of the marital relationship. However, that is not to say that a husband or wife is superior or inferior to the other which brings us to the separate and distinct but complementary roles of husbands and wives.

The Industrial Revolution emerged in the first half of the nineteenth century and brought huge changes to America in the form of urbanization, industrialization, and rapid social changes. Occurring simultaneously was a dramatic change in the political landscape of the country. Andrew Jackson's election in 1828 ushered in the age of the common man and severed the presidency from the domination of those with first hand remembrance of the American Revolution. The myths of Jackson as the hero of the common man and Jacksonian democracy as a watershed event in democratic processes is better described as a hypocritical reform movement steeped in corruption, spoils, and patronage. Jackson and his successors' actions "...ensured the dominance of a proslavery party in national politics..." which continued to exacerbate the problem of slavery until the beginning of the Civil War in 1860. It was during the Jacksonian period that significant attitudinal changes occurred with regard to slavery, health, prisons, education, social relationships, and the status of women. Out of this vortex of the Industrial Revolution and consequent political and social changes emerged two groups to assuage society's turmoil and bring order to the soul of Americans—the religiously awakened and the utopians. Between 1815 and 1860, religious renewal and fervor were hallmarks of American life. This was a more democratic brand of Protestantism than the more reserved Puritan variety with emphasis on the afterlife. The new enthusiastic Protestants believed in perfectionism, "...a belief that any sinner could be saved by Christ and, upon salvation, should pursue good works to ensure that saving grace, shifted the focus from the Puritan emphasis on the afterlife to the possibility of a sin-fee world in this life." For many the possibility of a sin-free world began to dominate their thinking and efforts if not totally jettisoning traditional understandings of sin and redemption. From these came hundreds of utopian communalist and transcendentalist societies bent on reordering social and economic systems while rejecting "...any social arrangements, tradition, church doctrine, or even familial relationships as expressions of power. Marriage, they held, constituted just another form of oppression, even slavery..."[662]

    Many utopians and religious perfectionists supported greater rights and roles for women. These included property rights, divorce, child custody, education, and greater opportunities and roles in the work place; although, not all groups supported all of these rights. Women increasingly saw political means as a way to solve personal problems. The temperance movement became their first foray into social activism. From the myriad of causes championed by women came the beginnings of the feminist movement. In 1848 Elizabeth Cady Stanton and a small band of Jacksonian feminists convened the

Seneca Women's Rights Convention in Seneca Falls, New York and issued a proclamation—a Declaration of Sentiments. With the exception of abortion, the proclamation touched on nearly all of the issues espoused by today's feminists. The proclamation included a call for greater educational opportunities, legal rights, marital rights, and the right to vote. However, interest in greater rights for women came from all corners of society, e.g., the first female college graduate in the United States came from Oberlin, headed by Charles Finney, the great evangelist of the first half of the nineteenth century.[663]

Following the Civil War, Elizabeth Stanton formed the National Woman Suffrage Association to press for a constitutional amendment to allow women the right to vote. Other goals of the group included birth control and easier divorce laws. Some women opposed the issues other than suffrage and formed the National American Woman Suffrage Association. The two groups merged in 1890, but it would be 30 years before suffrage was granted to women in 1920. The vote for women was delayed because feminism's radical activists, such as Margaret Sanger, packaged women's suffrage with controversial baggage such as birth control primarily through abortion and eugenics.[664]

To understand the deleterious effects of feminism on the modern nuclear family, one must track feminism's growth and inextricable historical ties to humanism. And in the pantheon of radical feminists, Margaret Sanger must be considered among the firsts and most radical of all. Sanger was born in 1879 in upstate New York to Michael Higgins and his wife. Although an Irish immigrant of Catholic heritage, he was a freethinker and skeptic and held radical socialist ideas. In spite of Margaret's father's constant undermining of her fledgling faith, she was baptized in 1893 in secret at St. Mary's Catholic Church in Corning, New York. Margaret was the sixth of eleven and grew up in an impoverished home filed with drudgery, fear, and unhappiness. With her faith wilting under constant assault by her father, she developed a passionate hatred of the Church by the age of seventeen. She soon experienced her first taste of freedom at boarding school in which she "…plunged into radical politics, suffragette feminism, and unfettered sex." She tried teaching but found it laborious. This was followed by nursing which she also found strenuous and difficult. She never finished her training. Her escape was found by marrying a well-off architect working for a prominent New York firm. William and Margaret Sanger soon had three children, but in spite of the demands of family life, William was eventually drawn back to old friends and acquaintances in radical politics. Margaret would occasionally accompany William when he attended socialist, anarchist, and communist meetings in Greenwich Village. Finding motherhood, domesticity, and the bourgeois life unfulfilling, Margaret adopted her husband's interests and was quickly consumed with the bohemian, the rebellious, and the revolutionary. Her life became a constant swirl of rallies and meetings with the foremost radicals of the day. She joined the Socialist Party that had consolidated almost all of the revolutionary elements of American politics and accounted for six percent of the vote in the 1912 election. As she became ever more consumed with the radical causes, home life deteriorated with the apartment in perpetual disarray and children often sent to neighbors and friends for care and keeping. It was at this point that Margaret came under the influence of Emma Goldman, an extreme radical with ties to the Bolsheviks in Russian, Fabians in England, Anarchists in Germany, and Malthusians in France. Goldman lectured and wrote on a wide range of subjects "...from the necessity of free love to the nobility of incendiary violence, from the evils of capitalism to the virtues of assassination, from the perils of democracy to the need for birth control." So enamored was Margaret of Goldman and her ideas, she told William that "...she needed emancipation from every taint of Christianized capitalism, including the strict bonds of the marriage bed." Shocked, William attempted but failed to keep his marriage intact. After a brief stint in labor activism, Margaret became a fiery evangelist for sexual freedom.[665]

With her divorce from William Sanger, Margaret's direction for the remainder of her life began to take shape. She began writing and publishing *The Woman Rebel*. The first issue called marriage a "degenerate institution", capitalism an "indecent exploitation", and sexual modesty an "obscene prudery." In other issues she wrote on contraception, sexual liberation, social revolution, and defended political assassinations. Having violated postal laws due to what was judged to be the obscene and lascivious content of her materials and facing up to five years in prison, she fled to England and immediately made contact with assorted radical groups. She spent a little over a year in England and made important institutional and intellectual contacts. She shared her ideas and her bed with such Fabian luminaries as H. G. Wells, George Bernard Shaw, and Havelock Ellis, author of the seven-volume *Studies in the Psychology of Sex*. She was especially influenced by Malthusian theories of population growth in which poverty and deprivation were thought to be the result of a population crisis because production of goods and services was forever doomed to trail the exponential growth of population. Malthus' theories became the basis for national and international social policy in the West. Malthusians and others believed the "physically unfit, the materially poor, the spiritually diseased, the racially inferior, the mentally incompetent" should be eliminated through benign neglect as opposed to proactive solutions to deal with the misery of the less fortunate. They believed that such proactive solutions would only aggravate the problem of sickness, crime, and privation. Other Malthus disciples saw a subtler, more practical means of achieving population control—education, contraception, sterilization, and abortion.[666] It was a German house painter by the name of Adolph Hitler that would take Malthus' theories to their ultimate conclusion which was neither benign nor subtle.

Margaret recognized that her goals of radical socialism and sexual liberation would not be readily accepted upon her return the United States. With the help of Havelock Ellis, she repackaged her revolutionary rhetoric and pro-abortion campaign under the banner of scientific and philanthropic-sounding terms that emphasized population control and eugenics. Upon return to the United States she launched a successful public relations campaign to get the criminal charges against her dropped, founded the Birth Control League, and began publication of The *Birth Control Review*. She opened her first abortion clinic but was quickly arrested and spent thirty days in the workhouse for distribution of obscene materials and prescription of dangerous medical procedures. However, her stature rose among the urban intelligentsia and subscriptions soared as articles from well-known authors such as H. G. Wells, Julian Huxley, and Karl Menninger were printed in the *Birth Control Review*. Her widespread fame only grew with the publication in 1922 of her book *The Pivot of Civilization*. The best-selling and highly controversial book openly proclaimed Malthusian and Eugenic goals and "...called for the elimination of 'human weeds', for the cessation of charity, for the segregation of 'morons, misfits, and the maladjusted' and for the sterilization of 'genetically inferior races'." Eventually, she became closely associated with German scientists who designed Nazi Germany's "race purification" plan and endorsed early Reich euthanasia, sterilization, abortion, and infanticide programs. Articles closely paralleling Nazi Aryan-White Supremacist propaganda were published in the *Birth Control Review*. However, World War II created a huge threat to Margaret and her organization as details begin to emerge of Nazi atrocities committed in the name of eugenics and racial purification. Aided by millions of dollars available from another "money" marriage, Margaret embarked on a three-pronged program to rescue herself and her organization from its infamous connection with Nazi Germany and its massacres: change the name of her organization to Planned Parenthood Federation of America, found a national birth control organization under which local and regional birth control leagues would affiliate and contribute their grassroots respectability, and initiate a massive propaganda campaign to emphasize patriotism and family values while hiding her scandalous personal life and political views. Although well hidden, most of her personal life was a disaster. Her daughter died of pneumonia, and her sons were neglected and forgotten. Much of her adult life had been a blur of sexual encounters and erotic fantasies and fetishes. She experimented with the occult, séances, Eastern meditation, and other esoteric philosophies. She became addicted to drugs and alcohol in 1949. Margaret Sanger died in 1966 at the age of eighty-seven, but she accomplished her goal of altering Western civilization.[667]

    The face of Planned Parenthood today continues to be that Margaret Sanger, and her goals remain its goals. Dr. Alan Guttmacher succeeded Sanger as the president of Planned Parenthood in 1962 and stated that Planned Parenthood's direction was essentially the same as the one Sanger had lain down. Faye Wattleton, the longest serving president of Planned Parenthood (1978-1992) other than Sanger, concurred when she said she was proud to be "walking in the footsteps of Margaret Sanger."[668] The close connection between the views of humanism and Planned Parenthood cannot be denied when two of its presidents, Margaret Sanger and Faye Wattleton, were named Humanist of the Year by the American Humanist Association: Sanger in 1957 and Wattleton in 1986.[669] Planned Parenthood's ties to humanism were reinforced when Alan Guttmacher, its second president, signed *Humanist Manifesto II* in 1973.[670]

The economic and political strength of the organization have few equals. For the fiscal year ended June 30, 2008, the organization had total annual revenue of $1.101billion and *net* assets of $.995 billion.[671]

When one counts all of those small human beings aborted in the cocoons of their mothers' wombs, Margaret Sanger's worldwide legacy of death far exceeds that of Joseph Stalin, Adolf Hitler, Benito Mussolini, and the Khmer Rouge combined.

In the post-World War II era, the feminist movement was in decline. Many in the media pronounced the demise of the movement and "…celebrated the happy, suburban housewife."[672] But the feminist movement would gain new life in the turbulent 1960s as it joined forces with other groups bent on fundamentally changing America. The spark for the rebirth of the women's movement in the 1960s was the *Feminine Mystique*, a book by Betty Friedan that appeared in 1963. Friedan wrote about "the problem that has no name," by which she meant the supposed alienation and meaninglessness experienced by the typical housewife.[673] The timing of the book could not have been better to advance the feminist movement and its humanistic principles.

The Civil Rights Act of 1964 included Title VII which prohibited sex discrimination in employment, and the Equal Employment Opportunity Commission was created in 1965 to enforce the Civil Rights Act. On June 28-30, 1966, the Third National Conference of Commissions on the Status of Women was held in Washington, D.C. Becoming frustrated with the course of events occurring during the conference, Betty Friedan and a group of other women met in her hotel room to discuss alternative strategies to achieve an end to sex discrimination in employment. Friedan had written the letters N O W on a napkin which became the acronym for the National Organization of Women founded at that meeting.[674] NOW's 1966 Statement of Purpose was clear in its efforts to change the role of women in American society.

NOW is dedicated to the proposition that women...must have the chance to develop their *fullest human potential*...it is no longer either necessary or possible for women to devote the greater part of their lives to child-rearing; yet childbearing and rearing, which continues to be a most important part of most women's lives—still is used to justify barring women from equal professional and economic participation and advance. We do not accept the traditional assumption that a woman has to choose between marriage and motherhood, on the one hand, and serious participation in industry or the professions on the other. True *equality of opportunity and freedom of choice* for women requires such practical, and possible innovations as a nationwide network of child care centers, which will make it unnecessary for women to retire completely form society until their children are grown...We reject the assumptions that a man must carry the sole burden of supporting himself, his wife, and family, and that a woman is automatically entitled to lifelong support by a man upon her marriage, or that marriage, home and family are primarily woman's world and responsibility—hers, to dominate—his to support...We will seek to open a *reexamination of laws and mores governing marriage and divorce*...We are similarly opposed to all policies and practices—in church, state, college, factory, or office—which, in the guise of protectiveness, not only deny opportunities but also foster in women self-denigration, dependence, and evasion of responsibility, undermine their confidence in their own abilities and foster contempt for women.[675] (emphasis added)

Written by Friedan, the stated goals of NOW carry the trademark language of the humanistic worldview, and like Margaret Sanger before her, Friedan was named Humanist of the Year in 1975.[676] Friedan was also a signor of the 1973 *Humanist Manifesto II*.[677] Feminist goals, like those of other humanistic social engineers and revolutionaries, attempt to redefine the roles of men and women in society. In 1981, Friedan called the early suffragette days the first wave that demanded a "full participation, power and voice in the mainstream" from which the Boomers benefited. She now called for the Boomers and their daughters to focus on a second wave of "embracing the family in new terms of equality and diversity."[678] Again, we must note the emphasis on *redesigning* the family structure. For the feminists of the 1960s and 70s, conventional marriage and family were at best an option for a few, but they questioned its allure in a "progressive" society in which "marriage and children limited women's career success and prevented them from the adventure and self-exploration that seemed men's privilege."[679] However, both humanists and feminists discovered the inflexibility of human universals such as marriage.

We have previously reported the grim statistics with regard to the age of un-marriage that began in the mid-1960s. However, these statistics are merely numbers and percentages and do not truly convey the devil's bargain made by the feminists bend on *redesigning* the family structure. Many in the Boomer generation and their elders listened to the humanists' siren song of freedom, individualism, autonomy, creativity, and growth that was to bring happiness through un-marriage. But it is the morning after in America, and we stare at the dissipated figure before us and see only the wreckage, misery, and unhappiness of divorce, cohabitation, out-of-wedlock births, poverty, and single family households. Not only was the feminist ideal bad for women and men, extensive research has revealed marriage was good for men and women and that a gender balance rather than gender bias existed within marriage. The benefits of marriage for *both* men and women include greater happiness and satisfaction in life, greater combined financial success, greater sexual satisfaction, better psychological and physical health, and less exposure to physical violence.[680]

What of the children raised under the newly designed humanist family construct? The price for those following the feminist mantra during the 1960s through the 1980s was high, and much of the price was paid by their children—"troubled parents, disordered homes, and diminished prospects."[681] We have observed that marriage is both a private or personal relationship as well as a social institution whose *primary* purpose was organization of rearing or training up the next generation. However, with the ascendency of the humanistic worldview, its values focused on the individual person and his/her independence, freedom, self-actualization, autonomy, growth, and creativity. With these humanistic goals in place beginning with the

1960s, children became secondary to matrimony's new primary objective—happiness.[682]

The dramatic transformation of American divorce laws during the last half of the twentieth century is a reflection of the triumph of the humanistic worldview that the individual is more important than the family which is based on the Enlightenment's understanding of human nature. Under the humanistic worldview, happiness and fulfillment of the adults who enter marriage is of primary importance. If one becomes unhappy in the marital relationship, then to disengage from the union should be made easy as in the no-fault divorce laws. Under the Judeo-Christian worldview, the well-being of the family (and ultimately society) is paramount, and therefore divorce should be made difficult.[683] However, C. S. Lewis writing in *Mere Christianity* questioned how far Christians should go in imposing their views of marriage and divorce on the rest of the community. Specifically, he wrote that just because Christians believed that divorce should be made difficult, that belief should not be imposed on society in general. His personal view was that churches should recognize that "the majority of British people are not Christians, and therefore, cannot be expected to live Christian lives." He also believed there should be two kinds of marriage: one for Christians and governed by the Church and one enforced on all citizens and enforced by the state. But, Lewis's views are both puzzling and wrong. His views are puzzling in that he wrote eloquently in *The Abolition of Man* of the Tao which "provides a common human law of action which can over-arch rulers and ruled alike." Lewis's Tao was literary shorthand for the permanent things, the universals such as marriage and family—"a norm to which the teachers themselves were subject and from which they claimed no liberty to depart." To *not* uphold universals in society as the standard by which we live begs disintegration and collapse of that society. Lewis was proved wrong by events of the five decades following his death (he died the same day as President Kennedy was assassinated in 1963).[684] If Lewis were still alive almost sixty years after he wrote *Mere Christianity,* he would undoubtedly recant with regard to his two-tier view of marriage and the ease with which divorce should be available through the secular state. Even secular family experts are surrendering to the weight of evidence coming from their own research that marriage is "central to the overall well-being of children."[685]

Why is marriage central to the overall well-being of children and why is divorce so destructive to that well-being? First we must address the relationship of the married couple to that of their children. For most of American history up to the 1960s, marriage consisted of "a self-reliant child-centered couple, who had freely chosen each other in a spirit of equality and mutual affection and who would pass on to their young not just property but also the qualities needed to live in freedom."[686] Here we refer to child-centeredness in the home and not of the humanist's definition of indulgent child-centeredness prevailing in America's elementary and high schools. The primary task of human beings is to maintain and continue the human order. This is done through the act of creation. But that maintenance and extension of the human order is more than a biological event. The primary duty of parents is to socialized their children, i.e., to imbue within those children the central vision of society that is consistent with the central and accepted truths of human history. It is through marriage and family in the classroom of the home that such socialization occurs and by which society achieves order and continuation. The rapid rise of the humanistic worldview beginning in the 1960s put forth monumental challenges to the transmission of the moral order upon which American society had flourished. Those challenges include illegitimacy, cohabitation, fatherlessness, homosexual lifestyle, and divorce.[687] It is those things that erode the foundation of marriage, family, and home and effectively cast children on a rootless quest for meaning in life.

The presence of two parents in a home with their children does not guarantee a nurturing environment. Marriage, family, and home are merely the elements necessary for socialization of children. Nurturing must be added, and that is difficult in modern society as family members are rarely together for extended periods of time. The demands on families in a fast-paced, technologically driven, and rapidly changing society makes the nurturing of children difficult at best. The difficulties expand considerably in households requiring two-incomes, particularly in families living with a humanistic worldview. Without concerted resistance, it is easy to become submersed in that worldview and its values which will be transmitted to the children. The home becomes merely a place to sleep and store stuff, and family members are reduced to tenant status where there is no mutual dependence, connection, or cohesiveness. Many will argue that we can't turn back the clock to the "good old days", but a return to simpler times is not being proposed even if it were possible. What is the solution to providing a nurturing home environment in the midst of a dominant worldview that dismisses its primacy? To accept one's children as priority is the beginning of an answer, and that priority is not expressed only through provision of the material things of life.

God's creation of man was an act of love, but He knew that act would cost Him the crucifixion of His son on the cross. The creation of life within the bonds of marriage is a reflection of that divine love. In marriage, a man and a woman become one and through an act of love create another human being for whom they have a responsibility. And as with God's creation, the creation of another human being will cost the creators. The cost is making one's children priority as self must become secondary for both the individual and the couple.

To provide the necessary nurturing and socialization of their children, American husbands and wives must examine their worldview and evaluate their priorities. If a man is working sixty hour weeks, skipping vacations, and rarely sees his family in order to provide for them the better things of life, he has wrong priorities and his family will suffer. Likewise, if a wife is working a full-time job and pursuing a career track as well as attempting to maintain some semblance of home life, the nurturing process will diminish. To correct the situation, compromise and adjustments must be made. The cost may involve not maximizing one's career potential for *both* the husband and wife. Humanists will shout about the importance of the husband's or wife's individual selves, and feminists will decry the greater sacrifice demanded of the wife. We have discussed the complementariness of the husband and wife in the marriage relationship and will not belabor the point other than to reiterate the following. For the husband-father, his strength lies in securing provision for his family. For the wife-mother, her strength lies is nurturing her small children, and the best day-care facility "…is no substitute for a parent's unqualified love and devotion, patience, empathy, and unhurried attention." It is also understood that some women have great emotional difficulty fulfilling the role of a full-time stay-at-home mom while others want to escape the working world outside of the home and simply be a mom. If circumstances are such that the wife must work or feels compelled to do so, many alternatives and combinations thereof are available that will allow time to spend as many non-work hours with her children as possible. These alternatives include working part-time, coordination of schedules such that one parent is home during part of the day, use of grandparents or nannies as opposed to institutional care, suspending pursuit of one's career during the early childhood years, and seeking employment in a field with hours corresponding to that of children in their school-age years (e.g., teaching). Other sacrifices may be necessary such as limiting the number of hours children are allowed to be involved with extra-curricular activities which keep them from spending time with parents. Whatever the sacrifices required, the nurturing and well-being of the child must take precedence over virtually every other aspect of family life.[688]

"Trust, love, loyalty, fidelity, commitment, and meaning" are basic human needs and are part of the nature of man. It is upon these basic human needs that universal social institutions are built of which the married couple is the foundation. What gives marriage and family centrality and power within the universal social institutions? In their superb book *The Case for Marriage*, Linda Waite and Maggie Gallagher wrote, "As a species, we have developed social institutions over eons to get the most out of these creatures that we are. The family, focused around the married couple, forms the keystone of these universal social institutions." And the foundation of the married couple is at its strongest when bound with those simple non-conditional commitments to "…love and cherish, till death do us part."[689] Waite and Gallagher conclude that:

> Decades of social-science research have confirmed the deepest intuitions of the human heart: As frightening, exhilarating, and improbable as this wild vow of constancy may seem, there is no substitute. When love seeks permanence, a safe home for children who long for both parents, when men and women look for someone they can

count on, there are no substitutes. The word for what we mean is *marriage*.[690] (emphasis in original)

Chapter 22

American Family – Abortion

We get a fleeting glance at the enormity of God's decision to create man from a reading of the second verse of the first chapter of Genesis. "And the earth was without form, and void; and darkness was upon the face of the deep. And the Spirit of God *moved* upon the face of the waters." (emphasis added)   In this passage, the verb "moved" is "rachaph", the transliteration from the original Hebrew and is variously translated as hovering, fluttering, or to brood as when a hen gently settles herself on her nest to incubate her creation. By implication, it means to sit quietly, thoughtfully, contemplatively—with a feeling of tender love and yet with sense of brooding or foreboding at the terrible cost of creation. Thus, the value of life is inextricably linked with the unfathomable creative act of God.[691]

One of the things within man that separates him from the animal world is an inborn sense of revulsion and rebellion at the taking of the innocent life of another human. That something is an inner feeling, perhaps ill-defined or even unrecognized, that to take innocent life is to destroy that which belongs to God, which was created in His image, and which cost Him immensely. Be it one's own or that of another, the authority to destroy innocent human life is withheld from humankind. Even among murderers in a murderous society, it is rare to find one with absolutely no qualms or remorse about taking the innocent life of another human being.

For those with Judeo-Christian beliefs, God is the creator of the universe and all within including man, and consequently God and His universal laws are the arbiters of the life and death of men and no one else. For the humanist, life and its origins have nothing to do with God. Humanists have devalued God, and "When man devalues God, he eventually comes to devalue man, as well as the animating factor we call life."[692]

Without doubt, the most contentious and emotional issue of our times in the war between humanist and Christian worldviews revolves around abortion of unborn babies. Perhaps this is understandable given that life itself is the most basic urge. Think of a drowning man who desperately lunges to the surface to gasp in essential oxygen that separates him from oblivion and death. Except for the giving of one's life for another, all else—power, pleasure, fame, possessions, yesterday, and tomorrow—are of absolutely no consequence at such a moment. Other than love, the most powerful of emotions is the compulsion to live. And it is the contrary understanding of life itself and its origin that is the root from which has grown the division between the humanist and Christian worldviews.

In virtually every culture, the pages of ancient pagan history are washed with the blood of innocent children destroyed through various means and for many reasons. In ancient Greece, pregnant women were given heavy doses of herbal potions to induce abortions, and the great Greek philosophers Plato and Aristotle promoted eugenics through the practices of abortion and infanticide. Persians practiced abortion through the use of surgical curette procedures. The abdomens of pregnant Polynesian women were beaten with large stones or hot coals were placed on their bodies. Arabs forced chemical abortifacients directly into the wombs of pregnant women through the birth canal. But the pagan view of life was not limited to the unborn child, and infanticide was a natural extension of abortion. The ancient Egyptians rid themselves of unwanted children by disembowelment and dismemberment, especially girls, and their collagen was harvested for the production of cosmetics. Children of the primitive Canaanites were sacrificed on flaming pyres to their god Molech. The Romans abandoned unwanted children, usually girls, in the public dumps outside city walls. Abandonment was also a common practice of the ancient Greeks.[693]

For all of ancient history few voices were raised against the wanton slaughter of children. It was the dramatic and rapid spread of Christianity in the second and third centuries throughout the Mediterranean world that propelled the new and novel notion that life was sacred. However, it was not the newness or novelty of the idea that captured the civilized world and achieved a cultural consensus. The power in the message of the sanctity of life came from the

Scriptural revelation and the universal affirmation *and* action of the church world. The message that abortion and infanticide were murder rang loudly and clearly from the foundation of Christianity and for nineteen centuries thereafter. At the end of the first century, a compilation of Apostolic moral teachings called the *Didache* stated that, "You shall not slay a child by abortion. You shall not kill that which has already been generated." Athenagoras, a second century Christian apologist, wrote, "We say that women who induce abortions are murderers…The fetus in the womb is a living being and therefore the object of God's care." In the third century Tertullian wrote in his *Apology* that, "…murder is forbidden once and for all. We may not destroy even the fetus in the womb…" A century later Basil the Great said, "She who has deliberately destroyed a fetus must bear the penalty for murder…Moreover, those who gave abortifacients for the destruction of a child conceived in the womb are murderers themselves…" On down through the centuries the Church spoke with one voice against abortion and infanticide and for the sanctity of life in accordance with God's revelation in the Bible. Not only did the Church affirm and proclaim its message, the most profound impact on the civilized world came as a result of the Church *living* its message. In Rome, Corinth, Caesarea, and wherever the Gospel spread it was the Christians' good works that changed lives—lives of those they helped and of those that observed. These works included the rescue of orphans and children abandoned outside of city walls; "…care for the poor, sick, the suffering, the lame, and the aged in clinics and hostels"; and the rescue and care of temple prostitutes who were despised, abused, and exploited. Christians established hospitals, orphanages, rescue missions, and a myriad of other means to reach out to a world with the message that life is sacred. And for nineteen centuries that message burned with intensity and clarity.[694]

With the resurgence of the hydra-headed monster of humanism during the Renaissance and Enlightenment, life was separated from God, and its charge was given to the whims of mortals. The third common principle of *Humanist Manifesto II* affirmed "that moral values derive their source from human experience. Ethics is *autonomous* and *situational*, needing no theological or ideological sanction. (emphasis in original) Ethics stem from human need and interest." Reason and intelligence are the means to human progress.[695] One can easily follow the thread—for the humanists, decisions of life depend on the current situation, human experience, needs of the moment, and interests of society. But who are these autonomous deciders? By what standards are their reason and intellects measured? Is one humanist's moral values heresy to another? Where do the humanists' acclaimed "preciousness and dignity of the individual person" fall within this amorphous, jumbled hierarchy of needs, interests, experience, and situations? Humanists promise "maximum individual autonomy *consonant* with social responsibility."[696] (emphasis in original) For a clearer understanding of what this means, we substitute *compatible* as a synonym for consonant. Therefore, using the humanists' definition, maximum individual autonomy is meaningless if that autonomy is not *compatible* with social responsibility as determined by the deciders. In other words, an individual's autonomy is always trumped if that autonomy is not *compatible* with the current deciders' ideas of social responsibility. Carrying abortion to its logical conclusion, if the decider decides an *unborn* child is unworthy of life, then he/she may also decide the mentally or physically deficient *infant or elderly person* is not worthy of life because of ___?___ (after analyzing the situation and needs of society, the reader may play the role of the decider and fill in the blank). Once again it must be reiterated that, "When man devalues God, he eventually comes to devalue man, as well as the animating factor we call life."[697]

After January 22, 1973, the lives of unborn babies were no longer sacrosanct in America but placed in the hands of the deciders. It is estimated that over fifty two million abortions have occurred in America from January 1973 through 2008. These estimates came from direct surveys of abortionists by the Guttmacher Institute, once a research affiliate of Planned Parenthood.[698] The number of abortions per day, if an average were calculated for the entire thirty-six year period, is over 3,900. This average number of abortions *per day* exceeds by over one thousand the number of lives lost in the terrorist attacks on September 11, 2001.

Numbers and statistics are sterile things and do not convey the horror of a single abortion. Euphemisms, platitudes, and legal arguments about rights, privacy, and choice attempt to soften the picture or divert attention from the horror surrounding the abortion of an unborn child. However, if a person is serious about deciding whether he or she can morally support such a practice, he or she must understand how abortion is accomplished and weigh that understanding against humanists' defenses of the practice.

In the litigation surrounding numerous abortion cases that have occurred since 1973, most have been wrapped in a fog of medical and legal terminology that tends to anesthetize rather than enlighten the reader of such legal documents. In 2000, a rare glimpse into the "plain English" mechanics of a late term abortion occurred in the dissenting opinion of Supreme Court Justice Anthony Kennedy. The Supreme Court had ruled 5-4 in its *Stenberg v. Carhart* decision to shield partial-birth abortion from legislative prohibition. In attempting to explain the majority's reasoning behind their decision, Justice Breyer used a number of medical definitions for the Dilation and Extraction procedure (D&X) provided by the American College of Obstetricians and Gynecologists including such phrases as "instrumental conversion of the fetus to a footling breech" and "partial evacuation of the intracranial contents of a living fetus."[699] However, Justice Kennedy filled in the gaps. He began with what happens after the cervix is dilated.

> ...the fetus' arms and legs are delivered outside the uterus while the fetus is alive; witnesses to the procedure report seeing the body of the fetus moving outside the woman's body...At this point, the abortion procedure has the appearance of a live birth. As stated by one group of physicians "as the physician manually performs breech extraction of the body of a live fetus, excepting the head, she continues in the apparent role of an obstetrician delivering a child."...With only the head of the fetus remaining in utero, the abortionist tears open the skull...scissors is "the appropriate instrument" to be used at this state of the abortion...
>
> Witnesses report observing the portion of the fetus outside the woman react to the skull penetration...The abortionist then inserts a suction tube and vacuums out the developing brain and other matter found within the skull. The process of making the size of the fetus' head smaller is given the clinically neutral term "reduction procedure."

> ...Brain death does not occur until after the skull invasion, and, according to Dr. Carhart, the heart of the fetus may continue to beat for minutes after the contents of the skull are vacuumed out...The abortionist next completes the delivery of a dead fetus, intact except for the damage to the head and missing contents of the skull.[700]

In a bizarre argument in support of the court's opinion, Justice Stevens stated that the D&X procedure was no "more brutal, more gruesome or less respectful of 'potential life' than the equally gruesome" D&E (Dilation and extraction) method used in second-trimester abortions.[701] Again Justice Kennedy went beyond medical jargon to illuminate the *literal* butchery involved.

> Dr. Carhart uses the traction created by the opening between the uterus and vagina to dismember the fetus, tearing the grasped portion away from the remainder of the body...[The unborn child] dies just as a human adult or child would: It bleeds to death as it is torn from limb from limb. The fetus can be alive at the beginning of the dismemberment process and can survive for a time while its limbs are being torn off. Dr. Carhart agreed that "when you pull out a piece of the fetus, let's say, an arm or a leg and remove that, at the time just prior to removal of the portion of the fetus...the fetus [is] alive.
>
> [Carhart] testified that mere dismemberment of a limb does not always cause death because he knows of a physician who removed the arm of a fetus only to have the fetus go on to be born "as a living child with one arm."...At the conclusion of a D&E abortion no intact fetus remains. In Dr. Carhart's words, the abortionist is left with "a tray of pieces.[702]

How does the humanist explain, justify, or defend this tragedy? The first justification of those supporting abortion is through the legal approach. For that we look at the Supreme Court Justices' majority opinion in *Roe v. Wade*. The landmark decision that legalized abortion was decided on the grounds of the right of personal privacy. Although Justice Blackmun stated that, "The Constitution does not explicitly mention any right of privacy," the majority of the court believed that the Fourteenth Amendment's concept of personal liberty and restrictions upon state action and the Ninth Amendment's reservation of rights to the people were "...broad enough to encompass a woman's decision whether or not to terminate her pregnancy." Immediately thereafter Justice Blackmun recited a litany of reasons as to why it would be detrimental if the state were allowed to interfere with a woman's choice to terminate her pregnancy. Several excerpts are instructive: "Maternity, or additional offspring, may force upon the woman a distressful life and future. Psychological harm may be imminent. Mental and physical health may be taxed by child care. There is also the distress...associated with the unwanted child...bringing a child into a family already unstable, psychologically and otherwise, to care for it...In other cases...the stigma of unwed motherhood..."[703]

Nonetheless, the littlest member involved in the case, completely ignored by Justice Blackmun in his defense of the mother's right to choose, eventually had to be addressed. In the litigation, it was the contention of those opposed to abortion that "life begins at conception and is present throughout pregnancy..." To this argument, Blackmun made a most remarkable statement.[704]

> We need not resolve the difficult question of when life begins. When those trained in the respective disciplines of medicine, philosophy, and theology are unable to arrive at any consensus, the judiciary at this point in the development of man's knowledge, is not in a position to speculate as to the answer.[705]

This is astonishing in that the essence of the case revolves around termination of a living organism, whether one chooses to call it a baby or fetus. Blackmun's arguments discount the status of the fetus as a "person" within the meaning of the Fourteenth Amendment. Blackmun admits that if the fetus attained personhood, the fetus' right to life would be guaranteed specifically by the Fourteenth Amendment. However, Blackmun eventually concluded that the term "person" under the law had application only post-natally. He follows with the statement that, "It should be sufficient to note briefly the wide divergence of thinking on this most sensitive and difficult question. There has always been strong support for the view that life does not begin until live birth." If that living organism within a mother's womb is not life, what is it? Blackmun called it "potentiality of human life."[706]

Writing for the majority, Blackmun's tortured logic asserts that the court need not resolve the question of when life begins; then he admits that if it began at conception the case for the proponents of abortion would fail. The court in effect ruled that life begins at birth and labeled anything preceding that event as "potentiality for human life." This was an epic victory for the humanist worldview. "The right to birth control, abortion, and divorce should be recognized" was codified as the fifth common principle in *Humanist Manifesto II* adopted the same year as the court legalized abortion under *Roe v. Wade*.[707]

A second defense of abortion is made on a scientific basis. For those favoring abortion, this battleground is to be avoided if at all possible as Blackmun attempted in writing the majority opinion for the court. It is apparent from reading Blackmun's opinion that he did not want to address the point at which life begins from a scientific perspective. From the perspective of the law, Blackmun refers vaguely to "…strong support for the view that life does not begin until live birth" and labels anything prior to that as an equally vague "potentiality for human life." Effectively, live birth became the abortionists' arbitrary line that separated potentiality for human life and the beginning of life itself. However, in their defense of abortion in the fields of science and logic, Blackman and the majority lose in both arenas.

One of the first arguments submitted by those supporting legalized abortion is an attempt to separate the existence of a human in the moral sense from the existence of a human being in the biological sense. Human beings exist in a moral sense and have rights at the point of consciousness. From the biological perspective, the pre-conscious human beings exist but do not have rights. Thus, pro-abortion proponents arbitrarily pin existence to consciousness. From scientific and logical standpoints, the abortionists' problem of defending abortion is compounded. To affix consciousness to the occurrence of some physical event other than the beginning of the continuum of life is wholly arbitrary. For the supporters of abortion, that arbitrary event at which consciousness occurs is at the point of live birth. But, is the in utero human being less conscious five minutes before birth than the ex utero human being five minutes after live birth? The post-natal child may be more active, breathe on his/her own, and have greater reaction to stimuli, but, it is no more conscious that the pre-natal child. If consciousness is not affixed to live birth, how then is the conscious being distinguished from the pre-conscious being? What is the trigger or tipping point at which one becomes the other? If that is not determinable by the abortionist, how does he/she keep from aborting a conscious being with "rights"?[708]

Pro-life proponents believe the beginning of life occurs at the moment of conception in which the zygote is created by the union of two gametes, an egg from the mother and a sperm from the father. Unlike the gametes and other cells in the human body, the zygote is a "...distinct, unified, self-integrating organism, which develops itself...in accord with its own genetic 'blueprint'." The zygote requires no outside genetic material to cause it "...to mature into an embryo, the embryo into a fetus, the fetus into an infant, the infant into a child, the child into an adolescent, the adolescent into an adult." The line between the zygote and adult human being is continuous, i.e., there are no "biological interruptions, or gaps" from embryo to adult. Being a distinct, self-integrating organism is the issue, not dependence on the mother (before or after birth).[709] There is no arbitrary line separating the fetus from personhood and no imaginary line separating something with the potential for human life from a post-natal baby. By any reasonable measure, the weight of pro-life arguments prevails and the abortionists' arguments fail from both scientific and logical standpoints.

The victims of abortion range far beyond the unborn. Blackmun's majority opinion focused on the psychological harm to the mother and families by not permitting the mother the right to terminate her pregnancy. The champions of women's rights have little to say about the lifelong psychological trauma suffered by mothers and families because of abortion. Grant reports that, "The *majority* of women who undergo abortions suffer significant psychological distress." (emphasis in original) The effects of post-abortion syndrome include women who become suicidal, attempt suicide, drink heavily, have nightmares, and have "nervous breakdowns."[710] Humanist attempts at counseling are a weak and imperfect solution for those who have psychological damage as a result of abortion of their babies. True forgiveness and restoration can only be found through the redemptive work of Christ.

The humanist victory in the 1973 abortion battle was only one campaign in the larger battle of worldviews. Abortion was merely "...the wedge used to split open the historic Western commitment to the dignity of human life."[711] Once unleashed, abortion coarsened society with regard to the sanctity of life. The issue of abortion quickly moved from a woman's right of privacy to a tool of public policy. This was demonstrated by Former Arkansas State Health Director Joycelyn Elders, later President Clinton's Surgeon General of the United States in the early 1990s, when she pointed to abortion's "...important and positive public health effect" through reduction of "the number of children afflicted with severe health defects."[712]

With abortion legalized, pro-abortion writers attempted to drive the wedge deeper by sanctioning the taking of innocent life as "justifiable homicide" which effectively dispenses with concerns as to when human life begins. Thus, the humanists' coveted right of choice moved across the line from abortion to infanticide in the 1982 case of "Baby Doe." In this case a Down's syndrome child was born with a deformed esophagus. With the concurrence of their doctor based on the Down's syndrome, the parents refused to allow a relatively simple operation that would have corrected the deformed esophagus and allow the child to eat and live. Two Indiana courts refused to intervene, and six days later a living child was allowed to die of starvation because it was retarded.[713]

Many scientists and academics would not stop at "allowing" children to die. Some such as Francis Crick, Nobel Prize winner for discovering the double helix in DNA, support screening newborns. For Crick, those that fail to meet certain health standards would be euthanized. Peter Singer, Princeton's DeCamp Professor of Bioethics, believes that parents ought to be allowed to kill their disabled children. His reasoning is "...that they are 'nonpersons' until they are rational and self-conscious." Singer extends his reasoning to the "...killing of incompetent persons of any age if their families decide their lives are 'not worth living'."[714] Some would scoff that Chick's and Singer's opinions are extreme and would never gain cultural acceptance. However, legalized abortion in America was also once thought extreme by most Americans.

During the Vietnam War, many discredited the domino theory that maintained if one small Southeast Asian nation fell to communism, their neighbor nations would be toppled also. History proved the truth of the domino theory in Southeast Asia. It also appears to have proven true in America with humanism's attack on the historic dignity of human life in Western civilization. The Supreme Court's creation of the right to abortion was the first domino to fall. Next came "Baby Doe" and the tacit approval of infanticide. Next to fall was the domino of assisted suicide in Oregon, legalized in 1997. The domino of euthanasia, the killing of another for his or her alleged benefit with or without consent, is wobbling as the line between assisted suicide and euthanasia has "become a legal fiction."[715] Robert Bork succinctly captures the ultimate end of humanism's quest to reduce life to a utilitarian unit, a product of biology or nature: "Modern liberalism's obsession with the autonomy of the individual is taking us to a culture of death. Ironically, the freedom of the individual to choose death has made it far easier for others to choose his death. The autonomy is often theirs, not his."[716]

Under the aegis of a majority of nine people on the United States Supreme Court, abortion became a choice in 1973, and unborn babies suddenly became mere fetal tissue with potentiality for human life. Contrast the words of the Psalmist with the court's decision and humanism's convoluted defenses of abortion through fictitious rights and irrational moralizing about choice and radical individualism.

> You made all the delicate, inner parts of my body, and knit them together in my mother's womb. Thank you for making me so wonderfully complex! It is amazing to think about. Your workmanship is marvelous—and how well I know it. You were there while I was being formed in utter seclusion! You saw me before I was born and scheduled each day of my life before I began to breathe. Every day was recorded in your Book! Psalm 139:13-16 Living Bible.

Chapter 23

American Family – Homosexuality

Homosexuality reaches far back into history and touches many cultures. Almost two thousand years before Christ, the Genesis account reveals God's abhorrence of homosexuality and is demonstrated by the destruction of Sodom. Probably the most important statement reflecting the Judeo-Christian view of homosexuality is given in the New Testament book of Romans (1:18-32) and specifically in verses 24-27.* In ancient Greek society homosexuality flourished, and the homosexual relationship between an adult male with a much younger male was considered the personification of true love. It was in the homosexual relationship that the Athenian man "expressed his better side, intelligence, will for self-improvement, and a higher level of emotions." Although Greece's glory declined with the Peloponnesian Wars ending in 404 BC, Greek philosophy, literature, and political theory would pass down to Rome and ultimately to Western civilization. Homosexual marriages in ancient Rome were rare and generally looked on with disfavor, not because that heterosexual marriage was sacred, but rather because no "real" Roman man would play the role of the subordinate Roman wife.[717] However, ancient precedent does not render support for cultural normalization of homosexuality in ordered societies, ancient or modern. Some will argue that "normal" is

---

* "Therefore God gave them up in the lusts of their hearts to impurity, to the dishonoring of their bodies among themselves, because they exchanged the truth about God for a lie and worshiped and served the creature rather than the Creator, who is blessed for ever! For this reason God gave them up to dishonorable passions. Their women exchanged natural relations for unnatural, and the men likewise gave up natural relations with women and were consumed with passion for one another, men committing shameless acts with men and receiving in their own persons the due penalty of their error." [Romans 1:24-27 RSV.]

whatever a culture says is normal. However, throughout this book it has been shown that cultures that forget, ignore, or unashamedly disregard the permanent things, the universals, will eventually disintegrate. It is on this premise that homosexuality is viewed and will be examined and discussed in the remainder of this chapter.

We have written much about marriage in earlier chapters and generally will not revisit those observations. However, we must return to certain aspects of marriage and children in order to properly contrast that with the agenda and demands of those who advocate acceptance of homosexuality in society. One of those agenda items is to redefine the meaning of family. We have said that the ordered family structure is part of the human constitution, a universal truth, one of the permanent things, and exists in every known society. The family attains status within society—legitimacy, social identity, legal recognition, cultural tradition, and an estate. Humans have fashioned numerous methods by which to organize their societies, but the common link to all is the family unit—a father, a mother, and children living together in bonds of committed caring. It is the fundamental unit upon which societies are built.

By contrast, homosexuality is a disorganizing concept with regard to human relationships and ultimately disorganizing in building stable, enduring societies. Proponents wish to lift the status of homosexuality in society through its attainment of legitimacy, legal identity, and respect as a cultural tradition, a place at the table so to speak. These efforts involve court challenges to long-standing and culturally established norms, enactment of laws which favor the homosexual agenda and that diminish marriage, and promotion of homosexuality in the popular culture.

As marriage is the central organizing concept in society, it is critical for proponents of homosexuality to redefine what it means to be a family, and this has become the primary field of battle. There are two general conceptions of marriage in society. The first is that marriage is at its core about the children born of that marriage and by default is limited to heterosexual marriage relationships. The second is that marriage is essentially a private relationship. This is from whence comes the attack by the proponents of the homosexual agenda. The legislative and legal efforts to redefine marriage to include homosexual couples of either gender, whether in law or culture, would weaken the idea of a mother and father for every child.[718] Marriage, under the homosexual definition, is "...a loving, self-determining couple engaging in an ordinary civil contract that has nothing to do with children." Under the homosexual definition of marriage, children are not central to the relationship. However, Shelby Steele (quoted by Kay Hymowitz) wrote, "The gravity of marriage as an institution comes from its demand that love be negotiated through these *larger* responsibilities [surrounding procreation]."[719] (emphasis added) The homosexual definition aligns with humanists' emphasis on the individual, not the family. To see the damage to marriage and the family from society's acceptance of radical individualism as promoted by the reigning humanistic worldview, one need only to look once again at the late Senator Moynihan's discerning observation that the family structure has come apart all over the Western world during the last forty years of the twentieth century.

Arguing for the right for homosexuals to marry, humanists deny that marriage is inherently heterosexual. As such reasoning goes, the value of sex derives from *either* procreation *or* pleasure. It would then follow that the motivation for heterosexual acts and homosexual acts may be similar for reasons other than procreation. Therefore, there is a bias in traditional matrimonial laws which unfairly penalize homosexuals by preventing them from attaining status through marriage.[720] This is one of the points by which humanists and other proponents of homosexuality attempt to redefine marriage.

In an attempt to redefine marriage, it is necessary for the proponents of homosexuality to change the purpose and value of sex. There are a number of *instrumental or extrinsic* reasons for sexual acts including individual or mutual sexual satisfaction, obtaining pleasure, releasing tension, and expressing various feelings such as esteem, friendliness, and affection. For the heterosexual marriage, pleasure in sexual union is rightly sought and perfects the marital union. However, in the traditional view of marriage, the value of sex is *intrinsic*, not merely to attain pleasure or some other extrinsic value. The principal intrinsic value and purpose of sexual union "...is *marriage itself*, considered as a bodily (one-flesh) union of persons consummated and actualized by acts that are reproductive in type." (emphasis in original) Why only *reproductive* acts? The heterosexual marriage relationship is "naturally ordered to the good of procreation (and to the nurturing and education of children)." In this relationship, two distinct individuals come together as a mated pair and through consummation of the reproductive act "the two become one flesh." The Apostle Paul called it a profound mystery.* The strength and depth of spousal commitment and unity that derives from a marriage consummated by the reproductive act, whether intended for purposes of procreation or not, cannot be matched by any other relationship. The nature of the reproductive acts in marriage are distinctly and intrinsically unitive. Reproductive acts under the marital veil achieve a meshing of persons that transcends the instrumental or extrinsic purposes of the act itself.[721] Thus, the "why" of reproductive acts (excluding all other sexual acts) is that the reproductive act rests on the complementarity of men and women— bodily, emotionally, spiritually, and temperamentally. From this we see that the reproductive act is more than just about sex, it is about marriage itself.

If the arguments of the proponents of homosexuality fail to diminish the importance and exclusivity of the reproductive act in defining marriage, the proponents fight on other fronts. One tactic with which they have been very effective and successful is casting the proponents of homosexuality and same-sex marriage as commanding the moral high ground. They present themselves and their cause as morally superior to their opponents who are cast as villains in the morality play widely disseminated in popular culture. To oppose homosexuality is deemed the moral equivalence of racism, bigotry, ignorance, and homophobia. Those persons who are not accepting of homosexuality are labeled as intolerant. But Bennett identifies the humanists' perversion of the concept of tolerance. He calls it "...the disfigurement of the idea of tolerance at the hands of the agenda-pushers of our day...that would brand as bigots those of us who exercise our elementary responsibility...to make firm moral judgments in matters touching on marriage and the raising of our children." The humanist would force all to worship at the shrine of tolerance, but their price of admission is a tolerance rooted in moral relativism with no room for finding truth or judging something based

---

* "For this reason a man shall leave his father and mother and be joined to his wife, and the two shall become one flesh. This mystery is a profound one..." Ephesians 5:31-32a RSV.

on the concept of right and wrong. For those that fail to enter the humanist shrine, they become the objects of intolerant harassment through restrictions on free speech (speech codes), coercion, and intimidation. To the proponents of homosexuality, tolerance means forced acceptance, and such acceptance necessitates "normalization, validation, public legitimation, and finally public endorsement."[722]

It is interesting and instructive to compare the humanists' definition of tolerance, used to force acceptance of homosexuality, with its proper definition. One dictionary gives three meanings, two of which are relevant to our discussion. In the first instance tolerance is said to be a "...sympathy or indulgence for beliefs or practices differing or conflicting with one's own..." The second refers to the "...allowable deviation from a standard..."[723] With the exception of a few, Americans have demonstrated remarkable tolerance or indulgence toward homosexuality, but a large majority still believe that it conflicts with their beliefs.[724] Those beliefs hold that traditional marriage between a man and a woman is the standard (universal). Homosexuality is a significant and fatal deviation from that standard and does not warrant normalization, validation, public legitimation, or public endorsement in the central vision of culture in America.

If God created man, then that creation includes those who commit homosexual acts as well as those who engage in heterosexual relationships outside of marriage, both in rebellion against God's laws. He loves each one. However, His love does not extend to their acts that stand in direct rebellion to his universal laws and the revelation to mankind. Then what should be the attitude be toward the homosexual if one holds the Judeo-Christian worldview? If God loves and respects the homosexual as an individual member of the creation, so should those that disagree with the homosexual's actions. That means we should treat them with respect and fairness that is due any other human being. However, like God, we do not accept or approve their actions. Nor should society allow the homosexual practices to be normalized, validated, endorsed, or given any form of legitimacy such as allowing same-sex marriages or homosexual adoptions.

Another front in the attack on traditional marriage is the advancement of homosexual "rights" through judicial efforts. The voting citizens of Colorado enacted a state referendum which denied *special* civil rights based on sexual orientation. Effectively, the people of Colorado said that homosexuals could not claim quota preferences, protected status, or discrimination based on their sexual orientation. Therefore, private persons and institutions that held homosexuality morally objectionable could discriminate (e.g., refusal to rent a room to homosexuals, refusing to hire a practicing homosexual by a religious organization that held homosexuality was morally wrong). However, the United States Supreme Court struck down the law in 1995 (*Romer v. Evans*) because it demonstrated "animus" (bigotry) against homosexuals. However, according to dissenting Justice Scalia, the law was modest effort "...to preserve traditional sexual mores against the efforts of a politically powerful minority to revise those mores through the use of the laws...[and] was an entirely reasonable provision which does not even disfavor homosexuals in any substantive sense, but merely denies them preferential treatment."[725] This was followed by the Court's striking down a Texas law banning sodomy (Lawrence v. Texas). Again, the Court ruled that the state was guilty of bigotry or prejudice because it adopted legislation prohibiting homosexual behavior. In his dissent, Justice Scalia severely criticized the majority's opinion which "...dismantles the structure of constitutional law that has permitted distinction to be made between heterosexual and homosexual unions..."[726]

The practical effect of rulings of unconstitutionality since the middle of the twentieth century is that the successful challenges to laws that maintain the mores and traditions upon which the nation were founded become the basis for policy initiatives of the "cultural elite on the far left of the American political spectrum."[727] These rulings result in policy initiatives that are humanistic in origin and spread throughout the various American institutions as judicially blessed laws, policies, directives, rules, and regulations of the land. And the *new* business of the government is to protect the individual's personal values. The elevation of the *individual and his personal values* (and the exclusion of any reference to the Judeo-Christian tradition) as the standard by which decisions of supreme importance are made occurred for the first time in *Roe v. Wade*. The centrality and importance of the humanistic view of the individual was further enhanced in the 1992 Supreme Court case *Casey v. Planned Parenthood*. Writing for the majority, Justice Kennedy stated, "At the heart of liberty is the right to define one's own concept of existence, of meaning, of the universe, and of the mystery of human life." This is a seismic shift not only in how one views life but of culture itself. We have stated that culture is the central vision that binds, unifies, and gives direction to society, without which a society disintegrates. Individuals may think, feel, and act upon their personal and private liberties in any society as long as their actions fall *within the limits* of the laws that express the central vision of that society.[728] With regard to rulings on abortion and homosexuality, the Supreme Court has uncoupled the nation from its cultural moorings that were established over the centuries and that has steadied the nation since our founding. In place of reliance on the Judeo-Christian tradition, the Court and the nation have embarked upon the turbulent waters of the humanistic cult of the individual. A few pertinent questions reveal the perilous course. Does Justice Kennedy place any limits on the individual who defines his own concepts of the meanings and mysteries of life? How will issues of marriage be addressed that involve polygamy, marriage between a mother and her adult son, or three persons of the same sex who wish to marry? What is the rationale for denying those individuals the realization of their own personal conceptions of marriage? Will the courts require a person to rent a home to these individuals or require the Boy Scouts to allow them to be troop leaders? The permutations continue to multiply as American society disintegrates.

    The universal cultural rejection of homosexuality through man's history flows from ancient to modern day and is derived from the permanent things or universals. However, it was from the revelation in both the Old and New Testament that these universals were given focus, clarity, and status. Yet, many in the modern church hierarchy champion various aspects if not all of the homosexual agenda. Many church leaders excuse or deny that homosexuality is contrary to scriptural admonitions and do so through reinterpretation or revision of biblical passages to fit their humanistic worldview. One example of such revision is that "…homosexual conduct is wrong only when you engage in it unnaturally—that is, only if you are by nature a *heterosexual*." (emphasis in original) It is one thing to disagree with the Bible's teaching on homosexuality or to reject biblical authority altogether in defending homosexual practices. However, it is blatantly disingenuous to revise or twist biblical teachings in order to excuse homosexual practices when the biblical record is unequivocally clear in its universal condemnation of homosexuality. Others argue that the basic thrust of Christ's teachings is that in the end we must place love above all other considerations. Basic doctrines are inherently divisive and must be pushed aside in favor of the non-judgmental love and acceptance of people as they are. They argue that such narrow and rigid doctrines as to how one must live are divisive and contrary to the inclusiveness demonstrated by the lives and teachings of Jesus and His disciples.[729] However, this argument is clearly false and strikes at the foundation of the Christian worldview regarding the Fall and man's need for redemption as chronicled from Genesis through Revelation. Man's disobedience led to his fall. The terrible price paid by Christ for man's redemption was not a hall pass to go do as one pleases. Rather, redemption is a key that is offered to man to enter into the door of fellowship with God once again. Entry requires repentance, acceptance of the status of Jesus as Lord of one's life, and walking thereafter in obedience to His universal laws as recorded in the Bible.

Why have so many of the religious elite fallen into the camps of the proponents of homosexuality? Tocqueville warned of religions that depend upon the principles of this world.

> …when religion aims to depend upon the principles of this world, it becomes almost as vulnerable as all other powers on this earth. By itself, it may aspire to immortality but, linked to fleeting powers, it follows their fortunes and often collapses together with those passions which sustain them for a day.[730]

Many of mainstream Christian churches have linked themselves to the humanistic worldview, and their affinity for the cause of homosexuality is one of the principles of this (humanistic) worldview upon which they have come to depend. Those churches which have embraced the homosexual agenda have seen their number of adherents decline dramatically. By contrast, those churches which have grown are the ones that have stood against the assaults of secular culture and taught unequivocal biblical morality and salvation.[731]

Proponents of homosexuality often cite various scientific studies that indicate sexual orientation is a matter of genetics, i.e., sexual orientation is involuntary, immutable, and rooted in nature." Based on such "facts," as this line of reasoning continues, moral distinctions between homosexual and heterosexual behavior would be invalid. First we must address the belief that sexual orientation is a matter of genetics. One 1993 study by the National Institutes of Health suggested that genes play a role in influencing sexual orientation and therefore "...homosexuality may not be *solely* a personal choice." (emphasis in original) However, the results of this study were brought into question by a more recent study whose results were published in *Science* in 1999. The new study indicated that if there was a genetic link to homosexuality, it is so small or weak as to be inconsequential. Others surrender on the issue of genetic *causation* but continue to hold to genetic *predisposition* to homosexuality. Here we move the second part of the argument: If homosexuality were to be found to have a genetic basis, then moral distinctions are invalid as it relates to differences between homosexuality and heterosexuality. But this too is an invalid argument for neither causation nor predisposition justifies cultural acceptance. For example, some people are genetically prone to alcoholism. Another study established a genetic link to criminal behavior. But such genetic links do not justify immoral behavior whether it be alcoholism, criminal activities, or homosexuality. People are not slaves to their passions, desires, and predispositions as humanists would have us believe. Some people will struggle with those forces more than others, but people have the ability to choose their behavior.[732] It is true that some behaviors descend into addictions, but the road to those addictions began with a choice.

In 2008 the Just the Facts Coalition published and mailed to all sixteen thousand public school superintendents a document entitled *Just the Facts About Sexual Orientation and Youth-A Primer for Principals, Educators, and School Personnel*. The coalition is comprised of thirteen organizations[*] with the stated purpose of

---

[*] The organizations comprising the coalition are: American Academy of Pediatrics, American Association of School Administrators, American Counseling Association, American Federation of Teachers, American Psychological Association, American School Counselor Association, American School Health Association, Interfaith Alliance Foundation, National Association of School Psychologists, National Association of secondary School Principals, National Association of Social Workers,

providing "...accurate information that will help you respond to a recent upsurge in promotion of efforts to change sexual orientation through therapy and religious ministries. This upsurge has been coupled with a demand that these perspectives on homosexuality be given equal time in schools." The document purports to give superintendents and their school personnel an authoritative answer regarding the school's approach to homosexuality of students. The document is particularly dismissive of reparative therapy and sexual orientation conversion therapy and state that coalition members "...do not support efforts to change young people's sexual orientation through therapy and have raised serious concerns about the potential harm from such efforts..." Additionally, those religious individuals and organizations that attempt to change sexual orientation "...tend to have negative attitudes toward homosexuality that are based in their particular religious perspectives." About one-fourth of the document addresses "Relevant Legal Principles" and warn school systems that because "...of the religious nature of ex-gay or transformational ministry, any endorsement or promotion of such ministry by officials or employees of a public school district in a school-related context *would likely* raise constitutional questions." (emphasis added) The not-so-subtle message to school systems is that any efforts to change sexual orientation from homosexual to heterosexual will be met with a lawsuit. The document lists various resources in support of the coalition's viewpoint (primarily from the coalition's own organizations) and includes at least a half dozen pro-gay or gay-advocacy groups.[733]

In December 1770, a young thirty-five-year-old John Adams addressed the court in his unpopular defense of British soldiers in the Boston Massacre trials. He stated, "Facts are stubborn things; and whatever may be our wishes, our inclinations, or the dictums of our passions, they cannot alter the state of facts and evidence."[734] It was in a similar and equally unpopular situation that the American College of Pediatricians (ACP) found itself after the Just the Facts Coalition published and distributed its pro-homosexual document. Like Adams, the ACP also found that facts are stubborn things, and in March 2010, the organization proceeded to correct the record with

---

National Education Association, and the School Social Work Association of America.

regard to sexual orientation by sending a letter to the superintendents of schools across the nation and pointed them to the FactsAboutYouth.com website for more information. The essence of the facts is best presented by extensively quoting from the ACP letter.

> Rigorous studies demonstrate that most adolescents who initially experience same-sex attraction, or are sexually confused, no longer experience such attractions by age 25. In one study, as many as 26% of 12-year-olds reported being uncertain of their sexual orientation, yet only 2-3% of adults actually identify themselves as homosexual...
>
> Even children with Gender Identity Disorder (when a child desires to be the opposite sex) will typically lose this desire by puberty, if the behavior is *not reinforced*...Even when motivated by noble intentions, schools can ironically play a detrimental role if they reinforce this disorder. (emphasis added)
>
> In dealing with adolescents experiencing same-sex attraction, it is essential to understand there is no scientific evidence that an individual is born "gay" or "transgender." Instead, the best available research points to multiple factors—primarily social and familial—that predispose children and adolescents to homosexual attraction and/or gender confusion. It is also critical to understand that these conditions *can respond well to therapy*. (emphasis added)
>
> Dr. Francis Collins, former Director of the Genome Project, has stated that while homosexuality may be genetically influenced, it is '...not hardwired by DNA, and that whatever genes are involved represent predispositions, not predeterminations.' He also states [that] '...the prominent roles[s] of individual free will choices [has] a profound effect on us.'
>
> The National Association for Research and Therapy of Homosexuality (NARTH) recently released a landmark survey and analysis of 125 years of scientific studies and

clinical experience dealing with homosexuality. This report...draws three major conclusions: (1) individuals with unwanted same sex attraction often can be successfully treated; (2) there is no undue risk to patients from embarking on such therapy and (3), as a group, homosexuals experience significantly higher levels of mental and physical health problems compared to heterosexuals...

In light of these facts, it is clear that when well-intentioned but misinformed school personnel encourage students to 'come out as gay' and be 'affirmed,' there is a serious risk of erroneously labeling students (who may merely be experiencing transient sexual confusion and/or engaging in sexual experimentation.)...

It is not the school's role to diagnose and attempt to treat any student's medical condition, and certainly not a school's role to 'affirm' a student's perceived personal sexual orientation.[735]

A coalition member, the American Academy of Pediatrics (AAP), fired back at the American College of Pediatricians less than two weeks later (April 13, 2010) by sending a letter to all superintendents criticizing ACP's professional standing and the facts contained in its March 31 informational mailing. However, ACP responded by giving additional support for its professional credibility and its science-based approach to the matter of homosexuality.

The American College of Pediatricians ...is a national professional medical organization of pediatricians with representation in 47 states and five countries.

The AAP letter accuses the *Facts* site [FactsAbout Youth.com] of not providing 'scientific and medical evidence regarding sexual orientation.' They make this claim even though there are more than one hundred references supporting the statements on the site. On the other hand, the *Just the Facts* brochure authored by the AAP and other organizations provides no references or research to support its extreme claims.[736]

Heterosexual marriage is a universal, and the strength and unity provided by it is the foundation of a strong and enduring society. Where traditional marriage is in broad disarray, as it is in most Western societies, it does not disprove the truth of the marriage universal but rather speaks of the ravages caused by the ascending humanist worldview. Where traditional marriage declines, so do those societies decline that allow it to occur.

Chapter 24

Popular Culture

We must include popular culture as one of the American institutions that has been greatly affected by the humanistic worldview. By popular (contemporary) culture is meant the well-known and generally accepted cultural patterns or lifestyles that are widespread within a culture. Every society has one. Except in times of revolt, popular culture is merely veneer that covers the core of a society's innards; perhaps better stated, popular culture is a reflection of that core. The veneer may change over time but still be supportive of the central cultural vision. However, the veneer may also change and be seen in *opposition* to the central cultural vision. Popular culture is not powerless or unimportant, and the disintegration of any society will be accelerated by a popular culture at odds with that central cultural vision. This has been occurring in America at an accelerated rate since the ascendency of the Boomers in the 1960s.

Unrestrained by tradition or other moral force, popular culture can lead to rebellion against the cultural central vision of a society. Tradition, by itself, can only maintain a central cultural vision for a time as the moral capital upon which the vision was built is eroded. If a society's central vision is corrupt or false, that rebellion may be a good thing if one assumes that there are moral absolutes of right and wrong, truth and falsity. But a popular culture that misreads and wars against the validity of a morally sound central cultural vision will either be destroyed or cause that society, to which popular culture stands in opposition, to disintegrate. As has been discussed in earlier chapters, a society's central vision not founded on universal truths (first principles) will eventually disintegrate.

Popular culture is not so much an institution of American life but rather a reflection of the combined faces of its institutions that shape popular culture. Nevertheless, as popular culture is being shaped by other forces, it attains a critical mass and power to shape or bend society's central cultural vision. Two of the greatest forces influencing popular culture are the arts and mass media. In an electronic age the line between the two forces is often blurred.

Some works of art inspire and ennoble a culture while others bring discord and disintegration. What makes the difference? In the classical understanding, the purpose of the arts was to represent something significant about reality and truth and thereby guide, enrich, and sustain culture. This was objectivism by which is meant belief in objective reality and in which moral good is objectively real. This reality is not one of static or restrictive repetition but of amplification, clarification, and inspiration. In this manner, as we have previously stated, the Bible uses history, hymns, letters, proverbs, parables, and even a love song to present truth and add substance, detail, and clarity to man's relationship with the Creator and His universal laws. A work of fiction may also present a powerful message of God's truth as it impacts the fallen nature of man. Thus, through the classical view of art we may see God rooted in the structure, orderliness, and harmony of His creation and its universals, and the classical view can be presented through various art forms such as painting, architecture, literature, dance, theater, and music.[737]

Describing the purpose of literature, Kirk wrote, "Every major form of literary art has taken for its deeper themes the norms of human nature…'the permanent things'…to teach human beings their true nature, their dignity, and their place in the scheme of things." As the eighteenth century came to a close and the religious view of life began to decay, this normative purpose of literature was replaced by "…the literature of nihilism, of pornography and of sensationalism…"[738]

The undermining of the authority of religion and the purpose of art through the influences of the Renaissance and Enlightenment had devastating effects by the end of the eighteenth century. The assault on the religious view of life and art continued in the nineteenth century as science became the sole source of knowledge. For the rationalists, art was a "falsification of reality" or "at best "merely an expression of personal emotion" rather than a means to represent something significant about reality and truth. The initial result of science's attack on art led artists to acquiesce and mimic science's general underlying principles which produced a trend toward abstract art (e.g., Cubism associated with mathematics and geometry). However, artists rebelled and built their own world separate from science in which their art took two forms. Some would be the avant-garde seers of society and offer a vision of an ideal world. Other artists became the scolds of society through the denunciation of the "ugliness of the bourgeois, materialistic, industrialized society…" which produced a "naturalism in art" that reflected the stark, gritty underbelly of society. Both forms were hostile toward the real world (i.e., objective reality of moral good) and ultimately both collapsed into unmitigated "…protests, criticism, and attacks on established morality and social structures." But as the artist-prophets attacked all standards, they sowed the seeds of their own destruction as even their standards were attacked and pushed aside. The end result of an art world without standards is that society is left with art that is purposeless and indistinguishable from the mundane sameness of life. Without standards, everything qualifies as art: the common place (a household appliance, an object retrieved from the dumpster, and other "found" art); the temporal (in time and influence); and the vulgar (the scatological, the obscene, and other forms of cultural pollution). No longer does art inspire and uplift culture through focus on the norms of human nature. Through the influence of humanistic worldview, the arts have lost focus and purpose (apart from any sensory, entertainment, or shock values), and in doing so the arts have declined and become a caricature of its own vacuous meaninglessness.[739]

The humanistic influence on the arts is called subjectivism (as opposed to Judeo-Christian objectivism). At the heart of subjectivism there are no standards of right or wrong, good or bad, and moral or immoral. Concepts of quality become irrelevant as the humanistic tenet of equality dictates that the art of the struggling beginner is just as good as the work of an accomplished artist with a lifetime of experience. Such demands for equality have led major museums to display such anti-art and experienced art critics to be unable to distinguish between the work of a trained artist and that of a child.[740]

The humanists' capture of the arts from the classical view was accomplished through the exaltation if the individual. What is the attraction of individualism as defined by humanists? Bork reports that one modern has stated that the "core of American ideology is a uniquely insistent and far-reaching individualism—a view of the individual person which gives unprecedented weight to his or her choices, interests, and claims."[741] This definition conforms nicely with the "maximum individual autonomy" as enounced by *Humanist Manifesto II* quoted elsewhere in this book. Weaver traced the source of the ravages of artistic expression to egotism. Modern man thinking only of his rights and desiring to be "equal" sinks into "self-absorption." Egotism then leads the exalted individual to a distorted view of the world and alienation from reality, that is, the individual can't see through his egotism to reality. The ravages to the arts occur because egotism *stands between art and enduring reality*. [742] Egotism's effects also extend beyond the arts to the larger realm. As Martin Buber put it, "Something has stepped between our existence and God to shut off the light of heaven...[and] that something is in fact *ourselves*, our own bloated selfhood..."[743] (emphasis in original) And, bloated selfhood is the hereditary disease of humanism.

As we have seen, artistic expression perishes without linkage to that reality (as expressed by the classic view of art and reality of the moral good). For the humanist, the arts are experiential, temporal, and valueless and whose appeal is based on its ability to stimulate the senses, to entertain, and to shock, all of which are inherently individualistic and therefore fragmentary to culture. For the Christian, the arts are meant to reflect the *reality* of God's glory, beauty, and truth, and through such we enhance our moral and spiritual development and understanding, all of which are inherently unifying to culture.

Perhaps an even more powerful shaper of modern popular culture is mass media. Yet, mass media and popular culture demonstrate a symbiotic relationship. Each feeds off of as well as reflects the other. Modern mass media, particularly the electronic variety, is an inherently humanistic and secularizing force in popular culture. To properly understand its impact on popular culture, we must briefly examine the origins of mass media, its inherent structure and worldview, and its vested power.

The "information revolution" is not of recent origin but began with Guttenberg in 1450, over a half millennium ago. Up until the American Revolution there was little "mass" to the media. At the beginning of the eighteenth century the emergence of independent journalism in Britain and on the European continent was spurred by political changes, the capitalistic impulse, and competition between opposition newspapers. As journalism and the postal system spread since the seventeenth century, Europeans and Americans were supplied with a regular source of information about the public world. However, in colonial America, the number of colonists exposed to journalism's window on the world was limited as compared to their European brethren. This changed dramatically at the end of the American Revolution as the number of printing presses multiplied rapidly and appeared not only in major seaports but in "principal inland towns and villages."[744]

The infant American press was democratized, quarrelsome, petty, partisan, scandalous, and rarely neutral. While these presses produced books, pamphlets, sheet music, handbills, and other printed material, the main business of these small enterprises was the printing of weekly newspapers which were dependent on both advertising and subscriptions. The growing importance of post-Revolution American newspapers is demonstrated by the dramatic increase in their numbers. Between 1790 and 1835, the American population grew slightly under four-fold (3.9 million to 15 million) while the number of newspapers increased eleven-fold (106 to 1,258). It was all the more remarkable when by 1834-1835 the number of daily newspapers in the United States (ninety) was compared to the number of dailies in Britain (seventeen). In the United States there were between eighteen and nineteen newspaper subscriptions per one hundred households in the 1780s compared with fifty subscriptions per hundred households in the 1820s (although some households had multiple subscriptions).[745]

Tocqueville believed that the extensive freedom of the American political process and the independence of the press had were *not* the primary reasons for the multiplication of post-Revolution American newspapers. He also believed that newspapers did not multiply because they were cheap (made possible through governmental subsidies relating to distribution). Rather, the "extraordinary subdivision of administrative power" was the main reason for the great number of newspapers. Tocqueville called these administrative subdivisions "associations" at the village, city, and province levels that are responsible for local administration as opposed to a national association. In other words, decentralized government fostered a greater number of newspapers. The multiplication of newspapers was necessary because "the more numerous local powers, the greater the number of people required by law to exercise them and the more insistently this necessity is felt, the more newspapers abound."[746] Yet this assumption conflicted with reality as local newspapers of the era carried a preponderance of national and world news and little local news.[747]

Several factors contributed to the spread and readership of newspapers. One factor was the development of an extensive postal system that was created at the very beginning of the republic. Revolutionary leader Benjamin Rush, speaking in support of the new Constitution in 1787, argued that "… 'knowledge of every kind' had to be circulated…in order to adapt the 'principles, morals, and manners of our citizens to our republican form of government'." To that end the foundations of the first national news network was created in 1792 with the adoption of laws granting subsidies to newspapers. These subsidies involved not only low distribution costs (one cent up to 100 miles) but newspapers also had the right of free exchange of copies with other newspapers through use of the postal system (by the 1840s this amounted to an average of 4,300 exchange copies per newspaper per year). America was a democracy, and voters involved themselves in the political process. This involvement required information. Political parties emerged in the 1820s and created newspapers to connect themselves to voters.[748]

As the nineteenth century came to a close, the centralization of American government under the auspices of the burgeoning progressive movement was well under way. Newspapers declined as American government moved toward centralization, but not for the reasons Tocqueville presented. Rather, the emergence of the electronic media in the early 1920s marked the beginning of the demise of the print-dominated age that had reigned for almost five centuries. In fairness, Tocqueville and his contemporaries could not have imagined broadcast media such as was created in the early twentieth century. Within twenty years of the first radio broadcast on November 2, 1920, newspapers were no longer the primary source of news. National political leaders used the new medium of radio to great effect in communicating directly with the public.[749] A little more than a decade after that first radio broadcast, Franklin Roosevelt became the first president to extensively and effectively use radio to communicate directly with the nation's citizens.

As has been previously stated, modern mass media is an inherently humanistic and secularizing force in popular culture. To understand mass media, we must examine the sources from which its secular and humanistic nature flow. The first source is the structural nature of the media themselves. The second source is the secular and humanistic worldviews of the individuals and institutions controlling the mass media.

We begin with the secular and humanistic tendencies that are embedded in structural framework of mass media. Recall our discussion of modern artistic expression and its loss of linkage with enduring reality. The loss of linkage with reality has also afflicted mass media. Malcolm Muggeridge contends that "modern mass media—and particularly television—insulate us from the reality of the moral order...the media have created, and belong to, a world of fantasy, the more dangerous because it purports to be, and is largely taken as being, the real world." What evidence do we have to support this conclusion? The structure of the media focuses on the *immediacy* of events which creates a disconnection between time and eternity. In other words, the drama of the journalistic moment has no connection to the wisdom of the ages. Life revolves around the twenty-four hour news cycle. Such demand for immediacy leads to *superficiality* in which only the shallow veneer of things or events are reported. Fact driven reporting trounces understanding, and information overwhelms wisdom. In addition to immediacy and superficiality, mass media is also *leveling or relativistic* by which is meant that trivial events of the moment receive attention beyond their importance. By doing so, journalism makes all things of relatively equal importance and thereby diminishes concepts of cultural and eternal importance such as "perseverance, fidelity, and hope" to the point that such concepts become meaningless in popular culture. As life rapidly, continuously, and graphically unfolds from the founts of mass media, we become numb or mesmerized and dreams and reality merge in a monotonic din of sounds and images. Mass media has lost its link with enduring reality. As a result contemporary culture drifts and is demoralized because the traditional standards and commitment—the concepts of good and evil—have been marginalized if not demonized.[750]

The second source of mass media's secular and humanistic influence on popular culture is the overwhelmingly predominant secular and humanistic worldviews of the individuals and institutions controlling mass media. In the twentieth century, the information revolution was dubbed "mass media" and tended to focus on electronic media—radio, television, and cinema. However, mass media, whether print or electronic, is not merely the means or type of communication, it is also the powerful personalities and institutions (both private and public) that organize and direct the means and content of that communication.[751] Until the mid to late 1800s, the print media were beholden to the government and political parties for their survival. As newspapers gained revenue from increased circulation and advertising, they were less dependent on government and politicians and thereby attained a measure of independence and a corresponding increase in wealth and power. Syndicated political columnists began to exert substantial influence in the 1920s. To this was added the broadcast and cinema personalities of vast cultural influence: radio commentators, radio personalities, and movie stars. Mass media had evolved into a powerful and autocratic industry with its own agenda.[752]

Certainly the growth of mass media into a powerful industry in its own right was neither what the Founders had anticipated nor what Benjamin Rush meant when he said "… 'knowledge of every kind' had to be circulated…in order to adapt the 'principles, morals, and manners of our citizens to our republican form of government'." Rather than reinforcing those principles, morals and manners, modern mass media molds public opinion by setting the agenda and influencing what people think about.[753] From such has come a cultural shift as the mass media's humanistic worldview has ascended while the Christian worldview is marginalized and demeaned through substantial and constant attack.

If mass media is overwhelmingly secular and humanistic in its structure and worldview, what does that portend for American culture? We have shown that the humanist's worldview is one of progress, and that progress is one that is defined and imposed (top-down) by society's humanistic elite, its conditioners. Our past protection from this demagoguery was the great diversity of opinion attained through thousands of media sources (bottom up). To American society's harm, the rise of mass media and its consolidation has resulted in an all-powerful and all-knowing media with a progressive, humanistic agenda. The following observation presents a telling picture of the mutually beneficial relationship between American mass media and the practices of centralized and socialistic governments.

> There is an ironic and interesting parallel between the modern media behemoths and the development of telecommunications in Russia following the 1917 revolution. Until its collapse in 1991 and irrespective of the differing levels of affluence, the Soviet Union and its satellites had substantially fewer telephones than North America and its European neighbors. The new Soviet leaders of 1917 consciously invested in loudspeakers, not a telephone system, and subsequently broadcast technologies, another form of loudspeaker. The totalitarian rulers were more interested in disseminating information to its citizens as well as limiting communications between citizens. In spite of the protestations of today's media giants as they wrap themselves in the self-righteous tunic of fairness, free speech, and a free press, a peek beneath this tunic reveals the harsh blare of the bull horn held by a mailed fist.[754]

Only in recent years have mass media outlets arisen with a conservative and generally pro-Judeo-Christian viewpoint. Along with the development of the Internet, these new mass media outlets have had a marked impact by challenging the near monolithic humanistic mass media of the twentieth century and its agenda.

To this point we have talked mainly about the informational/political component of mass media. The second member of the unholy trinity of mass media is popular entertainment. Little needs to be said to convince the average viewer of popular entertainment's hostility to the Judeo-Christian worldview. Regarding such, Robert Bork wrote, "In keeping with the progress of liberalism, popular entertainment generally—and the worst of it in particular—celebrates the unconstrained self, and savages those who would constrain."[755] And the unconstrained self is a hallmark of humanism.

The third member of the unholy trinity is advertising. Advertising, in and of itself, is a legitimate and often necessary form of communication. However, driven by winds of popular culture, advertising is often a willing accomplice in the propagation of the humanistic worldview. Advertising is not just a pawn reflecting the desires of popular culture, but it also influences it. And much of that advertising is aimed at children and young people.

The Purdue Opinion Panel conducted the most authoritative research into the attitudes of young Americans during the fifteen years following World War II. The results of the research reflected a dramatic growth in consumption by the rising youth culture. In an earlier chapter dealing with the creation of the boomer generation, it was noted that the phenomenal prosperity during the post-World War II years was a major shared cultural event that contributed to formation of the Boomer generation. The general prosperity fueled weekly allowances and after-school jobs that provided an unprecedented economic power to the youth market. This did not go unnoticed by American businesses. A vast array of products was targeted at the youth market and its newly acquired purchasing power, and advertising was the means of getting their attention. Out of this marketing of products to the youth culture appeared a surprising new development that was pivotal in challenging the established moral order.[756] Alan Petigny labeled this development "the glamorization of the young":

> ...the culture's valorization of youth or in the desire of adult men and women to remain young at heart. In the indulgence society accorded youth, and the rise of a commercial culture targeted to a burgeoning youth market, the teenage years came to be seen as a halcyon, carefree time. Reinforcing this glamorization was a scourging critique of American society-at-large...And because the world of adolescents was so tightly bound to consumption, millions of adults, flush with disposable income, were able to essentially shop for identity—in other words, they were able to purchase many of the symbols and trappings of the youth culture.[757]

Diane West described this phenomenon as "...the cultural seduction of grown-up Americans." Essentially, by adopting the styles of defiant youth, grown-up Americans rejected important components of the existing moral order in American life.[758]

At a convocation* of scholars and ministry leaders from all over the world, one break-out session was led by Robert Hoskins who presented six macro trends affecting Christianity throughout the world. One of those macro trends is the secularizing power of globalization. One aspect of this globalization is a developing a global youth culture that is becoming more alike and more connected.[759] This development is an advertiser's dream. How will the advertisers market to the growing global youth market? Hoskins described a marketing conference that he attended and which was primarily aimed at and attended by representatives of Fortune 100 companies. These companies represent the top 100 American public companies in terms of revenues and include Exxon-Mobil, Wal-Mart, General Motors, Microsoft, Time Warner, Sears, Walt Disney, Coca-Cola, and Macy's. In discussing the best ways to market to children and young people, the Fortune 100 advertisers were told that the key to reaching this group through advertising was to focus on sexuality, tribalism as the family is disintegrating, and rebellion-overthrow of the system.[760] The emphasis on sexuality, tribalism, and rebellion reflect the classic cultural imperatives of humanism and reprises the chorus of the Boomer hymn of the 1960s and 1970s.

American popular culture is the seminal influence on the globalized youth culture. An example of this global influence is found in the tiny African nation of Swaziland. Eighty-three percent of Swazi people have one or more television sets in their houses, and Swazi children watch twenty-two hours of television per week, more than older people watch. South African television strongly influences Swaziland and is consequently eroding viewership of Swaziland-based television programming. Following the Swaziland news, the highest rated program (highest percentage of total population watching) is *Generations* which features a homosexual in a relatively favorable light. Due to the normalization and veneration of homosexuality through the content of this and other programs, there has been a dramatic shift in the attitudes of young viewers toward homosexuality. Children and young people in Swaziland are much more willing to reject their parents' traditional view that homosexuality is immoral. Other influential and highly watched

---

* Empowered 21: Global Congress on Holy Spirit Empowerment in the 21st Century, Tulsa, Oklahoma, April 8-10, 2010.

programming includes *The Bold and the Beautiful*, *Smack Down*, and *The Oprah Show*.[761]

Regarding the transmission and globalization of Western culture, Peter Berger wrote:

> There exists an international subculture composed of people with Western-type higher education...This subculture is the principal "carrier" of progressive, Enlightenment beliefs and values...They are very influential, as they control the institutions that provide the "official" definitions of reality (notably in the educational system, the media of mass communications, and the higher reaches of the legal system)...there is, without question, a globalized *elite* culture. (emphasis in original)[762]

In the 1960s, Marshall McLuhan famously wrote "the medium is the message." As McLuhan postulated, it is the "medium that shapes and controls the scale and form of human association and action."[763] Five decades later, in Swaziland and around the world, McLuhan's words continue to be proven accurate as the secularizing effects of mass media become stronger each year.

The information age in the twenty-first century has become a flood in which we can drown if we are not careful. The source of this flood is mass media which dictates the cultural agenda and what people think about. Its broad channels of dissemination are information (news, politics, and minutia of popular culture), entertainment, and advertising. This flood of information hinders thoughtfulness and ultimately our understanding without which formless chaos reigns. In the torrents of chaos, if we are not diligent, we lose sight of our Judeo-Christian culture's central vision and perish. But how do we exercise the required diligence? Diligence begins when we recognize that the enemy is not information but a lack of understanding. Dean Riley, in his *Wisdom & God In The Age of Information*, wrote:

> Information gives form to our ideas, it adds flesh to the bones of thought—and in putting our thoughts into form or shape, we engage in a process as old as time—pulling together elements as the Creator, navigating a formless, chaotic

universe...[and] telling the difference between information and understanding will be all the more critical. We must remember our purpose as we navigate.[764]

With the exception of a few, mass media offers little help in navigating the torrents of chaos for it focuses on the temporal and immediate rather than eternity. The temporal assumes importance beyond its worth. Mass media demands attention, action, and that mass media demands a secularized society address the issues of the day. Mass media conveys secularized solutions to those issues that pour forth from secularized governments, schools, and other American institutions—all without the long view. Mass media is both mesmerizing and numbing—a carnival ride of dodgems. We proceed in one direction until we are bumped into another. The objective is movement, "progress" as it were, but there is no destination or goal. What is important is the "experience" as we ride through life in temporal happiness.

We began this chapter with the statement that popular culture is merely veneer that covers the core of a society's innards. In other words, popular culture is a reflection of society's central cultural vision. As that veneer begins to stand in opposition to the central cultural core, conflict results and one or the other will prevail for they cannot maintain equilibrium. By the 1920s the popular culture no longer reflected the core cultural vision that had prevailed since the arrival of Christendom with the Europeans. The Protestant establishment was no longer the cultural authority and became irrelevant except for the masses in grass roots America. The new cultural authorities in public life were the secular elites from education, social sciences, physical sciences, journalism, Hollywood, and the rest of the entertainment industry.[765]

The decay of American life is evident in almost every sphere of popular culture: crime, violence, family decay, loss of civility, obscenity in thought and word (art, music, print, film, and the Internet), an explosion of perversion (pornography to include fornication, pedophilia, sadomasochism, bestiality, and other acts that are beyond the comprehension of citizens of a truly civilized society). How do secular humanists explain and defend the direction of popular culture as one views its degenerative effects on society and America's central cultural core? On the one hand, liberals submit that such is the "price you pay for freedom of expression."[766] However, when the humanistic ideal of unrestrained freedom of expression is more important that the larger cultural central vision, something is amiss with that worldview. The second defense is that the root causes of crime and violence do not lay with popular culture. This is the central theme of a book Karen Sternheimer, *Connecting Social Problems and Popular Culture*. "The roots of the most serious problems American children face, problems like lack of a quality education, violent victimization, early pregnancies, single parenthood, and obesity, poverty plays a starring role; *popular culture is a bit player at best*." (emphasis added) Sternheimer presents the media culture (which she equates with popular culture) as merely "…a refracted social mirror, providing us with insights about major social issues such as race, gender, class, and the power and patterns of inequality." It is important for humanists and their cadre of defenders such as Sternheimer to defend popular culture. To allow indictment of popular culture for society's woes would be to point an accusing finger at humanist notions of individualism, unbridled personal liberty and license, and moral relativism.[767]

But as society wades neck-deep in the moral swamp of today's popular culture, how can thinking people not recognized the direct and suicidal cause-effect relationship between the most serious problems, as enumerated by Sternheimer, and popular culture? The answer is that the vast majority of society does recognize the decaying effects of popular culture. But Sternheimer dismisses the role of popular culture and believes it to be useful in pointing to the real culprit: "Because the media culture is so enchanting, so attention seeking, it can be used to redirect our attention to the sources of our society's problems and to provide us with a wake-up call about the persistence of inequality in the United States." Again, we see the humanistic call for equality that has been discussed extensively in this book and which has been shown to not be the solution to "…education, violence, teen pregnancy, family instability, health, substance use, sexism, racism, and homophobia…" as humanists would have us believe.[768] Sternheimer's humanistic worldview fails to see that these and other societal problems (as reflected in popular culture) are the result of the fallen nature of man. Without this recognition and application of biblical truths as a remedy, popular culture driven by a humanistic worldview will only exacerbate society's problems and ultimately result in disintegration.

The long established central cultural vision of America has eroded under the assault of a popular culture created in the image of a vigorous secular-humanistic worldview. The result is a chaotic and unhappy society swimming in a popular culture with little to no legal or moral restraints. American culture will continue to unravel until a crisis point is reached that will cause one of two courses of action. Either America will once again order its culture around the Judeo-Christian worldview, or the secular-humanistic worldview will reach its inevitable destination as "…an authoritarian and unhappy society."

Part IV – Ye shall be as gods – Summary, Status, and Direction

This book has covered a great deal of history, and the reader may feel somewhat overwhelmed. In Part IV, an attempt is made to pull together the information and arguments presented in this book. First, an elemental discussion of the differences between humanism and Christianity will be summarized as well as and some of the key concepts as redefined by humanists. The present-day status of the Christianity in America and America's central cultural vision will be examined. Finally, the cultural choices that lay before America will be examined along with the means by which the over-arching Judeo-Christian banner above the central cultural vision of America may be restored.

Chapter 25

Differences between Christian and Humanist Worldviews – A Summary

This book is about a clash of Christian and humanistic worldviews, principally in modern America. The origins of the opposing views and their impact on the major institutions of American have been documented and discussed throughout this book. Coincidental to these discussions, the tenets of each of these worldviews also have been examined and discussed. However, a parallel comparison of each tenet embedded in these competing worldviews will give clarity and sharpen the contrast between these competing positions. We shall discuss each major tenet in turn.

God and Creation

In the Christian worldview, God existed before time, creation of the universe, and all therein including the earth and mankind. He stood outside the universe and created matter out of nothing.

Humanism denies the existence of a supernatural, creative force in the creation of the universe. Its gospel is naturalism which insists that the unending universe of space and time are all parts of one great Nature including the earth and human beings. Existence and Nature are the same, and apart from Nature nothing exists. An explanation of everything that exists can be obtained through observation of the forces of nature. In the naturalistic explanation, the universe is an endless and unbroken series of causes and effects through time. Humanists claim that creative matter, the stuff of the universe, does not need a Prime Mover to jump start the universe and keep it going. On the contrary, humanists claim that the universe is auto-dynamic in its existence, development, operation, and continuation.

Man's Purpose

God created mankind for a special and mutual relationship with the Creator. God did not create man out of need. Rather, it was a will to love, an expression of the very character of God, to share the inner life of the Trinity. Therefore, in the Christian worldview, man's purpose is to glorify God, to love and be loved by Him, and to enjoy interacting with Him and His creation for eternity. As man was created in His image, he must develop those "image of God" qualities to be in harmony with God's purpose.

In the humanist worldview, the main purpose of human life is to advance the happiness of man through the development, enjoyment, and making available to all the abundant material, cultural and spiritual goods of this natural world. To advance happiness, man must strive for joyous service for the greater good of all humanity in this natural world through reason, science, and democracy.

Man's Creation and Free Will

In the Christian worldview, man was the noblest of God's creatures and singly endowed with reason and free will. Therefore, the Creator also laid down certain laws of "human nature"; the laws of good and evil to which the Creator and his all creation conform. Unlike the rest of creation, man through his free will was allowed to choose or not choose to constrain his actions and conform to and be in obedience to the Creator's laws of human nature. Therefore, man can and will be held accountable for right and wrong behaviors.

In the humanist worldview, man and his human nature were not created by a Supreme Being but are products of evolution. Man is merely a complex animal without notions of moral responsibility. Humans and other life forms are the products of an infinitely long process of evolution that exceeds three billion years. The body was primary and basic but with its increasing complexity came development and integration of animal behavior and control. This integration culminated with Homo sapiens and the "phenomenon of the mind" or man as we know him today. Speech arose from man's social nature and developed from "…elementary movements, grunts, and cries…" Moral standards were not sent down from a divine creator but were rather a social product that evolved through human association. Sin, soul, and conscience were fantasies that have been replaced by instincts and drives that evolved through time. Man's reason is a slave to desires and passions which carries an implicit denial of free choice or free will. Slave reason only produces rationalizations for morally wrong thoughts and behavior. If one can act only upon the impetus of internal passions and desires or external forces, then reason is powerless to restrain those passions, desires, or external forces. Therefore, man does not have free choice and consequently cannot be held accountable for right or wrong behavior. There are no absolutes and therefore no restraints on passions which rule reason.

Man's Nature

In the Christian worldview, man is a fallen creature. Mankind's free will allowed man to think and act in ways that were contrary to God's plan and will for His creation. When man acted in ways contrary to God's laws (truths), such disobedience was called sin, and as a result decay and death entered into God's creation. This is called the Fall, and it affected not only man but all of God's creation. Man's fall separated him from God.

For the humanist, man is continuously perfectible, a process whereby he will become progressively better and better. Man is not fallen and does not need redemption. Humanists assert there is no limit set to the perfecting of the powers of man other than the duration of the globe upon which nature has spawned us.

Man's Position and Destiny

Unregenerate man is positionally separated from God because of man's inherited sinful nature. The Christian worldview holds that man is inherently fallen because of the entry of sin in to the human race (original sin) and therefore is separated from God. But as God is a loving God, He created a way through His son, Jesus Christ, which allows man through an act of his free will to get out of the mess he created. This is the restoration, and therefore man who chooses Christ foresees an eternity spent with his Creator. For man who rejects God's son through his free choice, the gulf separating him from God remains un-crossable, and the emptiness and pain caused by his broken relationship and separation from his creator will torment his being for eternity. Thus, Christians and certain other religions adhere to a dualistic view that the soul (will, intellect, emotions) is separate and independent from the body and that the soul survives the body's death.

In the humanist worldview, man is the evolutionary product of Nature, and his mind is inextricably joined with the functioning of his brain. There is no conscious survival after death because of the unity of body and personality (which includes every aspect of the mind). Therefore, humanists embrace the monistic theory which sees a close and fundamental connection of body and personality that results in an indissoluble unity. Implicit in this theory is that the personality, like the body, is not immortal and that man's earthly existence is all there is.

Man's Relationship to Man

In the Christian worldview, man is made for relationship which implies dwelling together. It is one of the fundamental needs of mankind. Man was made in the image of God, and the importance of human relationships is a reflection of the Trinitarian relationship. It is a picture of His fundamental being as shown by the Father-Son relationship and the relationship of Christ with the Church. The reflection of God's image in mankind's relational patterns is present in marriage, family, community, nations, and the Kingdom of God. Such patterns of relationship are based on fraternity and kinship.

The humanist views man's relationship with man through the distorted lens of equality. The distortion arises as equality goes beyond equality of man before God (which humanism denies) and the law. It is also an equality that goes beyond equality of opportunity to equality of outcome. In the humanist view, man's relationship with man ultimately transcends gender, family, community, and national boundaries. In the words of *Humanist Manifesto II*, "What more daring goal for humankind than for each person to become, in ideal as well as practice, a citizen of a world community."[769]*

---

*While a candidate for President, Barak Obama spoke to a large crowd in Berlin, Germany, on July 24, 2008. In that speech, he called himself "...a

Man as an Individual

Each individual was created for a personal and loving relationship with God. Because man is born with the mark of sin that was transmitted to him down through history from his first ancestor, the relationship remains broken. The Christian worldview recognizes the fallen condition of humankind and that God has provided a means whereby man can return to Him through repentance and living in a proper orientation to His laws and plan. A personal (individual) relationship with God is possible only through recognition of who God is and obedience to his precepts. That relationship is restored through the acceptance of God's son, Jesus Christ, as man's Lord and Savior.

Humanists hold that the preciousness and dignity of the individual person is a central humanist value in which individuals should be encouraged to realize their own creative talents and desires and exercise maximum individual autonomy *consonant with social responsibility*. As to the individual, humanists promise a freedom from the mores, norms, tradition, and distant voices of the past. The freedom espoused by the humanists gives unbridled control to the self and senses. However, one must read the fine print in the humanists' promises, i.e., individual autonomy must be *consonant with social responsibility*. Therefore, humanists harness an individual's dignity, worth, and freedom to the principle of the greatest-happiness-for-the-greatest-number which is hitched to the humanist belief that the highest moral obligation is to humanity as a whole. The obligations of the individual are subservient to his obligations to the larger society, and those obligations are determined and defined by the humanist intellectual elite, i.e., God is replaced by man as the authority.

Societal Organization and Governments

In the Christian worldview, sustained order in society is possible only when its citizens achieve order of their individual souls

---

proud citizen of the United States, and a fellow citizen of the world." [http://edition.cnn.com/2008/Politics/07/24/obama.words/ (accessed November 9, 2010).]

within God's laws. As a man orders his individual soul in accordance with God's timeless truths, he also contributes to an orderly society that promotes harmonious relationships with nature and between individuals within that society. Society contains many elements of which governments are only one. The Christian worldview sees governments as ordained by God for its own distinctive civil purposes and not for church purposes. The Church and government are separate institutions, but that does not imply a wall of separation stands between them. The Church is not removed from involvement in governmental affairs from the perspective of principle. Nevertheless, the Church cannot be involved in government on the basis of power as contrasted with Islam which makes no distinction between church and state in the exercise of its power.[770]

Humanists link organization of society to the enhancement of freedom and dignity of the individual which occurs when a "full range of individual liberties" is experienced. A fully functioning humanistic society must provide "…alternative economic systems…to increase the sum of human satisfaction through reduction of …disproportions in wealth, income, and economic growth" throughout the world. Such humanistic societal reorganization "transcends the narrow allegiances of church, state, party, class, or race in moving toward a wider vision of human potentiality."[771] For the humanist, government must ultimately and inevitably assume a socialistic form in order to deliver the promised human satisfactions and eradication of disproportionate wealth, income, and economic growth.

Religion

Religion is man's feeble efforts to cross the gulf between fallen man and God. It is endemic to all of mankind, in every age and every people group. The religious impulse exists because it is not linked to human experiment, invention, or ideologies but to the permanent things or first principles. However, apart from the truth offered by the Judeo-Christian ethic, religion remains powerless to span the gulf that was created by sin. It was the revelation, initially to the Hebrews and continuing through the inspired writings of the Apostles, which gave clarity and foundation to those truths that mankind had struggled to apprehend and points the way to bridge the chasm between God and man.

In the humanist worldview, religion is a human social construction. Its presence merely occurs as means to draw people together and give meaning to their lives. There is no room for supernaturalism for religion is merely a form of human experience and values. Human justice, not a dead God, gives meaning to human experiences and values. Therefore, humanists deny the dualism that divides the universe into two separate realms—the material and the spiritual.

Marriage and Family

The supreme reflection of God's image in humankind is in the marriage relationship followed by family. The roles of husband and wife and father and mother (monogamous married couple living with their children) are not societal constructs. The surface *patterns* and *functioning* of family may vary markedly in various cultures and societies down through the ages. However, the divinely ordered family *structure* is intrinsically a part of the fundamental identity of the family in every society and for all time. It is one of those universals or permanent things that are imbedded in the foundation of creation.

The humanistic worldview and its values focus on the individual person and his/her independence, freedom, self-actualization, autonomy, growth, and creativity. Hence, marriage becomes secondary to the individual and is at best a contractual arrangement devoid of the requirements of covenantal "self-giving" as it interferes with humanistic values stated above. Further, marriage is only one of several relational choices open to the individual. Marriage is not central or necessary for nurturing and the transmission of moral and cultural values to children. The pair-bonding elements of monogamy and permanency are individual decisions and not cultural universals.

We have summarized the differences between the general tenets of the Christian and humanist worldviews. Now we turn to the means that humanists use to dislodge the Judeo-Christian worldview as the central vision of American culture—the attack on language. Richard Weaver believed that "...a divine element is present in language. The feeling that to have power of language is to have control over things is deeply imbedded in the human mind." Throughout the ages language has been the means of achieving order in culture. Knowledge of truth comes through the word which provides solidity in the "shifting world of appearances." Weaver called words the storehouse of our memory. In our modern age humanists have effectively used semantics to neuter words of their meaning in historical and symbolic contexts, that is, words now mean what men want them to mean. By removing the fixities of language (which undermines an understanding of truth), language loses its ability to define and compel. As the meaning of words is divorced from truth, relativism gains supremacy, and a culture tends to disintegration without an understanding of eternal truths upon which to orient its self.[772] In the battle of worldviews, certain words have gained power to obscure truth and history through the machinations of humanist redefinition.

Truth

In the Christian worldview, the Supreme Being (God) formed the universe and God created matter out of nothing. He impressed certain principles upon that matter, from which it can never depart, and without which it would cease to be. These principles dictate rules of action and applies to animate and inanimate objects. These "laws of nature" must invariably be followed by the universe and the created matter therein. One exception was allowed as man could choose to follow or depart from those principles as they relate to human nature. Those principles are truths that are intrinsic, timeless, and are essential elements that provide a coherent and rational way to live in the world. These absolutes are called by various names: permanent things, universals, first principles, eternal truths, and norms.

The humanistic worldview regarding truth is one of cultural relativism which requires a suspension of judgment since all belief systems contain some truth within while no one belief system has all the truth. For humanists, all social constructions are culturally relative as they are shaped by class, gender, and ethnicity. Thus, there can be no universal truths because all viewpoints, lifestyles, and beliefs are equally valid. As a result, no man or group can claim to be infallible with regard to truth and virtue. Rather, truth is produced by the free give and take of competing claims and opinions—i.e., truth can be manufactured.

Freedom

Simply put, freedom means an absence of coercion and constraint, but freedom does not mean an absence of consequences. God created man with a free will, that is, God gave man a choice as to whether to follow or not follow God's laws and commandments. The consequences of disobedience to God's laws are readily evident in society, but those consequences should not be confused with coercion or lack of freedom. Man must suffer the consequences for wrong choices. Yet, man often blames God for the pain and suffering in the world. As he joins himself with his like-minded fellowmen in an organized society, they impose restrictions on themselves to make life better. It is a freedom to restrain one's self.

Freedom, under the humanists' perverted definition, unbridled the self and senses from any control except within the strictures imposed by the greater good for humanity. The humanist definition of freedom presumes to loose man from the bondage of mores, norms, tradition, and distant voices of the past. However, the humanists' definition of freedom, which co-joins the maximization of individual autonomy with the humanist-created primacy of the greatest good for the greatest number, is a false freedom. A society organized around the tenets of humanism cannot remain free as it will be pushed to one end or the other of the anarchy-totalitarian continuum of government. In reality, such humanistic concepts of freedom coerce the individual through the requirement of a general commonality of thought and action which is forced downward from the state to the individual. However, the central cultural vision of any society must command unity to exist and prosper in ordered harmony. Such unity must filter up from individuals, not be coerced or forced down on society. Without such unity filtering up from individuals, there can be no order to the soul or society, and without such order society deteriorates over time and eventually disintegrates.

Democracy

Democracy is a form of government by the people, rule of the majority, and a means of voting. Democracy is not a synonym for freedom. Other definitions and descriptions of democracy include a means but not an end, a means whereby a society safeguards internal peace and individual freedom, a means of conveying power (but not a source of power), and on occasion a means by which freedom is threatened.

Humanists have appropriated, redefined the term, and have used it to arbitrarily consolidate power and limit individual freedom. The humanist definition of democracy has been infused with moral principles such as a commitment to liberty and equality, concern for the worth and dignity of the individual, an individual's right to do what he wishes and limits undue interference with his individual choice and action, opportunity for growth and personal realization, tolerance, and diversity. Each carries with it its own humanistic meaning. New rights, causes, and agendas wrapped in the humanistic apparel of false qualities and moral imperatives are given legitimacy as they are linked with democracy. Therefore, to oppose these rights, causes, and agendas is to oppose democracy. For humanists, democracy is both method *and* goal, a means *and* an end. In effect, democracy has been elevated to something of value in itself. This is a perversion of the meaning of democracy and a perversion of what the Founders meant.

Equality

Here we speak of equality in light of the individual within the Christian and humanistic worldviews. The founding Americans relied on order that rested upon a respect for prescriptive rights and customs as opposed to the egalitarian notions of the French philosophers during the French Revolution. This difference was made clear by John Adams' definition of equality which strikes at the heart of what it really means—a moral and political equality only—by which is meant equality before God and before the law. This definition does not teach that all men are born to equal powers, mental abilities, influence in society, property, and other advantages. Rather, all men are born to equal rights before God and the law and by implication equal opportunity.

The humanistic definition of equality is clearly stated in *Humanist Manifesto II's* eleventh common principal, "The principle of moral equality must be furthered...This means equality of opportunity..." But, the meaning of "equal opportunity" is immediately and drastically corrupted to mean an equality of outcome by humanist requirements. To further clarify the intent of the signors of the *Manifesto,* the document states that, "If unable, society should provide means to satisfy their basic economic, health, and cultural needs, including whatever resources make possible, a minimum guaranteed annual income."[773] This concept of human equality flows from the humanistic assumption of the perfectibility of man. Under this concept, what men are comes from experience. Therefore, men are equal at birth, and differences and inequalities arise due to environment. The goal of humanists was to achieve an egalitarian society (and eliminate inequalities due to environment) through political means in which man, achieving perfect equality in their political rights, would at the same time be perfectly equalized and assimilated in their possessions, their opinions, and their passions. When humanists failed to achieve equality of outcome through political equality, the levelers demanded economic democracy, a new and expanded humanist definition of equality. However, economic democracy still means an equality of condition as opposed to equality of opportunity and is to be achieved through recognition of invented or synthetic rights coupled with broad but non-specific egalitarian ideals. As society is leveled with guarantees of certain outcomes to its citizens, political equality suffers.

Justice

Justice is variously defined as fairness, impartiality, right action, and the principle or process by which every man and woman in society are accorded the things that inherently belong to them (their lives, dignity, property, and status or station in life). Justice implies standards by which its office is administered. Those standards were built up over the centuries and crafted by adherence to unchanging universal truths, a set of norms that derive from an authority above the state and a people's culture across the whole of life. The concept of justice is a universal, a thing of permanence that transcends the whole of man's time on this planet and pertains to all cultures. Because justice has permanence or status, it acts as a measure or standard rather than a tool to achieve a social function or change.

For the humanist, man is an economic being, and the definition of justice must be bent to recognized humanist social values. Those values—liberty and opportunity, income and wealth, and the bases of self-respect—are to be distributed equally unless an unequal distribution of any or all of these values is equally advantageous to everyone. These values, and therefore justice charged with upholding these values, are a thing rationally constructed by man. For the humanist, justice is achieved when there is a "fair" measure of economic distribution. No god, no tradition, no patrimony, and no settled law need apply. Humanists have changed the definition of justice to fit their worldview, but like order and freedom, justice is not of human construction, and no amount of humanist tinkering will change the heart of man with regard to a right understanding of fairness, impartiality, and right action in a civil society.

Multiculturalism

The Judeo-Christian ethic recognizes the common origin of man as described in Genesis of the Old Testament. In the New Testament the Apostle Paul spoke to the assembled Athenians that the God of the Hebrews "...made of one blood all nations of men for to dwell on the face of the earth..."[774] Christians understand that God created all peoples, but those peoples have developed different cultures and worldviews. Christianity far exceeds humanism and most other worldviews in its adaptation to and civil respect for diverse cultures and governments. From whence does this adaptation and respect come? First, Christianity offers truth and therefore provides the answers to life's basic questions which helps bring order to one's soul and ultimately order to those societies in which Christians dwell. Truth provides a measure of commonality between men, a set standard by which men may interact with one another. Truth also engenders trust as it is exhibited in the lives of people that are followers of Christ *and* followers of His example. Second, Christianity does not have a political agenda other that adherence to principle. Therefore, it enters and resides quietly in various societies—from free to totalitarian.

Humanistic multiculturalism is defined as a belief that all cultures are equally valid and valuable, and it claims that all cultures offer some truth while no one culture can claim to provide the answers to all of life's basic questions. The essence of multiculturalism is found in the denial of absolutes, one of the cardinal tenets of the humanistic faith. Without absolutes, societies descend to moral relativism, a values-free approach that makes it impossible to judge one period or era in relation to another or to say that one culture's ethic is superior to another. The multicultural movement is premised on the belief that America is too immersed in Western "Eurocentric" teachings to the detriment of other cultures. The imposition of the multicultural mindset, in the American educational system in particular, is an attempt to supplant America's white, male-dominated European history and the Judeo-Christian ethic which relies on absolutes. Challenges to multiculturalism are labeled as being opposed to freedom and paints Christianity as being repressive, bigoted, and intolerant.

Diversity

For the Christian view of diversity, the best explanation comes from Paul's letter to the Corinthians with regard to unity in the Church.

> For just as the body is one and has many members and all the members of the body, though many, are one body, so it is with Christ...But God so composed the body, giving the greater honor to the inferior part, that there may be no discord in the body, but that the members may have the same care for one another. If one member suffers, all suffer together; if one member is honored, all rejoice together. (1 Corinthians 12:12, 24-26 Revised Standard Version)

The Christian's focus is not on the individual's differences but upon diversity's contribution to the whole of society, and from this emphasis comes unity. Unity is made possible when each member is recognized as an indispensable contributor to the body.

Humanism's diversity is a close kin of multiculturalism and focuses on the differences within society and not society as a whole. With emphasis on the differences, mass culture becomes nothing more than an escalating number of subcultures within an increasingly distressed political framework that attempts to satisfy the myriad of demands of the individual subcultures. There is a loss of unity through fragmentation and ultimately a loss of a society's central cultural vision which leads to disintegration. Humanism's impulse for diversity is a derivative of relativism and humanism's perverted concept of equality.

Tolerance

One definition of tolerance is "...the allowed deviation from a standard."[775] This definition implies a standard by which to measure other cultures as well as a limit to the extent to which deviation from the prevailing culture's standard will be allowed. Because there is a standard, tension arises between tolerance and exclusivity (adherence to that standard) demanded by culture. Tolerance suggests acceptance and inclusiveness while exclusivity implies segregation and denial (by which is meant segregation *between* cultures, not *within* cultures). A culture that values its central vision welcomes integration of diverse groups that share that common central vision. However, the very essence of culture requires that it discriminate against those outside its boundaries that do not share its central vision.

Regarding tolerance, Christian teaching speaks unerringly in defense of the concept of universal human rights and why each is obligated to respect the rights of others. The conflict with the humanist worldview regarding toleration arises with the humanist belief that man is a social animal, and his morality results from his innate altruism, a moral instinct of selflessness, though not equally developed in all humans. For the humanist, the origin of man's morality evolved from his ability to connect value or benefit with behaving well toward others, but that value does not originate with the laws established by a supernatural God. The humanist solution to "chauvinistic ethnicity" and its consequent intolerance is to recognize a new inclusive ethnicity that certifies its membership in the world community. This transformation occurs through recognition that the state must be secular in nature, that there are concepts and methodologies for achieving tolerance that transcend individual cultural boundaries, and that an essential part of the new world morality requires adherence to humanist values beginning with a recognition of universal human rights. Therefore, toleration begins with the denial of absolutes as no man or group can claim ownership of truth which is often the product of the free give and take of conflicting opinions. The humanist stance towards toleration is a reflection of moral relativism which is the antithesis of Christian belief and that of many other religions.

Pluralism

A pluralistic society is one "…in which members of diverse ethnic, racial, religious, or social groups maintain an *autonomous participation* in and development of their traditional culture or special interest *within the confines of a common civilization*."[776] (emphasis added) By its very essence, culture must discriminate against those outside its boundaries that do not share its central vision. From its beginnings America was a pluralistic society in that it did not have a politically established national religion, i.e., one state sponsored denomination or sect. Although exhibiting a form of pluralism that denied government interference with their beliefs, America exhibited an exceptionally strong religious sanction. This sanction was the "…power of Christian teaching over private conscience [that] made possible the American democratic society."[777] This was the central cultural vision upon which America was founded.

For the secular humanist, pluralism demands all religion be removed from the public square. This is a different interpretation of pluralism than held by Americans of the Revolutionary era. Pluralism in modern America, as defined by humanists, must presuppose that there are no universals, i.e., no God, and that all cultures are equally worthy and valid. It is in this humanistic definition of pluralism that cultures are prone to failure. To attempt to meld together or co-mingle multiple cultures into one culture with *multiple centers of vision* is to create a powerless culture with little influence and place it on the road to disintegration.

In our world of progressive education, scientism, and mass media, the semanticists have captured the linguistic high ground through redefinition of key concepts. Regarding the consequences thereof, Weaver cut to the heart of the matter.

> Just as soon as men begin to point out that the word is one entity and the object it represents is another, there set in a temptation to do one thing with the word and another different thing with the object it is supposed to represent; and here begins that relativism which by now is visibly affecting those institutions which depend for their very existence upon our ability to use language as a permanent binder.[778]

However, in the end, cultures and their component institutions do not survive which rest on the false dialectical pronouncements, definitions, and dogma of humanism. On the contrary, the long-term survival and prospering of a culture depends on its apprehension and incorporation of those things we have called eternal and unchanging truths or universals.

Chapter 26

Christianity and Humanism – Endgame in America

As the second decade of the twenty-first century unfolds, American society remains more conflicted than ever. The most obvious evidence of the conflict is reflected by the media and our elected representatives' efforts to govern. Words like "gridlock" and "dead lock" are topics of daily discussion, and civil discourse may have been mortally wounded as debate has developed an ugly rancor and shrillness in the halls of government and channels of media. The root cause is the principal topic of this book—the clash of the Judeo-Christian and humanistic worldviews. As stated earlier, there can be no compromise or truce in this conflict. Coexistence is not an option as each holds irreconcilable basic tenets which are terminally toxic to the other. Why is this so? For the answer we must reiterate the importance of understanding of what culture is, how a culture is built, and what can cause a culture to disintegrate.

Man is a special being, if for no reason other than he is the only creature to ask why he is here. That very question presupposes his denial that he owes his existence to some fantastically improbable celestial *and* biological crap shoot. Man senses his specialness and cannot abide nothingness as the reason for his existence. He looks at himself and sees faint images of something far greater, and he is compelled to search for answers as to the meaning and purpose of his life. He yearns to be something above what he sees in the natural world. Unique to the earth and its living creatures, man thinks, verbalizes, and symbolizes his quest for connection to some greater purpose. These yearnings become the felt needs of the group and represent an ordering of life in the larger sense—how things fit together and work and man's place in the grand scheme of things. This ordering is a process whereby the group determines what is true and right and a rejection of the way things are that are contrary to order.

Out of the ordering process comes unity from which arises culture—the central vision of the group. Weaver attributes a number of traits to culture without which it will disintegrate: "It is the essence of culture to feel its own imperative and to believe in the uniqueness of its worth...[it] must insist on a pattern of inclusion and exclusion...[is] inward facing toward some high representation...Culture is by nature aristocratic...discriminating between what counts for much and what counts for little..."[779]

Robert Bork wrote that, "It is difficult to overstate the importance of the cultural unity that is being deliberately destroyed."[780] Not only is unity necessary for the establishment of order, that is, a society's central cultural vision, unity is the most important attribute for a culture's continued survival. At present we do not have that sustaining unity in America. In his 1858 speech accepting his party's nomination for the U.S. Senate seat representing Illinois, the young political candidate quoted from the gospel of Mark, "And if a house be divided against itself, that house cannot stand."[781] The dividing issue to which Abraham Lincoln referred was slavery. He lost the election but became a strong anti-slavery voice that propelled him to the Presidency two years later and the ensuing Civil War with its nearly fatal shattering of national unity.[782] Today, America faces a cultural crisis of even greater magnitude in which the nation's cultural unity is being undermined by a humanist worldview that has seeped into all aspects of American life. The American central cultural vision as known by the colonists, Founders, and citizens to the present day is in peril because the "...inward-looking vision and the impulse to resist the alien are lost." With such loss comes disruption and eventual disintegration.[783]

The central cultural vision held by the colonists, the Founders, and citizens was the set of blueprints for building the American form and practice of government, our national house so to speak. Those blueprints had been drawn largely from the Judeo-Christian tradition and its reliance on a transcendent God, His eternal truths, and His revelation to the Hebrews and first century Christians. To these central elements were added the proscriptions of history, custom, convention, and tradition—in essence, our patrimony. After a number of years certain wings of the house were demolished (e.g., slavery) and rebuilt to better adhere to those original blueprints.

Most of the governance of the house in the intervening years since its construction dealt with routine maintenance, interior decorations, and arrangement of furniture within. But the house was of sound construction, and apart from occasional errors in modification which were readily corrected, the structure served its inhabitants well. The house was large and had many rooms, and many were welcomed to live therein, even those that did not like the architecture and the central vision of its culture—the over-arching banner of the Judeo-Christian worldview. However, the Founders knew of the fallen nature of man and foresaw a time when men would attempt to change that which they had built on timeless truths. In their great wisdom, the Founders believed they should insure what they had built would not be changed capriciously by its inhabitants. So they devised the Constitution that limited those changes so the house would continue to function within the time-tested guidelines, or as Thomas Jefferson said, to "...bind him down with the chains of the Constitution."[784]

True to their prediction, several groups (humanists with varying philosophies and agendas) believed that the house should not be just maintained or periodically redecorated but be reconstructed in its entirety. They wished to tear down the structure and build a new house using a set of old blueprints based on the tenets of humanism (which the Founders had judged to be fundamentally flawed and structurally unsound). For the humanists, the center of the cultural vision would have to be shifted, and the old overarching banner of the Judeo-Christian worldview would have to go. Their demolition efforts began in earnest in the nineteenth century and rapidly progressed throughout the twentieth century. The structural supports of the old house were identified as the first to be demolished—belief in a transcendent God, hierarchy, moral truths, right and wrong, the fallen nature of man, and the sanctity of life to name just a few. However, the Founders' Constitution slowed the humanists' progress. So they took the Founders' words and invented new definitions and meanings to attach to those words. Once the new meanings were defined by their intellectual superiors, taught in our schools, and embedded in our media-saturated consciousness, the humanists insisted that the old Constitution was outdated and must be modified and modernized to fit the new progressive understanding of the world and its problems. The old structure still stands, but for how long we do not know. Its future depends on its inhabitants. In spite of humanist assaults, the great majority of the inhabitants still like the original plans but seem to not know how (or care enough to rise from their lethargy) to stop the demolition and rebuild the house as it once was.

    Before we address the answers as to how to reconstruct American society as it was originally envisioned and implemented by the Founders, we must separate the house from the blueprints. It is the house that is in danger of collapse from the wrecking ball of humanism. Whether the house stands or not, the Judeo-Christian worldview points to the ultimate truth, and that truth existed before the creation of this world and will exist after this world should God so choose to allow its demise. Cultures may disintegrate, but the truth of Christianity will not for it resides in the individual hearts of men and women. Christianity is not dependent on government sanction, and it does not have a political agenda apart from adherence to biblical principles. Western civilization and ultimately America with its unique freedoms were products of the tenets of Christianity as it flowered in Europe after the fall of the Roman Empire. The truth of Christianity's lack of dependence on government sanction and absence of political agenda is evident in the growth of Christianity under its initial duress and harsh persecution in the pagan Roman Empire. It is also evidenced when one examines Christianity's growth through the centuries and growth of Christianity in twentieth and twenty-first centuries in dictatorial and totalitarian countries such as the former Russian communist state, China, and other African, Asian, and South American countries. In fact, those nations in the southern and eastern hemispheres including countries that exhibit some of the greatest repression of freedom of religion will soon represent the center of world Christianity in terms of growth and adherents.[785] Malcolm Muggeridge wrote of this growth and the renewal of Christianity in many atheistic and materialistic countries. He called this growth and renewal of the Christian faith in its purist form in these brutal and oppressive regimes the most extraordinary single fact of the twentieth century.[786]

    The enormous conflict being witnessed in America results from the highly successful and advanced attempt to displace the overarching moral suasion of Christianity and Christian principles and in its place impose the humanist philosophy. The Christian worldview is in danger of utter removal from American culture because of a loss of an understanding of the uniqueness of its worth, the loss of America's ability to exclude those things which strike at the heart of its central cultural vision, and America's inability to distinguish that which counts for much and that which counts for little. With the steady dismantling and removal of the central cultural vision, America is sliding toward oblivion as it drinks the poison of humanism with its disintegrating notions of the autonomous individual, relativism, radical egalitarianism, progressivism, and denial of a supreme being.

Weaver wrote, "…when a culture has lost its will to live, outside ministrations are of no use."[787] Modern Europe is a prime example of the endgame of a failing humanistic culture as it grapples with the militaristic religion of Islam. Most of Europe long ago abandoned Christianity and embraced humanism. Following the lure of narcissistic freedoms and egotism, nanny state promises based on illusory and fictitious rights, the false definitions of tolerance and equality, and aimless movement mischaracterized as progress, Europeans have developed an invertebrate culture with neither the will or strength to combat the aggressors that storm its gates to enslave and devour it. European culture has lost the ability to discriminate and cohere, both necessary to survive. In essence, it is a loss of unity.

Even prominent humanists recognize the loss of order and unity in American society. One such was Benjamin Spock, whose life and huge contributions to the advancement of an American humanistic worldview was briefly chronicled at the beginning of this book. He remained a champion of humanism throughout his life, and his efforts were recognized when he was named Humanist of the Year in 1968.[788] In 1994, four years before the end of his life at age ninety, Spock wrote *A Better World for Our Children – Rebuilding American Family Values*. In the book Spock expressed considerable concern as he viewed the harmful effects of society on American children. "I am near despair. My despair comes not only from the progressive loss of values in this century, but from the fact that present society is simply not working. *Societies and people who live in them fall apart if they lose their fundamental beliefs, and the signs of this loss are everywhere.*" (emphasis added) As a result America was losing its way because of "a progressive relaxation of many of our standards of behavior and the souring of many commonly held beliefs." He listed a number of signs of this loss of fundamental values and beliefs and included the increasing instability of marriage, child neglect through excessive focus on careers, materialism, single parent households, failure of schools, progressive coarsening of the attitude towards sexuality due to mass media, and growth in family violence. The book contains a number of insightful observations and positive remedies for society's ills. He recognized that "our society has misplaced its values and lost its bearings," but he believed "the solution is not to rush backward, eyes closed, groping for the answers of the past, but instead to look for the causes of our problems and for realistic solutions that might fit those causes." Amazingly, Spock remained oblivious to humanism's disintegrating effects and did not see that the ills of society are a direct result of well over a century of humanism's dominance in American life. Spock continued to believe "strongly in the evolutionary, psycho-biological basis for the idealism that has allowed the human race to go as far as it has gone." But at the same time he wrote, "I now realize the truth of the Biblical declaration, 'man cannot live by bread alone'."[789] In many ways, Spock's book on values was an apologia but more so in the sense of justification or defense of humanism (with only a mild mea culpa). In spite of his defense of humanism, Spock's observations and concerns in the book repudiate, conflict with, or in the least are inconsistent with much of humanistic dogma that he endorsed, wrote about, taught, and fought for throughout his life. Yet, for solutions to the ills of society he chronicled, he continued to return to the polluted source from which those ills originated—humanism. There is a shop-worn cliché attributed to Albert Einstein regarding the definition of insanity: "Doing the same thing over and over again and expecting different results."[790] This definition would seem an apt description of the humanists' dilemma in dealing with American society's failings and its rapid demise.

Humanism under the labels of modern liberalism and progressivism is morally and intellectually bankrupt. Its policies are ill-conceived, incoherent, and have led to high rates of divorce, co-habitation, illegitimacy, abortion, single family households and consequential poverty, and drug abuse to name just a few. The nation has moved toward economic bondage in both government and private sectors as socialism and its entitlement mentality have become ingrained in the American consciousness. There has been a broad and deep coarsening of culture as lewdness, vulgarity, lawlessness, and violence have bled from the entertainment media into the streets and homes of America. Politically, economically, and morally, the nation is in significant distress. There are many books on the market that chronicle the decline of the West, and in particular America, that provide specific remedies, mostly of a political and economic nature that offer good and legitimate prescriptions for resuscitating American culture as it was once known. These prescriptions are helpful but often deal with symptoms, not the disease itself. That disease is humanism.

So where does one start in a recapture America's central cultural vision? In the political and economic arena, there must be elections and appointments of officials that understand the roots of the disintegration of American culture and who unswervingly implement policies that adhere to the founding principles under the over-arching banner of the Judeo-Christian ethic. This must include taking back positions of political power at the local school boards and city councils to the highest offices in the nation. It means demanding that judges must be held accountable for overstepping legitimate authority and imposing disintegrating cultural agendas that stand in opposition to founding principles and the wishes of the electorate. A burgeoning bureaucracy must be reined in at every level of government along with its consequent intrusiveness into the lives of Americans. Universities must be recaptured through staffing and program changes—either through legislative dictates or tightened purse strings. However, even if these objectives are accomplished at every level of government, political and economic conservatism remains fragile in a liberal culture.[791] In this regard Judge Bork described America as being two nations.

> It is well to remember the limits of politics. The political nation is not the same as the cultural nation; the two have different leaders and very different views of the world. Even when conservative political leaders have the votes, liberal cultural leaders operate and exercise influence where votes do not count. However many political victories conservatives may produce, they cannot attack modern liberalism in its fortresses…very little will change in Hollywood, the network evening news, universities, church bureaucracies, the *New York times*, or the *Washington Post*…Conservative political victories will always

be tenuous and fragile *unless conservatives recapture the culture.*[792] (emphasis added)

A conservative government will always be subject to unrelenting attacks of a liberal-dominated culture. A second constraining force on a conservative political agenda is the large body within the populace addicted to entitlement/welfare programs and who may balk at limitations and reductions during the painful weaning process.

We have identified the disease infecting America's culture as humanism, and like a cancer it has metastasized through the various institutions of American society. Although political and economic measures are important, ultimate and sustained healing must come from within, not just through the application of Band-Aids to the abrasions caused by modern secular society. Healing must proceed from a re-establishment of order. As we have seen, order allows the establishment of laws that support order. From just laws, justice is made possible, and from the possibility of justice flow freedom. Order in society can only be achieved from a right ordering of the soul of the individual. This order is achieved as man comes into a proper relationship with God. When individuals collectively order their souls and achieve a proper relationship with God, unity is advanced and the central cultural vision is restored. Here we speak of a moral and spiritual regeneration of America through spiritual renewal, often called a religious revival or awakening, that will set the "...moral tone in opposition to today's liberal relativism."[793] That is the prescription for America. That healing must begin with the individual and a subsequent national spiritual renewal—a remedy that has served America well during several periods of crisis in its colonial and national history. A brief examination of three religious awakenings will demonstrate the power and importance of spiritual renewal in American history.

History has proven that the years following protracted wars are generally periods of significant moral decline. This was true of the remaining years of the eighteenth century following the Revolutionary War (1776-1781). During the last decade of the century, six percent of the population (five million Americans) were confirmed drunkards. Crime had grown to such an extent that bank robberies were a daily occurrence and women did not go out at night for fear of assault. The churches were almost totally irrelevant in curbing the moral decline.[794] Although the state churches (Anglican, Congregational, and Presbyterian), declined precipitously during the 1760-1790 period, the religious impulse was alive and well in new religious denominations (Methodists, Baptists, and others).[795] Nevertheless, the war years would take toll on all churches, especially during the last decade of the century.

> The Methodists were losing more members than they were gaining. The Baptists said that they had their most wintry season. The Presbyterians in general assembly deplored the nation's ungodliness. In a typical Congregational church, the Rev. Samuel Shepherd of Lemnos, Massachusetts, in sixteen years had not taken one young person in fellowship. The Lutherans were so languishing that they discussed uniting with Episcopalians who were even worse off. The Protestant Episcopal Bishop of New York...quit functioning; he had confirmed no one for so long that he decided he was out of work, so he took up other employment. The Chief Justice of the United States, John Marshall, wrote to the Bishop of Virginia, James Madison, that the Church "was too far gone ever to be redeemed."...Tom Paine echoed, "Christianity will be forgotten in thirty years."[796]

Christianity at the universities was just as destitute. Students at Harvard were polled, and not one Christian was found. Two admitted to being Christians at Princeton while only five members of the student body were *not* members of the filthy speech movement of the times. Few if any campuses escaped the denigration of Christianity and general mayhem. Anti-Christian plays were presented at Dartmouth, a Bible taken from a local church was burned in a public bonfire, students burned Nassau Hall at Princeton, and students forced the resignation of Harvard's president. Christians on college campuses in the 1790s were so few "...that they met in secret, like a communist cell, and kept their minutes in code so that no one would know."[797]

In 1791, through the Union of Prayer that was begun with the efforts of William Carey, Andrew Fuller, John Sutcliffe, and other church leaders, the Second Great Awakening began sweeping began sweeping Great Britain. It was a New England Baptist pastor named Isaac Backus that played a pivotal role in igniting the Second Great Awakening in America. Backus was both a product of and participant in the Great Awakening led by Jonathan Edwards and George Whitefield. Born in 1724, he began preaching in 1746, initially as a Congregationalist. Struggling with the issue of the incompatibility of infant baptism and salvation through grace, Backus and a number of his church members organized a Baptist church in 1756 at which he was the pastor for fifty years until his death in 1806.[798] With spiritual conditions in America at their worst in 1794, Backus sent an urgent plea to pastors of all churches of every Christian denomination in America. His plea for prayer for revival was widely adopted, and a network of prayer meetings on the first Monday of each month soon led to revival. By 1800, revival had reached the western extremities of civilization in Logan County, Kentucky, if the wild and irreligious people of Rogue's Harbour (as it was known) could be called civilized. Lawlessness was so rampant that local citizens formed themselves into regiments of vigilantes that fought outlaws, often unsuccessfully, to establish a measure of law and order for the settlements. It was here that Presbyterian minister James McCready settled and became pastor of three small churches. All through the winter of 1799, McCready and several of his congregants joined the national monthly Monday meetings to pray for revival as well as holding weekly Saturday evening to Sunday morning prayer meetings. Following months of prayer, revival came in the summer of 1800. The spiritual hunger was so great eleven thousand came to a communion service. Overwhelmed, McCready called for help from all denominations.[799] Next came the famous Cane Ridge camp meeting in southern Kentucky during the summer of 1801. Six or seven ministers preached simultaneously from various points to reach crowds that were estimated to exceed 10,000. To give perspective to the significant size of the crowds, the largest city in Kentucky at the time was Lexington with a population of only 2,000.[800]

The Second Great Awakening restored a considerable measure of morality and initiated other civilizing influences on the young nation. Its fruits included popular education, Bible Societies, Sunday schools, the modern missionary movement, and ultimately sowed and nurtured the seeds that led to the abolition of slavery.[801]

The Revival of 1857-1858 is known by various names: the Great Revival of 1858, the Businessman's Revival, the Layman's Revival, the Union Prayer Meeting, and the Third Great Awakening. Several distinguishing features of this revival were the absence of any recognized clerical leadership, its broad interdenominational character, and the focus on prayer. However, the meetings included brief corporate prayers, religious testimony, and singing. The revival sprang from an initial meeting at the noon hour on September 23, 1857 in the upper room of the Dutch Reform Church in lower Manhattan. Jeremiah Lamphier had advertised the prayer meeting, but only six came that first day. Three weeks later, a financial panic that had been building since August exploded on October 13th when banks were closed and would not reopen for two months. Attendance soon mushroomed as businessmen from nearby Wall Street began attending. The prayer meetings quickly spread to other churches, auditoriums, and theaters. The greatest intensity of the revival occurred between February and April of 1858. The revival spread across the United States and lasted for about a year. Revival broke out in Canada and crossed the Atlantic to the British Isles where it lasted until 1862. The prayer revival also sparked local church revivals in New England, the Midwest, and upper South (beginning particularly with New Year's Eve "watch night" services); on college campuses across the nation; and separate Women's prayer groups. Net growth in membership of Protestant denominations for the period 1857-1859 was 474,000, more than twice the number of the preceding three years.[802]

Historians have debated the impact of the Revival of 1857-1858 as it related to nineteenth century social reform efforts. Some historians strongly connect the revival with concerns for the ills of society and the need for social reforms that were beginning to ferment in the last half of the century. Others pointed to the revival prayer meeting practice of avoiding any discussion of controversial topics such as slavery and abolitionism as evidence of little direct social impact caused by the revival.[803] The reality was that the 1857-1858 Revival was about personal religious transformation but with which society greatly benefited. As has been reiterated throughout this book, the ordering of society and the addressing of its social ills must begin with the individual and an ordering of his soul in right relationship with God. This must certainly be the greatest impact of the Revival of 1857-1858 as the nation was soon to be immersed in its greatest struggle to survive. It was the Revival of 1857-1858 that caused men and women, in both the North and South, to be spiritually prepared for the coming struggle in which the nation would exorcize the demon of slavery and recover its national unity. Large and widespread revivals continued during the Civil War in both Union and Confederate armies and can be said to be a continuation of the Revival of 1857-1858. Conversions during the war were estimated to be between 100,000 and 200,000 among Union troops and 150,000 in the Confederate Army. One may ask how this can be—brothers fighting and killing each other while both called on God for protection and to save their immortal souls. To answer, we must remember that slavery was an institutional cancer on the national body. Regardless of slavery's origins and protectors, it was slavery that was being cut from the body, not the Southern soldier and citizen. God was just as concerned for the individual Southerner as he was for those in the North. After the war, many of the faithful Civil War veterans on both sides of the conflict returned to their homes with their religious fervor intact, filled the pews, and brought healing to the nation.[804] Without this unifying force of a common religious view, the significant post-war tensions could easily and likely have led to a permanent balkanization of much of the country.

The last of the three revivals to be discussed also began as a movement of prayer in 1904. Evan Roberts was a student at Newcastle Emlyn College, Wales. Following attendance at a meeting where Presbyterian evangelist Seth Joshua spoke, Roberts asked permission to go back to his home church and speak. Such was the response to Roberts' prayer and preaching that the crowds grew and revival spread rapidly to other areas. The Welsh revival movement yielded one hundred thousand converts in five months, and its impact was profound and lasting. Judges had few if any cases to try as there "...were no robberies, no burglaries, no rapes, no murders, and no embezzlements, nothing." Policemen had so much time on their hands that they formed several quartets and sang in local churches upon request.[805] J. Edwin Orr, one of the foremost scholars on revivals, wrote of the astounding changes that occurred throughout Wales.

As the revival swept Wales, drunkenness was cut in half. There was a wave of bankruptcies, but nearly all taverns. There was even a slowdown in the mines, for so many Welsh coal miners were converted and stopped using bad language that the horses that dragged the coal trucks in the mines could not understand what was being said to them. That revival also affected sexual moral standards...the illegitimate birth rate had dropped 44% within a year of the beginning of the revival.[806]

Five years after the revival began, one critic wrote a book in which he reported that "...of a hundred thousand joining the churches in five months of excitement, after five years *only* seventy-five thousand still stood in the membership of those churches!" (emphasis added) From Wales the revival spread throughout Britain, Scandinavia, Germany, Australia, Africa, Brazil, Mexico, Chile, and the United States. In the U.S., the results were just as dramatic as in Wales. This was demonstrated in Portland, Oregon, where "...two hundred forty major stores closed from 11 to 2 each day to enable people to attend prayer meetings..."[807]

These examples of spiritual renewal are not only prescriptive but should be an encouragement to those that believe America's central cultural vision is beyond hope of restoration. Once again, we must state that the prescription for America's cultural decline is a spiritual renewal within the individual which can subsequently transform a nation. Only then can America's central cultural vision be restored. Spiritual renewals have restored America during several times of crisis in the nation's history. How do such revivals come? Throughout all of history, *the common and inextricable thread running through all spiritual awakenings is concerted prayer* as has been shown in the examples above.

Waves of spiritual renewal and moral decline have undulated across history's pages since man's initial fall. Spiritual renewal is not unique to America but has been a requisite in some form or fashion in many societies in every age. But spiritual renewal is not always chosen. For one example we look back to a time a thousand years before Jesus walked the streets of Jerusalem when God gave the ancient Hebrews blueprints for another house designed by Him. Solomon, son of King David, was charged with the task of building a house for God to dwell among His chosen people. The Temple was built precisely to God's specification and magnificently appointed. Upon completion, Solomon consecrated the Temple with a prayer which ended with certain petitions. He asked that God would: inhabit the house prepared for Him; hear and accept the prayers of his people; render judgment upon the people in an equitable manner; be merciful to his people who sought him, repented of their sin, and reformed their ways; accept strangers into His house and answer their prayers; plead the cause of His people against all who opposed their cause; dwell in the house; make the ministers of the house a blessing to the people and instruments to save others; and cause the house to serve the people and provide abundant joy and satisfaction.[808] God responded to Solomon's prayer with a covenant.

> When I shut up the heavens so that there is no rain, or command the locust to devour the land, or send pestilence among my people, *if my people who are called by my name humble themselves, and pray and seek my face, and turn from their wicked ways, then I will hear from heaven and will forgive their sin and heal their land.* Now my eyes will be open and my ears attentive to the prayer that is made in this place.[809] (emphasis added)

Much of American society in the twenty-first century cannot be called by His name for we are chiseling that name from our public buildings and monuments and silencing His mention in public discourse. Humility is no longer an American trait for God has been pronounced dead, and man is now the measure. Prayer is not only lacking but banned from our schools and the public square. The ways of the wicked are embraced wholeheartedly by a popular culture in which deference to maximum autonomy of the individual and abdication of the will to the senses reign supreme.

When Solomon died, his son Rehoboam became king. Having been banned by Solomon, Jeroboam returned from Egypt upon hearing of the king's death. Representing the ten northern tribes of Israel, Jeroboam sought relief from the heavy burdens placed on the people by Rehoboam's father. In considering the matter, Rehoboam sought council from the old men who counseled his father, and they encouraged the king to lighten the people's burden. However, Jeroboam rejected that council in favor of counsel from the young men who had grown up with him. Their advice was to not only maintain those burdens but to increase them. As a result the ten tribes rebelled and the kingdom was divided. Because of the wickedness and idolatry of Rehoboam and the Jewish people, God removed His presence, provision, and protection from their nation. Five years after Solomon's death, the temple was sacked by the Shishak, king of Egypt.[810] Even after three millennia, the parallels between America's national house and Solomon's house are striking.

Earlier in this book, Russell Kirk was quoted as he paraphrased the words of Fulbert, the French bishop of a thousand years ago. Kirk then applied Fulbert's words and wisdom to the dangers prevalent in modern America.

> Fulbert of Chartres, in medieval times, declared that we moderns—that is, the people of his own age—are dwarfs standing upon the shoulders of giants: we see farther than do the giants, but merely because we are mounted upon their shoulders. Those giants are the wise men of classical and early Christian epochs. *From them Americans have inherited the order of the soul and the order of the commonwealth.* If we think to liberate ourselves from the past by leaping off those giants' shoulders—why, we tumble into the ditch of unreason. If we ignore the subtle wisdom of the classical past and the British past, we are left with a thin evanescent culture, a mere film upon the surface of the deep well of the past. Those who refuse to drink of that well may be drowned in it.[811] (emphasis added)

We must reiterate that, as regarding our inheritance of order of the soul and order of the commonwealth, our preeminent concern must be for the restoration of order of the soul. How does that occur? Order of the soul can only be achieved through a right relationship with God who is the reason for our being. Only by ordering the soul can we order the commonwealth and restore the over-arching banner of the Judeo-

Christian ethic to American culture. The hallmarks of such an ordered commonwealth mirror God's covenant with Solomon and the Hebrews: humility, prayer, and a return to a virtuous and moral society.

The battle is not a one of political parties, campaigns, or clever sloganeering. Writing to the Ephesians, the Apostle Paul revealed the true identities of the aggressors. "For we are not contending against flesh and blood, but against the principalities, against the powers, against the world rulers of this present darkness, against the spiritual hosts of wickedness in the heavenly places."[812] The war will not be won with a single victory or a group of victories. The battle must be fought and won by every generation for ultimate victory in the war will not be achieved until the end of the age. Hence, the greatest contribution each generation can give is to maintain and transmit the values of their patrimony to their children, their children's children, and to every future generation. We must become the giants upon whose shoulders they will stand.

Ultimately, the preservation of the Judeo-Christian worldview as the dominant central cultural vision of America depends on her people's obedience to God's covenant, "…if my people who are called by my name humble themselves, and pray and seek my face, and turn from their wicked ways, then I will hear from heaven and will forgive their sin and heal their land."[813]

Notes

Part I – The Boomers

Introduction
[1] "40 Years Ago Vietnam: MG Keith Ware," *Bridgehead Sentinel*, Summer 2008, 13.

Chapter 1 – The Baby Boomers
[2] William Strauss and Neil Howe, *Generations – The History of America's Future, 1584 to 2069*, (New York: Quill William Morrow, 1991), p. 25.
[3] Tom Brokaw, *The Greatest Generation*, (New York: Random House, 1998), p. xx.
[4] Strauss and Howe, p. 8.
[5] Ibid., pp. 8-11, chart between pp. 96-97.
[6] Ibid.
[7] Ibid.
[8] Steve Gillon, *Boomer Nation*, (New York: Free Press, 2004), p.3.
[9] J. Walker Smith and Ann Clurman, *Generation Ageless*, (New York: Collins, 2007), p. xvii.
[10] Thomas Maier, *Dr. Spock – An American Life*, (New York: Harcourt Brace & Company, 1998), p. xii.
[11] Ibid., pp. 13-18.
[12] Ibid., pp. 8-10.
[13] Ibid., pp. 25-32.
[14] Benjamin Spock, *A Better World for Our Children*, (Bethesda, Maryland: National Press Books, 1994), p. 25; Maier, pp. 36-37.
[15] Maier, pp. 40, 47, 57.
[16] Ibid., pp. 71-76.
[17] Ibid., pp. 78-79.
[18] Spock, *A Better World for Our Children*, p. 20.
[19] Maier, pp. 43-44.
[20] Ibid., pp. 110-112.
[21] Ibid., pp. 77-80.
[22] Ibid., pp. 87-90.
[23] Ibid., pp. 91-98.
[24] Ibid., p. 98.
[25] Ibid., pp. 90-98, 132.
[26] Ibid., pp. 124, 127, 131, 133, 135.
[27] Spock, *A Better World for Our Children*, pp. 32-33.
[28] Maier, p. 138.

[29] Benjamin Spock, *The Common Sense Book of Baby and Child Care*, (New York: Duell, Sloan and Pearce, 1945, 1946), p. 270.
[30] Spock, *The Common Sense Book of Baby and Child Care*, pp. 266-272.
[31] Maier, p. 157.
[32] Maier, pp. 207-208.
[33] Benjamin Spock, M. D., and Michael B. Rothenberg, M.D., *Dr. Spock's Baby and Child Care*, (New York: Pocket Books, 1992), p. 426.
[34] Spock and Rothenberg, *Dr. Spock's Baby and Child Care*, pp. 426, 437.
[35] Donald Capps, ed., *Freud and Freudians on Religion – A reader*, (New Haven, Connecticut: Yale University Press, 2001), p. 56.
[36] Maier, pp. 202, 209.
[37] Sidney Hook, *John Dewey – His Philosophy of Education and Its Critics*, (New York: Tamiment Institute, 1959), p. 3.
[38] H. G. Rickover, *Education and Freedom*, (New York: E. P. Dutton & Co., Inc. 1959); H. G. Rickover, *American Education—A National Failure*, (New York: E. F. Dutton & Co., Inc., 1963).
[39] Robert B. Talisse, *On Dewey*, (Belmont, California: Wadsworth/Thompson Learning, 2000), pp. ix, 1, 4.
[40] Ibid., pp. 5-7.
[41] Ibid., pp. 7-8.
[42] Alan Ryan, *John Dewey and the High Tide of American Liberalism*, (New York: W. W. Norton & Company, 1995), p. 46.
[43] Talisse, pp. 2-3.
[44] Ibid., pp. 11-12.
[45] Robert J. Roth, *John Dewey and Self-Realization*, (Westport, Connecticut: Greenwood Press, Publishers, 1962), p. 100-101.
[46] Roth, p. 101.
[47] Ibid., pp. 4,6.
[48] Hook, p. 6-7.
[49] Ibid., p. 7.
[50] Ibid., pp. 13-15.
[51] Ibid., pp. 18-19.
[52] Charlotte Thomson Iserbyt, *the deliberate dumbing down of america*, (Ravenna, Ohio: Conscience Press, 1999), pp. 5-6, 345.

Chapter 2 – Boomers – The Fifties
[53] Maier, p. 201.
[54] Daniel J. Boorstin, *The Americans-The Democratic Experience*, (New York: Random House, 1973), pp. 396-397.
[55] Richard P. Adler, ed., *Understanding Television – Essays on Television as a Social and Cultural Force*, (New York: Praeger Publishers, 1981), p. xi.
[56] Cobbett S. Steinberg, *TV Facts*, (New York: Facts on File, Inc., 1980), p.

142.
[57] Adler, pp. xi-xii.
[58] Steinberg, pp. 150-151.
[59] Michael Novak, "Television Shapes the Soul," in *Understanding Television – Essays on Television as a Social and Cultural Force* ed. Richard P. Adler, pp. 20, 26-27.
[60] Richard Croker, *The Boomer Century 1946-2046*, (New York: Springboard Press, 2007), p. 20.
[61] Croker, p. 22.
[62] Gillon, p. 4, 8-9.
[63] Ibid., p. 1
[64] Ibid., p. 7.
[65] Strauss and Howe, p. 305.
[66] Live Births, Birth Rates, and Fertility Rates, by Race: United States, 1909-2000, Table 1-1, US Center for Disease Control, http://www.cdc.gov/ncha//data/statab/t001x01.pdf (accessed September 24, 2009).
[67] Strauss and Howe, p. 305.
[68] Susan Douglas quoted by Steve Gillon, *Boomer Nation*, p. 5.
[69] Gillon, pp. 5, 7.
[70] Croker, p. 7.
[71] Smith and Clurman, p. xxi.
[72] Ibid., p. xxii.
[73] Samuelson, pp. 46-47.
[74] Ibid., p. 35.
[75] "Little Boxes lyrics," Lyricsmode, http://www.lyricsmode.com/lyrics/m/malvina_reynolds/little_boxes.html (accessed September 26, 2009); "Folk Singing: Tacky into the Wind," Time.com, February 28, 1964, http://www.time.com/time/magazine/article/0,9171,873851,00.html?iid=digg_share (accessed October 14, 2009).
[76] Samuelson, p. 36.
[77] Richard A. Schwartz, *An Eyewitness History – The 1950s*, (New York: Facts On File, Inc., 2003), pp. 56-57.
[78] Samuelson, p. 11.
[79] Ibid., p. 35.
[80] Neil A. Hamilton, *Atlas of the Baby Boom Generation*, (New York: Macmillan Reference USA, 2000), pp. 68-69
[81] Gillon, p.3.
[82] James D. Watson, *The Double Helix*, (New York: Atheneum, 1968), p. 197; Richard A. Schwartz, *An Eyewitness History – The 1950s*, (New York: Facts On File, Inc., 2003), p. 193.

[83] Samuelson, pp. 38-39.
[84] Paul Dickson, *Sputnik – The Shock of the Century*, (New York: Walker & Company, 2001), pp. 1-2, 9.
[85] Dickson, pp. 2, 4-6, 9.
[86] Ibid., p. 4.
[87] Leonard Steinhorn, *The Greater Generation*, (New York, Thomas Dunne Books, 2006), p. 87.
[88] Ibid., p.19.
[89] Smith and Clurman, p. xxii.
[90] Schwartz, pp. 32, 74, 76, 162, 193, 229, 299, 337.
[91] Steinhorn, p. 13.
[92] Ibid., p. 69.
[93] Fred Kaplan, *1959-The Year Everything Changed*, (Hoboken, New Jersey: John Wiley & Sons, Inc.2009), p. xiii.

Chapter 3 – Boomers – The Sixties – Ye shall not surely die
[94] Genesis 3:5 (KJV)
[95] Croker, p. 4.
[96] Ibid., p. 112.
[97] Ibid., p. 60.
[98] J. Walker Smith and Ann Clurman, Generation Ageless, (New York: Harper Collins, 2007), pp. 18-19, 176-177.
[99] Ibid., pp. 177-178, 181, 183-184.
[100] Ibid., p. 181.
[101] Ibid., p. 179-180.
[102] Robert H. Bork, *Slouching Towards Gomorrah*, (New York: Regan Books, 1996), p. 51.
[103] Steinhorn, p. 42.
[104] Ibid., p. 13.
[105] 1 Corinthians 4:7 (RSV).
[106] Smith and Clurman, p. 115.
[107] Gillon, p. 20.
[108] Croker, p. 15.
[109] Kaplan, p. 1
[110] Alan Petigny, *The Permissive Society – America, 1941-1965*, (New York: Cambridge University Press, 2009), pp. 116-119, 130.
[111] Lara V. Marks, *Sexual Chemistry – A History of the Contraceptive Pill*, (New Haven, Connecticut: Yale University Press, 2001), pp. 3, 7, 186.
[112] Charles Rembar, *The End of Obscenity*, (New York: Perennial Library, 1968), pp. ix-x, xii.
[113] Gregory Baum and John Coleman, ed., *The Sexual Revolution*, (Edinburgh: Stichting Concilium and T. & T. Clark LTD, 1984), p. 66.

[114] Robert Cohen and Reginald E. Zelnik, ed., *The Free Speech Movement*, (Los Angeles, California: University of California Press, 2002), pp. 1, 40, 42.
[115] Samuelson, p. 8.
[116] Ibid., pp. 182-183.
[117] Martin Luther King, Jr., *A Testament of Hope-The Essential writings of Martin Luther King, Jr.*, ed. James Melvin Washington, (New York: Harper San Francisco, 1986), pp. 217, 289.
[118] Ibid., pp. 293-294, 302.
[119] Steinhorn, p. 75.
[120] King, *A Testament of Hope-The Essential writings of Martin Luther King, Jr.*, p. 302.
[121] Ibid., pp. 296-297.
[122] Gillon, pp. 97-98.
[123] Samuelson, pp. 184-187.
[124] Michael Maclear, *Vietnam*, (New York: Tess Press, 2003), pp. 1-3.
[125] Ibid., pp. 3, 6.
[126] Ibid., pp. 3-4, 6.
[127] Ibid., pp. 4, 6.
[128] Ibid., p. 6.
[129] Ibid.
[130] Ibid., pp. 8-9.
[131] Ibid., p. 8.
[132] Ibid., pp. xiv-xvi.
[133] David L. Anderson, *The Columbia Guide to the Vietnam War*, (New York: Columbia University Press, 2002), pp. 108-109, 112-113.
[134] Maclear, pp. xiv-xvi.
[135] Ibid., p. 456.
[136] "The Whole World Was Watching: an oral history of 1968," South Kingstown High School and Brown University's Scholarly Technology Group, http://www.stg.brown.edu/projects/1968/reference/timeline.html (accessed October 9, 2009).
[137] Maclear, p. 466.
[138] Ibid., pp. xiv-xvi.
[139] Ibid., p. 769.
[140] Ibid., p. 729.
[141] "The Genocide," Cambodian Genocide Group, New York, New York, http:// www.cambodiangenocide.org/ genocide.htm (accessed October 14, 2009).
[142] Richard Dean Burns and Milton Leitenberg, *The Wars in Vietnam, Cambodia and Laos, 1945-1982*, (Santa Barbara, California: ABC-Clio Information Services, 1984), pp. xxvi-xxvii.

[143] Martin Stuart-Fox, ed., *Contemporary Laos*, (London: University of Queensland Press, 1982), pp. 17-18.
[144] Elliott Kulick and Dick Wilson, *Thailand's Turn*, (London: The MacMillan Press LTD, 1992), pp. 11-41, 163-164.
[145] David L. Anderson, *The Columbia Guide to the Vietnam War*, (New York: Columbia University Press, 2002), p. 289.
[146] "Draft-age Americans in Canada, "*Forging Our Legacy: Canadian Citizenship & Immigration – 1900-1977,* Citizenship and Immigration-Canada, http://www.cic.gc.ca/english/resources/publication/legacy/chap6-14 (accessed December 9, 2010).
[147] Gillon, p. 1.
[148] Steinhorn, p.82.
[149] "Baby Boom Bust," *World*, June 6, 2009, 9.

Part II – Worldview

Chapter 4 – Worldview: Christianity vs. Humanism
[150] *Webster's Seventh New Collegiate Dictionary*, (Springfield, Massachusetts: G. & C. Merriam Company, Publishers, 1963).
[151] *Webster's Revised Unabridged Dictionary*, (Plainfield, New Jersey: MICRA, Inc., 1996).
[152] Albert M. Wolters, *Creation Regained*, 2nd Edition, (Grand Rapids, Michigan: Wm. B. Eerdmans Publishing Co., 1985, 2005), pp. 2-3.
[153] Ibid., p. 4-6.
[154] Ibid., p. 5.
[155] James Kurth, "The Real Clash," *The National Interest 3* (fall 1994): 3-15. Quoted by: Robert P. George, *Clash of Orthodoxies*, (Wilmington, Delaware: ISI Books, 2001), p. 3.
[156] George, p. 4.
[157] C. S. Lewis, *The Complete C. S. Lewis Signature Classics, Miracles*, (New York: Harper One, 2002), p. 116.
[158] Wolters, pp. 78-81.
[159] George, p. 20.
[160] Aleksandr Solzhenitsyn quoted by: James E. Person, Jr., *Russell Kirk, A Critical Biography of a Conservative Mind*, (Lanham, Maryland: Madison Books, 1999), p. 174.
[161] Whittaker Chambers, *Witness*, (New York: Random House, 1952), p. 4.
[162] Ibid., pp. 9-10.

Chapter 5 – The Fingerprints of God
[163] L. M. Nesbitt, *Hell-Hole of Creation – The Exploration of Abyssinian Danakil*, (New York: Alfred A Knopf, 1934), pp. v-vi, 48-49, 312-319.

[164] Russell Kirk, *The Essential Kirk – Selected Essays*, ed. George A. Panichas, (Wilmington, Delaware: ISI Books, 2007), pp. 76-77.
[165] Wolters, p. 10.
[166] Genesis 3:22 (KJV).
[167] William Blackstone, *Commentaries on the Laws of England*, Vol. I-Book I & II, (Philadelphia: J. B. Lippincott Company, 1910), pp. 25-28; Acts 17:30 RSV.
[168] Marcus Tullius Cicero, *The Laws*, quoted by Russell Kirk, *The Roots of American Order*, (Washington, D. C.: Regnery Gateway, 1991), pp. 106, 108.
[169] W. Cleon Skousen, *The 5000 Year Leap*, (www.nccs.net: National Center for Constitutional Studies, 1981), pp. 37-39.
[170] Russell Kirk, *The Roots of American Order*, (Washington D. C.: Regnery Gateway, 1991), pp. 3-5.
[171] C. S. Lewis, *The Complete C. S. Lewis Signature Classics, Mere Christianity,* (New York: Harper One, 2002), pp. 30, 34.
[172] Skousen, p. 17.
[173] Blackstone, p. 25.
[174] Ibid., pp. 25-28.
[175] Wolters, p. 16.
[176] Ibid., pp. 16-19.
[177] Christopher Badeaux, "Faith, Fear and Cormac McCarthy," *The City*, Vol. 1, Issue 3, (Winter 2008), 84-85.
[178] Diederik Aerts, et.al., "World views: from fragmentation to integration," *Center Leo Apostel*, Vrije Universiteit Brussell in Belgium, http://www.vub.ac.be/CLEA/pub/books/worldviews/ (accessed May 19, 2009).
[179] Colson and Pearcey, *How Now Shall We Live?* p. xiii.
[180] Lewis, *The Complete C. S. Lewis Signature Classics, Mere Christianity,* pp. 39-40.
[181] Colson and Pearcey, *How Now Shall We Live?* pp. 20, 22-23, 25.
[182] Lewis, *The Complete C. S. Lewis Signature Classics, Mere Christianity,* p. 39.

Chapter 6 – The Judeo-Christian Tradition and the Rise of Western Civilization

[183] Kirk, *The Roots of American Order*, pp. 160-161.
[184] Ibid., pp. 147-148.
[185] John Herman Randall, Jr., *The Making of the Modern Mind*, (New York: Columbia University Press, 1926, 1940), pp. 10-15.
[186] Ibid., pp. 13-14.
[187] Ibid., p. 15.

[188] Ibid., p. 111.
[189] Kirk, *The Roots of American Order*, p. 223.
[190] J. M. Roberts, History of the World, (Oxford: Oxford University Press, 2003), pp. 164, 170.
[191] Kirk, *The Roots of American Order*, pp. 225-226.
[192] Alan Schreck, Phd., *The Compact History of the Catholic Church*, (Cincinnati, Ohio: Servant Books, 2009), p. 61.
[193] Kirk, *The Essential Russell Kirk – Selected Essays*, pp. 97-100; Kirk, *Roots of American Order*, pp. 209, 211.
[194] Randall, p. 14.
[195] Sherwood Eddy, *The Kingdom of God and the American Dream*, (New York: Harper &Brothers Publishers, 1941), pp. 14-15.
[196] Roberts, p. 537.
[197] Kirk, *The Roots of American Order*, pp. 223, 230-231.
[198] Ibid., pp. 230-234.
[199] Roberts, pp. 689-690.
[200] Kirk, *The Roots of American Order*, pp. 348-349.
[201] Roberts, pp. 686-688.
[202] Ibid., p. 688.
[203] Randall, pp. 381-383.
[204] Ibid., pp. 381-383.

Chapter 7 – The Renaissance and Enlightenment: Progress and Perfection – Science and Reason

[205] John Dewey, *The Influence of Darwin on Philosophy*, (New York: Henry Holt and Company, 1910; New York: Peter Smith, 1951), pp. 1-2. Citations are to the Peter Smith edition.
[206] Roberts, pp. 877-880.
[207] Randall, pp. 510-511.
[208] Keith G. Meador, "My Own Salvation," in *The Secular Revolution*, ed. Christian Smith, (Berkeley, California: University of California Press, 2003), p. 270.
[209] Donald Capps, ed., *Freud and Freudians on Religion – A Reader*, (New Haven, Connecticut: Yale University Press, 2001), pp. 56-57.
[210] Hans Kung, *Freud and the Problem of God*, trans. Edward Quinn, (New Haven, Connecticut: Yale University Press, 1979, 1990), p. 48.
[211] Colson and Pearcey, *How Now Shall We Live?* p. 176.
[212] Richard Webster, *Why Freud was Wrong*, (New York: Basic Books, 1995), p. 506.
[213] Colson and Pearcey, *How Now Shall We Live?* pp. 425-426.
[214] Timothy Keller, The Reason for God (New York: Dutton, 2008), p. 89.
[215] Colson and Pearcey, *How Now Shall We Live?* pp. 425-426.

[216] Ibid., pp. 419-421.
[217] Keller, pp. 85-86.
[218] Ibid., p. 127.
[219] Kirk, *The Essential Russell Kirk – Selected Essays*, p. 243.
[220] Randall, p. 517.
[221] Ibid., p. 517.
[222] Kirk, *The Essential Russell Kirk – Selected Essays,* p. 355.
[223] Roberts, p. 882.
[224] Karl Marx and Frederick Engels, *The Communist Manifesto*, Eric Hobsbawm, intro., (London: Verso 1998), pp. 6-7, 52, 56, 58, 60-61.
[225] Randall, p. 659.
[226] Kirk, *The Essential Russell Kirk – Selected Essays*, pp.355-356; Colson, *How Now Shall We Live?* p. 544.
[227] "Marx of Respect," The Friends of Charles Darwin, http//friendsofdarwin.com/articles/2000/marx/ (accessed December 16,2010).
[228] Lewis, *The Complete C. S. Lewis Signature Classics, Miracles*, pp. 316-317, 319.
[229] Randall, pp. 381-383.
[230] Ibid., pp. 383-384.
[231] Ibid., pp. 382-283
[232] Kirk, *The Roots of American Order*, pp. 360-362.
[233] Lewis, *The Complete C. S. Lewis Signature Classics, Miracles*, pp. 320, 324-326.
[234] Hunter Baker, "A Republic of Letters," *The City,* Vol. IV, No. 1, (Spring 2011), 98.
[235] George, pp. 15-16.
[236] Lewis, *The Complete C. S. Lewis Signature Classics, Mere Christianity*, p. 116.
[237] Ibid., pp. 115-117.
[238] Ibid., pp. 117-119, 121.
[239] George, p. 313.
[240] Ibid., p. 313.
[241] Marvin Olasky, "Paine's brain," *World*, Vol. 25, No. 3, January 30, 2010, 76.
[242] Schreck, p. 61.
[243] Roberts, pp. 536-537.
[244] Schreck, pp. 61-62.
[245] Francis A. Schaeffer, *Escape from Reason*, (Downers Grove, Illinois: IVP Books, 1968), pp. 16, 22, 24, 27.
[246] Roberts, pp. 539, 545.
[247] Schaeffer, pp. 27-28.

[248] Olasky, "Paine's brain," *World*, Vol. 25, No. 3, January 30, 2010, 76.
[249] Blackstone, p. 28.
[250] Watchman Nee, *The Normal Christian Life*, Hendrickson Christian Classics Edition, (Peabody, Massachusetts: Henrickson Publishers, 1961), pp. 3, 17.
[251] Ibid., p. 149.
[252] Schreck, p. 159.
[253] Frank Bartleman, *Azusa Street*, (New Kensington, Pennsylvania: Whitaker House, 1982), pp. 161-162.
[254] Randall, p. 227.
[255] John 18:36 KJV.

Chapter 8 – Colonial American Heritage

[256] M. Stanton Evans, *The Theme Is Freedom*, (Washington, D.C.: Regnery Publishing, Inc., 1994), pp. 78-79, 166.
[257] Ibid., pp. 149-151.
[258] Ibid., pp. 152-158.
[259] Ibid., p. 160.
[260] Kirk, *The Roots of American Order,* pp. 239-240, 257-258.
[261] Evans, p. 160.
[262] Kirk, *The Roots of American Order*, p. 302-304.
[263] Eddy, pp. 74-75.
[264] Evans, pp. 40-41.
[265] Ibid., pp. 186, 188-191.
[266] Eddy, pp. 48-49, 56.
[267] Kirk, *The Roots of American Order*, p. 333.
[268] Eddy, pp. 78-79.
[269] Kirk, *The Roots of American Order*, p. 338.
[270] Ibid., pp. 347-349.
[271] Eddy, pp. 79-80.
[272] Alexis de Tocqueville, *Democracy in America*, trans. Gerald E. Bevan, (New York: Penguin Books, 2003), p. 345.
[273] Evans, pp. 271-272, 274-275.
[274] Ibid., pp. 274-275.
[275] Eddy, pp. 54-56.
[276] Ibid., pp.89-91, 93-95, 97, 103.
[277] Kirk, *The Roots of American Order*, pp. 303, 311-312
[278] Ibid., pp. 303, 311-312.
[279] Evans, pp. 217, 220-221.
[280] Eddy, p. 115.

Chapter 9 – The American Founders and Their Beliefs

[281] Rowland Berthoff, *An Unsettled People: Social Order and Disorder in American History*, (New York: Harper & Row, Publishers, 1971), pp. 83-86.
[282] Gordon S. Wood, "Religion and the American Revolution," in *New Directions in American Religious History*, ed. Harry S. Stout and D. G. Hart, (New York: Oxford University Press, 1997), pp. 174-175.
[283] Ibid., pp. 176-177.
[284] Ibid., pp. 185-188.
[285] Kirk, *The Roots of American Order*, p. 398.
[286] Ibid., pp. 394-398.
[287] Ibid., pp.389-390.
[288] Eddy, p. 109.
[289] Skousen, pp.10, 19.
[290] Orrin G. Hatch, introductory remarks for the book by: W. Cleon Skousen, *The 5000 Year Leap*, (www.nccs.net: National Center for Constitutional Studies, 1981), p. xxi.
[291] Clinton Rossiter, ed., *The Federalist Papers*, (New York: Signet Classic, 1961), p. 48.
[292] Ibid., pp. 73-74.
[293] Ibid., p. vii.
[294] Skousen, pp. ii-iii.
[295] James E. Person, Jr., *Russell Kirk, A Critical Biography of a Conservative Mind*, (Lanham, Maryland: Madison Books, 1999), p. 105.
[296] Eddy, p. 124.
[297] Kirk, *Roots of American Order*, p. 29.
[298] Kirk, *The Essential Russell Kirk – Selected Essays*, pp. 229-230.

Chapter 10 – The Roots and Rise of Modern Humanism
[299] Psalm 14:1 (KJV)
[300] Roberts, pp. 171, 174, 188-192.
[301] Ibid., pp. 199-200.
[302] Jim Herrick, *Humanism – An Introduction*, (Amherst, New York: Prometheus Books, 2005), p. 5.
[303] "sophist," *Webster's Seventh New Collegiate Dictionary*, (Springfield, Massachusetts: G. & C. Merriam Company, 1963), p. 833.
[304] Kirk, *The Roots of American Order*, pp. 73-74.
[305] Herrick, pp. 5-6.
[306] Kirk, *The Roots of American Order*, p. 74.
[307] Randall, p. 47.
[308] Kirk, *The Roots of American Order*, pp. 73-75, 78, 81.
[309] Ibid., pp. 86, 88-90.
[310] Corliss Lamont, *The Philosophy of Humanism*, (Amherst, New York:

Humanist Press, 1947, 1957, 1965, 1982, 1992), pp.35-37.
[311] Roberts, p. 211.
[312] Kirk, *The Roots of American Order*, pp. 51-53.
[313] Alfred Zimmern quoted by Russell Kirk, The *Roots of American Order*, p.55.
[314] Kirk, *The Roots of American Order*, pp. 75, 77-78, 85, 93..
[315] Roberts, pp. 222-223.
[316] Herrick, p. 6.
[317] Randall, pp. 594-595.
[318] Roberts, pp. 222-223.
[319] Ibid., pp. 222-223.
[320] Matthew Henry, *Commentary on the Whole Bible*, (Grand Rapids, Michigan: Zondervan Publishing House, 1961), pp. 1705-1706.
[321] Ibid., pp. 1706-1708.
[322] Roberts, *History of the World*, pp. 273-274.
[323] Ibid., pp. 274.
[324] Randall, p. 46.
[325] Kirk, *The Roots of American Order*, p. 74.
[326] Ibid., p. 85.
[327] Ibid., p. 81.
[328] Roberts, p. 537.
[329] Francis A. Schaeffer, *Escape from Reason*, (Downers Grover, Illinois: IVP Books, 1968), p. 15.
[330] Roberts, pp. 539, 545.
[331] Lamont, pp. xii, xxiii, 3, 12-13, 16, 24-25.
[332] Ibid., pp. 12-15.
[333] Ibid., p. 3.
[334] Paul Kurtz, ed., *The Humanist Alternative: some definitions of Humanism*, (Buffalo, New York: Prometheus Books, 1973), p. 15.
[335] Lamont, p. 35.
[336] Ibid., pp. 37, 39-40.
[337] Ibid., pp. 41, 44-47.
[338] "humanism," "secular," *Webster's Seventh New Collegiate Dictionary*, (Springfield, Massachusetts: G. & C. Merriam Company, Publishers, 1963), pp. 404, 780.
[339] Kurtz, *The Humanist Alternative: some definitions of Humanism*, pp. 177-178.
[340] Ibid., p. 15.
[341] Ibid., pp. 177-178.
[342] Ibid., pp. 177-178, 180, 183.
[343] Ibid., pp. 181- 183.

Chapter 11 – The "Why" – Worldview of Humanism and Christianity

[344] Genesis 1:26 (KJV)
[345] Wilfred McClay, "The Soul & the City", *The City*, Vol. II, No. 2, (Summer 2009), 8-9.
[346] Loren E. Wilkinson, "Immanuel and the Purpose of Creation," in *Doing Theology for the People of God*, ed. Donald Lewis & Alister McGrath, (Downers Grove, Illinois: InterVarsity Press, 1996), pp. 251, 253.
[347] Badeaux, "Faith Fear and Cormac McCarthy", *The City*, Vol. 1, No.3, (Winter 2008), 84-85.
[348] C. S. Lewis, *The Timeless Writings of C. S. Lewis*, ed. Walter Hooper, (New York: Inspiration Press, 1967) p. 208.
[349] C. S. Lewis, *The Complete C. S. Lewis Signature Classics, The Abolition of Man*, (New York: Harper One, 2002), p. 727.
[350] Roberts, pp. 61-61.
[351] Lamont, pp. 126-127.
[352] Ibid., p. 127; Lewis, *The Complete C. S. Lewis Signature Classics, The Abolition of Man*, pp. 233-234.
[353] Lamont, pp. 129, 134.
[354] Stephen Hawking, *A Brief History of Time*, (New York: Bantam Books, 1988, 1996), pp. 12-13, 187.
[355] Ibid, pp. 34, 189.
[356] Ibid., pp. 34-35, 189-191.
[357] Keller, pp. 129-131; Hawking, pp. 128-129.
[358] Donald E. Johnson, PhD., *Probability's Nature and Nature's Probability*, (Charleston, South Carolina: Booksurge Publishing, 2009), p. 98.
[359] Joao Magueijo, *Faster Than the Speed of Light*, (Cambridge, Massachusetts: Perseus Publishers, 2003), pp. 3-4.
[360] Hawking, pp. 128-129.
[361] Herrick, p. 44.
[362] Lamont, p. 127; Lewis, *The Timeless Writings of C. S. Lewis, Christian Reflections*, p. 134.
[363] Hawking, pp. 42, 53.
[364] Jim Herrick, *Humanism – An Introduction*, (Amherst, New York: Prometheus Books, 2005), p. 46.
[365] Phillip E. Johnson, *Darwin on Trial*, (Downers Grove, Illinois: IVP Books, 1991, 1993), pp. 15-16.
[366] Lamont, pp. 88-90, 96-97, 102-103.
[367] Ibid., pp. 108-109.
[368] Ibid., p. 117.
[369] Ibid., p. 120.

Part III – Humanism and American Institutions
[370] Christian Smith, pp. 2-3.
[371] Ibid., p. 363.
[372] Leo Bogart, *Over the Edge*, (Chicago, Illinois: Ivan R. Dee, 2005), p. x.

Chapter 12 – Religion – The Power of Religion in American History
[373] Paul Kurtz, ed., *Humanist Manifestos I and II*, (Buffalo, New York: Prometheus Books, 1973) p. 8.
[374] Richard M. Weaver, *Visions of Order*, (Wilmington, Delaware: Intercollegiate Studies Institute, 1964), pp. 9-10.
[375] Tocqueville, pp. 346-347.
[376] Paul Kurtz, *Toward a New Enlightenment – The Philosophy of Paul Kurtz*, (New Brunswick, New Jersey: Transaction Publishers, 1994), p. 49.
[377] Herrick, p. 35; Lamont, p. 143.
[378] Colson and Pearcey, *How Now Shall We Live?* p. 314.
[379] "imagination," *Webster's Seventh New Collegiate Dictionary*, (Springfield, Massachusetts: G. & C. Merriam Company, Publishers, 1963), p. 416.
[380] Craig M. Gay, *The way of the (modern) world*, (Grand Rapids, Michigan: Wm. B. Eerdmans Publishing Co., 1998), p. 246.
[381] Kirk, *The Essential Russell Kirk – Selected Essays*, p. 23.
[382] Herrick, p. 34.
[383] Roger Nicole, "James I. Packer's Contribution to the Doctrine of Inerrancy of Scripture," in *Doing Theology for the People of God*, ed. Donald Lewis & Alister McGrath, (Downers Grove, Illinois: InterVarsity Press, 1996), p. 176.
[384] Robert W. Smith, *The Space Telescope*, (Cambridge: Cambridge University Press, 1993), pp. 5, 7, 13-14,105-108.
[385] Nicole, "James I. Packer's Contribution to the Doctrine of Inerrancy of Scripture," in *Doing Theology for the People of God*, ed. Donald Lewis & Alister McGrath, pp. 176-177.
[386] Roger T. Beckwith, "Toward a theology of the Biblical Text," in *Doing Theology for the People of God*, ed. Donald Lewis & Alister McGrath, pp. 48, 50.

Chapter 13 – Religion in the Public Arena – Mention Jesus Christ and "…all hell breaks loose"
[387] Joel Belz, "Politeness police," *World*, Vol. 25, No. 2, January 30, 2010, 4, 10; Cal Thomas, "Something about that name: Jesus," *Tulsa World*, January 8, 2010, A-16.
[388] Belz, "Politeness police," *World*, January 30, 2010, 10.

[389] Thomas, "Something about that name: Jesus," *Tulsa World*, January 8, 2010, A-18.
[390] Lewis, *The Complete C. S. Lewis Signature Classics, Mere Christianity*, pp. 41-42.
[391] Marvin Olasky, "Zen violence," *World*, Vol. 25, No. 3, February 13, 2010, 80.
[392] "pluralism," *Webster's Seventh New Collegiate Dictionary*, (Springfield, Massachusetts: G. & C. Merriam Company, Publishers, 1963), p. 653.
[393] Kirk, *The Roots of American Order*, pp. 94-95.
[394] Tocqueville, pp. 341-345.
[395] Ibid., pp. 340-341, 344.
[396] Ibid., p. 342.
[397] Ibid., p. 348.
[398] "Call to Renewal – Keynote Address." Welcome to obamaspeaches.com http://obamaspeaches.com/o81-Call-to-Renewal-Keynote-Address-Obama-Speech.htm (accessed June 10, 2009).
[399] *World Almanac and Book of Facts 1999*, (Mahwah, New Jersey: World Almanac Books, 1998), p. 379.
[400] "Twelve Percent of U.S. Population is Foreign Born," America.gov, August 9, 2004, http://www.america.gov/st/washfile-english/2004/August/20040809150255cmretrop0.7581903.html (accessed December 18, 2010); "American Migration: 1776 to 2006," The Globalist, November 29, 2006, http://www.theglobalist.com/StoryId.aspx?StoryId=5759 (accessed December 18, 2010).
[401] Kurtz, *Toward a New Enlightenment*, p. 101.
[402] Evans, pp. xiii-xv.
[403] Gene Edward Veith, "Suicidal ideology," *World*, February 23/March 1, 2008, 33.
[404] Emily Belz, "Wilders' side," *World*, November 7, 2009, 38.
[405] Alexander G. Higgins, "vote," Associated Press, November 29, 2009, http://news.yahoo.com/s/ap/20091129/ap_on_re_eu/eu_switserland_minaret_ban (accessed December 1, 2009).
[406] "CAN Wins Legal Battle Against Maine," Christian Action Network, April 10, 2010, http://christianaction.org/node/14 (accessed December 18, 2010).
[407] Evans, pp. 40-42.
[408] Keller, pp. 40-41.
[409] Acts 17:26 (KJV)
[410] Kurtz, *Toward a New Enlightenment*, p. 70.
[411] Weaver, *Visions of Order*, pp. 10-12.
[412] Ibid., pp. 11-13.
[413] Emily Belz, "Identity crisis," *World*, May 8, 2010, 40.

[414] Ted Olsen and Trevor Persaud, "Christian Legal Society Loses in Supreme Court Case," Christianity Today, (December 18, 2010), http://www.christianitytoday.com/ct/2010/juneweb-olly/e6.11.0.ht (accessed December 18, 2010); Ginsburg, R., Opinion of the Court, Supreme Court of the United States, 561 ___ (2010), Christian U.S. Legal Society Chapter of the University of California, Hastings College of the Law, aka Hastings Christian Fellowship v. Martinez et. al. (no.08-1371), http://www.supremecourt.gov/opinions/09pdf/08-1371.pdf (accessed December 18, 2010).

[415] Weaver, *Visions of Order*, p. xv.

[416] Kurtz, *Toward a New Enlightenment*, pp. 99-100.

[417] Ibid., pp. 100-101.

[418] George, pp. 18-20.

[419] Herrick, p. 2.

[420] Kurtz, *Toward a New Enlightenment*, pp. 101-104.

Chapter 14 – Government – "…America is not a Christian nation

[421] "Fox News figures outraged over Obama's 'Christian nation' comment," Media Matters for America, April 9, 2009, http://mediamatters.org/research/200904090033 (accessed June 6, 2009).

[422] Kirk, *The Roots of American Order*, pp. 223-224; Randall, p. 164.

[423] "secular," "secularism," *Webster's Seventh New Collegiate Dictionary*, (Springfield, Massachusetts: G. & C. Merriam Company, Publishers, 1963), p. 780.

[424] President Obama made essentially the same statement in 2006. "Whatever we once were, we are no longer just a Christian nation; we are also a Jewish nation, a Muslim nation, a Buddhist nation, a Hindu nation, and a nation of nonbelievers." http://obamaspeaches.com/o81- C all-to-Renewal-Keynote- Address-Obama-Speech.htm (accessed June 10, 2009).

[425] Skousen, p. 89.

[426] Gingrich, p. 83.

[427] Res. 397, 111th Cong., 1st session, May 4, 2009 http://www.govtrack.us/congress/billtext.xpd?bill=hr111-397&page (accessed June 10, 2009).

[428] Newt Gingrich, *Rediscovering God in America*, (Nashville, Tennessee: Integrity House, 2006), p. 39.

[429] Kirk, *Roots of American Order*, p. 343.

[430] Stout and Hart, p. 174.

[431] Gingrich, pp. 46-47, 83.

[432] Tocqueville, p. 426.

[433] David Barton, *The Myth of Separation*, (Aledo, Texas: WallBuider Press,

1989), pp. 47-50.
434 Ibid, p. 50.
435 Blackstone, p. 27.

Chapter 15 – Government – Liberalism and Progressivism in America
436 Roberts, p. 693.
437 Paris Reidhead, "Ten Shekels and a Shirt," Remnant Resource Network, http://remnantradio.org/Archives/articles/TenShekels/tenshekels.htm (accessed December 18, 2010).
438 Christian Smith, pp. 52-55, 58, 66-67.
439 George, pp. 232-233, 251.
440 Evans, pp. 146-148.
441 Kirk, *The Essential Russell Kirk – Selected Essays*, p. 26
442 Ibid., pp. 28-30.
443 Ibid., pp. 7-9.
444 Richard M. Weaver, *Ideas Have Consequences*, (Chicago, Illinois: The University of Chicago Press, 1948), p. 52.
445 Randall, pp. 440, 444.
446 "President Obama's speech at Nobel ceremony", Thompson Reuters, December 10, 2009, http:www.reuters.com/article/idUSTRE5B92KK 20091210? WT.scrh=1&WT.MC_id=obamaobel (accessed December 21, 2009).
447 Lamont, pp. 14-15.
448 Lewis, *The Complete C. S. Lewis Signature Classics, The Abolition of Man*, pp. 721-722.
449 Weaver, *Ideas Have Consequences*, p. 51.
450 Ibid., p. 52.
451 Kirk, *The Essential Russell Kirk – Selected Essays*, p.355.
452 Weaver, *Ideas Have Consequences*, pp. 1, 51.
453 Kurtz, *Humanist Manifestos I and II*, p. 18.
454 Kurtz, *In Defense of Secular Humanism*, p. 72.
455 Ibid., pp. 68-69.
456 Lamont, pp. 12-13.
457 Evans, pp. 146-148.
458 Weaver, *Visions of Order*, pp. 136-145.
459 Evans, p. 22.
460 "coerce," *Webster's Seventh New Collegiate Dictionary*, (Springfield, Massachusetts: G. & C. Merriam Company, Publishers, 1963), p. 160.
461 Evans, pp. 28-19.
462 Ibid., p. 317.
463 F. A. Hayek, *The Road to Serfdom*, ed. Bruce Caldwell, (Chicago, Illinois: The University of Chicago Press, 1944, 2007), pp. 109-111.

[464] Kurtz, *In Defense of Secular Humanism*, pp. 76-78.
[465] Lamont, pp. 285-297.
[466] Ibid., p. 120.
[467] Weaver, *Ideas Have Consequences*, pp. 41-42.
[468] Samuelson, pp. 172-174, 184-185.
[469] Weaver, *Ideas Have Consequences*, p. 42.
[470] Randall, pp. 315-316.
[471] Kirk, *The Roots of American Order*, pp. 29, 397.
[472] Russell Kirk, *The Conservative Mind*, (www.bnpublishing.net, 2008), pp. 82.83.
[473] Weaver, *Ideas Have Consequences*, p. 41.
[474] Ibid., p. 40.
[475] Rossiter, p. 76.
[476] Weaver, *Ideas Have Consequences*, p. 44.
[477] Samuelson, pp. 177-178, 182-184.
[478] Person, p. 97.
[479] Herrick, p. 38.
[480] Weaver, *Visions of Order*, pp. 22-23.

Chapter 16 – Government – Humanism and the Rise of Socialism
[481] Kurtz, *Humanist Manifestos I and II*, p. 10.
[482] Ibid., pp. 20-22.
[483] Roberts, pp. 693-694; Randall, pp. 350-355.
[484] Edmund Burke, *Reflections on the Revolution in France*, ed. L. G. Mitchell, (Oxford: Oxford University Press, 1993, 1999), pp. vii, xiv-xvi, 269-271.
[485] Roberts, pp.750-751, 759.
[486] Marx and Engels, pp. 3-7.
[487] Roberts, p. 757-758.
[488] Marx and Engels, pp. 6-7.
[489] Ibid., pp. 51, 56, 58, 60-61.
[490] Hayek, pp. 76-77.
[491] Ibid., pp. 83-85.
[492] Ibid., pp. 76-77.
[493] Schweikart and Allen, pp. 444-445, 497-498.
[494] Ibid., pp. 422, 426-427.
[495] Ibid., pp. 460, 475, 480, 503.
[496] Ibid., pp. 538-539.
[497] Ibid., p. 18.
[498] Eddy, pp.36-37.
[499] Steven Thomma, "Politicians, pundits aim to rewrite history," *Tulsa World*, April 4, 2010, A 13.

[500] Eddy, pp. 40, 43, 46.
[501] Skousen, p. 173.
[502] Weaver, *Ideas Have Consequences*, pp. 131, 134-135.
[503] Evans, pp. 299-300.
[504] Skousen, pp. 173-176.
[505] Ibid., p. 175.
[506] Rossiter, p. 559.
[507] George Will, "Eminent domain issue threatens free speech," *Tulsa World*, August 21, 2009, A-11.
[508] Essel R. Dillavou, Charles G. Howard, Paul C. Roberts, and William J. Robert, *Principles of Business Law*, 7th edition, (Englewood Cliffs, New Jersey: Prentice Hall, Inc., 1962), p.14.
[509] Timothy Lamer, "Out of tune," *World*, May 23, 2009, 33; "White House Denies Charge by Attorney that Administration Threatened to Destroy Investment Firm's Reputation," abcNews.com. http://blogs.abcnews.com/politicalpunch/2009/05/bankruptcy-atto.html (accessed April 13, 2010).
[510] Weaver, *Ideas Have Consequences*, p. 129.
[511] Samuelson, pp. 144-145, 177-178.
[512] Ibid., pp. 141, 143-144, 152.
[513] 2009 Single and Married Individuals Tax Rate Schedule, Internal Revenue Service.
[514] "Who Doesn't Pay Federal Taxes?" Tax Policy Center, July 9, 2009. http://www.taxpolicycenter.org/taxtopics/federal-taxes-households.cfm (accessed May 6, 2010).
[515] Rossiter, pp. 212-213.
[516] Kurtz, *Humanist Manifestos I and II*, p. 21.
[517] Andrée Seu, "Agent John," *World*, (July 3, 2010), 95.
[518] Ibid.
[519] Ibid.
[520] Gerald Klingaman, "Kudzu, Mile-a-Minute Vine," University of Arkansas, Division of Agriculture, Cooperative Extension Service, August 30, 2002, http://www.arhomeandgarden.org/plantoftheweek/articles/Kudzu.htm. (accessed January 7, 2011). "Kudzu", *Wikipedia*, http://en.wikipedia.org/wiki/kudzu (accessed May 6, 2010).
[521] Janie Cheaney, "Knowledge and power," *World*, May 9, 2009, 30.

Chapter 17 – Science – Naturalistic Evolution
[522] Colson and Pearcey, *How Now Shall We Live?* pp. 52, 55, 59.
[523] Ray Comfort, "Special Introduction," Charles Darwin, *The Origin of Species, 150th Anniversary Edition*, (Alachua, Florida: Bridge-Logos, 2009), pp. 1-2.

[524] Ibid., pp. 5-7.
[525] Phillip E. Johnson, *Darwin on Trial*, pp. 15-16
[526] Donald E. Johnson, *Probability's Nature and Nature's Probability*, p. 41.
[527] Ibid., pp. 41-42.
[528] Phillip E. Johnson, *Darwin on Trial*, p. 129.
[529] Lewis, *The Complete C. S. Lewis Signature Classics, Mere Christianity*, p. 31.
[530] Donald E. Johnson, *Probability's Nature and Nature's Probability*, pp. 89, 105.
[531] Comfort, "Special Introduction," Darwin, *The Origin of Species, 150th Anniversary Edition*, p. 20.
[532] Phillip E. Johnson, *Darwin on Trial*, pp.68-68
[533] Comfort, "Special Introduction", Darwin, *The Origin of Species, 150th Anniversary Edition*, p. 13.
[534] Charles Darwin, *The Origin of Species, 150th Anniversary Edition*, (Alachua, Florida: Bridge-Logos, 2009), p. 142.
[535] Phillip E. Johnson, *Darwin on Trial*, pp.46-49.
[536] Ibid., p. 50.
[537] Ibid., pp. 49, 57; Comfort, "Special Introduction," Darwin, *The Origin of Species, 150th Anniversary Edition*, p. 13.
[538] Phillip E. Johnson, *Darwin on Trial*, pp.52, 58.
[539] Colson and Pearcey, *How Now Shall We Live?* p. 26.
[540] Phillip E. Johnson, *Darwin on Trial*, p. 53.
[541] Comfort, "Special Introduction", Darwin, *The Origin of Species, 150th Anniversary Edition*, pp. 18-19.
[542] Ibid., p. 19.
[543] Ibid., p. 18.
[544] Darwin, *The Origin of Species, 150th Anniversary Edition*, p. 284-285.
[545] Phillip E. Johnson, *Darwin on Trial*, p. 50.
[546] Michael J. Behe, *Darwin's Black Box*, (New York: Free Press, 1996, 2006), p. 24-25.
[547] Colson and Pearcey, *How Now Shall We Live?* pp. 85-87.
[548] Comfort, "Special Introduction", Darwin, *The Origin of Species, 150th Anniversary Edition*, pp. 21-23.
[549] Ibid., pp. 21-22.
[550] Colson and Pearcey, *How Now Shall We Live?* pp. 85-87.
[551] Darwin, *The Origin of Species, 150th Anniversary Edition*, pp. 158-159.
[552] Behe, p. 39.
[553] Ibid., pp. 39, 42, 45-46.
[554] Ibid., pp. 46, 203.
[555] Comfort, "Special Introduction", Darwin, *The Origin of Species, 150th Anniversary Edition*, pp. 9-10.

[556] Donald E. Johnson, *Probability's Nature and Nature's Probability*, p. 64.
[557] Ibid., p. 69.
[558] Behe, pp. 232-233.
[559] Ibid., p. 243.
[560] Paul Davies, *The Mind of God*, (New York: Touchstone, 1992), pp. 14-15, 23.
[561] Darwin, *The Origin of Species, 150th Anniversary Edition*, pp. 282-283.
[562] Herrick, p. 44.
[563] Malcolm Muggeridge, *The End of Christendom*, (Grand Rapids, Michigan: William B. Eerdmans Publishing Company, 1980), p. 59.
[564] Lewis, *The Timeless Writings of C. S. Lewis, Christian Reflections*, pp. 233-234.

Chapter 18 – Human Sciences and the Secularization of America

[565] Billie Davis, "A Perspective on Human Nature," in *Elements of a Christian Worldview*, comp. & ed. Michael D. Palmer, (Springfield, Missouri: Logion Press, 1998), pp. 180-181.
[566] Ibid., p. 181.
[567] Ibid., pp. 181-182.
[568] Darwin, *The Origin of Species, 150th Anniversary Edition*, p. 287.
[569] Bradley C. S. Watson, *Living Constitution, Dying Faith*, (Wilmington, Delaware: ISI Books, 2009), p. 56.
[570] Christian Smith, p. 1.
[571] Watson, pp. 55-56.
[572] Schweikart and Allen, pp. 444-445, 497-498.
[573] Watson, pp. 56, 58-59.
[574] Ibid., pp. 58, 60-61.
[575] Meador, "My Own Salvation," in *The Secular Revolution*, ed. Christian Smith, p. 282.
[576] Christian Smith, p. 3.
[577] Davis, "A Perspective on Human Nature," in *Elements of a Christian Worldview*, ed. Michael D. Palmer, pp. 182-188.
[578] Meador, "My Own Salvation," in *The Secular Revolution*, ed. Christian Smith, p. 295.
[579] Ibid., pp. 273, 276-277, 298-299.
[580] Ibid., pp. 273-276, 298-299.
[581] Ibid., pp. 278-282, 295, 301.
[582] Ibid., p. 302.
[583] Ibid., p. 269.
[584] Ibid., pp. 269, 303.
[585] Palmer, pp. 190-192.
[586] Christian Smith, p. 282.

[587] Davis, "A Perspective on Human Nature," in *Elements of a Christian Worldview*, ed. Michael D. Palmer, pp. 192, 194, 197-198.
[588] Ibid., Palmer, p. 200.
[589] Ibid., pp. 200, 204-207, 213-214.
[590] Kirk, *The Essential Russell Kirk – Selected Essays*, pp.355-356; Colson and Pearcey, *How Now Shall We Live?* pp. 176-177.
[591] Lewis, *The Complete C. S. Lewis Signature Classics, The Abolition of Man*, pp. 721-722.
[592] Davis, "A Perspective on Human Nature," in *Elements of a Christian Worldview*, ed. Michael D. Palmer, p. 215.

Chapter 19 – American Education
[593] Weaver, *Visions of Order*, pp. 10-11, 113-114, 132.
[594] Ibid., pp. 115-116.
[595] Gay, pp. 204-205.
[596] George M. Thomas, Lisa R. Peck, and Channin G. De Haan, "Reforming Education, Transforming Religion, 1876-1931," in *The Secular Revolution*, ed. Christian Smith, (Berkeley, California: University of California Press, 2003, pp. 355-356, 362, 365, 377.
[597] Ibid., pp. 356-357.
[598] Ibid., pp. 367-369, 372.
[599] Ibid., p. 372.
[600] Ibid., pp. 375, 377, 380-381, 386-387.
[601] Gay, pp. 205-208.
[602] Ibid, pp. 207-208.
[603] "UT System Fast Facts." Fast Facts 2010, The University of Texas System, February 2010, http://utsystem.ed/News/Files/FastFacts 2010.pdf (accessed July 8, 2010).
[604] Robert C. Koons, "Robert C. Koons: Autobiographical Sketch," The Virtual Office of Dr. Robert C. Koons, July 8, 2010, http://www.leaderu.com/offices/koons/menus/autobiography.html (accessed: July 8, 2010).
[605] Robert C. Koons, "Ideologically driven humanities faculty at the University of Texas overwhelmed a tradition-focused cultural center", Clarion Call, The John William Pope Center for higher Education Policy, August 4, 2009, http://www.popecenter.org/clarion_call/article.html?id=2213 (accessed: July 8, 2010).
[606] Barbara Moeller, "The Texas Mugging of Western Civ", *Our Essays*, July 6, 2009, http://www.mindingthecampus.com/originals/2009/07/by_barbara_moeller_last_novemb.html (accessed July 8, 2010)
[607] Ibid.
[608] Ibid.

[609] Ibid.
[610] Robert C. Koons, "Ideologically driven humanities faculty at the University of Texas overwhelmed a tradition-focused cultural center", Clarion Call, The John William Pope Center for higher Education Policy, August 4, 2009, http://www.popecenter.org/clarion_call/article.html?id=2213 (accessed: July 8, 2010).
[611] Ibid.
[612] Kirk, *The Essential Russell Kirk - Selected Essays*, pp. 398-399.
[613] Ibid., p. 400.
[614] Ibid., p. 400.
[615] Weaver, *Ideas Have Consequences*, p. 58.
[616] Lewis, *The Complete C. S. Lewis Signature Classics, The Abolition of Man*, pp. 702, 704.
[617] David French, "Tenured bigots," *World*, August 18, 2007, 27.
[618] Sarah Netter, "Georgia Grad Student Sues University Over Gay Sensitivity Training," abcNews/US, July 27, 2010, http://abcnews.go.com/US/georgia-student-sues-university-lgbt-sensitivity-training/story?id=11261490 (accessed August 7, 2010); Kate Schwartz, "School Wants Student to Alter Religious View on Gays," July 27, 2007, http://www.newser.com/story/96566/school-wants-student-to-alter-religious-view-gays.html (accessed August 7, 2010)
[619] "Home-Schooler Ordered to Attend Public Classes," *Pentecostal Evangel*, November 15, 2009, 23.
[620] Weaver, *Visions of Order*, p. 117.
[621] Ibid.

Chapter 20 – American Family – Marriage and Family
[622] Weaver, *Ideas Have Consequences*, pp. 41-42.
[623] Ibid., p. 41-42.
[624] "egalitarian," *Webster's Seventh New Collegiate Dictionary*, (Springfield, Massachusetts: G. & C. Merriam Company, Publishers, 1963), p. 264.
[625] Weaver, *Ideas Have Consequences*, pp. 35, 41-42.
[626] Wolters, p. 96.
[627] Colson and Pearcey, *How Now Shall We Live?* pp. 324-325.
[628] Blackstone, p. 28.
[629] Kay S. Hymowitz, *Marriage and Caste in America*, (Chicago, Illinois: Ivan R. Dee, 2006), pp. 3, 5.
[630] William J. Bennett, *The Broken Hearth*, (New York: Doubleday, 2001), p. 68.
[631] Exodus 20:3 RSV.
[632] Bennett, pp. 44, 67.
[633] Ibid., p. 44.

[634] Stephanie Coontz, *Marriage, a History*, (New York: Penguin Group, 2005), p. 7.
[635] Bennett, pp. 44-45, 174-178.
[636] Ibid., pp. 45-50, 53.
[637] Ibid., pp. 184-188.
[638] Ibid., pp. 186-187.
[639] Gary Chapman, *Covenant Marriage*, (Nashville, Tennessee: Broadman & Holman Publishers, 2003), pp. 6-10.
[640] Ibid., pp. 11-16.
[641] Kurtz, *Humanist Manifestos I and II*, p. 18.
[642] Chapman, pp. 17-21.
[643] Robert Rector, "The Collapse of Marriage and the Rise of Welfare Dependence," Panel Discussion, Lecture #959, The Heritage Foundation (May 22, 2006). www.heritage.org/research/welfare/hl959.cfm (accessed September 17, 2010).
[644] Robert Rector, "Marriage: America's Greatest Weapon Against Child Poverty," The Heritage Foundation, September 16, 2010, http://www.heritage.org/Research/Reports/2010/09/Marriage- America's-Greatest-Weapon-Against-Child-Poverty/ (accessed September 21, 2010).
[645] Marriage and divorce rates: 1920-1995, Table Ae507-513, *Historical Statistics of the United States, Earliest Times to the Present*, Millennial Edition, Vol. One, Part A, Population, pp. 1-688 – 1-689.
[646] Barbara Dafoe Whitehead, PhD, "The Collapse of Marriage and the Rise of Welfare Dependence," Panel Discussion, Lecture #959, The Heritage Foundation, May 22, 2006, www.heritage.org/research/welfare/hl959.cfm (accessed September 17, 2010).
[647] Marriage and divorce rates: 1920-1995, Table Ae507-513, *Historical Statistics of the United States, Earliest Times to the Present*, Millennial Edition, Vol. One, Part A, Population, pp. 1-688 – 1-689.
[648] Families below poverty threshold, by family type and the sex, race, and Hispanic origin of the household head: 1959-1999, Table Be283-309, *Historical Statistics of the United States, Earliest Times to the Present*, Millennial Edition, Vol. Two, Part B, Work and Welfare, (New York: Cambridge University Press, 2006), p. 2-678.
[649] Robert Rector, "Marriage: America's Greatest Weapon Against Child Poverty," The Heritage Foundation, September 16, 2010, http://www.heritage.org/Research/Reports/2010/09/Marriage- America's-Greatest-Weapon-Against-Child-Poverty/ (accessed September 21, 2010).
[650] Labor force participation rate for married women, by age and presence of

children: 1948-1999, Table Ba579-582, *Historical Statistics of the United States, Earliest Times to the Present*, Millennial Edition, Vol. Two, Part B, Work and Welfare, p. 2-94.

[651] Children in primary child care arrangements used by employed mothers, by type of care: 1958-1994, Table Ba5086-5090, *Historical Statistics of the United States, Earliest Times to the Present*, Millennial Edition, Vol. Two, Part B, Work and Welfare, p. 2-366.

[652] Robert Rector, "Marriage: America's Greatest Weapon Against Child Poverty," The Heritage Foundation, September 16, 2010, http://www.heritage.org/Research/Reports/2010/09/Marriage-America's-Greatest-Weapon- Against-Child-Poverty/ (accessed September 21, 2010).

[653] Bennett, pp. 2, 85.

[654] Lee Rainwater and William L. Yancey, *The Moynihan Report and the Politics of Controversy*, (Cambridge Massachusetts: M.I.T. Press, 1967), p. 3.

[655] Bennett, pp. 1-2.

[656] Ibid., p. 67.

Chapter 21 – American Family – Feminism and the Roles of Men and Women

[657] Coontz, pp. 4-5.

[658] Ibid. pp. 6-7.

[659] Ibid., pp. 154-156.

[660] Ibid., pp. 145-146.

[661] Linda J. Waite and Maggie Gallagher, *The Case for Marriage*, (New York: Doubleday, 2000), p. 1.

[662] Schweikart and Allen, pp. 205, 207, 219, 221, 224-226.

[663] Ibid., pp. 226-227, 530.

[664] Ibid., p. 530.

[665] George Grant, *Grand Illusions – The Legacy of Planned Parenthood*, (Brentwood, Tennessee: Wolgemuth & Hyatt, Publishers, Inc., 1988), pp. 44-47.

[666] Ibid., pp. 49-53.

[667] Ibid., pp. 52-58.

[668] Ibid., p.59.

[669] About the AHA, American Humanist Association, http://www.americanhumanist.org/who_we_are/about_the_AHA/Humanist_of_the_Year (accessed September 16, 2010).

[670] Kurtz, *Humanist Manifestos I and II*, p. 25.

[671] "Annual Report 2008-2009," Planned Parenthood Federation of America,. 28-29. http://www.plannedparenthood.org/files/PPFA/

PPFA_Annual_Report_08-09-FINAL-12-10-10.pdf (accessed January 7, 2011).

[672] "The Founding of NOW," National Organization of Women, http://www.now.org/history/the_founding.html (accessed September 10, 2010).

[673] Charles Colson, *Lies that Go Unchallenged In Popular Culture*, comp. James Stuart Bell, (Wheaton, Illinois: Tyndale House Publishers, Inc., 2005), p. 73.

[674] "The Founding of NOW," National Organization of Women website, http://www.now.org/history/the_founding.html (accessed September 10, 2010).

[675] "The National Organization for Women's 1966 Statement of Purpose," National Organization of Women, http://www.now.org/history/purpos66.html (accessed September 10, 2010).

[676] About the AHA, American Humanist Association website, http://www.americanhumanist.org/who_we_are/about_the_AHA/Humanist of_the_Year (accessed September 16, 2010).

[677] Kurtz, *Humanist Manifestos I and II*, p. 28.

[678] Gillon, p. 192.

[679] Hymowitz, p. 125.

[680] Waite and Gallagher, pp. 170-171.

[681] Hymowitz, p. 125.

[682] Ibid., pp. 13-14.

[683] Keller, pp. 17-18.

[684] Lewis, *The Complete C. S. Lewis Signature Classics, Mere Christianity and The Abolition of Man*, pp. 95, 721, 727.

[685] Hymowitz, p. 30.

[686] Ibid., p. 41.

[687] Bennett, p. 69.

[688] Ibid., pp.26-27.

[689] Waite and Gallagher, p. 203.

[690] Ibid.

Chapter 22 – American Family - Abortion

[691] "7363 rachaph," Biblios.com, http://strongsnumbers.com/hebrew/7363.htm (accessed September 22, 2010); http://www.blueletterbible.org/lang/lexicon/lexicon.cfm?Strongs=H7 (accessed September 22, 2010); "The Heavens," Genesis Research, http://www.accuracyingenesis.com/heavens.html (accessed September 22, 2010); Janie B. Cheaney, "To Breed or Not to Breed?" *World*, (July 17, 2010), 20.

[692] Janie B. Cheaney, "To Breed or Not to Breed?" *World*, (July 17, 2010), 20.

[693] Grant, p. 189; James Hernando, "Legacy of Life," *Today's Pentecostal Evangel*, (January 19, 2009), 16.
[694] Grant, pp. 190-195.
[695] Kurtz, *Humanist Manifestos I and II*, p. 17.
[696] Ibid., p. 18.
[697] Janie B. Cheaney, "To Breed or Not to Breed?" *World*, (July 17, 2010), 20.
[698] "U.S. Abortion Statistics by Year (1973-Current)", National Right to Life Committee, 2010, http://www.christianliferesources.com??/ library/view.php&articleid=1042 (accessed September 25, 2010)
[699] John E. Dunsford, "Like a Startle...Like a flinch," *Touchstone* (November 2000), 10.
[700] Ibid., 11.
[701] Ibid.
[702] Ibid., 11-12.
[703] Blackmun, J., Opinion of the Court, Supreme Court of the United States, 410 U.S. 113, Roe v. Wade (no. 70-18), VIII, January 22, 1973, Cornell University Law School, Legal Information Institute. http://www.law.cornell.edu/supct/html/historics/USSC_CR_0410_0113_Z.html (accessed September 27, 2010).
[704] Blackmun, J., Opinion of the Court, Supreme Court of the United States, 10 U.S. 113, Roe v. Wade (no. 70-18), IX. http://www.law.cornell.edu/supct/html/historics/USSC_CR_0410_0113_Z.html (accessed September 27, 2010).
[705] Ibid.
[706] Blackmun, J., Opinion of the Court, Supreme Court of the United States, 410 U.S. 113, Roe v. Wade (no. 70-18), IX-X. http://www.law.cornell.edu/supct/html/historics/USSC_CR_0410_0113_Z.html (accessed September 27, 2010).
[707] Kurtz, *Humanist Manifestos I and II*, p. 8.
[708] George, pp. 67-69.
[709] Ibid., pp. 70-71.
[710] Grant, pp. 180-181.
[711] Colson and Pearcey, *How Now Shall We Live?* p. 120.
[712] Ibid., p. 121.
[713] Ibid., pp. 120-121.
[714] Ibid., pp. 122-123.
[715] Ibid., p. 125.
[716] Bork, p. 186.

Chapter 23 – American Family - Homosexuality
[717] Coontz, pp. 11, 77.

[718] David Blankenhorn, *The Future of Marriage*, (New York: Encounter Books, 2007), p. 175.
[719] Hymowitz, p. 46.
[720] George, p. 81.
[721] Ibid., pp. 77-79, 81-82
[722] Bennett, pp. 105-107, 121, 138.
[723] "tolerance," *Webster's Seventh New Collegiate Dictionary*, (Springfield, Massachusetts: G. & C. Merriam Company, 1963), p. 930.
[724] Bennett, p. 107.
[725] Bork, pp. 113-114.
[726] Charles Colson, *God & Government*, (Grand Rapids, Michigan: Zondervan, 2007), pp. 241-242.
[727] Bork, p. 114.
[728] Colson, *God & Government*, pp. 241-242.
[729] Bennett, pp. 127-229-131.
[730] Tocqueville, p. 348.
[731] Bork, p. 286.
[732] Bennett, pp. 22-25; Colson, *Lies That Go Unchallenged*, pp. 26-27.
[733] "Just The Facts About Sexual Orientation and Youth," Just the Facts Coalition, (Washington, D.C.: Just the Facts Coalition, 2008), http://apa.org/pi/lgbt/resources/just-the-facts.pdf (accessed October 8, 2010).
[734] David McCullough, *John Adams,* (New York: Touchstone, 2001), p. 68.
[735] "Facts About Youth," American College of Pediatricians, http://factsaboutyouth.com/wp- content/uploads/Superintendent-LetterC_3.311.pdf (accessed October 8, 2010).
[736] "Superintendents: Don't be confused by the AAP," American College of Pediatricians, /http://factsaboutyouth.com/superintendents-don't- be-confused-by-the-aap/ (accessed October 8, 2010).

Chapter 24 – Popular Culture
[737] Colson and Pearcey, *How Now Shall We Live*, pp. 441, 453; "objectivism," *Webster's Seventh New Collegiate Dictionary*, (Springfield, Massachusetts: G. & C. Merriam Company, 1963), p. 582.
[738] Kirk, *The Essential Russell Kirk - Selected Essays,* pp. 208-210.
[739] Colson and Pearcey, *How Now Shall We Live?* pp. 445-449.
[740] Ibid., pp. 441, 448-449.
[741] Bork, p. 133.
[742] Weaver, *Ideas Have Consequences*, pp. 70-71, 79.
[743] Gay, p. 196.
[744] Paul Starr, *The Creation of The Media*, (New York: Basic Books, 2004),

pp. 46, 83-84.
[745] Ibid., pp. 85-87.
[746] Tocqueville, pp. 602-603.
[747] Starr, p. 87.
[748] Ibid., pp. 85-90.
[749] Ibid., p. 327.
[750] Gay, pp. 200-202.
[751] Starr, pp. 1-2, 25.
[752] Ibid., pp. 385-386, 395.
[753] Ibid., pp. 395, 398.
[754] Larry G. Johnson, *Tar Creek*, (Mustang, Oklahoma: Tate Publishing & Enterprises, LLC, 2008) p. 280.
[755] Bork, p. 125.
[756] Petigny, , pp. 204, 206.
[757] Ibid., pp. 220-221.
[758] Ibid., pp. 222-223.
[759] Robert Hoskins, "Six Macro-Trends in Global Missions," One Hope, 600 SW 3rd Street, Pompano Beach, FL 33060
[760] Author's notes from Empowered 21 breakout session, Tulsa, Oklahoma, April 9, 2010: Six Macro Trends chaired by Robert Hoskins, One Hope, 600 SW 3rd Street, Pompano Beach, FL 33060.
[761] "Welcome to the Swazi-Media audience Measurement Survey (Report) Television Section," infoshopSwaziland.com, http://infoshopswaziland.com/swazi_mams/Mams_television_vierwership_in_swaziland.htm (accessed October 26, 2010); Author's notes from Empowered 21 breakout session, Tulsa, Oklahoma, April 9, 2010: Six Macro Trends chaired by Robert Hoskins, One Hope, 600 SW 3rd Street, Pompano Beach, FL 33060.
[762] Christian Smith, p. 85.
[763] "Marshall McLuhan," The Estate of Corinne and Marshall McLuhan, http://www.marshallmcluhan.com/faqs.html (accessed October 13, 2010).
[764] Dean M. Riley, "Wisdom & God In The Age of Information," *The City*, Vol. 3, No. 2, (Fall 2010), 51.
[765] Christian Smith, pp. 28-29.
[766] Bork, p. 131.
[767] Karen Sternheimer, *Connecting Social Problems and Popular Culture*, (Boulder, Colorado: Westview Press, 2010), pp. 3-4, 17.
[768] Ibid., p. 299.

Part IV – Ye shall be as gods – Summary, Status, Direction

Chapter 25 – Differences between Christian and Humanist Worldviews – A Summary

[769] Kurtz, *Humanist Manifestos I and II*, p. 23.
[770] Colson and Pearcey, *How Now Shall We Live?* p. 417.
[771] Ibid., pp. 19-22.
[772] Weaver, *Ideas Have Consequences*, pp. 148-149, 152, 158, 163..
[773] Kurtz, *Humanist Manifestos I and II*, p. 20.
[774] Acts 17:26 (KJV)
[775] "tolerance," *Webster's Seventh New Collegiate Dictionary*, (Springfield, Massachusetts: G. & C. Merriam Company, Publishers, 1963), p. 930.
[776] "pluralism," *Webster's Seventh New Collegiate Dictionary*, (Springfield, Massachusetts: G. & C. Merriam Company, Publishers, 1963), p. 653.
[777] Kirk, *The Roots of American Order*, pp. 94-95.

Chapter 26 – Christianity and Humanism – Endgame in America

[778] George M. Curtis, III, and James J. Thompson, Jr., eds., *The Southern Essays of Richard M. Weaver*, (Indianapolis, Indiana: Liberty Fund, 1987), pp. 195-196.
[779] Weaver, *Visions of Order*, pp. 4, 9-12.
[780] Bork, p. 296.
[781] Mark 3:25 KJV
[782] Jim Cymbala, *Fresh Power*, (Grand Rapids, Michigan: Zondervan, 2001), p. 93.
[783] Weaver, *Visions of Order*, p. 13.
[784] Kirk, *Roots of the American Revolution*, p. 29.
[785] Keller, p. 41.
[786] Muggeridge, p. 38.
[787] Weaver, *Visions of Order*, p. 6.
[788] "About the AHA," American Humanist Association website, http://www.americanhumanist.org/who_we_are/about_the_AHA/Humanist_of_the_Year (accessed September 16, 2010).
[789] Dr. Benjamin M. Spock, *A better World for Our Children - Rebuilding American Family Values*, (Bethesda, Maryland: National Press Books, 1994), pp. 15-16, 93, 99, 124-125, 139.
[790] "Insanity," Quotation #26932. Michael Moncur's (Cynical) Quotations, http://www.quotationspage.com/quote/ 26032.html (accessed November 8, 2010).
[791] Bork, pp. 338-339.
[792] Ibid., p. 339.
[793] Ibid., p. 336.
[794] J. Edwin Orr, "Prayer brought Revival," oChristion.com, http://articles.ochristian.com/article8330.shtml (accessed November 26,

2010).
[795] Stout and Hart, pp. 186-187.
[796] J. Edwin Orr, "Prayer brought Revival," http://articles.ochristian.com/article 8330.shtml (accessed November 26, 2010).
[797] Ibid.
[798] Michael McClymond, ed., *Encyclopedia of Religious Revivals in America*, Vol. 1, A-Z, (Westport, Connecticut: Greenwood Press, 2007), pp. 43-44
[799] J. Edwin Orr, "Prayer brought Revival," http://articles.ochristian.com/article8330.shtml (accessed November 26, 2010).
[800] Marshall W. Fishwick, *Great Awakenings*, (New York: Harrington Park Press, 1995), p. 19.
[801] J. Edwin Orr, "Prayer brought Revival," http://articles.ochristian.com/article8330.shtml (accessed November 26, 2010).
[802] McClymond, *Encyclopedia of Religious Revivals in America*, Vol. 1, A- Z, pp. 362-363; Vol. 2, Primary Documents, p. 168; Random facts about 1857, Yahoo! Answers, http://answers.yahoo.com/question/index?qid =1129053708AAhiObt (accessed December 1, 2010).
[803] McClymond, *Encyclopedia of Religious Revivals in America*, Vol. 1, A- Z, p. 365.
[804] McClymond, *Encyclopedia of Religious Revivals in America*, Vol. 1, A- Z, pp. 117-121.
[805] J. Edwin Orr, "Prayer brought Revival," http://articles.ochristian.com/article8330.shtml (accessed November 26, 2010).
[806] Ibid.
[807] Ibid.
[808] II Chronicles 6:12-41 RSV; Henry, pp. 455-456.
[809] II Chronicles 7:13-15 RSV.
[810] II Chronicles 9:31, 101-18, 12:9 RSV.
[811] Kirk, *The Essential Russell Kirk*, p. 90.
[812] Ephesians 6:12 RSV.
[813] II Chronicles 7:14 RSV.

Bibliography

Books

Adler, Richard P., Editor. *Understanding Television – Essays on Television as a Social and Cultural Force*. New York: Praeger Publishers, 1981.

Anderson, David L. *The Columbia Guide to the Vietnam War*. New York: Columbia University Press, 2002.

Aquinas, Thomas. *Aquinas's Shorter Summa*. Manchester, New Hampshire: Sophia Institute Press, 1993, 2002.

Barm, Gregory, and John Coleman, ed. *The Sexual Revolution*. Edinburgh: Stichting Concilium and T. & T. Clark LTD, 1984.

Bartleman, Frank. *Azusa Street*. New Kensington, Pennsylvania: Whitaker House, 1982.

Barton, David. *The Myth of Separation*. Aledo, Texas: WallBuilder Press, 1989.

Behe, Michael J. *Darwin's Black Box*. New York: Free Press, 1996, 2006.

Bennett, William J. *The Broken Hearth*. New York: Doubleday, 2001.

Berthoff, Rowland. *An Unsettled People: Social Order and Disorder in American History*. New York: Harper & Row, Publishers, 1971.

Bible. Scripture quotations marked KJV are taken from the Holy Bible, King James Version.

Bible. Scripture quotations marked RSV are taken from the Holy Bible, Revised Standard Version. Copyright 1946, 1952, 1971 by the Division of Christian Education of the National council of the Churches of Christ in the United States of America.

Bible. Scripture quotations marked LB are taken from the Living Bible. Copyright 1971 by Tyndale House Publishers, Inc., Wheaton, Illinois.

Blackstone, William. *Commentaries on the Laws of England*, Vol. I-Book I & II. Philadelphia: J. B. Lippincott Company, 1910.

Blankenhorn, David. *The Future of Marriage*. New York: Encounter Books, 2007.

Bogart, Leo. *Over the Edge*. Chicago, Illinois: Ivan R. Dee, 2005.

Boorstin, Daniel J. *The Americans-The Democratic Experience*. New York: Random House, 1973.

Bork, Robert H. *Slouching Towards Gomorrah*. New York: Regan Books, 1996.

Brokaw, Tom. *The Greatest Generation*. New York: Random House, 1998.

Burk, Edmund. *Reflections on the Revolution in France*. Edited by L. G. Mitchell. Oxford: Oxford University Press, 1993, 1999.

Burns, Richard Dean, and Milton Leitenberg. *The Wars in Vietnam, Cambodia and Laos 1945-1982*. Santa Barbara, California: ABC-Clio Information Services, 1984.

Capps, Donald, ed. *Freud and Freudians on Religion – A reader*. New Haven, Connecticut: Yale University Press, 2001.

Chambers, Whittaker. *Witness*. New York: Random House, 1952.

Chapman, Gary. *Covenant Marriage*. Nashville, Tennessee: Broadman & Holman Publishers, 2003.

Cohen, Robert, and Reginald E. Zelnik, ed. *The Free Speech Movement*. Los Angeles, California: University of California Press, 2002.

Colson, Charles. *God & Government*. Grand Rapids, Michigan: Zondervan, 2007

_____. *Lies that Go Unchallenged In Popular Culture*. Compiled by James Stuart Bell. Wheaton, Illinois: Tyndale House Publishers, Inc., 2005.

Colson, Charles, and Nancy Pearcey. *How Now Shall We Live?* Wheaton, Illinois: Tyndale House Publishers, Inc., 1999.

Coontz, Stephanie. *Marriage, a History*. New York: Penguin Group, 2005.

Croker, Richard. *The Boomer Century 1946-2046*. New York: Springboard Press, 2007.

Curtis, George M., III, and James J. Thompson, Jr., eds. *The Southern Essays of Richard M. Weaver*. Indianapolis, Indiana: Liberty Fund, 1987.

Cymbala, Jim. *Fresh Power*. Grand Rapids, Michigan: Zondervan, 2001.

Darwin, Charles. *The Origin of Species, 150th Anniversary Edition*. Special Introduction by Ray Comfort. Alachua, Florida: Bridge-Logos, 2009.

Davies, Paul. *The Mind of God*. New York: Touchstone, 1992.

Davis, Billie. "A Perspective on Human Nature." In *Elements of a Christian Worldview*, compiled and edited by Michael D. Palmer, Springfield, Missouri: Logion Press, 1998.

Dewey, John. *The Influence of Darwin on Philosophy*. New York: Henry Holt and Company, 1910.

Dickson, Paul. *Sputnik – The Shock of the Century*. New York: Walker & Company, 2001.

Dillavou, Essel R., Charles G. Howard, Paul C. Roberts, and William J. Robert. *Principles of Business Law*, 7th edition. Englewood Cliffs, New Jersey: Prentice Hall, Inc., 1962.

Eddy, Sherwood. *The Kingdom of God and the American Dream*. New York: Harper & Brothers Publishers, 1941.

Evans, M. Stanton. *The Theme Is Freedom*. Washington, D.C.: Regnery Publishing, Inc., 1994.

Fishwick, Marshall W. *Great Awakenings*. New York: Harrington Park Press, 1995.

Gay, Craig M. *The way of the (modern) world*. Grand Rapids, Michigan: Wm. B. Eerdmans Publishing Co., 1998.

George, Robert P. *Clash of Orthodoxies*. Wilmington, Delaware: ISI Books, 2001.

Gillon, Steve. *Boomer Nation*. New York: Free Press, 2004.

Gingrich, Newt. *Rediscovering God in America*. Nashville, Tennessee: Integrity House, 2006.

Grant, George. *Grand Illusions – The Legacy of Planned Parenthood*. Brentwood, Tennessee: Wolgemuth & Hyatt, Publishers, Inc., 1988.

Hamilton, Neil A. *Atlas of the Baby Boom Generation*. New York: Macmillan Reference USA, 2000.

Hawking, Stephen. *A Brief History of Time*, (New York: Bantam Books, 1988, 1996.

Hayek, F. A. *The Road to Serfdom*. Edited by Bruce Caldwell. Chicago, Illinois: The University of Chicago Press, 1944, 2007.

Henry, Matthew. *Commentary on the Whole Bible*. Grand Rapids, Michigan: Zondervan Publishing House, 1961.

Herrick, Jim Herrick. *Humanism – An Introduction*. Amherst, New York: Prometheus Books, 2005.

Historical Statistics of the United States, Earliest Times to the Present. Millennial Edition. Vol. One, Part A, Population, Table Ae507-513, pp.1-688 – 1-689. Vol. Two, Part B, Work and Welfare, Table Be283-309, p. 2-678. New York: Cambridge University Press, 2006.

Hook, Sidney. *John Dewey – His Philosophy of Education and Its Critics*. New York: Tamiment Institute, 1959.

Hymowitz, Kay S. *Marriage and Caste in America*. Chicago, Illinois: Ivan R. Dee, 2006.

Iserbyt, Charlotte Thomson. *the deliberate dumbing down of America*. Ravenna, Ohio: Conscience Press, 1999.

Johnson, Donald E. PhD. *Probability's Nature and Nature's Probability*. Charleston, South Carolina: Booksurge Publishing, 2009.

Johnson, Larry G. *Tar Creek*. Mustang, Oklahoma: Tate Publishing & Enterprises, LLC, 2008.

Johnson, Phillip E. *Darwin on Trial.* Downers Grove, Illinois: IVP Books, 1991, 1993.

Kaplan, Fred. *1959-The Year Everything Changed.* Hoboken, New Jersey: John Wiley & Sons, Inc., 2009.

Keller, Timothy. *The Reason for God.* New York: Dutton, 2008.

King, Jr., Martin Luther. *A Testament of Hope-The Essential writings of Martin Luther King, Jr.* Edited by James Melvin Washington. New York: Harper San Francisco, 1986.

Kirk, Russell. *The Essential Kirk – Selected Essays.* Edited by George A. Panichas. Wilmington, Delaware: ISI Books, 2007.

_____. *The Roots of American Order.* Washington D. C.: Regnery Gateway, 1991.

Kulick, Elliott, and Dick Wilson. *Thailand's Turn.* London: The MacMillan Press LTD, 1992.

Kung, Hans. *Freud and the Problem of God.* Translated by Edward Quinn. New Haven, Connecticut: Yale University Press, 1979, 1990.

Kurtz, Paul, ed. *Humanist Manifestos I and II.* Buffalo, New York: Prometheus Books, 1973.

_____, ed. *The Humanist Alternative: some definitions of Humanism.* Buffalo, New York: Prometheus Books, 1973.

_____. *Toward a New Enlightenment – The Philosophy of Paul Kurtz,* (New Brunswick, New Jersey: Transaction Publishers, 1994.

Lamont, Corliss Lamont. *The Philosophy of Humanism.* Amherst, New York: Humanist Press, 1947, 1957, 1965, 1982, 1992.

Lewis, C. S. *The Complete C. S. Lewis Signature Classics, Mere Christianity.* New York: Harper One, 2002.

_____. *The Complete C. S. Lewis Signature Classics, Miracles.* New York: Harper One, 2002.

_____. *The Complete C. S. Lewis Signature Classics, The Abolition of*

Man. New York: Harper One, 2002.

_____. *The Four Loves*. New York: Harcourt, Brace, Jovanovich, Publishers, 1960, 1988.

_____. *The Timeless Writings of C. S. Lewis*. Edited by Walter Hooper. New York: Inspiration Press, 1967.

Lewis, Donald, and Alister McGrath, ed. *Doing Theology for the People of God*. Downers Grove, Illinois: InterVarsity Press, 1996.

Maclear, Michael. *Vietnam*. New York: Tess Press, 2003.

Magueijo, Joao. *Faster Than the Speed of Light*. Cambridge, Massachusetts: Perseus Publishers, 2003.

Maier, Thomas. *Dr. Spock – An American Life*. New York: Harcourt Brace & Company, 1998.

Marks, Lara V. *Sexual Chemistry – A History of the Contraceptive Pill*. New Haven, Connecticut: Yale University Press, 2001.

Marx, Karl, and Frederick Engels. *The Communist Manifesto*. Introduced by Eric Hobsbawm. London: Verso, 1998.

McClymond, Michael, ed. *Encyclopedia of Religious Revivals in America*. Vol. 1, A-Z. Vol. 2, Primary Documents. Westport, Connecticut: Greenwood Press, 2007.

McCullough, David. *John Adams*. New York: Touchstone, 200.

Meador, Keith G. "My Own Salvation." In *The Secular Revolution*, edited by Christian Smith, Berkeley, California: University of California Press, 2003.

Merton, Robert K. *On the Shoulders of Giants*. Chicago: University of Chicago Press, 1965.

Muggeridge, Malcolm. *The End of Christendom*. Grand Rapids, Michigan: William B. Eerdmans Publishing Company, 1980.

Nee, Watchman. *The Normal Christian Life*. Hendrickson Christian Classics Edition. Peabody, Massachusetts: Henrickson Publishers, 1961.

Nesbitt, L. M. *Hell-Hole of Creation – The Exploration of Abyssinian Danakil.* New York: Alfred A. Knopf, 1934.

Nicole, Roger. "James I. Packer's Contribution to the Doctrine of Inerrancy of Scripture." In *Doing Theology for the People of God,* edited by Donald Lewis & Alister McGrath. Downers Grove, Illinois: InterVarsity Press, 1996.

Novak, Michael. "Television Shapes the Soul." In *Understanding Television – Essays on Television as a Social and Cultural Force,* edited by Richard P. Adler. New York: Praeger Publishers, 1981.

Palmer, Michael D., comp. & ed. *Elements of a Christian Worldview.* Springfield, Missouri: Logion Press, 1998.

Person, Jr., James E. *Russell Kirk, A Critical Biography of a Conservative Mind.* Lanham, Maryland: Madison Books, 1999.

Petigny, Alan. *The Permissive Society – America, 1941-1965.* New York: Cambridge University Press, 2009.

Rainwater, Lee, and William L. Yancey. *The Moynihan Report and the Politics of Controversy.* Cambridge Massachusetts: M.I.T. Press, 1967.

Randall, Jr., John Herman. *The Making of the Modern Mind.* New York: Columbia University Press, 1926.

Rembar, Charles. *The End of Obscenity.* New York: Perennial Library, 1968.

Rickover, H. G. A*merican Education—A National Failure.* New York: E. F. Dutton & Co., Inc., 1963.

_____. *Education and Freedom.* New York: E. P. Dutton & Co., Inc. 1959.

Roberts, J. M. *History of the World.* Oxford: Oxford University Press, 2003.

Rossiter, Clinton, ed. *The Federalist Papers.* New York: Signet Classic, 1961.

Roth, Robert J. *John Dewey and Self-Realization*. Westport, Connecticut: Greenwood Press, Publishers, 1962.

Ryan, Ryan. *John Dewey and the High Tide of American Liberalism*. New York: W. W. Norton & Company, 1995.

Samuelson, Robert J. *The Good Life and Its Discontents – The American Dream in the age of Entitlement 1945-1995*. New York: Vantage Books, 1995, 1997.

Samuelson, Robert J. *The Good Life and Its discontents*. New York: Vintage Books, 1995,1997.

Schaeffer, Francis A. *Escape from Reason*. Downers Grove, Illinois: IVP Books, 1968.

Schreck, Alan, Phd. *The Compact History of the Catholic Church*. Cincinnati, Ohio: Servant Books, 2009.

Schwartz, Richard A. *An Eyewitness History – The 1950s*. New York: Facts On File, Inc., 2003.

Skousen, W. Cleon. *The 5000 Year Leap*. www.nccs.net: National Center for Constitutional Studies, 1981.

Smith, Christian, ed. *The Secular Revolution*. Berkeley, California: University of California Press, 2003.

Smith, J. Walker, and Ann Clurman. *Generation Ageless*. New York: Collins, 2007.

Smith, Robert W. *The Space Telescope*. Cambridge: Cambridge University Press, 1993.

Spock, Benjamin. *A Better World for Our Children*. Bethesda, Maryland: National Press Books.

_____. *A better World for Our Children - Rebuilding American Family Values*. Bethesda, Maryland: National Press Books, 1994.

_____. *The Common Sense Book of Baby and Child Care*. New York: Duell, Sloan and Pearce, 1945, 1946.

Spock, Benjamin, M. D., and Michael B. Rothenberg, M.D. *Dr. Spock's Baby and Child Care.* New York: Pocket Books, 1992.

Starr, Paul. *The Creation of The Media.* New York: Basic Books, 2004.

Steinberg, Cobbett S. *TV Facts.* New York: Facts on File, Inc., 1980.

Steinhorn, Leonard. *The Greater Generation.* New York, Thomas Dunne Books, 2006.

Sternheimer, Karen. *Connecting Social Problems and Popular Culture.* Boulder, Colorado: Westview Press, 2010.

Stout, Harry S., and D. G. Hart, ed. *New Directions in American Religious History.* New York: Oxford University Press, 1997.

Strauss, William, and Neil Howe. *Generations – The History of America's Future, 1584 to 2069.* New York: Quill William Morrow, 1991.

Stuart-Fox, Martin, ed. *Contemporary Laos.* London: University of Queensland Press, 1982.

Talisse, Robert B. *On Dewey.* Belmont, California: Wadsworth/Thompson Learning, 2000.

Thomas, George M., Lisa R. Peck, and Channin G. De Haan. "Reforming Education, Transforming Religion, 1876-1931." In *The Secular Revolution*, edited by Christian Smith. Berkeley, California: University of California Press, 2003.

Tocqueville, Alexis de. *Democracy in America.* Translated by Gerald E. Bevan. New York: Penguin Books, 2003.

Waite, Linda J., and Maggie Gallagher. *The Case for Marriage.* New York: Doubleday, 2000.

Watson, Bradley C. S. *Living Constitution, Dying Faith.* Wilmington, Delaware: ISI Books, 2009.

Watson, James D. *The Double Helix.* New York: Atheneum, 1968.

Weaver, Richard M. *Ideas Have Consequences.* Chicago, Illinois: The University of Chicago Press, 1948.

_____. *Visions of Order*. Wilmington, Delaware: Intercollegiate Studies Institute, 1964.

Weaver, Richard Webster. *Why Freud was Wrong*. New York: Basic Books, 1995.

Webster's Revised Unabridged Dictionary. Plainfield, New Jersey: MICRA, Inc., 1996.

Webster's Seventh New Collegiate Dictionary. Springfield, Massachusetts: G. & C. Merriam Company, Publishers, 1963.

Wilkinson, Loren E. "Immanuel and the Purpose of Creation." In *Doing Theology for the People of God*, edited by Donald Lewis & Alister McGrath. Downers Grove, Illinois: InterVarsity Press, 1996.

Wolters, Albert M. Creation Regained. Grand Rapids, Michigan: Wm. B. Eerdmans, 1985, 2005.

World Almanac and Book of Facts 1999. Mahwah, New Jersey: World Almanac Books, 1998.

Wood, Gordon S. "Religion and the American Revolution." In New Directions in American Religious History, edited by Harry S. Stout and D. G. Hart. New York: Oxford University Press, 1997.

Magazines

Belz, Emily, "Identity crisis," *World*, May 8, 2010, 40.

Belz, Emily, "Wilders' side," *World*, November 7, 2009, 38. Belz, Joel,

"Politeness police," *World*, January 30, 2010, 4, 10; Cheaney, Janie B.,

"Knowledge and power," *World*, May 9, 2009, 30.

Cheaney, Janie B., "To Breed or Not to Breed?" *World*, July 17, 2010, 20.

Editors, "Baby Boom Bust," *World*, Vol. 24, No. 11, June 6, 2009, 9.

French, David, "Tenured bigots," *World*, August 18, 2007, 27.

"Home-Schooler Ordered to Attend Public Classes," *Pentecostal Evangel*, November 15, 2009, 23.

Hernando, James, "Legacy of Life," *Today's Pentecostal Evangel*, January 19, 2009, 16.

Lamer, Timothy, "Out of tune," *World*, May 23, 2009, 33.

Olasky, Marvin, "Paine's brain," *World*, January 30, 2010, 76.

Olasky, Marvin, "Zen violence," *World*, February 13, 2010, 80.

Seu, Andrée, "Agent John," *World*, July 3, 2010, 95.

Veith, Gene Edward, "Suicidal ideology," *World*, February 23/March 1, 2008, 33.

Journals

Badeaux, Christopher. "Faith, Fear and Cormac McCarthy." *The City*, Vol. 1, No. 3 (Winter 2008): 84-85.

Baker, Hunter. "A Republic of Letters." *The City,* Vol. IV, No. 1 (Spring 2011): 98.

Dunsford, John E. "Like a Startle...Like a flinch." *Touchstone* (November 2000): 10.

McClay, Wilfred. "The Soul & the City", *The City*, Vol. II, No. 2 (Summer 2009): 8-9.

Riley, Dean M. "Wisdom & God In The Age of Information," *The City*, Vol. III, No. 2 (Fall 2010): 51.

Newspapers

"40 Years Ago Vietnam: MG Keith Ware," *Bridgehead Sentinel*, Summer 2008, 13.

Thomas, Cal, "Something about that name: Jesus," *Tulsa World*, January 8, 2010, A-16

Thomma, Steven, "Politicians, pundits aim to rewrite history," *Tulsa World*, April 4, 2010, A 13.

Will, George, "Eminent domain issue threatens free speech," *Tulsa World*,

August 21, 2009, A-11.

Electronic Sources

"About the AHA." American Humanist Association. http://www.americanhumanist.org/who_we_are/about the_AHA/Humanist of_the_Year (accessed September 16, 2010).

"Administration Threatened to Destroy Investment Firm's Reputation." abcNews.com. http://blogs.abcnews.com/politicalpunch /2009/05/ bankruptcy-atto.html (accessed April 13, 2010).

Aerts, Diederik,et.al. "World views: from fragmentation to integration." *Center Leo Apostel*, Vrije Universiteit Brussell in Belgium. http://www.vub.ac.be/CLEA/pub/books/worldviews/(accessed May 19, 2000).

"American Migration: 1776 to 2006." The Globalist. November 29, 2006. http://www.theglobalist.com/StoryId.aspx?StoryId=5759 (accessed December 18, 2010).

"Annual Report 2008-2009." Planned Parenthood Federation of America. http://www.plannedparenthood.org/files/PPFA/PPFA_Annual_ Report_08-09-FINAL-12-10-10.pdf (accessed January 7, 2011).

"Call to Renewal – Keynote Address." Welcome to obamaspeaches.com. http://obamaspeaches.com/o81-Call-to-Renewal-Keynote- Address-Obama-Speech.htm (accessed June 10, 2009).

"CAN Wins Legal Battle Against Maine." Christian Action Network. April 10, 2010. http://christianaction.org/node/14 (accessed December 18, 2010).

Blackmun, J. Opinion of the Court, Supreme Court of the United States, 410 U.S. 113, Roe v. Wade (no. 70-18), VIII, IX, X. January 22, 1973. Cornell University Law School, Legal Information Institute. http://www.law.cornell.edu/supct/html/historics/USSC_CR_0410_0113 _Z.htmlml (accessed September 27, 2010).

Blue Letter Bible. http://www.blueletterbible.org/lang/lexicon/ lexicon.cfm?Strongs=H7 (accessed September 22, 2010).

"Draft-age Americans in Canada." *Forging Our Legacy: Canadian*

Citizenship & Immigration – 1900-1977. Citizenship and Immigration-Canada. http://www.cic.gc.ca/english/resources/publication/legacy/chap6-14 (accessed December 9, 2010).

"Facts About Youth." American College of Pediatricians. http://factsaboutyouth.com/wp-content/uploads/Superintendent-LetterC3.311.pdf (accessed October 8, 2010).

"Folk Singing: Tacky into the Wind." Time.com. February 28, 1964. http://www.time.com/time/magazine/article/0,9171,873851,00.html?iid=digg_share (accessed October 14, 2009).

"The Founding of NOW." National Organization of Women. http://www.now.org/history/the_founding.html (accessed September 10, 2010).

"Fox News figures outraged over Obama's 'Christian nation' comment." Media Matters for America. April 9, 2009. http://mediamatters.org/research/200904090033 (accessed June 6, 2009).

"The Genocide." Cambodian Genocide Group, New York, New York. http://www.cambodiangenocide.org/genocide.htm (accessed October 14, 2009).

Ginsburg, R. Opinion of the Court, Supreme Court of the United States, 561 U.S.___(2010), Christian Legal Society Chapter of the University of California, Hastings College of the Law, aka Hastings Christian Fellowship v. Martinez et. al. (no.08-1371). http://www.supremecourt.gov/opinions/09pdf/08-1371.pdf (accessed December 18, 2010).

H.Res. 397, 111th Cong., 1st session. May 4, 2009. http://www.govtrack.us/congress/billtext.xpd?bill=hr111-397&page (accessed June 10, 2009).

"The Heavens." Genesis Research. http://www.accuracyingenesis.com/heavens.html (accessed September 22, 2010); Higgins, Alexander G. "vote." Associated Press. November 29, 2009. http://news.yahoo.com/s/ap/20091129/ap_on_re_eu/eu_switserland_minaret_ban (accessed December 1, 2009).

"Insanity." Quotation #26932. Michael Moncur's (Cynical) Quotations. 43-44. http://www.quotationspage.com/quote/26032.html (accessed November 8, 2010).

"Just The Facts About Sexual Orientation and Youth." Just the Facts Coalition, Washington, D.C. 2008. http://apa.org/pi/lgbt/resources/just-the-facts.pdf (accessed October 8, 2010).

Klingaman, Gerald. "Kudzu, Mile-a-Minute Vine." University of Arkansas, Division of Agriculture, Cooperative Extension Service. August 30, 2002. http://www.arhomeandgarden.org/plantoftheweek/articles/ . Kudzu.htm (accessed January 7, 2011).

Koons, Robert C. "Ideologically driven humanities faculty at the University of Texas overwhelmed a tradition-focused cultural center." *Clarion Call.* The John William Pope Center for higher Education Policy. August 4, 2009. http://www.popecenter.org/clarion_call/article.html?id=2213 (accessed: July 8, 2010).

_____. "Robert C. Koons: Autobiographical Sketch." The Virtual Office of Dr. Robert C. Koons. July 8, 2010. http://www.leaderu.com/offices/ ml koons/menus/autobiography.html (accessed: July 8, 2010).

"Kudzu." *Wikipedia.* http://en.wikipedia.org/wiki/kudzu (accessed May 6, 2010).

"Little Boxes lyrics." Lyricsmode. http://www.lyricsmade.com/lyrics/m/malvina_reynolds/littleboxes.html (accessed September 26, 2009).

Live Births, Birth Rates, and Fertility Rates, by Race: United States, 1909-2000. Table 1-1. US Center for Disease Control. http://www.cdc.gov /ncha//data/statab/t001x01.pdf (accessed September 24, 2009).

"Marshall McLuhan."The Estate of Corinne and Marshall McLuhan. http://www.marshallmcluhan.com/faqs.html (accessed October 13, 2010).

"Marx of Respect." The Friends of Charles Darwin. http//friendsofdarwin.com/articles/2000/marx/ (accessed December 16,2010).

Moeller, Barbara. "The Texas Mugging of Western Civ." *Our Essays.* July 6, 2009. http://www.mindingthecampus.com/originals/2009/07/by_ barbara_Moeller_last_novemb.html (accessed July 8, 2010)

"The National Organization for Women's 1966 Statement of Purpose." National Organization of Women. http://www.now.org/history/purpos66

.html (accessed September 10, 2010).

Netter, Sarah. "Georgia Grad Student Sues University Over Gay Sensitivity Training." abcNews/US. July 27, 2010. http://abcnews.go.com/US/georgia-student-sues-university-lgbt-sensitivity-training/story?id=11261490 (accessed August 7, 2010).

Olsen, Ted, and Trevor Persaud. "Christian Legal Society Loses in Supreme Court Case." Christianity Today. December 18, 2010. http://www.christianitytoday.com/ct/2010/juneweb-olly/e6.11.0.ht (accessed December 18, 2010).

Orr, J. Edwin. "Prayer brought Revival." oChristian.com. http://articles.ochristian.com/article8330.shtml (accessed November 26, 2010).

"President Obama's speech at Nobel ceremony." Thompson Reuters. December 10, 2009. http:www.reuters.com/article/idUSTRE5B92KK20091210?WT.scrh=1&WT.MC_id=obamaobel (accessed December 21, 2009).

Random facts about 1857. Yahoo! Answers. http://answers.yahoo.com/question/index?qid=20101129053708AAhiObt (accessed December 1, 2010).

Rector, Robert. "Marriage: America's Greatest Weapon Against Child Poverty." The Heritage Foundation. September 16, 2010. http://www.heritage.org/Research/Reports/2010/09/Marriage-America's-Greatest-Weapon-Against-Child-Poverty/ (accessed September 21, 2010).

_____. "The Collapse of Marriage and the Rise of Welfare Dependence." Panel Discussion. Lecture #959. The Heritage Foundation. May 22, 2006. http://www.heritage.org/research/welfare/hl959.cfm (accessed September 17, 2010).

Reidhead, Paris. "Ten Shekels and a Shirt." Remnant Resource Network. http://remnantradio.org/Archives/articles/TenShekels/tenshekels.htm (accessed December 18, 2010).

Schwartz, Kate. "School Wants Student to Alter Religious View on Gays." July 27, 2007. http://www.newser.com/story/96566/school-wants-student-to-alter-religious-view-gays.htm (accessed August 7, 2010).

"Superintendents: Don't be confused by the AAP." American College of Pediatricians. http://factsaboutyouth.com/superintendents-don't-be- confused-by-the-aap/ (accessed October 8, 2010).

"Twelve Percent of U.S. Population is Foreign Born." America.gov. August 9, 2004. http://www.america.gov/st/washfile-english/2004/August/20040809150255cmretrop0.7581903.htm (accessed December 18, 2010).

"U.S. Abortion Statistics by Year (1973-Current)." National Right to Life Committee, 2010. http://www.christianliferesources.com??/library/view.php&articleid=1042 (accessed September 25, 2010)

"UT System Fast Facts." Fast Facts 2010. The University of Texas System. February 2010. http://utsystem.ed/News/Files/FastFacts2010.pdf (accessed: July 8, 2010).

"Welcome to the Swazi-Media audience Measurement Survey (Report) Television Section." infoshopSwaziland.com. http://infoshopswaziland.com/swazi_mams/Mams_television_vierwership_in_swaziland.htm (accessed October 26, 2010); Author's notes from Empowered 21 breakout session, Tulsa, Oklahoma, April 9, 2010.

"White House Denies Charge by Attorney that Administration Threatened to Destroy Investment Firm's Reputation." abcNews.com. http://blogs.abcnews.com/politicalpunch/2009/05/bankruptcy-atto.html (accessed April 13, 2010).

Whitehead, Barbara Dafoe, PhD. "The Collapse of Marriage and the Rise of Welfare Dependence." Panel Discussion. Lecture #959. The Heritage Foundation. May 22, 2006. www.heritage.org/research/welfare/ hl959.cfm (accessed September 17, 2010).

"Who Doesn't Pay Federal Taxes?" Tax Policy Center. July 9, 2009. http://www.taxpolicycenter.org/ taxtopics/federal-taxes-households.cfm (accessed May 6, 2010).

"The Whole World Was Watching: an oral history of 1968," South Kingstown High School and Brown University's Scholarly Technology Group, http://www.stg.brown.edu/projects/1968/reference/timeline.html (accessed October 9, 2009).

"7363 rachaph." Biblios.com. http://com/hebrew/7363.htm (accessed

September 22, 2010).

Author's Notes

Author's personal notes from presentation by Robert Hoskins: "Six Macro-Trends in Global Missions," One Hope, 600 SW 3rd Street, Pompano Beach, FL 33060.   Presented at: Empowered 21: Global Congress on Holy Spirit Empowerment in the 21st Century, Tulsa, Oklahoma, April 8-10, 2010.

INDEX

A

Abortion, 71, 194, 201, 214, 228, 307, 315, 328, 330-331, 341, 342-351, 359, 406
Adams, John, 129, 362; constitution, 136; equality, 231-232, 394; happiness of society, 248; sanctity of private property, 248.
Adler, Richard, 28
Advertising, 371, 374-378
Albert the Great (Albertus Magnus), 89, 148
AAP (American Academy of Pediatrics), 361n, 364
ACP (American College of Pediatricians), 362,364
American Humanist Association, 332
Anglican, 119-120, 226, 132, 409
Anglo-Saxon law, 80
anthropic principle, 163-165. *See also* fine-tuning argument.
anti-war protests, 50
Aquinas, Saint Thomas, 53, 89, 108-109, 108n, 148
Aristotle, 90, 141-142, 176; Catholicism 108; eugenics 342
Armey, Dick: socialism at Jamestown, 246-247
Athenagoras, 343

B

Backus, Isaac, 410
Badeaux, Christopher, 83
Baptists, 19, 132, 202n, 203, 244, 409-410; Danbury Baptist Association, 202-203
Basil the Great, 343
Behe, Michael, 268, 272
Benedict XVI (pope), 111
Bennett, William, 310, 313, 320-321, 356
Benson, Herbert, 173
Berger, Peter, 378

Bernard of Chartres, 137n
Breyer, Stephen, 345
Big Bang, 162, 164-165, 259, 266
birth control, 49, 238, 315, 328-329, 331, 348
Birth Control League, 330
Blackmun, Harry, 346-349
Blackstone, William, 80, 82, 110-111, 210, 308
Boorstin, Daniel, 28
Bork, Robert, 46, 351, 369, 375, 402, 407
Bradford, William, 247
Brainerd, David, 124
Britain, 88, 115, 120, 129, 176, 371, 410, 413
Buber, Martin
Burbank, Luther, 269
Burke, Edmund, 133, 239-240
Bush, George H. W., 44
Bushnell, Horace, 13, 15

C

Cambodia, 61, 62
Cambrian Explosion, 266
Carey, William, 410
Carroll, Robert, 266
Castro, Fidel, 132-133
Catholic Church, 91, 95, 116-118, 122, 206, 292, 302, 328; Catholic Reformation, 91, 95; humanism in, 90, 108109, 111
central cultural vision, 9, 10, 367-368, 379, 381, 383, 393, 398-399, 402, 405, 407-408, 413, 416
Chambers, Whittaker, 73-75
Charles (king), 119
child-centeredness, 293-294, 336
Chinese Nationalists, 57
Christendom, 87-88, 111, 115-117, 132-133, 146, 148, 185, 189, 191, 226-227, 229, 311, 379, 405
Christianity, ix, x, 78, 86, 113,190-

193, 195, 197, 213-215, 232,383, 404, 409; abortion, 343; America as Christian nation, 200, 203n, 204-205, 210, Aristotle's teaching, influence of, 90; attack on, 95, 97, 101, 161, 169, 171, 174, 218, 225-227, 229; Colonial America, 115, 120-122; Dewey, John, 23; Enlightenment and, 95; faith, 111-112; Founders, 186; individualism, 223; liberal, 282; marriage, 311-312, 314; multiculturalism, 396-397; popular culture, 377; public education, 292; public square and, 187-188; reason, 105-106; Roman Empire, growth in, 87-88; social gospel, 279; socialism, 244; Spock, Benjamin, 14; tenets, 85; Tocqueville's view, 173, 185; traditions, 73 Western civilization, growth in, 145-147; worldview, 85, 157, 305

Christian Century, 281-283
Church of England, 118-119, 125
Cicero, Marcus Tullius, 79
Civil Rights Act of 1964, 40, 51, 332
Clinton, Bill, 44, 350
Clurman, Ann, 32, 39, 46
Collins, Francis, 163, 363
Colson, Charles, 84, 97, 150, 173
Columbia University, 22, 25, 148, 151
Comfort, Ray, 263
Commission on National Goals, 38
common law, 15, 117, 160, 208, 234, 248, 250
Common Sense Book of Baby and Child Care, 12, 16, 17, 20

Communist Manifesto, 102-103, 240-241
Communist Party, 14, 50, 56, 63, 73, 240-241
Comte, Auguste, 213, 285
Condorcet, 93, 104
Congregationalists, 23, 119, 122
Conservative, 14, 16, 45, 136, 216-217, 219, 220, 246, 291, 294-295, 298-300, 303, 375, 407-408
Coontz, Stephanie, 323
Council of Trent, 91
covenant relationship, 313-315
creation, ix, 71, 74, 77, 80-81, 84, 86, 97-98, 111, 132, 146, 148, 157-158, 161, 165, 170, 172, 176-180, 178n, 222-223, 259-262, 283, 286, 306-308, 312-313, 336-337, 341, 357, 368, 385-387, 391, 404
Crick, Francis, 35
Croker, Richard, 44, 48
Crusades, 88
Custis, Nelly, 205

D

Danakil Depression, 77
Danakils, 77
Daniels, Mitch, 66
Dark Ages, 88-89
Darwin, Charles, 15, 96, 102-103, 151, 165, 223, 259-261, 263-271, 273-274, 278-280, 283-287; influence on Dewey, 95
David (king), 139, 314, 414
Davies, Paul. 273
Davis, Billie, 285
Davis, Paul, 163
Declaration of Independence, 53, 57, 122, 130, 134, 207-208, 252
deism, 120-121, 123
deists, 120, 122
democracy, 22, 24-25, 40, 47, 125, 149, 154, 191-192, 197,

201-202, 214, 227-229, 231-233, 242-243, 290-291, 327, 329, 372, 386, 394-395
Dewey, John, 16, 21-25, 37, 95, 148, 151, 189, 280, 282, 294, 301; influence on Spock, 11
Dey of Tunis, 205
Didache, 343
Diderot, 151
Diehl, Randy, 297-299
Dingell, John, 251
discrimination, 39, 51-52, 215, 233, 302, 332, 358
diversity, 47, 71, 109, 166, 187, 196-197, 228, 261, 264, 303, 307, 334, 374, 394, 397-398
divorce, 160, 312-313, 315, 319, 327-329, 333-336, 348, 392, 406; statistics, 30, 317
DNA, 35, 268, 270-271, 350, 363
domino theory, 58, 61, 63, 351
Douglas, William O., 204
dualistic worldview, 73
Durkheim, Emile, 285

E

Eddy, Sherwood, 124, 126, 134, 136, 189, 246-247
Edwards, Jonathan, 124, 410
egalitarianism, 216, 306, 405
Einstein, Albert, 162-165, 406
Eisenhower, Dwight D., 4, 21, 36, 38-39, 43, 58-59, 60
Elders, Joycelyn, 159, 350
Elizabeth (queen), 118, 327
Ellis, Havelock, 330
eminent domain, 249-250
empiricism, 23, 284
Encyclopedia, 92
Engels, Frederick, 151, 240, 254
Enlightenment, 19, 67, 90, 92-93, 95, 97-98, 102-103, 105, 112-113, 115-117, 120-123, 125-126, 148, 207, 213-214, 217, 231-232, 238, 246, 293, 310,
321, 325, 335, 343, 368, 378
Epicureans, 144
Epicurus, 143
Equalitarianism, 232, 306
Equality, 24-25, 39-40, 47, 51-52, 54-55, 93, 104, 130, 188, 197, 314, 225, 227-234, 237, 239, 242, 256, 304, 306-307, 326, 333-334, 336, 369, 380, 388, 394-395, 398, 405
Erdogan, Recept Tayip, 190
euthanasia, 194, 228, 307, 331, 351
Evans, M. Stanton, 223, 226
evolution, 15, 96-97, 99, 104, 157, 164-168, 175, 219, 223, 259-274, 278, 281-283, 287, 307, 386, 388, 406; creative evolution (also called emergent evolution) 262; macroevolution, 263, 268, 271; microevolution, 263, 271, mosaic evolution, 265-266
experimentalism, 23

F

faith, 1, 9, 23, 53, 72-75, 80, 89, 90-91, 93, 95-96, 100, 104-109, 111-113, 119, 123, 127, 139, 143, 145-146, 152, 154, 169, 172-173, 177, 179-186, 188, 194, 200-202, 205, 208-210, 215, 217-218, 220, 225, 247, 257, 259, 273, 284, 303, 308, 316, 328, 397, 404, 412
Federalist Papers, 135, 232, 254
feminism, 72, 189, 307, 326, 328
feudal barons, 116-117
Feuerback, Ludwig, 151
fine-tuning argument, 163, 165. *See also* anthropic principle
Finney, Charles, 328
First Amendment, 49, 200, 203, 203n, 206, 208
First Cause, 52, 98, 161, 260

First Infantry Division, 260
Flores, Richard, 298
fossil record, 264-267, 271
Founders, ix, 9, 40, 67, 86, 115, 118, 123-127, 129, 131-136; American cultural vision, 402-404; church and state, 185-186, 201-207, 209-210; Cicero's influence on, 79; Deism, 121, democracy, 374; French philosophers, views on, 122; religious views, 230-232; socialism, views on, 245, 248, 252, 257, 279
Fox, George, 124
Fox News, 181, 181n
France, 36, 258, 329; Burke, Edmund, 239; Christendom, 88; Communist Party, 56l; Deism, 120; Enlightenment, 92; Materialist Philosophy, 151; Vietnam, 58, 60
fraternity, 229-231, 239, 306-307, 388
FSM (Free Speech Movement), 50
free will, 9, 81, 86, 105, 108, 158-160, 215, 223-225, 286, 363, 386-387, 393
freedom, 40, 47, 53, 197, 162, 306, 393; Christianity, 184-195; democracy, 394; free will, 132; individual, 149, 166, 213-216, 221-222, 224-227, 229, 239, 281, 313, 333-334, 351, 390, 389-391, 405; justice, 233-235, 396, 408; multiculturalism, 397; New Freedom, 242-243; political, 116-117, 125,-126, 200, 207, 224-227, 371; private property, 248, 252, 254; religious, 121n, 122-123, 184-195, 204, 210, 404; sexual freedom, 328-329; socialism, 237; worldview, 71
French Huguenots, 118
French Revolution, 93, 102, 104, 132-134, 136, 151, 231-232, 238-239, 241, 394
Freud, Sigmund: discredited, 101-102; psychoanalysis, 96, 189; religion, 96; Spock, influence on, 15-18, 20-21
Friedan, Betty, 332-333
Fulbert, Bishop of Chartres, 137, 137n, 155, 415
Fuller, Andrew, 410
Functionalism, 28, 282

G

G.I. generation, 10
Gallagher, Maggie, 338
Gay, Craig M., 175, 294-295,
genocide, 62
George, Robert P., 72-73, 107-108, 209
Gergen, David, 44
German Lutherans, 119
Germany, 88, 90, 120, 151, 220, 241, 258, 329, 389n, 413; Nazi, 331
Giap, Vo Nguyen, 50
Gillon, Steve, 30
Glorious Revolution of 1688, 118
Goldman, Emma, 329
Great Awakening, 123-124, 131-132, 410-411
Great Depression, 3, 9-10, 15, 22, 30, 32, 38, 252, 256, 277
Great Society, 245
Greatest Generation, 3, 9-10, 30, 38, 40-41, 43, 47, 65, 69, 245
Greece, 61, 88-89, 142, 148, 220, 342, 353
Greek civilization, 89, 139-140
Guth, Allen, 164
Guttmacher, Allan, 331-332, 344

H

Hamilton, Alexander, 135, 249, 254
Hammurabi (king)159-160
Hawking, Stephen, 162-165
Hayek, F. A., 226-227, 242
Hebrews, 78-79, 81n, 87, 105, 111, 133, 139, 143, 146-147, 157, 159-160, 176, 191, 195, 311, 391, 396, 402, 414, 416
Henry VIII (king), 117
Herbart, Johann Friedrich, 280
Herrick, Jim, 165, 168, 174, 177, 234-235, 274
Hiss, Alger, 74
Hitler, Adolf, 330, 332
Hobbes, Thomas, 151, 189
Holy Trinity Church v. United States, 1892, 208
homosexuality, 71, 193, 303, 307, 311-313, 353-364, 377
Hook, Sidney, 24
Hoover, Herbert, 245
Hoover, J. Edgar, 50
Hoskins, Robert, 377
Hovenkamp, Herbert, 278
Hubel Space Telescope, 178-179
human sciences, 278-281, 291-292
humanism, 67, 87, 213, 217, 220, 228, 351, 370, 377, 383, 408; American institutions, in, x; 169-170; Catholic Church, 109; church, enemy of, 111; destructive force, 404, 407; diversity, 398; doctrines, 190, 400, 403; Enlightenment, 97, 232, 343; evolution, 259; feminism, 328, 331-332; freedom, 393; God, 385; individual, 221-222; influence, 188; liberalism, 216-217; man's relationships, 388; Marxism, 103; modern, 139, 141, 148-149, 152-154; multiculturalism, 396; progressivism, 218; religion, humanism as, 86, 171; science, 161-162, 165; self, 375; socialism, 237, 244, 254; Spock, 405; worldview, 157, 197, 202, 209-210, 305-307
humanism, types: Christian, 89; ethical, 150; Greek, 89; humanistic Judaism, 150; naturalistic, 142; rationalistic, 150; religious, 150; scientific, 102, 150; secular, 152, 195, 210, 226-227, 295
Humanist Manifesto I, 103, 171, 220, 225, 237, 254, 314, 332-333, 343, 348, 370, 388, 395
Humanist Manifesto II, 220, 237, 254, 314, 332-333, 343, 348, 370, 388, 395
Hume, Brit, 181, 181n
Hume, David, 104
Huxley, Julian, 330
Hymowitz, Kay S., 308, 355

I

individualism, 167, 215, 223, 334, 351, 355, 369-370, 380; social, 91
Industrial Revolution, 217, 326-327
inerrant, 177, 179. *See also* literal
instrumentalism, 23
International Working Men's Association, 241
irreducible complexity, 269-271

J

Jackson, Andrew, 244, 326
James I (king), 118-119
James II (king), 118
James, William, 96, 151, 280, 282
Jamestown, 118, 206, 246-147
Jane Addams Hull House, 22

Jefferson, Thomas, 129, 136, 202-206, 202-203n, 249, 252, 299, 403
Jeroboam, 414-415
Jesus Christ, 53, 86-87, 90, 139, 146, 159, 181-183, 225, 261, 314, 387, 389
John (king), 116
John Paul II (pope), 107
Johnson, Donald E., 26, 271
Johnson, Lyndon, 61, 319
Judeo-Christian: abortion, 353, 358-359; arts, 369; banner, 10, 383, 403; creation, 272; Creator, 341 culture, 378; ethic, 85, 122n, 147, 150, 171, 174, 191, 194-195, 197, 200, 202, 210, 213, 125, 218, 221, 228, 294, 305, 390, 396-397, 415; free will 225; heritage, 289; homosexual, 357; marriage, 325-326; term, 85; tradition, 20, 54, 80, 82, 87, 115, 133, 137, 139, 157, 162, 201, 402; worldview, ix, 67, 72-73, 83, 225, 308, 313, 316, 375, 381, 391, 401, 403, 416; writings, 159
Judaism, 73, 78, 150
Just the Facts Coalition, 361-362, 364
justice, 47, 197, 215, 225, 234-235, 237, 248-249, 256, 395-396, 408; environmental justice, 255; social justice, 243

K

Kaplan, Fred, 48
Kaskaskia Indian tribe, 206
Keeton, Jennifer, 303
Keller, Timothy, 99-100, 163, 191
Kennedy, Anthony, 345-346, 358-359
Kennedy, John, 4, 9-10, 36, 43-44, 58-59, 60, 335
Kennedy, Robert, 61
Khmer Rouge, 61, 62, 332
King, Martin Luther, Jr., 52, 54, 59, 61
Kirk, Russell, 79-80, 85, 87, 89, 132, 136-137, 233, 300, 368, 415
Koons, Rob, 296-300, 302
Kudzu, 256-257, 304
Kurth, James, 72, 137
Kurtz, Paul, 152-154, 191-192, 194-196, 221, 227-228

L

Lai Khe, 5-6
Lamont, Corliss, 142, 148-150, 152-154, 161, 165-168, 216, 220-221, 227-228
Lamphier, Joseph, 411
Laos, 61, 63
League of the Just, 240
Leax, John, xi
leveling, 52-53, 833, 230-231, 243, 306, 373
Lewin, Bertram, 16
Lewis, C. S., 80, 84, 86, 105, 112, 183, 219, 262, 274, 287, 301, 335
liberal, 21, 45, 154, 204; Constitution, 136, 249; culture, 407-408; education, 295- 298, 300; government, 213-217; obscenity, 49; political theories, 169; progressivism, 257; progressives, 206, 234; protest demonstrations, 279; sexuality, 50; social gospel, 73; values, 220
liberalism, 29, 72, 180, 351, 375, 407; government, 213-217; progressivism, 406
liberty, 57, 104, 106, 115, 121, 186, 189-190, 192, 206, 208, 224, 227, 231, 235, 239, 242,

248-249, 251-252, 335, 347, 358, 380, 396; intellectual, 91; multiculturalism, and, 394; religious, 118, 120, 125-127, 130; spiritual 90
Lincoln, Abraham, 22, 247-248, 402
literal, 177, 260, 346. See also inerrant
"Little Boxes", 33
Lowell, James Russell, 300
Luther, Martin, 90

M

Maa, Suni, 77-78
Madison, James, 72, 122, 135, 136, 206, 232, 248
Magna Carta, 16, 147
Magueijo, Joao, 177-178n
Maier, Thomas, 16, 18
Mannheim, Karl, 11 marriage, 158, 305, 315-317; cultural universal, 308-314; family unit, and, 320-321; humanistic philosophy, and, 314; intermarriage, 196; same-sex, 214; statistics, 30, 32, 316-321; worldview, 307
Mars' Hill, 144-145, 147-148
Marx, Karl, 14, 56, 73, 102-103, 151, 165, 189, 240-241, 285
Mary (queen), 118
mass media, 368, 370, 373-375, 378-379, 400, 406
materialism, 37-39, 75, 103, 150-152, 172, 406
Mayflower Compact, 119
McClay, Wilfred, 158
McLuhan, Marshall, 378
Mediterranean culture, 88
Menninger, Karl, 330
Mere Christianity, 183, 335
Methodists, 132, 204, 244, 409
Middle Ages, 88-89, 9, 95, 115-116, 123

Minh, Ho Chi, 55-58, 60-61
modernism, 84-85
Moeller, Barbara, 297-299
monistic theory, 166, 388
Moore, Neil, 10
Morowitz, Harold, 261
Morrison, Charles Clayton, 281-284
Moynihan Report, 320-321
Moynihan, Daniel Patrick, 319-321, 355
Muggeridge, Malcolm, 107n, 274, 373, 404
multiculturalism, 72, 188-190, 194, 196-197, 397-398
Murray, Charles, 257
Mussolini, Benito, 332
Mutations, 263, 268, 271

N

National American Woman Suffrage Association, 328
NAACP (National Association for the Advancement of Colored People), 22
NOW (National Organization of Women), 189, 332
National Woman Suffrage Association, 328
natural law, 79, 83, 108, 177, 219, 234, 269, 287
naturalism, 23, 84-85, 91, 99, 103, 142, 150-152, 173, 223, 259-261, 263, 273, 291-292, 369, 385, 391
Nazi, 37, 331
Nee, Watchman, 110, 110n
neo-Darwinist, 263, 265, 268, 271
Nesbitt, Lewis M., 77
New Deal, 245
newspapers, 21, 28, 371-372, 374
Newton, Isaac, 98, 137n, 176, 178
1950s, 21, 29-41, 44, 48-49, 51-

52, 256, 323
1960s, 11, 17, 29, 34, 37, 40, 44-50, 52, 58, 63-65, 69, 79, 229, 233, 245, 316, 319, 323, 325, 332, 334-337, 377-378
1970s, 48-50, 63-65, 79, 377 nominalism, 90, 173n
norms, 53-54, 78-80, 82, 159, 215, 219, 222, 234, 287, 354, 368-369, 389, 392-393, 396
North Vietnam, 6-7, 57-63 noumenal,100
Novak, Michael, 29
nuclear family, 34, 82, 308-311, 321, 325-326, 328

O

O'Reilly, Bill, 181, 181n
Obama, Barak, 187, 199-202, 204, 210, 217-218, 251
Orr, J. Edwin, 412

P

Packer, J. I., 177, 180
Pangle, Tom,
299 pantheists,
84
Paris Commune, 241
Pascal, Blaise, 107n
Patterson, James, 32
Patti, Archimedes L. A., Major, 55-57, 60, 62
Paul, Apostle, 47, 53, 78, 87, 90, 311, 316, 356, 396-397, 416; Mars' Hill, at, 144-145,
147 permanent things, 78-80, 105,
111, 122n, 158, 173, 195, 217, 305, 307-308, 335, 354, 359, 368, 390, 392
Petigny, Alan, 48, 376
Pilgrims, 119, 126, 247
Planned Parenthood Federation of America, 331-332, 344, 358
Plato, 141-142, 146-147, 247, 342

pluralism, 184-185, 188, 190, 193-194, 294, 399, 429
Plymouth Colony, 247 post-Christian, 84-85, 184
postmodernism, 84-85
pre-marital sex, 49
Presbyterian, 14, 119, 122, 124, 132, 204, 409-410
Prigogine, Ilya, 261
Prime Mover, 142, 161, 385
progressive, 154, 213, 220, 372, 387, 400, 403, 405-406; income tax, 241; liberal, 136; marriage, 334; movement, 21; philosophical view, 16; pop culture, 375, 378; social action, 257
progressives, 15, 206, 218-220, 234, 253-254, 291-294, 296; presidents, 244-245
progressive education, 16, 21, 37, 289-296, 303-304
Protagoras, 141
Protestantism, 91, 118, 130-131, 281, 283-284, 291, 294, 327
psychoanalysis, 14-16, 96, 275, 281
psychology, 14, 15, 22, 25, 96, 102, 278, 280-286, 292-294, 330
punctuated equilibrium,265-266
Puritans, 10, 15, 119-120, 124, 126

Q

Quakers, 118-119, 122

R

rachaph (moved), 341
radical, 45-46, 49, 241, 328-330
radicalism, French, 231
Randall, John Herman, Jr., 101-103, 112, 143, 146, 148
Rawls, John, 234
reason, 23, 72-73, 79, 81, 92-93, 95, 100, 103-113, 115, 120-

121, 140-141, 144, 149-150, 163, 174, 213-216, 281, 220
Reformation, 90-92, 109, 115, 126, 132
regulation, 194-195, 249, 254-256, 258, 297, 358
Rehoboam, 414-415
Reich, Charles, 33
relativism, 111, 142, 190-192, 195, 197, 301, 356, 380, 392, 397-400, 405, 408
Rembar, Charles, 49-50
Renaissance, 5, 67, 88-92, 95, 98, 108, 113, 115-117, 123, 126, 148, 343, 368
reversion to average, 271
Revival of 1857-1858, 411-412
Revolutionary War, 115, 129, 131, 408
Reynolds, Malvina, 33
Rickover, Hyman G., 22
right of contract, 249-251
Riley, Dean, 378
Roberts, Evan, 412
Roberts, J. M., 93, 140
Roe v. Wade, 346, 348, 358
Roman Empire, 87-88, 90, 113, 115, 404
Roosevelt, Franklin, 9, 245, 372
Roosevelt, Theodore, 43, 244
Roth, Robert J., 23-24
Rousseau, Jean Jacques, 189, 238-240
Rush, Benjamin, 136, 206, 372, 374

S

Saigon, 5-6, 57, 61, 62
Saint-Simon, Claude, 240, 243
same-sex marriages, 214, 356-357
Samuelson, Robert, 52, 55, 230, 233, 253
Sanger, Margaret, 328-329, 331-333

Savio, Mario, 50
Schaffer, Francis, 108
Schweikart, Larry, 245
science, 22-24, 36, 48, 75, 78, 82, 84, 93, 95-99, 101-103, 105, 107, 112-113, 120, 124, 142, 149, 151, 154, 161-163, 165-166, 168-169, 173-178, 214, 219, 221, 259, 261, 263-264, 272-273, 275, 278-288, 291-295, 338, 348, 361, 364, 368-369, 379, 386
scientific naturalism, 99, 292
scientism, 99, 102, 219, 287, 400
Scotch-Irish Presbyterians, 118
Second Great Awakening, 131-132, 410
secular humanists, 73, 112, 150, 184, 187-188, 191-195, 197, 203, 225, 246, 285, 379
Seneca Women's Rights Convention, 328
Seu, Andrée, 255-256
sexual revolution, 48-49
Shaw, Bernard, 330
significant shared events and formative experiences, 11, 29, 48
Silent generation, 10, 38, 40
Singer, Peter, 350
Smith, Christian, 169, 280
social contract theory, 239
social engineering, 43, 52, 54, 188, 218, 325, 333
social gospel, 73, 244, 279, 281, 283, 291
Socialist Party, 329
Socrates, 141
Sodom, 353
Solomon, 414-416
Solzhenitsyn, Aleksandr, 73, 209
Sophists, 141-142
soul, dualistic view, 166, 388
Spencer, Herbert, 213
Spetner, Lee, 271

Spinoza, Benedict, 151
spiritual love, 309, 309n, 315
Spock, Benjamin, 11-17, 19-21, 25, 37, 405-406
Spock, Jane Cheney, 13-16
Sputnik, 22, 35-36
stabilizing selection, 266
Stalin, Joseph, 14, 23, 332
Stanton, Elizabeth Cady, 327-328
statutory law, 234
Steele, Shelby, 355
Steinhorn, Leonard, 37-38, 40-41, 47, 53
Sternheimer, Karen, 380
Stevens, John Paul, 346
Stewart, Jon, 182
stoicism, 143
Strauss, William, 10
suicide, 351
Supreme Being, 80-81, 120, 161, 204, 386, 391, 405
Sutcliffe, John, 410
Swaziland, 377-378
Swiss Pietists, 119

T

Taft, William Howard, 245
Tao, 335
Taxation, 117, 139, 194, 252-254
television, 4, 27-31, 35-37, 44, 63, 181, 233, 373-374, 377
Tennent, Gilbert, 124
Terror of 1792-1794, 239
Tertullian, 343
Tet Offensive, 5, 60-61
Thailand, 61, 63, 65
Thales, 140
Tocqueville, Alexis de, 121, 121-122n, 272, 185-186, 207, 243, 360, 371-372
tolerance, 71, 92, 183, 190-191, 193-194, 196-197, 253, 303, 356-357, 394, 398-399, 405
Troubled Asset Relief Program (TARP), 251
Truman, Harry, 39, 43, 61
truth, ix, 1, 70-72, 77-78, 80, 82-83, 85-87, 89-92, 87-102, 104, 106-108, 111-112, 121, 122-123, 122n, 126, 133, 139, 141, 143, 147, 157-160, 176, 178-179, 186, 190-192, 195, 200, 213, 216-227, 220, 228, 235, 260, 272-274, 280, 285-286, 288, 290, 294-296, 298, 301-302, 305, 308, 315, 336, 351, 353n, 354, 365, 367-368, 370, 381, 387, 390-393, 396-397, 399-400, 402-404, 406
Turkey, 61, 199-200, 199n, 204-205

U

Uncurriculum, 300-301
universe, 70-71, 74, 78-80, 83-84, 86, 97-98, 100, 112, 120, 132, 141, 143, 146-147, 149-150, 152-153, 157-158, 160-165, 167, 173, 178n, 179, 218-219, 223, 259, 262, 272-273, 275, 287, 306, 341, 358, 379, 385, 391-392
University of Chicago, 22, 282
University of Texas, 295-298

V

van Gogh, Theo, 189
varying speed of light theory (VSL), 178n
Viet Minh, 56-57
Vietnam, 4-7, 44, 50, 55-65, 351
Voting Rights Act of 1965, 51

W

Waite, Linda, 338
wall of separation, 169, 185, 202-204, 202n, 206, 390
Ware, Keith, 5-6
Washington, George, 122, 205
Watson, Bradley C. S., 278

Watson, Bradley C. S., 278
Watson, James, 35
Watson, John B., 15
Wattleton, Faye, 331-332
Weaver, Richard, 78, 171-172,
    192, 223, 229-231, 235, 248,
    289-290, 303-305, 307, 370,
    392, 400, 402, 405
Weber, Max, 285
Weil, Simone, 79
Wells, H. G., 35, 330
Wesley, John, 124
West, Diane, 376
Western civilization, 43, 67, 87-
    89, 97, 103, 111, 113, 141,
    146, 189, 196, 226-227, 250,
    289, 296-300, 311, 332, 351
Western Europe, 88, 92, 115,
    213-214, 323
Whig theory of history 220
Whitefield, George, 124, 410
Wilders, Geert, 189
William of Ockham, 90, 173n
Wilson, James Q., 33
Wilson, Woodrow, 245
Wolters, Albert M., 71, 78
Wood, Gordon, 132
Woods, Tiger, 181-183
Woodstock, 7, 44, 61
World Council of Churches, 111
Wundt, Wilhelm, 96

Y

Yankelovich, Inc., 45

Z

Zedong, Mao, 56, 63
Zeitz, Joshua, Dr., 32
Zinzendorf, Count Nikolaus von,
    124

www.ingramcontent.com/pod-product-compliance
Lightning Source LLC
Chambersburg PA
CBHW071958150426
43194CB00008B/917